MEDICAL RECORDS AND THE LAW

MEDICAL RECORDS AND THE LAW

William H. Roach, Jr.
Gardner, Carton & Douglas
Chicago

Susan N. Chernoff
Gardner, Carton & Douglas
Chicago

Carole Lange Esley
Northeast Health, Inc.
Camden, Maine

with the special assistance of
**Chris J. Mollet and
David A. Rubenstein**
Gardner, Carton & Douglas
Chicago

AN ASPEN PUBLICATION®
Aspen Publishers, Inc.

1985

Rockville, Maryland
Royal Tunbridge Wells

Library of Congress Cataloging in Publication Data

Roach, William H.
Medical records and the law.

"An Aspen publication."
Includes bibliographies and index.
1. Medical records—Law and legislation—United States. I. Chernoff,
Susan N. II. Esley, Carole Lange. III. Title. [DNLM: 1. Medical
Records—United States—legislation. WX 33 AA1 R6M]
KF3827.R4R63   1985   344.73'041   85-3975
ISBN: 0-87189-098-4   347.30441

Editorial Services: Jane Coyle

Printed in the United States of America

3   4   5

Table of Contents

Acknowledgments

Producing this work while pursuing our professions proved for us to be a sizable enterprise, one we could hardly have managed without the help of others. We are most appreciative of research assistance furnished by the following law students who worked as summer associates at Gardner, Carton & Douglas: Mary Layne Ahern (DePaul University), S. Naseem Anjam (DePaul University); Stephanie E. Balcerzak (Yale University), Darien Creamer (DePaul University), Wendy Freyer (Northwestern University), Deborah L. Gersh (George Washington University), Edwin A. Getz (Washington University), Stephen G. Gilles (University of Chicago), Frederic R. Gumbinner (University of Michigan), Treazure Johnson (University of Virginia), Jonathan Levin (Northwestern University), Joyce McArdle (University of Chicago), Pamela Nehring (University of Pittsburgh), Paul J. Novack (University of Michigan), David D. Peterson, Jr. (Northwestern University), Michael Regier (University of Virginia), Jill Sugar (Northwestern University), Klaus U. Thiedmann (Cornell University), Ann L. Vix (University of Michigan), Adrian Von Hassell (Vanderbilt University), G. Andrew Watson (Northwestern University), Bettina Weis (Vanderbilt University), Steven Wright (University of San Diego), and Cora Yang (New York University). In addition, Robin C. Friedman, James D. McDonough, Helen J. McSweeney, and Thaddeus J. Nodzenski, associate attorneys, and Patrice Maloney, a legal assistant, all of Gardner, Carton & Douglas, were extremely helpful in providing legal research for the project.

Frank Pace, Director of Medical Records at Michael Reese Hospital and Medical Center in Chicago and an experienced records practitioner and teacher, gave us his considered and careful evaluation of the manuscript. Cheryl K. Smith, RRA, Director of Medical Information Service at Penobscot Bay Medical Center, reviewed an early manuscript and gave us useful direction for the final work. Our inestimable secretaries, Mary L. Born, Rose Davis-Duffy, Danielle LaVine, Marcia Neilis, Deborah Raymond, and Genevieve Perpall, were throughout understanding, tireless, and patient. The director of the Word Processing Center at Gardner, Carton & Douglas, Pat Agema, and her staff provided valuable assistance in producing the manuscript. Our editor, Michael Brown, gave us unending encouragement with unfailing patience. To all these individuals we are deeply indebted.

William H. Roach, Jr.
Susan N. Chernoff
Carole Lange Esley
Chicago, Illinois
Rockland, Maine
May 1985

Note on Legal Citations

This book includes references to numerous court decisions. The numbers and letters following each case name indicate where to find the court's decision in the volumes of cases contained in law libraries. The name, numbers, and letters together are called the *citation* for the decision. For example, in *Natanson v. Kline,* 186 Kan. 393, 350 P.2d 1093 (1960), "P.2d" is the abbreviation for the reporter system: it means the *Pacific Reporter, Second Series.* The first number, 350, refers to volume 350 of the *Pacific Reporter, Second Series.* The next number, 1093, is the page number in volume 350. The date of the decision is given in parentheses. Sometimes the case is reported in more than one reporter system, so there will be another set of numbers and letters before the parentheses. Here, the decision is reported also in volume 186 of the *Kansas Reports* at page 393.

Where there is another set of numbers and letters after the parentheses, they refer to another court's decision concerning the same case. If the second court is a higher court, it will be preceded by letters such as *aff'd, rev'd,* or *cert. denied,* which indicate that the court affirmed, reversed, or declined to review the lower court's decision. *Mikel v. Abrams,* 541 F. Supp. 591 (W.D. Mo. 1982), *aff'd* 716 F. 2d 907 (8th Cir. 1983), shows that this case was decided in 1982 by the Federal District Court for the Western District of Missouri, whose decision may be found in volume 541 of the *Federal Supplement* reporter at page 591, and that the Federal Court of Appeals for the Eighth Circuit affirmed the lower court's decision in 1983. The appellate court's decision can be found in volume 716 of the *Federal Reporter, Second Series,* at page 907. In some situations the order of the references is reversed, so that the higher court is listed first. In those situations the abbreviations will be *aff'ing* or *rev'ing,* indicating whether the higher court is affirming or reversing the lower court.

Decisions are found in numerous reporter services, and citations vary widely. If you are looking for a particular decision, ask your law librarian or your legal counsel to assist you.

Chapter 1

Patient Record Requirements

RECORDS THAT MUST BE KEPT

The medical record consists of four types of data concerning an individual patient: (1) personal, (2) financial, (3) social, and (4) medical. Personal information is usually obtained upon admission and will include name, birth date, sex, marital status, next of kin, occupation, identification of physicians, and other items needed for specific patient identification. Financial data include the name of the patient's employer, the patient's health insurance company, types of insurance and policy numbers, Medicare and Medicaid numbers, if any, and other information that will enable the hospital to bill for its services. Social data include the patient's race and ethnic background, family relationships, life style, any court orders or other directions concerning the patient, community activities, and other information related to the patient's position in society. Medical data form the patient's clinical record, a continuously maintained history of the treatment provided to the patient in the hospital. These data include the results of physical examinations, medical history, the treatment administered, progress reports, physician's orders, clinical laboratory reports, x-ray reports, consultation reports, anesthesia record, operation record, signed consent forms, nurses' notes, and other reports that may be generated during the patient's treatment.[1]

The medical record may be written, typed, or computer generated. The computerized record can aid the information network on a patient, enhancing completeness and accuracy as well as immediate availability of the record to authorized personnel.[2] Whether written, typed, or in computer form, the medical

[1]See K. WATERS & G. MURPHY, MEDICAL RECORDS IN HEALTH INFORMATION, 39–95 (1979).

[2]See generally Wynstra, Computerized Medical Records: Legal Problems and Implications, 2:2 TOPICS IN HEALTH RECORD MANAGEMENT, 75–84, (Dec. 1981).

record should be a complete, accurate current record of the history, condition, and treatment of the patient and the results of the patient's hospitalization.

The medical record is used not only to document chronologically the care rendered to the patient, but also to plan and evaluate the patient's treatment and to enhance communication among the patient's physician and other health care professionals treating the patient. The record also provides clinical data for medical, nursing, and scientific research. In addition, individuals who conduct medical and nursing audits and peer review evaluations rely heavily on documentation in medical records.

Hospital medical records are also important legal documents to the hospital and the patient. For example, where hospital bylaws designate standards of care to be established by individual departments, examination of patient records can provide verification that the standards are being maintained. Also, administrative and clinical assessment programs may be targets of legal scrutiny, and patient records can again aid evaluation and justification of the programs.[3]

The key to the importance of medical records as legal documents is that they are essential to the defense of professional negligence actions. Since such actions are often litigated two to five years after the plaintiff received the treatment in question, the hospital record is frequently the only detailed record of what actually occurred during the hospitalization. Persons who participated in the plaintiff's treatment may not be available to testify on behalf of the defendants or may not remember important details of the case. A good record enables the hospital to reconstruct the patient's course of treatment and to show whether the care provided was acceptable under the circumstances.[4] The contents of the hospital record are usually admissible in evidence for or against the hospital and physicians. It is essential that everyone involved in medical record documentation and management understand the legal implications of the record so that they will create and maintain a record that will be useful to them in any future litigation. (For a discussion of admissibility of medical records, see Chapter 5.)

LEGAL REQUIREMENTS FOR CONTENT OF A MEDICAL RECORD

The requirement that hospitals maintain medical records is found in state and federal statutes and regulations, municipal codes, and hospital accreditation

---

[3]See K. WATERS & G. MURPHY, supra note 1, at 247.

[4]See, e.g., Foley v. Flushing Hosp. and Medical Center, 34 N.Y. 2d 863, 359 N.Y.S. 2d 113 (1974) (infant plaintiff's medical records provided evidence sufficient to prevent dismissal of malpractice suit).

standards. In a few states, hospital-licensing statutes set forth the minimum record requirements.[5] The Utah statute is illustrative:

§26–15–58 Licenses—Minimum Requirements

. . . In order to qualify as a licensed hospital, the following minimum requirements must be met:

. . . (4) All tissues removed at surgery must be submitted for examination to a pathologist approved by the department [of health] and the pathologist's written report shall be made part of the permanent record of each patient operated upon.

(5) Each patient shall have a clinical record which shall include: detailed clinical history, description of physical examination, reports of laboratory tests and of pathology and X-ray examinations, admission (provisional) and prerogative diagnosis, clear description of treatments given, including all operative procedures, postoperative diagnosis, progress notes by the physician, final complete diagnosis, and results of treatment at the time of discharge from the hospital and other reports as specified by the department in regulations. These records shall be properly indexed and filed in the hospital.[6]

In most states, the regulatory agency for hospitals has the power to promulgate rules and regulations governing the content of hospital medical records.[7] These rules and regulations set forth the specific information that must be kept in medical records of a licensed hospital.[8] The pertinent Illinois regulation, for example, reads:

For each patient there shall be an adequate, accurate, timely, and complete medical record. Minimum requirements for medical record content are as follows: patient identification and admission information; history of patient as to chief complaints, present illness and pertinent past history, family history, and social history; physical examination report; provisional diagnosis; diagnostic and therapeutic reports on laboratory tests results, x-ray findings, any surgical procedure per-

---

[5]*See, e.g.,* N.Y. Pub. Health Law §4165 (McKinney 1977); Tenn. Code Ann. §68–11–302 (1983).

[6]Utah Code Ann. §26–15–58 (1953).

[7]*See, e.g.,* Mass. Gen. Laws Ann. ch. 111, §70 (West Supp. 1983); Miss. Code Ann. §41–9–63 (1972).

[8]*See, e.g.,* Tenn. Minimum Standards and Regulations for Hospitals ch.1200.8.3.05; Rules and Regulations for the Licensure of General and Special Hospitals in Virginia §208.6 (1982); Wash. Hosp. Rules and Regulations §248–18–440 (1979).

formed, any pathological examination, any consultation, and any other diagnostic or therapeutic procedure performed; orders and progress notes made by the attending physician and when applicable by other members of the medical staff and allied health personnel; observation notes and vital sign charting made by nursing personnel; and conclusions as to the primary and any associated diagnosis, brief clinical resume, disposition at discharge to include instructions and/or medications and any autopsy findings on a hospital death.[9]

State licensing regulations are divided into three groups: those detailing specific information required; those specifying the broad areas of information required; and those stating simply that the medical record shall be adequate, accurate, or complete.[10] (The state licensing regulations are summarized in Appendix B.)

The law and regulations setting forth conditions of participation in federal reimbursement programs also require hospitals to maintain medical records and specify minimum content requirements for such records. The conditions of participation in Medicare programs state that:

The medical records contain sufficient information to justify the diagnosis and warrant the treatment and end results. The medical records contain the following information: Identification data; chief complaint; present illness; past history; family history; physical examination; provisional diagnosis; clinical laboratory reports; X-ray reports; consultations; treatment, medical and surgical; tissue report; progress notes; final diagnosis; discharge summary; autopsy findings.[11]

In some cities, municipal codes require certain information not otherwise required by state law or regulation.[12] In addition, some state statutes have special provisions concerning certain specific types of information to be maintained. In Illinois, for example, there is a special section of the Public Health Statutes that

[9]Ill. Hosp. Licensing Requirements §12–1.2(b) (1979).

[10]Arkansas, California, Colorado, Georgia, Idaho, Maryland, Massachusetts, Michigan, Nevada, New Mexico, New York, North Carolina, Tennessee, Utah, Washington, West Virginia, Wisconsin, Wyoming, and Puerto Rico have detailed provisions. Alabama, Alaska, Florida, Illinois, Kansas, Louisiana, Minnesota, Mississippi, Missouri, Montana, Nebraska, New Hampshire, New Jersey, Oregon, Rhode Island, South Dakota, and Vermont specify broad areas. Arizona, Connecticut, Hawaii, Indiana, Iowa, Kentucky, Maine, Ohio and Virginia contain only a general statement.

[11]42 U.S.C. §1395x(e)(2) (1974); 42 C.F.R. §405.1026(g) (1982).

[12]See, e.g., Chicago, Ill., Code §137–14 (1978).

requires retention of x-rays "as part of the regularly maintained records" for a period of five years.[13]

The Joint Commission on Accreditation of Hospitals (JCAH) requires hospitals to maintain patient care records as a standard of accreditation.

> An adequate medical record shall be maintained for every individual who is evaluated or treated as an inpatient, ambulatory care patient, or emergency patient, or who receives patient services in a hospital-administered home care program.[14]

The JCAH also specifies in considerable detail the information that should appear in the medical record.[15] In the absence of specific statutory or regulatory direction, hospitals should adopt institutional policies concerning the content of medical records. The policy may be a detailed list of data required, or may reference some other policy, such as the JCAH standards and interpretations. Generally, detailed policies require closer periodic review to keep them current, while broad policies remain applicable as circumstance and practice change. Hospitals should balance the need for providing enough specificity to guide medical records practitioners and hospital staff against the desire to avoid continual policy revisions. Most accredited hospitals in states that provide no statutory or regulatory direction concerning patient record content rely on the JCAH accreditation standards as a guide to record content policy.

In all states, however, hospitals should keep abreast of state, federal, and JCAH medical records requirements. State and local associations of medical record practitioners often publish changes in the applicable law and accreditation standards. Hospitals also receive notice of these changes from state and national hospital associations and from hospital legal counsel. All health care institutions should develop reliable ways of communicating new laws and regulations to the individuals responsible for making policy recommendations concerning medical record content, particularly to medical record practitioners and the medical staff.

In addition, these individuals should understand the various functions of the medical record and their interrelationships as well as how those functions are affected by the nature of the specific institution and current legislative, regulatory, and licensing requirements. Creating effective record content policy requires the involvement of a variety of disciplines within the institution. Policy makers must be willing to find ways to make practical adjustments to medical record content. In

---

[13]Ill. Ann. Stat. ch. 111–1/2, §157–11 (Smith-Hurd 1977).

[14]JOINT COMMISSION ON ACCREDITATION OF HOSPITALS, ACCREDITATION MANUAL FOR HOSPITALS 79 (1984).

[15]*Id.* at 84–88.

doing so, they should strike a balance between the administrative, financial, and other demands placed upon the medical record and the record's basic patient care function.

RECORD RETENTION REQUIREMENTS

The length of time a medical record is retained will be determined by federal or state law and regulations, or by sound hospital administrative policy and medical practice. It will also be greatly influenced by the nature of the institution and resources available to maintain a long retention period. Achieving a practical and workable solution to medical record retention policy becomes more difficult in an era of reduced financial resources. In the past, state-of-the-art microfilming and computer systems were considered a means for improving the medical information collection and retention capabilities of the organization. The extent to which that solution can be applied becomes a question of trading the cost of that solution off against the cost of basic patient care needs for a growing number of organizations today. Certainly expenditures for medical record retention are being more closely scrutinized to determine the clear justification and cost/benefit ratios. The cost of originating and maintaining records in any form will be looked at more closely as the institution's financial performance becomes more critical. With that scrutiny will come the review of basic assumptions concerning medical record content and maintenance with a more clear differentiation between the "need to have" and the "nice to have." These kinds of questions cannot be answered without a good understanding of the statutory and regulatory requirements governing medical record maintenance and the record's various functions in the health care environment.

The hospital-licensing acts and regulations of a few states establish specific medical record retention requirements that govern medical records generally[16] or certain parts of the medical record, such as x-rays.[17] (See Appendixes A and B.) Some states have established different retention requirements for different classifications of patients, such as minors, the mentally ill, and the deceased.[18] Several state regulations require hospitals to keep records in accordance with hospital policy for a period equal to the statute of limitations for contract or personal injury actions.[19] In four states that have adopted the Uniform Preservation of Private

---

[16]*See, e.g.*, N.M. Stat. Ann. §14–6–2 (1978), 7 Pa. Admin. Bull. 3657 (1977).

[17]Ill. Ann. Stat. ch. 111–1/2, §157–11 (Smith-Hurd 1977); Tenn. Minimum Standards and Regulations for Hospitals ch. 1200.8.3.05(3)(b).

[18]Miss. Code Ann. §41–9–69 (1972): Rules and Regulations for the Licensure of General and Special Hospitals in Virginia §208.9 (1977).

[19]Ill. Hosp. Licensing Requirements §12–1.4 (1979); N.M. Licensing Regulations, pt. 2, at H24 (1965); N.C. Hosp. Licensing Regulations, pt. XIII, §.1400 *et seq.* (1964).

Business Records Act,[20] the three-year records preservation requirement of the act may apply to the medical records of private hospitals, even though there are no specific statutory medical records retention provisions. As a condition of participation in federal reimbursement programs, hospitals must retain their medical records for a period "not less than that determined by the statute of limitations in the respective State,"[21] presumably the statute of limitations for tort actions. However, discharge summaries and clinical and other medical records relating to Medicare health insurance claims must be retained for "a period of five years after the month the cost report to which the materials apply is filed with the intermediary."[22]

In the absence of regulatory requirements, each hospital should establish its own policy governing medical records retention. It is clear that hospitals should retain medical records for as long as there is a medical or administrative need for them, e.g., for subsequent patient care, medical research, review and evaluation of professional and hospital services, and defense of professional or other liability actions.

There are several factors that the hospital should consider in establishing a retention policy: statutory and regulatory requirements, statutes of limitations and future litigation, extent of medical research, storage capabilities, microfilming and other processes, and recommendations of hospital associations.

Clearly, the hospital must first comply with all applicable statutory and regulatory retention requirements. Where the hospital considers it prudent to have a retention period longer than statutory or regulatory requirements, however, it may establish one.

It has often been suggested that a key factor to be considered when establishing a record retention policy is the statute of limitations on contract and tort actions. Except in the case of minors' records, retaining the record for the longer limitations period would not likely impose a burden on the hospital medical records department, since limitations periods are generally shorter than the period the record would be retained for medical reasons. If the statute of limitations were used as a guide, the medical record of a minor would have to be kept until the patient reached the age of majority plus the period of the statute. In states in which the age of majority is 18 years and the statute of limitations for torts is 2 years, the retention period for a newborn's record would be 20 years. While the possibility

---

[20]Ill. Ann. Stat. ch. 116, §59–64 (Smith-Hurd Supp. 1980); Md. Ann. Code art. 15B, §1–6 (1976); N.H. Rev. Stat. Ann. §§337–A:1–337–A:6 (1966); Okla. Stat. Ann. tit. 67. §§251–256 (West Supp. 1983–84).

[21]42 C.F.R. §405.1026(b) (1982).

[22]1 Medicare and Medicaid Guide (CCH) 6420.85 (1983).

of an infant's waiting until majority to bring suit is slight, it can happen.[23] Although most suits by minors are brought soon after the accident causing the injury, a hospital is best protected if it retains records until the minor reaches majority and for an additional time equal to the applicable state statute of limitations on tort actions.

In most professional negligence actions against a hospital, the institution must show that the care it provided was consistent with accepted medical practice at the time and reasonable under the circumstances. (For a discussion of the principles of hospital liability, see Chapter 10.) The hospital's medical records usually are essential to its defense of such actions. Moreover, in at least one case, in which the plaintiff alleged that the hospital negligently lost portions of her medical record, thereby depriving her of the evidence necessary to meet her burden of proof, the court found a duty upon the hospital to maintain its patients' records.[24] In another instance, however, a negligence action was dismissed for failure to state a duty owed to plaintiff by the hospital to preserve x-rays taken of plaintiff.[25] The action was brought after plaintiff's complaint of malpractice had been rejected by the Medical Malpractice Review Panel, which considered only those x-rays still available. The court stated that plaintiff had failed to show any damages resulting from the alleged negligence of the hospital. While there is little law on this point, it is clear hospitals should maintain their medical records at least for the period required by any statute or regulation.

If the hospital's staffs engage in extensive medical research, especially retrospective investigations that require detailed medical record data, the hospital may wish to establish a long retention period. Moreover, if the medical research conducted in the hospital involves experimental or innovative patient care procedures, the hospital is well advised to retain its medical records for at least 75 years. Hospitals that routinely provided head and neck radiation in the 1930s were fortunate if they had their medical records when lawsuits were filed in the 1970s alleging that the institutions negligently increased the plaintiffs' susceptibility to thyroid cancer. In one case arising from the experimental administration of diethylstilbestrol (DES) between 1950 and 1952, the plaintiffs alleged that the hospital and the drug company were negligent in failing to warn them of the danger to their children until more than 20 years after administering the DES and 4 years after becoming aware of the drug's dangers.[26] Although the court dismissed the complaint because no physical injury to the former patient was alleged, it did recognize a duty on the part of the hospital to notify patients of the ". . . risks

---

[23]*See, e.g.*, Johns Hopkins Hospital v. Genda, 255 Md. 616, 258 A. 2d 595 (1969); Bettigole v. Diener, 210 Md. 537, 124 A.2d 265 (1956); Hubach v. Cole, 133 Ohio St. 137, 12 N.E. 2d 283 (1938).

[24]Fox v. Cohen, 84 Ill. App. 3d 744, 406 N.E. 2d 178 (1980).

[25]Hryniak v. Nathan Littauer Hospital Ass'n, 86 A.D. 2d 699, 446 N.Y.S. 2d 558 (1982).

[26]Mink v. Univ. of Chicago, 460 F. Supp. 713 (N.D. Ill. 1978).

inherent in DES treatment when they became aware, or should have become aware, of the relationship between DES and cancer."[27] To discharge such a duty, hospitals must be able to identify patients who have received experimental drugs or treatment. The patients' medical records enable hospitals to identify such patients and, if necessary, assist hospitals in defending suits arising from experimental treatments. Even if the duty to notify is not owed to the patient, retention periods far longer than provided by limitation statutes are advisable. A growing body of authority holds that operation of the statute does not commence until the patient has discovered, or reasonably should have discovered, the causal relation between the injury and the treatment or drug administered.[28]

A major consideration for a hospital in establishing a retention policy is its capability to store a large number of records. Available space, expansion rates, the endurance of the paper and folders used, the cost of microfilming, and storage safety requirements all affect the hospital's ability to retain records.

The statutes and regulations of several states authorize microfilming or other photographic reproduction of records,[29] and at least one state specifically authorizes retention of medical records on a computer.[30] In Louisiana, where hospital records are public documents,[31] a hospital may, but need not, microfilm its records before they are destroyed at the expiration of the statute of limitations.[32] Therefore, where possible, the hospital might alleviate its retention problem by microfilming the records and destroying the original copies. Such a procedure has at least once been sanctioned by statute.[33] This would reduce the need for storage space but might raise other administrative problems. Members of the medical staff, for example, might object to the restrictions on the availability of particular records for purposes of research and review. Moreover, the hospital would incur additional reading and printing equipment costs. Where state law and regulations do not specifically authorize microfilming, hospitals may microfilm their medical records and may destroy the original records in accordance with law or regulations governing record destruction.

The hospital may microfilm its records itself, provided it has the proper staff and equipment, or it may send its records to an outside contract service to be filmed. If

---

[27]*Id.* at 720.

[28]Dawson v. Eli Lilly & Co., 543 F. Supp. 1330 (D.D.C. 1982); Girard v. U.S., 455 F. Supp. 502 (D.N.H. 1978); Raymond v. Eli Lilly & Co., 117 N.H. 164, 371 A. 2d 170 (1977).

[29]*See, e.g.,* Ark. Stat. Ann. §§16–501 (Repl. Vol. 1979), Cal. Evid. Code §§1550 (West 1966); Mass. Gen. Laws Ann. ch. 111, §70 (1983 and West Supp. 1984–1985); N.J. Stat. Ann. §26:8–5 (West Supp. 1983–1984); Va. Code §8.01–391 (Supp. 1983).

[30]*See* Ind. Code Ann. §34–3–15.5–1 *et seq.* (West Supp. 1983).

[31]La. Rev. Stat. Ann. §44:7 (West Supp. 1983).

[32]Op. Atty. Gen. Louisiana, Jan. 8, 1964; La. Rev. Stat. Ann. §44:39 (West Supp. 1983).

[33]Ill. Ann. Stat. ch. 116, §61 (Smith-Hurd Supp. 1983–84).

it elects to use a contract service, it should do so pursuant to a written agreement that specifies, among other things, the method of record transfer, the method of reproduction, the quality and cost of the service, the time within which the service will be performed, safeguards against breach of confidentiality, indemnification of the hospital for loss resulting from the contractor's improper release of information or loss of records, and subsequent destruction of the records.

The American Hospital Association (AHA) and the American Medical Record Association (AMRA) have adopted a policy on record retention that recommends retaining complete records in original or reproduced form for a period of ten years after the most recent patient care entry and retaining certain parts of the record permanently. The AMRA recommends that after a period of ten years, the complete record may be destroyed, unless destruction is prohibited by statute, ordinance, regulation, or law, provided that the institution:

1. Retains basic information such as dates of admission and discharge, names of responsible physician, records of diagnoses and operations, operative reports, pathology reports, and discharge resumes for all records so destroyed.
2. Retains complete medical records of minors for the period of minority plus the applicable period of statute of limitations in the state in which the health care institution is located.
3. Retains complete medical records of patients under mental disability in like manner as those of patients under disability o[r] minority.
4. Retains complete patient medical records for longer periods when requested in writing by one of the following:
   a. An attending or consultant physician of the patient,
   b. The patient or someone acting legally in his behalf,
   c. Legal counsel for a party having interest affected by the patient medical records.[34]

In addition, some state hospital associations have issued record retention guidelines that may be useful in developing a hospital record retention policy.[35]

In the final analysis, no blanket record retention rule can be devised. The length of time medical records should be retained after they are no longer needed for medical and administrative purposes should be determined by the hospital administration with the advice of legal counsel, taking into account all factors, including the feasibility and cost of microfilming, the availability and cost of storage space, and the possible future need for such records, as well as the legal considerations

---

[34]AMERICAN HOSPITAL ASSOCIATION AND AMERICAN MEDICAL RECORD ASSOCIATION, *Statement on Preservation of Patient Medical Records in Health Care Institutions* (August 1977).

[35]ILL. HOSP. ASSN. RECORD RETENTION GUIDE FOR ILLINOIS HOSPITALS (1977).

just discussed in the event of a suit by the patient against the hospital or a third party. It should be noted that, except in a case involving the hospital's negligent loss of the patient's records,[36] there is no reported instance of hospital liability for failing to retain hospital records.

DESTRUCTION OF THE RECORD

The method of medical record destruction is controlled by statute and regulation in some states. The Tennessee statute states:

> Upon retirement of the record as provided in . . . this section, the record or any part thereof retired shall be destroyed by burning, shredding, or other effective method in keeping with the confidential nature of its contents. Destruction of such records must be made in the ordinary course of business and no record shall be destroyed on an individual basis.[37]

Other states require hospitals to create, in accordance with applicable regulations, an abstract of any pertinent data in the medical record prior to destroying the record.[38] Although the states that have specified the method of record destruction generally permit destruction by shredding or burning, the Environmental Protection Agency recommends shredding and recycling.[39] Hospitals that deliver their medical records to a commercial enterprise for destruction should do so pursuant to a written agreement that sets forth the method of destruction, establishes safeguards against breach of confidentiality, includes indemnification provisions to protect the hospital from loss due to unauthorized disclosure, and requires the contractor to certify that records delivered to it have been properly destroyed.

Hospitals that destroy their own records must establish procedures to protect confidentiality of record information and ensure that records are completely destroyed. The hospital employee responsible for record destruction should certify that the records have been properly destroyed. Whether its records are destroyed commercially or by the hospital, the hospital should retain certificates of destruction permanently as evidence of its record disposal.

The hospital's medical records policies should include provisions governing destruction of records, and these provisions should be uniformly applied. Where it can be shown that a hospital has failed to apply such a policy uniformly or where

[36]Fox v. Cohen, 84 Ill. App. 3d 744, 406 N.E. 2d 178 (1978).
[37]Tenn. Code Ann. §68–11–305(c) (1983); *see also* Ind. Code Ann. §34–3–15.5–1 (Burns 1973).
[38]Miss. Code Ann. §41–9–75 (1972).
[39]*See* 40 C.F.R. §246 (1983).

destruction was contrary to hospital policy, the courts may allow the jury in a negligence suit to infer that, if the records were available, they would show the hospital acted improperly in treating the plaintiff.[40]

---

[40]Carr v. St. Paul Fire & Marine Ins. Co., 384 F. Supp. 821, 831 (W.D. Ark. 1974).

Chapter 2

Medical Record Entries

The quality of medical records created in hospitals depends largely upon the individuals making record entries. Hospital medical, nursing, and other professional personnel, as well as students and others who write in patient records, must understand the importance of creating legible, complete, and accurate records and the legal and medical implications of failing to do so. Court decisions have shown that a hospital's exposure to negligence liability increases if it permits its staff to make improper entries. Moreover, federal regulations and some state laws require certain record entries to be made within a specified period following the patient's discharge.

Corrections to records, while perfectly permissible, can create serious problems for hospitals, especially those involved in negligence litigation, if appropriate changes are made in an improper manner. Significant alterations made simply to improve the defense of a lawsuit or to defraud reimbursement agencies can have serious adverse consequences for the hospital, including the imposition of criminal sanctions. Hospitals should establish policies that encourage their staffs to create appropriate medical records in a timely fashion.

IMPORTANCE OF A LEGIBLE, COMPLETE MEDICAL RECORD

The medical record is often the single most important document available to a hospital in the defense of a negligence action and ordinarily is admissible as evidence of what transpired in the care of the patient. (For a discussion of the admissibility of medical records, see Chapter 5.) Without a legible and complete medical record, the hospital may be unable to defend itself successfully against allegations of improper care. Therefore, hospitals must take great care to ensure that entries made in its medical records are thorough and proper.

Medical record entries should be made in clear and concise language that can be understood by all professional staff attending the patient. An ambiguous or illegible record is often worse than no record since it documents a failure of the hospital and professional staff involved to communicate clearly, and thus may impair the ability of the staff to provide proper treatment to the patient.[1] In addition, an illegible record entry introduced into evidence in a court action against the hospital may create suspicion in the minds of the jury that the entry was improper and may thereby weaken the hospital's defense.

A person making entries should place his or her signature and position or title after each entry. Anyone who reads the medical record must be able to determine who participated in the patient's care, should the need arise to consult on a treatment question or to reconstruct the hospitalization in defense of a professional negligence action. Including appropriate titles also helps a reader evaluate the contents of the record entry.

The medical record should contain a complete account of the treatment given the patient. A record is complete if it contains information sufficient to show clearly what treatment the patient received, why it was given, and, if some routine procedure was not given, the reason it was not. The statutes and regulations of several states require hospitals to maintain a complete record of the care rendered to a patient during hospitalization.[2] In addition, the Joint Commission on Accreditation of Hospitals (JCAH) requires accredited hospitals to maintain complete records of the care they provide.[3]

Maintaining a complete record is important not only to comply with licensing and accreditation requirements but also to enable the hospital to establish that adequate care was provided. If a hospital can demonstrate by testimony as to its policy, procedures, and routine practices that it regularly keeps complete and accurate records, the absence of certain notations may be used in the hospital's defense. In *Smith v. Roger's Memorial Hospital*,[4] the fact that the hospital's records did not show that the patient had complained of certain symptoms, in light of testimony that the hospital's records were generally reliable, was important

---

[1]*See* Larrimore v. Homeopathic Hospital Ass'n of Del., 54 Del. 449, 181 A. 2d 573 (1962).

[2] *See, e.g.*, N.J. Stat. Ann. §26:8–5 (West Supp. 1982–83); Tenn. Code Ann. §53–121 (1977); Tenn. Minimum Standards and Regulations for Hospitals ch. 1200–8–3.05(1)(d) (1974); Ill. Hosp. Licensing Requirements §12–1.2(b) (1983).

[3]*See* JOINT COMMISSION ON ACCREDITATION OF HOSPITALS, ACCREDITATION MANUAL FOR HOSPITALS 79–87 (1984) for the minimal requirements for the contents of hospital records. Under JCAH standards all medical records must include the following: identification data; medical history; report of physical examination; diagnostic and therapeutic orders; evidence of informed consent when applicable; clinical observations; reports and results of procedures and tests; and conclusions drawn at the termination of hospitalization or treatment. *Id.* at 80.

[4]382 A.2d 1025 (App. D.C.), *cert. denied*, 439 U.S. 847 (1978).

evidence in rebutting the patient's claim that she had complained of the symptoms and did not receive proper care.

Similarly, the failure to maintain a complete record may lead to a finding that the hospital was negligent in its treatment of the patient. In *Collins v. Westlake Community Hospital*,[5] the plaintiff alleged that the hospital's nursing staff negligently failed to observe the condition and circulation of his leg during the time it was in a cast and that their failure caused the patient to lose the leg. The Illinois court examined the patient's medical record and concluded that the absence of nursing notes documenting observations of the leg during seven critical hours, particularly in view of the physician's order to "watch condition of toes," could reasonably have led the jury to infer that no observations were made during that time. The hospital's nurses testified in *Collins* that nurses do not always record observations on the chart when patients are checked, that usually they record only abnormal findings, and that this procedure is consistent with the principles of problem-oriented medical records, which many hospitals have adopted. Nonetheless, the court allowed the jury to draw an inference from the absence of documented observations that no observations had been made.[6]

As some courts have not kept pace with recent trends in medical records documentation, hospitals must be certain that, when careful observations are essential, all staff document their contacts with patients. The hospital's efforts to increase efficiency should never prevent its staff from keeping records sufficiently detailed to enable it to show the type and quality of care rendered.

REQUIREMENTS FOR ACCURACY AND TIMELY COMPLETION

Both the JCAH standards of accreditation[7] and many state statutes and regulations[8] require that accurate medical records be kept. An inaccurate record not only

---

[5] 557 Ill. 2d 388, 312 N.E. 2d 614 (1974). *See also* Fatuck v. Hillside Hospital, 45 A.D.2d 708, 356 N.Y.S. 2d 105 (1974) *aff'd* 36 N.Y. 2d 736, 368 N.Y.S. 2d 161 (1975). (Absence of nursing notes documenting observation after order that psychiatric patient be checked every 15 minutes constituted prima facie case of negligence when patient escaped and committed suicide.) Hansch v. Hackett, 190 Wash. 97, 66 P.2d 1129 (1937). (Hospital held liable for negligent failure of nurse to observe and record patient's symptoms so that doctor could diagnose patient's condition.)

[6] The opposite result was reached in Topel v. Long Island Jewish Medical Center, 55 N.Y. 2d 682, 431 N.E.2d 293 (1981), a similar case in which the plaintiff alleged that a psychiatric patient who committed suicide in his room had not been checked every 15 minutes as ordered. In this case the court noted the hospital's explanation that worksheets containing the records of routine checks were destroyed each week and held that even if the jury disbelieved the hospital's explanation, the lack of records documenting the room checks was not sufficient to establish a prima facie case.

[7] JCAH, ACCREDITATION MANUAL FOR HOSPITALS 79 (1984).

[8] *See, e.g.*, Miss. Code. Ann. §41–9–63 (1972); 7 Pa. Admin. Bull. 3657–58 (1977); N.J. Manual of Standards for Hosp. Facilities §702 (1981); Hawaii Pub. Health Regulations, ch. 12, §10 (1979).

may be detrimental to patient care and in violation of licensing statutes and accreditation standards, but also may allow a plaintiff in a professional negligence action to destroy the credibility of the entire record. In *Hiatt v. Groce*,[9] a Kansas court found that the clear discrepancy between what the medical record stated and what actually happened to the patient could justify the jury's finding that, if the medical record was erroneous in one respect, it could be erroneous in other respects as well and could be considered generally invalid.

Medical records must not only be accurate but must be completed in a timely manner. Entries should be made when the treatment they describe is given or the observations to be documented are made. Regulations governing participation in federal reimbursement programs require that hospital records be complete within 15 days following the patient's discharge.[10] JCAH accreditation standards require the hospital's medical staff regulations to state the time limit for completion of the record after discharge.[11] The bylaws or regulations of hospital medical staffs should require staff members to complete their patients' records within a specified time and should provide an automatic suspension of clinical privileges of members who fail to comply.[12]

Incomplete records can be disastrous to a hospital's or physician's defense in a professional negligence action. Entries made in a record weeks after the patient's discharge have less credibility than those made during or immediately after the patient's hospitalization. If an entry is made after a lawsuit is threatened or filed, it may appear to have been made self-servingly for purposes of establishing a defense rather than for documenting the actual treatment rendered.

In *Foley v. Flushing Hospital & Medical Center*,[13] the physician amended the patient's medical record to show that medication was given orally after the patient's father complained of injuries caused by injection of medication. The change in the record was dated to show when it was made, and there was no attempt to conceal the change. Nonetheless, the change, along with proof of the injury, was ultimately found to constitute sufficient evidence to go to the jury on the question of whether the medication was administered orally or by injection.

It is generally the responsibility of the individual practitioner and the hospital's medical staff organization to ensure that patient records are complete within a reasonable time after the patient's discharge from the hospital.[14] The medical rec-

---

[9]215 Kan. 14, 523 P. 2d 320, 326 (1974).

[10]42 C.F.R. §405.1026(j)(2) (1981).

[11]JCAH, ACCREDITATION MANUAL FOR HOSPITALS 85 (1984).

[12]*See, e.g.*, Board of Trustees of Mem. Hosp. v. Pratt, 72 Wyo. 120, 262 P. 2d 682 (1953).

[13]41 A.D.2d 769, 341 N.Y.S. 2d 917 (1973), *rev'd*, 34 N.Y. 2d 863, 359 N.Y.S. 2d 113 (1974). *See also* Libbee v. Permanente Clinic, 268 Or. 258, 520 P. 2d 361 (1974).

[14]See JCAH, ACCREDITATION MANUAL FOR HOSPITALS 85 (1984); HUFFMAN, MEDICAL RECORDS MANAGEMENT 152–54 (6th ed. 1972).

ords department customarily is delegated responsibility for making sure records are completed within the time specified by the hospital and for collating them into the permanent medical records. This department should establish procedures for notifying attending physicians when records are incomplete and for followup when a physician fails to respond.

The final responsibility for completeness of the record rests with the patient's attending physician and the medical staff through enforcement of its bylaws and regulations. A hospital that fails to have and enforce proper medical record completion policies subjects itself and its medical staff to liability for breach of its duty to monitor a patient's treatment and for any ensuing injuries. For example, in *Bost v. Riley*,[15] the court found that the hospital had breached its duty to the patient in failing to act when his physicians neglected to record progress notes on the patient's medical record. No recovery was allowed, however, because there was no causal link between the hospital's failure to act and the plaintiff's injuries.

PERSON MAKING ENTRIES

As the number and types of people making entries in patient medical records increases, so does the potential for increased liability. Unnecessary or improper entries can give rise to negligence liability exposure, problems involving unlicensed persons practicing nursing or medicine, and poor patient relations. Hospitals should have policies governing who may enter information in a record in order to diminish this exposure. These policies should be carefully developed so that hospitals do not compromise patient care as they attempt to reduce liability exposure.

Most states do not restrict the type of professionals who may write entries in the chart; who may do so is a matter of individual hospital policy.[16] The patient's attending physician certainly may write in the patient's chart in accordance with hospital medical staff and medical records policies. Under JCAH accreditation standards, hospitals may permit house staff to write orders in patient charts but may not prohibit a patient's attending physician from writing orders also.[17] However, federal regulations governing Medicare state that only attending and resident physicians are competent to write medical histories and physical examinations in the chart.[18]

Given these broad legal and accrediting requirements, any person providing care to a patient should be permitted to document that care in the patient's medical

[15]44 N.C. App. 638, 262 S.E. 2d 391, *appeal denied*, 300 N.C. 194, 269 S.E. 2d 621 (1980).

[16]JCAH, ACCREDITATION MANUAL FOR HOSPITALS 85 (1984).

[17]*Id.* at 84.

[18]42 C.F.R. §405.1026(h) (1981).

record, regardless of the person's position in the hospital. It is the hospital's responsibility to establish policies that require individual practitioners to function within the scope of practice as authorized by state licensing or certification statutes, or, in the absence of such statutes, as defined by their professional competence. Hospitals should also define the level of record documentation expected of practitioners working in the institution. To the extent the hospital permits nurse midwives, podiatrists, dentists, clinical psychologists, physicians' assistants, and other nonphysician practitioners to provide treatment, it should require them to document their treatment in accordance with hospital medical records policy.

The entries of certain individuals require a physician's countersignature. The purpose of countersignatures is to require a professional to review and, if appropriate, indicate approval of action taken by another practitioner. Usually, the person countersigning a record entry is more experienced or has received a higher level of training than the person who made the original entry. In any case, the person required to countersign should be the individual to whom the authority to evaluate the entry is given. Countersignatures should not be viewed as so much paperwork but as a means for carrying out delegated responsibility.

In most hospitals, licensed house staff may make entries in the patient charts, but attending physicians are required to countersign some or all such entries. Medicare regulations require attending physicians to countersign at least the histories, physical examinations, and summaries written by the house staff.[19] Each hospital's medical staff should determine the extent to which countersignatures are required beyond these minimum regulatory requirements. What is important is that the medical record show clear evidence of the attending physician's supervision of house staff engaged in patient care.[20]

When undergraduate medical students and unlicensed house staff make record entries that show the application of medical judgment, medical diagnosis, the prescription of treatment, or any other act defined by applicable state law to be the practice of medicine, these entries should be countersigned by a licensed physician, who may be an attending or a resident physician. In most states, it is a violation of the medical licensure act for anyone to practice medicine without a license, unless he or she is practicing under the direct, proximate supervision of a physician licensed to practice in the state. Therefore, without evidence of such supervision, the student or unlicensed resident might be held to have violated state law. The rules governing physicians' countersignature of medical record entries made by other authorized personnel should be set forth in the hospital's medical staff rules and regulations.[21]

---

[19]42 C.F.R. §405.1026(i) (1981).

[20]JCAH, ACCREDITATION MANUAL FOR HOSPITALS 84 (1984).

[21]*Id.*

Similarly, the entries of undergraduate nursing students should be counter-signed by a licensed professional nurse, if such entries document the practice of professional nursing as defined by the state's nursing licensure act. Without evidence of proper supervision, a nursing student practicing professional nursing could be held in violation of the state's nursing licensure act, unless the act specifically authorizes nursing students to practice nursing in the course of their studies toward a registered nurse (RN) degree.[22] The nursing licensure acts of some states also authorize graduate nurses who have applied for a license to practice professional nursing for a limited time without a license.[23] Graduate, unlicensed nurses in these states may make entries in medical records without countersignature by a licensed nurse. However, in states that have no specific allowances for practice by such graduates, their entries should be properly countersigned. Moreover, hospitals may establish rules governing nursing student record entries that are more stringent than state law.

While state and federal law is generally silent with regard to the entries of other students in the hospital, hospitals generally should require licensed professionals to countersign the record entries of students. The patient's medical record should show careful monitoring of students' scope of practice and competence.

In many hospitals, social workers participate in the care of patients and request that they be allowed to make entries in their patients' charts. Generally, there is no prohibition against entries by members of an institution's social service department, so long as the information placed in the record is relevant to the patient's treatment. Entries by social service staff should be limited to relevant factual observations or to data and judgments that such staff are competent to make; highly subjective remarks, if essential to the record, must be carefully worded and clearly relevant to the patient's care.

Authentication of Records

The requirement that records or a portion of them be signed by the physician or other medical practitioner exists to ensure authenticity. Most state regulations require a signature or other authentication for the record. Authentication is the key element in system reliability and security. The JCAH has recognized the potential applicability of computer technology to medical records by including in its glossary the following definition:

---

[22]*See, e.g.*, Ill. Ann. Stat. ch. 111, §3402 (Smith-Hurd Supp. 1984–85).
[23]*Id.*

"Authenticated"
To prove authorship, for example, by written signature, identifiable initials, or computer key. The use of rubber stamp signatures is acceptable only under the following conditions:

1. The individual whose signature the rubber stamp represents is the only one who has possession of the stamp and is the only one who uses it; and
2. The individual places in the administrative offices of the hospital a signed statement to the effect that he is the only one who has the stamp and is the only one who will use it.[24]

The JCAH's interpretations of its standards are both specific and general on the question of authentication. The interpretation for JCAH Medical Record Standard III provides in part:

All entries in the record must be dated and authenticated, and a method must be established to identify the authors of entries. . . . The parts of the medical record that are the responsibility of the medical practitioner shall be authenticated by him. For example, when specified professional personnel have been approved for such duties as taking medical histories and documenting some aspects of a physical examination, such information shall be appropriately authenticated by the responsible physician or dentist. The responsible medical staff member's own pertinent observations and significant physical findings should be added whenever necessary, or he may record his own history and physical examination of the patient. When members of the house staff and other specified professional personnel are involved in patient care, sufficient evidence should be documented in the medical record to substantiate the active participation in, and supervision of, the patient's care by the responsible attending physician or dentist. . . . Each clinical event, including the history and physical examination, shall be documented as soon as possible after its occurrence. Records of discharged patients shall be completed following discharge, within a reasonable period of time to be specified in the medical staff rules and regulations.[25]

Taken together, the JCAH standards indicate a clear intention to maintain the requirement of system reliability. This is so even where the JCAH recognizes the potential use of automated data processing.

---

[24]JCAH, ACCREDITATION MANUAL FOR HOSPITALS 211 (1984); *see also Id*. at 84.
[25]*Id*. at 85.

The Medicare Conditions of Participation require that records be authenticated and signed by a licensed physician. The physician must sign the entries he or she makes; a single signature on the face sheet of the record will not suffice to authenticate the entire record. Furthermore, the attending physician must countersign at least the history, physical examination, and summary written by the house staff.[26]

The majority of states requires that entries in the medical record be authenticated *and* signed by a medical staff member, thereby necessitating a written signature. However, a growing number of state regulations provide that entries must be authenticated *or* signed, thus permitting authentication by a variety of means, including written signature, identifiable initials, computer key, or rubber stamp signature.

Fifteen states now expressly provide in their hospital regulations for authentication by means of computer keys or rubber stamp signatures. However, all of the states that permit this type of authentication do require that control be exercised to limit access to and use of the authenticating devices to the properly authorized individuals to safeguard against abuse. With regard to rubber stamp signatures, these 15 states have adopted controls identical or very similar to those set forth in the JCAH's definition of authentication. (For a discussion of access to automated medical records, see Chapter 4.)

Alabama requires that entries in the medical record be made in ink or be typewritten, and that they be authenticated and signed or initialed by the attending physician.[27] In Arizona, the person responsible for each entry "shall be identified by initials or signature."[28] Arkansas permits physicians to use rubber stamp signatures if the method is approved in writing by the hospital administrator and the medical records committee.[29] In addition to the JCAH restrictions on the use of such stamps, Arkansas requires that the stamp be locked in the medical records department when the physician is not using it.[30]

California permits authentication by a signature stamp or computer key in lieu of a physician's signature only when the physician has placed a signed statement in the hospital administrative offices to the effect that "he is the only person who (1) has possession of the stamp or key and (2) will use the stamp or key."[31] Indiana requires that all physicians' orders for medication and treatment be in

---

[26]42 C.F.R. §405.1026(i)(3).

[27]Rules of Alabama State Board of Health Bureau of Licensure and Certification §420–5–7.07(1)(g) (1970).

[28]Arizona Hospital Licensing Regulations §Rg–10–221 L. (1979).

[29]Rules and Regulations for Hospitals and Related Institutions in Arkansas pt. 6, §V(E) (1979).

[30]*Id.* pt. 6, §V(E)1.

[31]Cal. Health and Safety Code §70751(g) (1984).

writing or acceptable computerized form and be signed by hand or computer key by the attending physician within 24 hours.[32]

In Kansas, each clinical entry must be signed or initialed by the attending physician, who must be properly identified in the record.[33] Kentucky requires that all orders for diet, diagnostic tests, therapeutic procedures, and medications be written, signed, and dated by the medical staff member.[34] Nebraska provides that "facsimiles" of physician's signatures and initials be permitted "where appropriate safeguards have been taken to limit access and use of the facsimile or code to the individual physician."[35]

New Jersey requires that all orders for medication and treatment be in writing, signed by the prescribing physician, and dated.[36] Telephone and verbal orders must be countersigned by the physician within 24 hours.[37] North Carolina provides that orders for medication or treatment be dated and recorded directly in the patient's chart or "in a computer or data processing system which provides a hard copy printout of the order for the patient's chart."[38] The hospital must establish a method "to identify all persons who record such orders and to safeguard against fraudulent recordings."[39] Authentication may be by signature, initials, computer entry or code, or "other method(s) not inconsistent with the laws, rules, and regulations of any other applicable jurisdictions."[40]

Oklahoma expressly prohibits the use of signature stamps as a substitute for the signature of the authorizing doctor.[41] Pennsylvania requires that all entries in the record be dated and authenticated by the person making the entry, and it has adopted the JCAH definition of authentication.[42] South Carolina permits the use of rubber stamp signatures provided that the JCAH limitations are observed.[43]

---

[32]Indiana State Board of Health, Regulations for General and Special Hospitals §9.1(d) (1977).

[33]Kansas Department of Health and Environment, Hospital Regulations §28–34–9(f) (1974).

[34]Kentucky Health Facilities and Health Services Licensing Requirements for Hospitals §3(11)(d)7 (1983).

[35]State of Nebraska Department of Health Regulations and Standards for Hospitals §3(d)(i)(c) (1979).

[36]New Jersey Department of Health Manual of Standards for Hospital Facilities §702(c)(10) (1981).

[37]*Id.* at 702(c)(10)b.

[38]Laws, Regulations and Procedures Applying to the Licensing of Hospitals in North Carolina §.0405(b) (1983).

[39]*Id.*

[40]*Id.* at §.0405(c).

[41]Standards and Regulations for Licensure of Hospitals and Related Institutions of Oklahoma pt. 2, A.4c(iii)b.

[42]Pennsylvania Department of Health, Bureau of Quality Assurance, Division of Hospitals Rules and Regulations for Hospitals §115.33(b) (1982).

[43]Minimum Standards for Licensing of Hospitals and Institutional General Infirmaries in South Carolina §601.1 (1982).

However, the regulations forbid their use on orders for drugs listed as controlled substances in the South Carolina Code.[44]

Tennessee requires that all orders for diagnostic procedures, treatments, medication, and transfer or disposition be recorded legibly in ink or by typewriter, and that they be dated and signed by the physician.[45] Verbal and telephone orders may be taken only by licensed nurses and must be countersigned by the physician no later than his or her next visit to the institution.[46] The person recording the orders must also sign his or her name and title.[47] The Washington statute provides that each entry in a patient's medical record be dated and authenticated by the person who either gave the order or provided the care to which the entry pertained.[48] However, authentication is defined as "authorization of a written entry in a record by means of a signature which shall include, minimally, first initial, last name, and title."[49] West Virginia similarly requires that all orders for medication and treatment be in writing and be signed in ink by the physician.[50]

It is obvious that the signature requirement is a major consideration. But the word "signature" may not necessarily mean one's name written by hand. For example, in several states the legislative definition of "signature" or "written" is broad enough to include printed signatures. Other states make an exception in the case of written signatures. For example, a Massachusetts statute reads:

MASS. GEN. LAWS ANN ch. 4 §7 (1980)
§7. DEFINITIONS

"Written" and "in writing" shall include printing, engraving, lithographing and any other mode of representing words and letters; but if the written signature of a person is required by law, it shall always be his own handwriting or, if he is unable to write, his mark.

The language of the statute is clear, and several cases[51] have construed that language to mean that where a statute or a regulation requires a written signature, it means a direct personal act of the person whose name is to be signed.

---

[44]*Id.* §601.1(B).

[45]Rules of Tennessee Department of Public Health, Bureau of Health Resources and Division of Health Care Facilities ch. 1200.8.3. 02(6)(a).

[46]*Id.*

[47]*Id.*

[48]Wash. Hosp. Rules and Regulations §248–18–440(3)(d)(1984).

[49]*Id.* §248–18–001(7).

[50]West Virginia Regulations and Law for Licensing Hospitals §603.1(i).

[51]*See, e.g.,* Irving v. Goodimate Co., 320 Mass. 454, 70 N.E. 2d 414 (1946); Finnegan v. Lucy, 157 Mass. 439, 32 N.E. 656 (1892).

The Massachusetts statute may also be broad enough to include computer-generated writings. Note the language, "and any other mode of representing words and letters." The Nebraska hospital regulations clearly allow for computer-generated writings by defining the term "signed" to include "handwritten signature or the use of an assigned computer code in any institution in which medical records are entered into or maintained on computer."[52]

The statutes may be interpreted by the courts to reflect modern techniques of communication based on certain business practices which have recognized a change in the meaning of the word "signature." For example, *Joseph Denunzio Fruit Co. v. Crane*[53] was a complicated contracts case involving, in part, the proper interpretation to be placed on written communications via teletype messages exchanged between certain parties. The court cited with approval several cases that indicated that a signature may take a variety of forms, including handwritten, printed, stamped, typewritten, engraved, photographed, or cut from one instrument and attached to another. The court recognized the teletype machine as a modern device, the use of which satisfied the California statute of frauds, which requires written instruments and signatures for certain types of transactions. The court stated:

> The court must take a realistic view of modern business practices, and can probably take judicial notice of the extensive use to which the teletype machine is being used today among business firms, particularly brokers, in the expeditious transmission of typewritten messages . . . this court will hold that the teletype messages in this case satisfy the statute of frauds in California.[54]

The New Jersey Supreme Court has adopted a rule which appears to recognize modern technology. While no interpretations of its language have been found, the rule is broad and virtually all-encompassing.

Rule 1. (13). WRITING

"Writing" means handwriting, typewriting, printing, photostating, photography and every other means of recording upon any tangible

[52]Nebraska Department of Health, Regulations and Standards for Hospitals, Rule 30–(1)(b)(xi) (1979).

[53]188 F.2d 569 (9th Cir. 1951), *cert. denied*, 342 U.S. 820 (1951), *aff'g* 79 F.Supp. 117 (S.D. Calif. 1948).

[54]*Id.* 79 F.Supp. at 128

thing any form of communications or representation, including letters, words, pictures, sounds or symbols, or combinations thereof, provided that such recording is (a) reasonably permanent and (b) readable by sight. When information or data [are] recorded by means of a generally accepted method or system, which is operated with suitable controls to safeguard the reliability and accuracy of the information or data, and which is equipped with means for providing a reproduction that is a "writing," such reproduction shall be treated as the equivalent of the information or data, notwithstanding that the form of recording does not itself constitute a "writing" as defined by this rule.[55]

It would appear that a computer tape library of medical record information would be, in the language of the New Jersey rule, (1) recorded by means of a generally accepted method or system, (2) operated with suitable controls to safeguard the reliability and accuracy of the information and data, and (3) equipped with means for providing a reproduction that is a "writing." If the court rule were made applicable to all writings in New Jersey, an automated medical record information system could be operated without a requirement of a backup manual system. This speculation is buttressed to some extent by the language of the hospital regulations of that state, which require merely that medical records be properly written.[56] However, there has so far been no ruling on the specific question of the applicability of the rule to this kind of system.

While several states, including Pennsylvania, Missouri, and Oregon, have adopted the JCAH definition of "authenticated" in their hospital regulations, it is not possible to state as a general rule that authentication of medical records may be accomplished by other than a written signature. Any health care institution that intends to automate its medical records information should confer with legal counsel to determine how its medical records may be authenticated in the proposed computer system. If state law requires a written signature for authentication, the institution must provide for such authentication in its automated system or obtain an amendment of the applicable, restrictive state law.

Verbal Orders

A physician's verbal orders should be limited as much as possible to telephone orders and in all cases must be transcribed in the medical record and signed by the physician within 24 hours.[57] JCAH accreditation standards and hospital licensing

---

[55]New Jersey Rules of Evidence, Rule 1(13).

[56]New Jersey Department of Health Manual of Standards for Hospital Facilities §701(C) (1981).

[57]JCAH, ACCREDITATION MANUAL FOR HOSPITALS 85 (1984).

regulations in some states require all physician orders to be written in the patient's medical record.[58] Irrespective of laws or accrediting standards, hospitals should require all verbal orders to be transcribed within a specified time. A physician's signature on a transcribed verbal order authenticates the order and indicates that it was written correctly. Who may receive and transcribe a physician's verbal order is a matter of hospital policy and should be set forth in hospital policies or in the medical staff rules and regulations.[59] The policies should be predicated on the concept that only personnel who are qualified to understand physicians' orders should be authorized to receive and transcribe verbal orders.

In view of the increased potential for error in the transcription of verbal orders, hospitals should discourage all verbal orders except those that must be issued by telephone. Physicians should be responsible for writing their orders in the medical record, unless they are not present when the order must be given. If circumstances make this impossible, the physician should authenticate the orders before leaving the unit. Nursing or house staff in most hospitals receive and transcribe telephone orders from attending physicians. Although not practicable in all cases, having a second person at the hospital on the telephone to witness the conversation reduces error and controversy concerning the order given. For especially sensitive orders, such as "do-not-resuscitate" orders, hospitals should require a witness to the order.

CORRECTIONS AND ALTERATIONS

As medical record entry errors are inevitable, hospitals should establish clear procedures for correcting errors. Generally, there are two kinds of errors: (1) minor errors in transcription, spelling, etc., and (2) more significant errors involving test results, physician orders, inadvertently omitted information, and similar substantive entries. As a general rule, the person who made the incorrect record entry should correct the entry. If the correction is a significant one, a senior person designated by hospital policy should review the correction to determine that it complies with the institution's guidelines for record amendments. Hospital personnel should make changes that are within their scope of practice as defined by state licensing and certification laws. A registered nurse, for example, should not amend a physician's medication order unless directed to do so by the physician or by a senior hospital official pursuant to established hospital policy. Obvious minor errors in spelling and the like do not require intervention by senior personnel. The person who made the error should correct it, if possible, but any practitioner working with the record may correct such a minor error.

The person correcting a charting error should cross out the incorrect entry, enter the correct information, initial the correction, and enter the time and date the

[58]Id.; Ill. Hosp. Licensing Requirements §3–3(a) and §12–1.2 (b) (1979).

[59]JCAH, ACCREDITATION MANUAL FOR HOSPITALS 85 (1984).

correction was made (if not otherwise shown in the entry). Mistakes in the chart should not be erased or obliterated, since erasures and obliterations will likely create suspicion in the mind of a jury concerning the original entry. A single line through incorrect entries leaves no doubt as to the original information being corrected. Where a correction requires more space than is available near the original entry, the person correcting the record should enter a reference to an addendum to the record and enter the more lengthy correction in the addendum.

If the patient requests that the record be amended, hospital personnel should advise the patient's attending physician of the changes requested. The physician should discuss the matter with the patient, if the physician considers the requested amendment inappropriate. If the record is amended, the amendment should be made in an addendum to the record, and the physician should add an entry to document that the change was made at the request of the patient, who will thereafter bear the burden of explaining the change. The hospital should establish a policy governing such amendments.

After a claim has been made or a lawsuit has been threatened or filed against the hospital or a member of its staff, hospital personnel and medical staff should make no changes in the complainant's medical record without first consulting their defense counsel. Attempts to alter medical record entries in a way that might be favorable to the defendants are always inappropriate and do not necessarily help the defense, particularly if the patient has obtained a copy of the chart prior to the time the changes are made. If the plaintiff can show that the record was altered without justification by a defendant, the plaintiff may be able to destroy the credibility of the entire record. In a 1980 Connecticut case in which the hospital's nurses rewrote an entire section of the patient's medical record following the patient's injury in the hospital, the court held in the subsequent negligence action that:

> [i]n addition to all the other evidence in the case, the significance of the revised hospital record should not be overlooked. Although the defendant understandably attempts to minimize what was done by characterizing the action as merely one of ordering expanded notes and by attributing it to poor judgment, the trier [of fact] was not required to be so charitable. An allowable inference from the bungled attempt to cover up the staff inadequacies on the morning of January 24 was that *the revision indicated a consciousness of negligence*. The court so charged and the jury could so find. [Emphasis added.][60]

---

[60]Pisel v. Stamford Hosp., 180 Conn. 314, 340, 430 A. 2d 1,15(1980). *See also* Libbee v. Permanente Clinic, 268 Or. 258, 520 P. 2d 361 (1974). (Jury could infer that the nurse who had falsified the patient's chart to show that she had checked the fetal heartbeat every half hour made that entry because she knew such procedure was good nursing practice. Such knowledge, along with other evidence, could be used to establish the appropriate standard of care.) Hiatt v. Groce, *supra* note 9 (clear discrepancy between the medical record and the facts could justify jury's disbelieving entire record).

If, after a claim has been made or a lawsuit threatened, an original record entry is found to be inaccurate or incomplete, the hospital should request that clarifications or additions to the record be placed in a properly signed and dated addendum to the record.

Deliberately altering a medical record or writing an incorrect record may subject the individual and the hospital to statutory sanctions. In some states, for example, a practitioner who makes a false entry on a medical record is subject to license revocation for unprofessional conduct.[61] In other states, falsifying a medical record for purposes of cheating or defrauding is a crime.[62] Under federal statutes and regulations, altering or falsifying a chart for purposes of wrongfully obtaining government funds is a crime and subjects the violator to a substantial fine or imprisonment.[63]

---

[61]*See, e.g.*, Ky. Rev. Stat. §311.595 (Supp. 1980).

[62]Tenn. Code Ann. §39–3–944 (1982 and Supp. 1983), making it a crime to falsify a hospital medical record for the purpose of cheating or defrauding.

[63]42 U.S.C. §1395nn (1983); 42 U.S.C. §1395y(d) & (e); 42 U.S.C. §§139cc(b)(2)(D)–(G).

Chapter 3

Special Medical Records
Problems

This chapter discusses selected special medical records problems arising frequently in hospital settings. While we have chosen to discuss only a few of the infinite situations a hospital may encounter, the issues raised here will apply to a broad range of medical records problems. In some instances, the hospital must deal with special types of patients, such as child abuse victims, celebrities, or hostile patients. In other situations discussed in this chapter, the hospital is forced to deal with particularly difficult issues surrounding dying patients. Some of the documentation problems discussed in this chapter, such as the treatment of a child abuse victim or differences of opinion among professional staff, also require documentation of the potentially competing interests.

Although these situations require physicians and other hospital personnel to adhere to the general legal standards discussed throughout this book, they also demand additional attention to careful documentation. Individuals making medical records entries relating to these special problems must be extraordinarily precise and objective in their documentation. These situations also suggest that the hospital, with the assistance of legal counsel, should develop a workable and appropriate hospital policy to provide hospital personnel and medical records practitioners with a consistent protocol.

RECORDS OF CHILD ABUSE

Every state has mandatory reporting laws obligating hospital personnel who have reason to believe that a child has been abused to report their findings to a designated state agency. These reporting requirements, which are discussed in more detail in Chapter 4, specify the nature and content of the report submitted to the state agency. Most state laws require that a hospital staff member covered by the statute who suspects child abuse notify the person in charge of the institution, who in turn makes the necessary report.

When the physician assesses a child to determine whether reasonable cause exists to believe the child is abused or neglected, careful notations must be made in the medical record. Specifically, a detailed and objective documentation and description of all pertinent physical findings should be clearly noted in the record. In addition, any tests performed or photographs taken to document the suspected abuse should be carefully noted in the record. This detailed information will be the basis upon which a determination of abuse is made. Therefore, it is essential that it be accurate, specific, and thorough.

The record should include a history of the injury, including details reported by the parent or guardian of how the injury allegedly happened, the date and time of the injury, sequence of events, names of witnesses, and time interval between the injury and the time medical attention was sought. If the parents, guardians, and child are interviewed separately, the date, time, and place of the interviews should also be documented in the record.

CONFLICT BETWEEN CHILD ABUSE REPORTING AND PATIENT CONFIDENTIALITY

Courts continue to struggle with the conflict between state mandatory child abuse reporting statutes and state and federal statutes prohibiting disclosure of certain medical records.[1] The trend seems to be for courts to allow disclosure in cases involving possible child abuse, but courts still disagree concerning the extent of disclosure.

Patient Confidentiality Statutes

As a general rule, information in a patient's medical record may not be disclosed without the patient's consent.[2] State and federal statutes support this rule. For example, the evidentiary statutes of many states establish a privilege that protects statements made in the course of treatment by a physician where a physician-patient relationship exists. This physician-patient privilege enables a patient (and, in some states, a physician or hospital) to object to any attempt to introduce such statements in a court proceeding.[3]

---

[1]For a discussion of the requirements for a court order for disclosure in child abuse cases, *see* Cosgrove, *Substance Abuse Record Confidentiality and Child Abuse Reporting Requirements*, 2 TOPICS IN HEALTH RECORD MANAGEMENT 81 (Sept. 1981).

[2]*See* IIA HOSPITAL LAW MANUAL, "Medical Records" 18 (1983).

[3]*Id.* at 68. *See* Ill. Ann. Stat. ch. 110, §8–802 (Smith-Hurd 1984).

Some states also have enacted statutes that prohibit or restrict disclosure of certain types of patient information in court or elsewhere. The Illinois Mental Health and Developmental Disabilities Act,[4] for example, prohibits the disclosure of information concerning a person undergoing treatment for mental illness or developmental disabilities (as defined by the act) except under certain circumstances. The statutes state that all records kept by a therapist or agency in the course of providing mental health or developmental disabilities service to a patient concerning the patient and the service provided are confidential and may not be disclosed, except as provided in the act.[5]

Federal law also protects certain patient information. Persons receiving treatment for alcoholism or drug abuse are protected by the federal Comprehensive Alcoholism Prevention, Treatment and Rehabilitation Act and the Drug Abuse Office and Treatment Act, both of which establish strict confidentiality requirements for patient records maintained by federally assisted treatment centers.[6] (For a detailed discussion of these statutes and the regulations issued pursuant to them, see Chapter 4.) A health care facility may not disclose record information of patients protected by these acts except under circumstances specifically described in the statutes[7] or unless a court has found "good cause" for authorizing disclosure and has entered an appropriate order to that effect.[8] The statutes do not define the term "good cause," and courts have been seeking a proper definition since the statutes were enacted.[9]

The public policy underlying these special confidentiality rules is to encourage people to seek medical or psychiatric treatment when they need it. The rules rely upon the assumption that, if statements made to physicians and other health care providers will not be disclosed, people will be more willing to discuss highly personal and confidential matters relating to their illnesses.

Child Abuse Reporting Laws

Most states have enacted child abuse reporting statutes. (For a more detailed discussion of such statutes, see Chapter 4.) Common to many of these enactments are the mandatory reporting of suspected or actual abuse and a grant of immunity to persons who make reports in good faith.[10] Increasingly, child abuse statutes

---

[4]*See* Ill. Ann. Stat. ch. 91–1/2, §§801 *et seq.* (Smith-Hurd Supp. 1984–85).

[5]*Id.* §803.

[6]A more detailed discussion of these statutes can be found in 1 Topics in Health Record Management (March and June 1981).

[7]42 C.F.R. §§2.51–2.53 (1983).

[8]*Id.* §2.61.

[9]*See* Cosgrove, *supra* note 1, at 82.

[10]*See, e.g.,* Ill. Ann. Stat. ch. 23, §2059 (Smith-Hurd Supp. 1984–85).

have broadened the definition of "abuse" to include emotional injury as well as physical and sexual abuse.[11] A typical child abuse statute authorizes a designated state agency to intervene for the child's protection and to assist the person committing abuse in finding appropriate counseling or treatment. As the known incidence of child abuse has increased with better reporting, the public's interest in child abuse prevention has grown.[12] As a result, some statutes now declare that any evidence of a child's injuries may be admitted into evidence in any legal proceeding arising from the alleged abuse.[13] The public policies supporting child abuse reporting statutes are the protection of children and the reduction of abuse through appropriate counseling.

Conflicting Policies

The public policies underlying mandatory child abuse reporting and protection of patient confidentiality appear to conflict. If the patient discloses information in the course of treatment for mental illess or alcoholism that suggests or confirms that he or she abused a child, the question arises of how the state agency may obtain such information as evidence in a legal proceeding instituted to protect the child from further abuse.

In *State of Minnesota v. Andring*,[14] the Supreme Court of Minnesota grappled with this apparent conflict. In this case, the defendant was charged with three counts of criminal sexual conduct involving his 10-year-old stepdaughter and his 11-year-old niece. State authorities learned of the abuse from sources other than the defendant's medical records. The defendant was released on bond and voluntarily entered a crisis unit, where he was diagnosed as suffering from acute alcoholism and depression. During (1) one-on-one counseling sessions, (2) the taking of his social history, and (3) group therapy sessions, the defendant described his sexual contact with young girls. The state moved for discovery and disclosure of the defendant's medical records and statements made to crisis unit personnel. The trial court denied the state's motion for discovery of statements made during his medical history and individual therapy and granted the motion for discovery of disclosure made in group therapy sessions. Given the conflicting policies involved, the trial court certified the issue to the Minnesota Supreme Court.

The defendant argued that (1) the federal Comprehensive Alcohol Abuse and Alcoholism Prevention, Treatment and Rehabilitation Act and regulations protect

---

[11]*Id.* §2053.

[12]For a thorough discussion of child abuse reporting statutes and their history, *see* Fraser, *A Glance at the Past, a Gaze at the Present, a Glimpse at the Future: A Critical Analysis of the Development of Chilid Abuse Reporting Statutes*, 54 CHICAGO-KENT L.REV. 635 (1978).

[13]*See, e.g.*, Ill. Ann. Stat. ch. 23, §2060 (Smith-Hurd Supp. 1984–85).

[14]342 N.W. 2d 128 (Minn. 1984).

the statements made during his treatment at the crisis unit, and (2) the state's physician-patient privilege covers all of the statements he made at the unit and, thus, protects them from disclosure in court. The state argued that the Minnesota Maltreatment of Minors Reporting Act requires health care personnel to report suspected child abuse and prohibits use of the physician-patient privilege to exclude evidence concerning a suspected child abuse victim's injuries.

The Minnesota Supreme Court held that the federal alcoholism treatment act and regulations do not preempt the state's child abuse reporting law. Examining the legislative history of the two statutes, the court found that the state law was enacted in response to the federal Child Abuse Prevention and Treatment Act, which requires a state to enact a child abuse reporting law in order to qualify for federal funds for child abuse programs. It also found that Congress enacted the federal child abuse statute and the federal alcoholism treatment statute in the same year. The court concluded that Congress could not have intended one statute to preempt the very state law it had itself mandated in another statute, and the court held that:

> the confidentiality of patient records provision of the alcohol treatment act does not preclude the use of patient records in child abuse proceedings to the extent required by [the state child abuse reporting statute].[15]

However, the court limited the extent to which such records could be disclosed. Pointing to the public policy of encouraging persons who abuse children to seek treatment voluntarily, the court held that the child abuse reporting statute abrogates the physician-patient privilege:

> only to the extent that it would permit evidentiary use of the information required to be contained in the maltreatment report—the identity of the child, the identity of the parent, guardian, or other person responsible for the child's care, the nature and extent of the child's injuries, and the name and address of the reporter.[16]

Thus, the court permitted some erosion of the physician-patient privilege, but only to the extent necessary to give force and effect to the abuse reporting statute. The court confirmed that, since the state had obtained through other sources the information required to be reported by the statute, the lower court was correct in this case to prohibit discovery of the medical history and individual therapy. Moreover, holding that the physician-patient privilege also extends to protect

[15]*Id.* at 132.
[16]*Id.* at 133.

confidential group therapy sessions where they are an integral and necessary part of a patient's diagnosis and treatment, the court overturned the lower court decision to permit discovery of the defendant's group therapy sessions.

The Minnesota Supreme Court was able in *Andring,* therefore, to preserve the integrity of the state child abuse reporting statute without mandating an invasion of the defendant's confidential statements made to health care personnel. The court chose to make the federal alcoholism treatment act and the Minnesota child abuse reporting statute work together, even though the alcoholism treatment act and regulations contain explicit language stating that the act preempts conflicting state law. The court cites no Congressional committee reports or other specific legislative history that support its position that the alcoholism treatment act is not preemptive. It appears the court simply viewed the public policy of protecting children as more important than that of protecting absolutely the records of alcoholism and drug abuse patients. It is interesting to note, however, that while the court rejected the preemption provision of the federal alcoholism treatment act, it did not order disclosure of information in this case in contravention of that statute. The key was that the state had already obtained information it needed to identify the abused children. If in future cases the state of Minnesota seeks such information from similar patient records, the court's holding in *Andring* will permit the state to pierce the shield provided by the federal alcoholism treatment act and the state physician-patient privilege, at least to the extent necessary to protect the children involved.

Resolving the Conflict without Court Action

In some cases, it may be possible for health care personnel, the hospital, and the hospital's attorney to resolve apparent conflicts between confidentiality and reporting statutes without resorting to formal legal action. Some years ago, for example, in a large Illinois teaching hospital, an unwed teenage mother disclosed during a therapy session with her psychologist that she had suffocated one of her infant twins and was afraid she would harm the remaining child. Alarmed, the psychologist telephoned the hospital's general counsel, reported the situation without disclosing the patient's identity, and sought his advice.

The apparent dilemma facing the psychologist and the attorney was whether the practitioner could comply with the Illinois mandatory child abuse reporting statute in light of the confidentiality protections established by the Illinois Mental Health and Developmental Disabilities Confidentiality Act, which at that time stated that patient information could be disclosed to protect a person from a clear, imminent risk of harm. After a close examination of the statutes, counsel determined that the psychologist could file a child abuse report in order to protect the surviving twin infant from imminent harm threatened by the mother. The psychologist filed the report with the appropriate state agency, which took protective custody of the infant and brought law enforcement personnel into the case. The mother was confined for psychiatric evaluation and, eventually, treatment.

In this case, the practitioner and the hospital attorney were able to use the imminent harm exception to the confidentiality statute to permit compliance with the child abuse reporting statute. While a solution was available in this case, it may not be in all cases. Recently, the Illinois legislature recognized this problem and enacted into the confidentiality act a provision specifically authorizing disclosure of patient records when necessary to comply with the child abuse reporting law, even if no imminent peril exists. Here, the principle that patient information is confidential, except where a greater public policy demands disclosure, was upheld.

Statutes may not always fit so nicely together, as demonstrated by the Minnesota situation. If legal counsel advise that under similar facts conflicting statutes cannot be reconciled, health care institutions should seek the courts' direction. Decisions such as *Andring* suggest that courts will find a way to obtain information needed to protect threatened children.

PATIENT ACCIDENT AND INCIDENT REPORTS

For a discussion of patient accident and incident reports, and guidelines regarding their composition and use, see Chapter 5.

EMERGENCY ROOM RECORDS

Various state and federal regulations and laws discussed throughout this book govern hospital records, including emergency room records. Some state statutes and regulations specify the information to be recorded; other states specify which broad areas of information concerning the patient's treatment must be included; some states simply declare that the medical record shall be adequate, accurate, or complete. State hospital licensure rules and regulations may also provide requirements and standards for the maintenance, handling, signing, filing, and retention of hospital records generally. For a summary of state hospital licensing regulations concerning medical records, see Appendix B.

Medicare regulations governing the Conditions of Participation for hospitals specifically address emergency service or emergency department records. The Medicare regulations provide for the following:

Standard; medical records. Adequate medical records on every patient are kept. The factors explaining the standard are as follows:

(1) The emergency room record contains:
    (i) Patient identification.
    (ii) History of disease or injury.
    (iii) Physical findings.
    (iv) Laboratory and X-ray reports, if any.
    (v) Diagnosis.
    (vi) Record of treatment.
    (vii) Disposition of the case.
    (viii) Signature of a physician.
(2) Medical reports for patients treated in the emergency service are organized by a medical record librarian or her equivalent.
(3) Where appropriate, medical records of emergency services are integrated with those of the inpatient and outpatient services.
(4) A proper method of filing records is maintained.
(5) At a minimum, emergency service medical records are kept for as long a time as required in a given state's statute of limitations.[17]

In addition to specific Medicare requirements applicable to emergency room records, the Joint Commission on Accreditation of Hospitals (JCAH) has published Standard VII on emergency services and recordkeeping: "A medical record shall be maintained on every patient seeking emergency care and shall be incorporated into the patient's permanent hospital record. . . ."[18] JCAH stipulates the minimum information that must be included in the emergency room record. The JCAH standard resembles the Medicare regulations closely. JCAH requires:

Each time a patient visits the emergency department/service, the following information shall be entered in the patient's medical record:

- Patient identification. When not obtainable, the reason shall be entered in the medical record.
- Time and means of arrival.
- Pertinent history of the illness or injury, and physical findings, including the patient's vital signs.
- Emergency care given to the patient prior to arrival.
- Diagnostic and therapeutic orders.
- Clinical observations, including results of treatment.
- Reports of procedures, tests, and results.
- Diagnostic impression.

---

[17]42 C.F.R. §405.1033(d)(1983).
[18]JCAH, ACCREDITATION MANUAL FOR HOSPITALS 30 (1984).

- Conclusion at the termination of evaluation/treatment, including final disposition, the patient's condition on discharge or transfer, and any instructions given to the patient and/or family for followup care.
- A patient's leaving against medical advice.

The medical record shall be authenticated by the practitioner who is responsible for its clinical accuracy.

It is recommended that the ambulance record of the patient be available to the practitioner providing emergency care and that it be filed with, but not necessarily as a part of, the patient's medical record.[19]

It is also essential that hospital emergency room policies and procedures address the completion of hospital records by emergency room personnel. These policies should be followed scrupulously. Penalties for violators should be written into the policies and uniformly enforced.

While hospitals must comply with all rules applicable to emergency room medical records, they should take special care to ensure that, where the patient receives emergency treatment, the record documents the circumstances that demonstrated that an emergency existed. This is essential if the patient was unable to give express consent to the treatment. If the hospital or emergency room physician has any doubt that a true emergency exists in such cases, the physician should obtain another physician's confirmation that an emergency exists, and the record should include that confirmation.

As in all medical records, complete documentation is important. For example, in *Louisville General Hospital v. Hellmann*,[20] the facts revealed that the patient was admitted to the defendant hospital for treatment of a head injury. He remained in the hospital for approximately 2½ weeks before his death. His widow sued the hospital, claiming negligent care. The emergency room record contained only two entries with regard to the medical care the decedent received in the emergency room between 8 p.m. and 6 a.m. on the day of admission. The physician testified that he had monitored the decedent's vital signs every 30 minutes during the time he was in the emergency room and that his failure to record each examination was customary procedure at the hospital.

In view of the physician's testimony, the plaintiff moved that the trial court enter an order directing the hospital to produce for inspection and copying all emergency room records compiled and prepared in the ordinary course of business of the hospital for each of the 30 days immediately preceding and including the

---

[19]*Id.*

[20]500 S.W. 2d 790 (Ky. 1973).

date the decedent was admitted. The court issued the order, and the defendant hospital moved that it be set aside. In support of its motion, the hospital filed the affidavit of the director of medical records, which stated that it was physically impossible to produce such records, as they were filed by patient number, not by month, and that there were approximately 5,000 records involved in that 30-day period. The trial court overruled this motion. On appeal, the appellate court stated that it appeared that the order would place an undue burden on the hospital, which was not commensurate with the results that might be obtained. Therefore, the trial court's order was modified to provide that the examination of the emergency room records be confined to no more than 100 of such records selected at random. Any personal information that might identify the patient was to be concealed.

The modified court order demonstrates the willingness of the court to look for a pattern of recording treatment in the emergency room of a defendant hospital and emphasizes the importance of maintaining complete emergency room records.

RECORDING DISAGREEMENTS AMONG PROFESSIONAL STAFF

All members of the medical team have a duty to take reasonable actions to safeguard the lives of their patients. Nurses as well as other medical professionals other than physicians are often given the responsibility of monitoring and coordinating patient care. As a result, in the exercise of reasonable professional judgment and in order to minimize possible liability for negligence, nonphysician medical professionals may be expected to intervene to clarify or object to those physicians' orders they believe are improper. For example, in *Carlsen v. Javurek*,[21] a nurse anesthetist refused to follow a physician's orders prescribing an anesthetic that the nurse knew was contraindicated. Although the nurse is usually obligated to follow physicians' orders, the court recognized that if, for example, the two professionals fail to agree on proper anesthetic, the surgery should be cancelled. If a nurse and physician are unable to agree, the nurse should obtain the intervention of a responsible medical or administrative officer according to the hospital policy.

It is essential for the nurse and other medical professionals to document their efforts to fulfill their duty to object to improper orders and to obtain responsible intervention to settle a professional disagreement. At the same time, it is important to create a medical record that is sufficiently objective and factual that it could not be used as evidence against the physician or the institution in a negligence action.

---

[21]526 F.2d 202 (8th Cir. 1975).

Although there are no clear answers to the medical records issues presented, in instances of disagreements among physicians and other medical professionals, several suggested approaches may be helpful.

If hospital policy requires that resolution of disagreements be documented in the medical record, the basic guideline for making these entries is that they be objective, concise, and completely factual rather than judgmental. The medical record is no place for vindictiveness or groundless opinion. All persons making entries into the records should be taught how to document these problems. For example, consider the following hypothetical case:

At 10:00 A.M. Ms. Jones, a staff nurse, finds on the order sheet an order from Dr. Smith to give 0.5 mg. of Digoxin intravenously to an infant patient. Recognizing that 0.5 mg. is a lethal dose, Ms. Jones telephones Dr. Smith at 10:10 A.M. and advises him that in her opinion the order is incorrect. Dr. Smith immediately acknowledges an error in the placement of a decimal and tells Ms. Jones the order should read "0.05 mg." Ms. Jones amends the order in accordance with the hospital's telephone order policy and administers the correct dosage, 0.05 mg.

Ms. Jones might document this incident in the nurse's notes as follows:

10:10 A.M. Called Dr. Smith concerning his order of 0.5 mg. of Digoxin IV. Dr. Smith directed that the order be changed to 0.05 mg. of Digoxin IV and be administered this A.M. Physician order sheet amended accordingly.

/s/ M. Jones, R.N.

Now, assume that Dr. Smith disagreed with Ms. Jones that the order was incorrect and told her to follow the order as written. Ms. Jones informed Dr. Smith that she could not follow the order without seeking further advice through the institution's responsible intervention procedure. Following the intervention procedure, Ms. Jones contacted Dr. Brown, chairman of the department of pediatrics, at 10:15 A.M. and described the situation. At 10:30 A.M. Dr. Smith telephoned Ms. Jones and directed her to change the order to "0.05 mg. Digoxin IV." We can assume that Dr. Brown had a brief, but effective, conversation with Dr. Smith between 10:15 and 10:30 A.M.

Ms. Jones might properly document the incident in the nurses' notes as follows:

10:10 A.M. Called Dr. Smith concerning his order of 0.5 mg. of Digoxin IV. Dr. Smith confirmed the order.

10:15 A.M. Called Dr. Brown concerning Dr. Smith's order of 0.5 mg. of Digoxin IV.

10:30 A.M. Received telephone order from Dr. Smith to change order to read 0.05 mg. Digoxin IV. Physician order sheet amended accordingly.

/s/ M. Jones, R.N.

In another hypothetical case, Ms. Jones finds a written order in the chart of a 55-year-old patient for 125 mg. of Propranolol orally every six hours. In her experience, this is an unusually large dose. At 10:00 A.M. she calls the prescribing physician, Dr. Smith, to discuss the order. Although Dr. Smith tells Ms. Jones that this is a proper dosage for this patient, Ms. Jones is still uneasy about the order. In accordance with her hospital's intervention procedure, she contacts the chairman of the department of medicine, Dr. Black, at 10:15 A.M. Dr. Black calls Ms. Jones at 10:45 A.M. and advises her that he has discussed the case with Dr. Smith and that he, Dr. Black, believes the order is proper. Ms. Jones administers the Propranolol and might document her actions in the nursing notes as follows:

10:00 A.M. Called Dr. Smith concerning his order of 125 mg. of Propranolol q6hrs. Dr. Smith confirmed his order.

10:15 A.M. Called Dr. Black concerning Dr. Smith's order of 125 mg. of Propranolol q6hrs.

10:45 A.M. Dr. Black telephoned and stated that he had discussed the order of 125 mg. of Propranolol q6hrs. with Dr. Smith and confirmed Dr. Smith's order.[22]

Although these hypothetical cases are obviously simplified, they provide an example of how medical records entries documenting intervention procedures should appear: concise, objective, and, above all, factual. The more complex the intervention, the more care the nurse or other professionals must take in documenting the facts. Statements such as "Dr. Smith is negligent again" or "Dr. Smith's order is incorrect" are unnecessary, inappropriate, and, should any legal action arise from the case, possibly harmful not only to the physician and the institution but also to the nurse involved.[23]

There are varying opinions among health care professionals concerning whether these kinds of professional discussions and disagreements should be documented in a medical record, and, if so, in what manner. Regardless of the position one takes on the issue, it is clear that a health care institution must have a policy on the question. Otherwise practitioners are left to work out their differences on their own. This inevitably leads to inconsistent patient care and record documentation practices and can result in dangerous medical records entries made by professionals in the heat of anger.

MEDICAL RECORDS ISSUES INVOLVING TERMINALLY ILL PATIENTS

Do-Not-Resuscitate Orders

The term "cardiopulmonary resuscitation" (CPR) describes a procedure developed over the past two decades to reestablish breathing and heartbeat after cardiac

---

[22]Roach, *Responsible Intervention: A Legal Duty To Act*, JOURNAL OF NURSING ADMINISTRATION 7, at 23–24 (July 1980).

[23]*Id.*

or respiratory arrest. The most basic form of CPR, which is being taught to the public, involves recognizing the indications for intervention, opening an airway, initiating mouth-to-mouth breathing, and compressing the chest externally to establish artificial circulation. In hospitals, and in some emergency transport vehicles, CPR can also include the administration of oxygen under pressure to the lungs, the use of intravenous medications, the injection of stimulants into the heart through intravenous medications, the injection of stimulants into the heart through catheters or long needles, electric shocks to the heart, insertion of a pacemaker, and open heart massage. Some of these procedures are highly intrusive and even violent in nature. These interventions are all medically justified and indicated for patients whose conditions are not yet diagnosed or for those who have a hopeful prognosis. However, as the national Conference on Cardiopulmonary Resuscitation and Emergency Cardiac Care, sponsored by the American Health Association and the National Academy of Sciences National Research Council, concluded that "[t]he purpose of CPR is the prevention of sudden, unexpected death. CPR is not indicated in certain situations, such as in cases of terminal irreversible illness where death is not unexpected."[24]

To ensure that CPR is not initiated where it is not indicated, it is common practice to write "Do not resuscitate" (DNR) or "No CPR" on the orders concerning treatment of the patient. Many institutions call the CPR team by announcing "Code Blue," so the order might read "No Code Blue." JCAH standards and some hospital-licensing rules can be interpreted to require documentation of all major actions regarding the patient's care. The JCAH Standards specify that all "significant clinical information pertaining to the patient" shall be documented in the medical record, including "diagnostic and therapeutic orders."[25] A written DNR order documents the fact that a decision has been made and by whom; it ensures that the decision is communicated to the staff so that inappropriate CPR is not initiated. When CPR is clearly not part of the planned care, staff members can act in accordance with the decision without concern that they misunderstood the decision or will later be thought to have neglected the patient. Written orders take into account the fact that these decisions are an appropriate part of medical practice and have been made after careful deliberation.

Although some physicians are still reluctant to write DNR orders because they fear legal liability, numerous courts have recognized the practice of writing such orders.[26] In *Matter of Dinnerstein*,[27] the earliest reported case in which a court

---

[24]*Standards and Guidelines for Cardiopulmonary Resuscitation (CPR) and Emergency Cardiac Care*, 244 J.A.M.A. 453, 506 (1980).

[25]JCAH, Accreditation Manual for Hospitals 79–81 (1984).

[26]Matter of Quinlan, 70 N.J. 10, 355 A. 2d 647, 657, 663 (1976); Eichner v. Dillon, 73 App. Div. 2d 431, 426 N.Y.S. 2d 517, 542, 550 (1980); Severns v. Wilmington Medical Center, Inc., 421 A. 2d 1334, 1338 (Del. 1980).

[27]6 Mass. App. 466, 380 N.E. 2d 134 (1978). This result was approved in Matter of Spring, 380 Mass. 629, 405 N.E. 2d 115, 120 (1980).

ruled directly on the appropriateness of DNR orders without prior court authorization, the practice was upheld. The court in *In re Severns*[28] authorized a DNR order but did not state whether court authorization is always required. The District of Columbia Court of Appeals has also stated its approval of the practice without court authorization.[29] Furthermore, risk of legal liability from a failure to resuscitate is much more limited when there is a written order or explanation than when no order is in the record.

The importance of proper documentation is illustrated by the one case in which a DNR order was legally challenged. In *Hoyt v. St. Mary's Rehabilitation Center*,[30] a Minnesota District Court ordered a hospital to remove a patient's name from the DNR list. Because of irreversible brain damage following neurological surgery, the 41-year-old patient functioned at approximately the level of a 2 year old. Her parents, who had received court appointment as her guardians, had agreed with the physicians that resuscitation was not appropriate. Hoyt, who met the patient after the brain damage and visited her daily, challenged the DNR order. In a unique departure from the principles regarding who may bring cases to court, the court created a new basis for standing to sue. It said that "third parties with a sincere interest in the ward and an ability to present the matter to the court" have standing and found that Hoyt had the requisite interest and ability. The court held that resuscitation decisions are within the authority of the guardian and that the only role of the court is to ensure that the decisions be made "only after appropriate consideration." The role of the third party with standing was limited to suggesting the need for court review of the guardians' consideration. In this particular case, the court found that the guardians were unaware of the nature of the treatment to be denied and did not demonstrate sufficient consideration of what the patient would have wanted. The court focused on whether the patient would have wanted to continue indefinitely at her present level in four areas: (1) pain, (2) intellectual activity, (3) happiness, and (4) personal relationships. The court also mentioned that consideration should be given to whether payment would be of concern to the patient. The court ordered the patient's name to be taken off the DNR list until "knowledgeable approval" by the guardian to put her name back on the list.

The *Hoyt* case is important for at least two other reasons. First, it illustrates that there is an acceptable range of opinion regarding when DNR orders are appropriate. It demonstrates judicial acceptance of such orders when patients are neither comatose nor near death, if there is knowledgeable concurrence by the physician and the patient's guardian. Second, it demonstrates that such decisions must be carefully made after due consideration because it may be necessary to justify the

---

[28]425 A. 2d 156, 160 (Del. Ch. 1980).

[29]Matter of J.N., 406 A. 2d 1275, 1282 (D.C. App. 1979).

[30]No. 774555 (Dist. Ct., Hennepin County, Minn., February 13, 1981).

decision in a subsequent court action. It is doubtful that many other courts will grant standing to third parties with a "sincere interest" because of the traditional deference to family and physician decision making in these matters and the desire of courts to control their dockets. However, there are other channels, such as professional licensing boards, through which questions could be raised.

New Veterans Administration (VA) guidelines for withholding emergency resuscitation from terminally ill hospital patients whose heart or breathing fails now explicitly permit—contrary to past practice—VA hospital physicians to write DNR orders in patient records.[31] The guidelines stipulate, in part, that a DNR order may be placed in the chart of a competent, terminally ill patient after the senior attending physician and the patient agree that the order is appropriate. When the patient is comatose or incompetent, the decision should be reached after consultation with the patient's family or guardian. One noteworthy aspect of the new guidelines is the recognition given to state "living will" or "natural death" statutes. (Living wills and natural death acts are discussed later in this chapter.) Patient compliance with their requirements may be considered evidence of that patient's wishes concerning DNR orders. However, the guidelines emphasize that "[u]nder no circumstances should DNR orders be written where they are in compliance only with a request for assisted suicide or voluntary euthanasia." While these guidelines are not binding, each VA facility is urged to formulate similar protocols for dealing with terminally ill patients. Notwithstanding any DNR protocols that may be adopted, VA policy continues to be that resuscitation will be administered to every patient who sustains cardiopulmonary arrest if the medical record does not contain a DNR order that conforms to established policy.

Natural Death Acts and Living Wills

Several states, starting with California,[32] have enacted laws providing that a patient's wishes may be followed with some degree of immunity if the patient has executed a special directive regarding treatment of terminal illness. Recognizing that, in some instances, the physician may be unwilling to follow the patient's directive, several of these laws require reasonable efforts to transfer the patient to the care of another physician who will abide by these wishes.

Other provisions of the acts vary with respect to who may sign, the content and execution of the directive, the sanctions and immunities, and the effect of the

---

[31]Veterans Administration, Department of Medicine and Surgery, Circulai 10–83–140 (Aug. 25, 1983).

[32]Ala. Code §22–8A–4 (Supp. 1980); Cal. Health and Safety Code §§7185–7193 (West Supp. 1982); D.C. Code Ann. §6–2422 (Michie Supp. 1983); Idaho Code §39–4504 (Michie Supp. 1983); Tex. Rev. Civ. Stat. Ann. art. 4590h §3 (Vernon Supp. 1983); Wash. Rev. Code Ann. §70.122.03(1) (West Supp. 1983–1984).

absence of a directive. Most of the natural death acts authorize only competent adults to sign directives. Thus, most of these laws do not cover a large part of the population, such as minors and incompetent adults who have not previously executed a directive.

Each of the laws specifies either the precise wording of the directive or the elements that must be included. In states that specify the wording, the patient who wants to express more detailed or different wishes must forego the benefit of the statute and rely on state common law and state and federal constitutional principles as a basis for his or her request. Furthermore, the physician must have the wording checked carefully to determine that it satisfies the statute's requirements. There can also be problems with individualized documents, however, because the patient's intent may not be clear. Each of the natural death acts specifies the formality with which the directive must be executed. All the acts require witnesses, and some disqualify certain people as witnesses. Some states require that the directive be notarized. Most acts specify the means to revoke a directive. Regardless of the technicalities, it is best not to carry out a directive if there is any reason to believe the patient has changed his or her mind.

The effect of the directive also varies among states. In some states, the directive appears to be binding, but no sanction is specified for physicians who do not follow it. In several other states, the directive is binding, and there are sanctions for not following it if the patient was diagnosed as terminally ill before he or she signed the directive. In most states, the directive is not binding if signed before diagnosis, so it is only to be given weight in the physician's decisions regarding care. When the directive is binding, the physician who does not wish to follow the directive has a duty to arrange a transfer to another physician. The specified sanction for failure to arrange this transfer is discipline under medical licensing acts for unprofessional conduct. All of the natural death acts provide some immunity for those who act or refrain from acting in accordance with a directive that complies with the act. In most states, however, it is questionable whether the immunity provisions offer substantially more protection than applicable common law and constitutional principles. The primary issue in most controversies will be the diagnosis of terminal illness. Since this diagnosis is viewed as a professional responsibility for which physicians should be accountable, none of the statutes provides any protection for liability that arises from negligent diagnosis. Of course, immunity by statute is easier to establish than immunity under common law or constitutional law principles. Thus, when practical, it is best to attempt to comply with the statutory requirements.

Most natural death acts specify that they do not affect other statutory or common law rights to refuse treatment. The Arkansas statute,[33] however, could potentially

---

[33]Ark. Stat. Ann. §82–3801—82–3804 (Supp. 1982).

be interpreted to supersede nonstatutory approaches because it is comprehensive and does not specifically preserve other approaches. Thus, with the possible exception of cases in Arkansas, it is reasonable to follow the wishes of the patient and/or family in accord with common law and constitutional law principles whenever there is no valid statutory directive.

Although many statutes specify that the directive is to be placed in the medical record, it is recommended that any physician or nurse who receives a proper directive should place the document in the medical record whether or not required by the statute. In addition, if medical or nursing staff obtains clarification of certain terms of the directive from the patient, the information obtained should be documented in the medical record. Specifically, the patient's instructions concerning specific procedures, such as blood transfusion, amputation, etc., about which the patient has expressed definite desires, should be entered into the record, even though they may not be valid elements of a directive under the state's natural death act. This information should not be included in the directive itself if the statute specifies the exact wording to be used in the directive.

The hospital staff should also be advised that, if the original declaration is contained in the patient's medical record, a patient will not be able to revoke the declaration by physical destruction. If a copy of the declaration is in the medical record and the hospital staff or physician receives notice of revocation, a note should be entered on the declaration stating that the patient has revoked it.

Most natural death acts make it a crime to interfere with the proper use of directive forms. Unauthorized cancellation or concealment of a directive in order to interfere with a patient's wish not to be treated is generally made a misdemeanor. Falsification or forgery of a directive or withholding knowledge of revocation in order to cause actions contrary to the patient's wishes, when these actions hasten death, is declared to be a felony. Since the natural death acts are still relatively new, there have been no reported cases involving use or misuse of the forms.

Whether or not the applicable state statute places a time limit on the effectiveness of a declaration, it may be advisable for persons in good health to revise their declarations periodically. The obvious disadvantage of this concept is that, if the declaration itself imposes an automatic time limit, a patient's directive contained in the medical record could lapse when the patient would like it to remain in effect. The need for such renewals is demonstrated by a Florida appeals court decision that held that a comatose, terminally ill patient who executed a living will six years before he became incompetent could not be removed from life-sustaining apparatus without court authorization, despite the patient's documented desire not to have such apparatus employed.[34] When a hospital was requested to terminate

---

[34]John F. Kennedy Memorial Hospital, Inc. v. Bludworth, 432 So.2d 611 (Fla. Dist. Ct. App. 1983).

artificial life-support measures for the patient in accordance with the living will, the facility petitioned the court to determine whether it would incur civil or criminal liability by complying with the request.

Although the Florida court recognized the right of a conscious, mentally competent but terminally ill patient to order the removal of life-support measures, it distinguished that situation from one in which such a patient is comatose and the request for termination of life support comes from the patient's guardian. A conscious patient who requests to die with dignity is the prime and direct beneficiary of the decision, the court explained, but an unconscious patient—unable to feel pain—benefits only indirectly. Because the benefits of a living will run more directly to the family of a comatose patient through financial savings and an end to the emotional drain of awaiting the death of a loved one, the state must protect the comatose, terminally ill patient from potentially self-serving requests made by the family. To do so requires a judicial determination of whether the patient would want life support suspended, the court explained. Although a living will is evidence of a patient's desire, the weight assigned to that expressed intention will depend on when the living will was executed, the circumstances of its execution, its content, and any evidence of a contrary intent on the part of the patient.

GENERAL DOCUMENTATION ISSUES

Hospitals, with the assistance of their medical staffs, should develop guidelines for managing the difficult situations associated with the dying process. Guidelines are not required by law, but they can help to avoid controversies that can add to the strain on patients, families, and staff in the already stressful situation of terminal illness. It is essential, however, that the guidelines preserve flexibility within the limits of propriety and the boundaries established by law. The situations surrounding terminal illness are as varied as the individual patients involved and do not fit well into fixed patterns.

The core of the guidelines should be a reaffirmation that decisions are to be made by the physician and the patient. If the patient is unable to participate or desires family involvement, the patient's family should be consulted. The nature of the patient and family involvement should be discussed in the guidelines, along with the alternatives available when they are unable to be involved.

The use of medical consultants in difficult cases should be encouraged because consultation provides some protection for both the physician and the hospital in the event questions arise later concerning the diagnosis. Some hospitals have created a consultative committee with members who may be consulted individually or collectively. Some persons have advocated that a hospital committee make final decisions concerning life-supporting treatment because they do not trust decisions made by physicians, patients, and families. Other persons have opposed mandatory committee decision making because it interferes with the physician-patient relationship and it is difficult to enforce, potentially increasing the risk of liability in situations in which the committee is not involved. A few states require committee involvement in some decisions regarding the terminally ill. Based on local circumstances, a hospital could reasonably conclude that this or other conditions require confirmation by a committee. Even if confirmation is not required, prudent physicians seek the support of a committee or other consultants voluntarily because some courts will be persuaded by the concurrence of qualified physicians on issues of good faith and good medical practice.[35]

One important feature that should be required in any hospital policy is proper documentation. The minimum documentation necessary should be an order or note in the medical record specifying the treatment to be withheld or withdrawn and an indication of the concurrence of the patient and/or family (or the reasons they were not involved, such as unavailability or incapacity). The record should document the prognosis and any other rationales for the decision. Just as with other actions for which written orders are required, emergency situations may arise in which oral orders are appropriate. However, oral orders must be written or countersigned within 24 hours.

The guidelines should also indicate how the medical staff should approach situations in which the patient's condition is possibly due to criminal activities. The hospital should try to accommodate the law enforcement needs of the prosecutor and medical examiner. (For a discussion of access to medical records by law enforcement agencies, see Chapter 4.)

In developing guidelines, hospitals should consider whether a form should be drafted for the patient and/or patient's family to sign if they concur with the decision to withhold or withdraw treatment. There is disagreement concerning the appropriateness of such forms. Some believe a signed form can heighten the awareness of the decision being made and is the best way to prove the concurrence of the patient and/or patient's family. They also point to the legislative preference for a signed form in the natural death acts. Others believe the use of such a form appears to place the entire decision-making burden on the patient or family. They prefer to present the physician's decision regarding treatment for patient and/or family concurrence, preserving their opportunity to veto the physician's decision while minimizing the strain on family and the potential for future family guilt feelings. They believe that the humaneness of this approach is worth the possibility of slightly increased difficulty in proving concurrence.

Autopsy Authorizations

Autopsies are the most frequent cause of litigation involving dead bodies and hospitals. Autopsies are performed primarily to determine the cause of a patient's

---

[35]Matter of Spring, 380 Mass. 629, 405 N.E. 2d 115 (1980).

death. This finding can be crucial in detecting crime or ruling out transmittable diseases that may be a threat to the public health. More frequently, the cause of death can determine whether death benefits are payable under insurance policies, workers' compensation laws, and other programs.

Community mores and religious beliefs have long dictated respectful handling of dead bodies. Societal views have now evolved to the point that a substantial portion of the population recognizes the benefit of autopsies. Out of respect to those who continue to find autopsies unacceptable, the law requires appropriate consent before an autopsy can be performed, except when an autopsy is needed to determine the cause of death for public policy purposes.

The consent to the autopsy, whether given by the decedent, by family members, or by other persons authorized to give consent in the particular state, must be documented in the patient's medical record. A few states require that an autopsy be authorized in writing. Many states include telegrams and recorded telephone permissions as acceptable forms of authorization. Common law does not require that the authorization be documented in a particular way, so evidentiary considerations are the primary basis for deciding the appropriate form of consent. A written authorization or recorded telephone authorization is obviously the easiest to prove. In *Lashbrook v. Barnes*,[36] the mother of the deceased claimed, although she had signed an autopsy authorization, that the body had been mutilated. The court quoted the authorization in its entirety and directed a verdict for the physician, which was affirmed on appeal. As a result of the written authorization, the sole remaining issue was whether the autopsy had been performed in the usual manner, and there was no evidence that it was not performed in the usual manner. This case demonstrates the benefits of securing and including in the medical record written authorization for an autopsy.

Hostile Patients

Hostile patients present problems for everyone in a health care facility. Whether the hostility arises from the patient's condition, general nature, or the treatment received at the institution, a patient is often more inclined to take legal action if a problem in treatment actually occurs. Moreover, hostile patients may be less inclined to remember all the facts of a treatment situation or to view them in a light favorable to the hospital. Therefore, hospital staff should take greater care in documenting the hostile patient's treatment.

Practitioners should take a common-sense approach to such documentation. No special rules of law apply to records of hostile patients. If the patient is hostile, the hospital should simply take care to create a detailed medical record that leaves

---

[36]437 S.W.2d 502 (Ky. 1969).

little ambiguity about the patient's care. Practitioners should avoid making derogatory remarks about a hostile patient in the medical record. They add nothing to the ability of other practitioners to care for the patient, and the patient will likely interpret them as further proof of the practitioners' bad faith. If hostility is clinically significant, it should be described clinically in the medical record.

Celebrity Patients

When patients who are subject to close scrutiny by news media are hospitalized for conditions that might be embarrassing for them, special care must often be taken to protect their confidentiality. While news media take an interest in patients who may have temporarily become newsworthy, they often use more aggressive tactics in obtaining information concerning celebrities. Therefore, some hospitals have established special procedures for handling celebrity patient records.

As an extra precaution against unauthorized disclosure, some hospitals omit the patient's name from the record or use a code name that corresponds to a master code maintained by the medical records director and hospital chief executive officer. While this device may give added protection to the patient, it may conflict with state statutes and regulations and should be employed only with the advice of the institution's counsel. Some hospitals place the medical records of celebrity patients in a special secure file accessible only to the medical records director and other designated persons. This approach may not provide the same degree of protection as the former method, but it will not likely violate record content requirements of state law.

ADOPTION RECORDS

Medical records practitioners in health care institutions may not frequently encounter requests from individuals seeking to inspect a medical record where the request is either primarily or incidentally premised on a desire to obtain information about the natural parents of an individual who has been adopted (the "adoptee"). Clearly the primary focus of attention on such requests to inspect medical records will usually concern the birth records of the adoptee. But when such requests are received, formulating an appropriate response may be troublesome. A response to a request of this kind may be difficult because of the policy conflict between laws that permit patient access to medical records and adoption laws that typically require that court records pertaining to an adoption be sealed and made confidential to protect the privacy of the natural parents of the adoptee.

Most states permit patients to inspect their records. (See Chapter 4 for a more detailed discussion of the rules governing patients' access to medical records.) In states that still restrict the patients' access to their medical records, the issue of who may inspect a medical record to obtain information about the natural parents of an adoptee is less relevant. Where patient access to medical records is permitted, however, and the law permitting such access does not expressly address the issues involved in obtaining access to the medical records of an adoptee, the resolution of the problem of who is permitted to inspect and obtain access to what kind of medical record should be sensitive to the competing policy interests described above. The problem presents several dimensions, the most significant of which are the following three:

1. Do the natural parents of the adoptee have and retain a right to inspect part or all of the adoptee's medical records?
2. Do the adopting parents of the adoptee acquire a right to inspect part or all of the adoptee's medical records?
3. Does the adoptee ever aquire a right to inspect part or all of his or her medical records?

Adoption Laws and Confidentiality

To appreciate fully the potential policy conflict between adoption laws and laws that permit patients to inspect their medical records, one must understand some fundamentals about the laws governing adoption.

Adoption laws in this country are statutory; frequently involve court action; and state in explicit detail the procedures governing adoption, the rights of all concerned parties, and the process by which an adoption is accomplished. More than 40 states currently provide that the court records pertaining to the adoption and the adoptee's original birth certificate may or must be sealed and made confidential by court order. Only three states, Alabama, Florida, and Kansas, grant the adoptee access to such records, and a few states grant no access to the records but expressly permit medical and other information to be given to the adoptee, so long as the identities of the natural parents are not disclosed.[37]

Typical of states' statutes that seal adoption records is the adoption statute in Illinois, which provides that on the request of:

> any party to an adoption proceeding the court shall [or may itself] order that the file relating to such proceeding shall be impounded by the clerk of the court and shall be opened for examination only upon specific order of the court, which order shall name the person or persons who are to be permitted to examine such file. Certified copies of all papers and

---

[37]Ala. Code §§26–10–5 and 38–7–13 (Supp. 1984); Kan. Stat. Ann. §65–2423 (1983); Fla. Stat. Ann. §63.162 (West Supp. 1984); *see* N.C. Gen. Stat. §48–25 (Supp. 1983).

documents contained in any file so impounded shall be made only on like order.[38]

Similarly, where the adopting parents have requested a new birth certificate for their adopted child, Illinois law provides that the original birth certificate "and the evidence of adoption . . . shall not be subject to inspection or certification except upon order of the circuit court or as provided by regulation."[39]

Vigorous court challenges to these adoption laws have been filed by individuals and adoptee advocacy organizations (one of the better known organizations is Yesterday's Children based in Evanston, Illinois), arguing on various grounds that statutes that generally prohibit them from obtaining access to the court records relating to their adoption are improper.

Challenges to the confidentiality have taken several forms legally. A principal claim of these organizations and individuals is that they have a fundamental constitutional right to receive information and to develop family ties with natural parents. Other claims have been based on the adoptee's need to identify his or her natural parents for medical treatment, although these claims have usually arisen in the context of the adoptee's effort to demonstrate that he or she comes within the "good cause" exception found in many statutes that permit access to the court records. Courts have typically rejected all such claims, even though the adoptee's life may be jeopardized if the identity of the natural parents is not disclosed.

Courts are seldom confronted with the issue of whether adult adoptees should be permitted to inspect the hospital medical records relating to their birth, which typically contain identifying information about their natural parents. Moreover, no reported court decisions in any state have specifically addressed this issue. Nevertheless, the issue deserves consideration because the balancing-of-interests policy analysis the courts have used in determining whether adoptees should be permitted to inspect judicial records concerning their adoption should presumably apply with equal force to the issue of whether adoptees should be permitted to inspect their medical records related to their birth.

Constitutional Challenges

In *In re Roger B.*,[40] the plaintiff challenged the Illinois adoption statute, asserting that his status as an adult adoptee "who had feelings of inadequacy and uncertainty as to his background be permitted access to his adoption records, and that the statute was unconstitutional." The court upheld the statute and held that

---

[38]Ill. Ann. Stat. ch. 4, §9.1–18 (Smith-Hurd 1975).

[39]Ill. Ann. Stat. ch. 111–1/2, §73–17 (Smith-Hurd 1980).

[40]84 Ill. 2d 323, 418 N.E. 2d 751 (1981).

adoptees have no "fundamental right to examine [their] adoption records."[41] The court determined that confidentiality was required to protect the privacy of the natural parents as well as for the privacy of the adopting parents, and that these interests do not cease when the adoptee reaches adulthood. The court concluded its discussion by stating that:

> confidentiality performs the socially and legally vital role of balancing the interest of the child, the interest of the natural parents, and the interest of the adopting parents. The prohibition against seeing the records is not restricted to the adoptees. It applies equally to the adoptees, the adopting parents, natural parents, and to any curious third party who seeks to look at the record.[42]

In *Mills v. Atlantic City Department of Vital Statistics,*[43] the plaintiffs challenged the constitutionality of a New Jersey statute that requires the state registrar to place under seal the original birth certificate of any child who is adopted, thereby concealing the identity of the natural parents. Such a procedure terminates the legal relationship between the natural parent and the child, and a new birth certificate containing the names of the adoptive parents is issued. The statute provides that the seal of secrecy may only be broken upon the order of a court for good cause shown. The plaintiffs in *Mills* challenged these statutes as abridging their right to privacy and right to receive information and as a denial of equal protection of the law, contrary to the Fourteenth Amendment to the United States Constitution.

The court rejected the plaintiffs' contentions, and in doing so discussed the purpose of the New Jersey Adoption Act—the promotion of "policies and procedures socially necessary and desirable for the protection not only of the child placed for adoption but also for the natural and adopting parents."[44] If this information is kept confidential, all three parties are helped. The natural parents will place the child with a reputable agency because they know their actions and motivations will not become public. The adoptive parents may raise the child without fear of interference from the natural parents and without fear that the birth status of an illegitimate child will be revealed. Lastly, the child is protected from the stigma of illegitimacy, which, though fading in modern society, may still exist.[45]

---

[41]*Id.* at 329.

[42]*Id.* at 335.

[43]148 N.J. Super. 302, 372 A. 2d 646 (1977).

[44]*Id.*, 372 A. 2d at 649.

[45]*Id.*

In examining the plaintiffs' claim of privacy the court concluded:

> that while information regarding heritage, background and physical and psychological heredity of a person is essential to that person's identity and self image, nevertheless it is not so intimately personal as to fall within the zones of privacy implicitly protected in the penumbra of the Bill of Rights.[46]

Moreover, the court pointed out that the natural parents have their right to privacy, the right to be left alone, which is expressly set out in the New Jersey statutes and has been recognized as a vital interest by the United States Supreme Court.[47] The court rejected the plaintiffs' claim of a right to receive information because first, such a right is not unconditional, and second, the plaintiffs could obtain the information by showing good cause, which they had failed to do. The court found that the protection of the integrity of the adoption process is a valid state interest, and such a desire to receive information must be read in accordance with it.[48]

Lastly, the court rejected the equal protection claim. The plaintiffs argued that the statutory classification that requires adoptees to secure a court order before they can inspect their birth records is suspect. They compared this to discriminations based on race, national origin, sex, and illegitimacy. The court denied this claim because:

> [a]n adoptee does not derive that status from an accident of birth but as the result of a legal proceeding which has as the very essence of its purpose the protection of that adoptee's best interest. Rather than vilify or relegate the adoptee to an inferior status, the adoption process of which the challenged statutes are an integral part, often improves the situation of the child, insuring a home, family unit and loving care which otherwise might not be guaranteed.[49]

In the *Application of Gilbert*,[50] the plaintiff made the same three arguments asserted in *Mills*, but in addition presented religious beliefs constituting good cause. He was a member of the Church of Jesus Christ of Latter Day Saints, and "a fundamental belief of that church is that in order to be saved and exalted after death

---

[46]*Id*. at 650.

[47]*See* Stanley v. Georgia, 394 U.S. 557 (1969).

[48]372 A. 2d at 653.

[49]*Id*. The same equal protection argument is made in Application of Maples, 563 S.W. 2d 760 (Mo. 1978).

[50]563 S.W.2d 760, 769 (Mo. 1978).

every person must trace their ancestry and perform certain ordinances for their blood relatives."[51] Thus, he needed the names of his natural parents. The appellate court remanded the case so that the parties could offer evidence concerning the fundamental beliefs of the church but cautioned the lower court to be "mindful that evidence of one's religious beliefs may not require opening the record if it results in preferential treatment for one professing such belief, because the granting of privilege to one religious denomination not enjoyed by others could be constitutionally suspect."[52]

Adoptees have also challenged sealed record statutes on the basis of the Thirteenth Amendment and the due process clause of the Fourteenth Amendment.[53] The plaintiff's due process argument that an adult adoptee's interest in learning his natural parents' identities is a fundamental right was rejected by the court. In *Alma Society v. Mellon*,[54] the plaintiffs made no showing of cause. Rather, they argued that the sealed record statutes imposed badges of slavery on them and that the Thirteenth Amendment prohibition of slavery and involuntary servitude gave them an absolute right to the records. The plaintiffs asserted that the Thirteenth Amendment covered this situation because their situation was similar to slave children who were sold at a young age and grew up separated from their parents because they could not communicate with them. They argued that, even though they were literate, they could not communicate with their parents and thus were in the same position as the slaves. The court rejected both arguments.

Challenges for Cause

Medical Problems. Courts are often sympathetic to adoptees who need to see their adoption records for medical reasons. A medical necessity generally satisfies the "good cause" requirement of many statutes. In *Chattman v. Bennett*,[55] the court held that a female adoptee who was considering having children could have access to any medical reports or related matter contained in the records of her adoption. Her concern that some genetic or hereditary factor in her background might foretell a medical problem for any children constituted "good cause." In providing the plaintiff with such medical information (her medical records and those of her natural parents, as well as any other material therein relating to possible genetic or hereditary conditions), the court required the deletion of any nonpertinent information including the names of the natural parents.

---

[51]*Id.* at 770.

[52]*Id.*

[53]*See, e.g.,* Alma Society v. Mellon, 601 F.2d 1225 (2d Cir.), *cert. denied,* 444 U.S. 995 (1979); Yesterday's Children v. Kennedy, 569 F.2d 431 (7th Cir. 1977).

[54]Alma Society v. Mellon, 601 F.2d at 1230.

[55]339 N.Y.S. 2d 768 (N.Y. App. Div. 1977).

While courts are likely to consider fears of potential hereditary diseases, etc., as satisfying the "good cause" requirement of most statutes, the medical records of the natural parents will not be released on the mere mention of hereditary diseases. Such allegations must be supported with detailed descriptions. In *Application of William Sage,*[56] the plaintiff wanted to inspect his adoption records because he felt an "inner compulsion" to reacquaint himself with his natural family, and he was concerned that his natural father may have died of hereditary heart disease. The court asked Mr. Sage to supply an affidavit setting forth more detailed information regarding his concern over the possibility of hereditary disease. The plaintiff produced no affidavits, however. The court indicated that it would release the records if either both of the adoptive parents or both of the natural parents consented. At least one of the adoptive parents objected. Thus, Mr. Sage did not establish good cause. Mr. Sage also made equal protection and due process arguments, which the court rejected.

Similarly, in *Rhodes v. Laurino,*[57] the plaintiff sought the medical histories of his natural parents and their forebears to assist his physician with diagnosis and possible prevention of degenerative diseases. The relevant New York statute provided in part that "[n]o order for disclosure or access shall be granted except on good cause shown and due notice to both adoptive parents." In this case both adoptive parents were deceased, and such medical information could be disclosed only upon evidence from competent medical authority that such information was urgently needed. The plaintiff's physician's response that "the urgency of some ailments (e.g., cardiac) do [sic] not permit for court petitions upon attack's unexpected occurrence, and any time delay might well prove fatal or seriously disabling to the patient" was not satisfactory. Because the plaintiff never produced a more satisfactory description of the urgent need for such information, the request was denied.

Psychological Needs. Courts have been less sympathetic to adoptees' psychological needs for such information than to their medical needs. The courts seem to be suspicious that psychological need is nothing more than curiosity. In *Matter of Linda F.M.,*[58] the adoptee sought both the records of her adoption and the sealed Board of Health records relative to her birth. (This adoption took place through a private agency.) She asserted that she satisfied the good cause requirement of the applicable statute for three reasons: because she did not know who her natural parents were, she was (1) experiencing psychological problems that impaired her musical skills, (2) fearful of entering into an incestuous marriage, and (3) unable to establish her religious faith. The court held that the plaintiff had only demon-

---

[56] 21 Wash. App. 803, 586 P.2d 1201, 1206 (1978).

[57] 444 F.Supp. 170 (E.D.N.Y. 1978).

[58] 95, Misc. 2d 581, 409 N.Y.S. 2d 638 (1978).

strated curiosity about the identity of her natural parents, and curiosity would not satisfy the good cause requirement.

In *Application of Anonymous*,[59] the adoptee alleged as good cause the fact that he is suffering from a psychological disorder caused by not knowing his true identity and that obtaining that knowledge would be "beneficial to his present emotional state." The court held that, to make a determination of good cause pursuant to the applicable statute, the natural parents were necessary parties because the anonymity of the natural parents is something the statute seeks to protect. The court decided it could designate a party to serve on their behalf.

In *In re C.A.B.*,[60] the adoptee, a woman who had been adopted at age three, petitioned the court for leave to inspect her adoption records because of "an emptiness and confusion about who I am" and for family health protection gained from the knowledge of any inherited diseases. The court recognized that this was a valid good cause, but stated that it could make no decision unless there was further evidentiary support of the petitioner's claims.

In *Matter of Maxtone-Graham*,[61] the adoptee's psychiatrist submitted an affidavit stating that all adoption records would be necessary for her treatment. The adoptee's natural mother had been located and consented to the release of the records concerning her. The adoption agencies, however, would not give the adoptee the names, addresses, and information about her foster parents because the adoptee had not made a showing of good cause with regard to those records.

Inheritance. In Louisiana, adopted children retain the right to inherit from their natural parents and other blood relatives. Thus, Louisiana courts may consider the right of an adoptee to inherit from his parents and other blood relatives a "compelling necessity." In Louisiana, a compelling necessity is one of the factors a court considers in determining whether to open sealed adoption records. Generally, the court appoints a curator who determines whether blood relatives were named, whether any inheritance rights existed, and how the adoptee's rights could be assured while giving full consideration to protecting the confidentiality of the blood parents.[62]

In *Kirsch v. Parker*,[63] the court treated the situation of an adoptee, who was nearly five years old when she was adopted, differently from a child who was adopted at birth. Because the adoptee was older when she was adopted, her situation was not governed by the statute described above that provides for sealed

---

[59]390 N.Y.S. 2d 779 (1976).

[60]384 A. 2d 679 (D.C. App. 1978).

[61]90 Misc. 2d 107, 393 N.Y.S. 2d 835 (1975).

[62]Massey v. Parker, 369 So. 2d 1310 (La. Sup. Ct. 1979); Prentice v. Parker, 376 So. 2d 568 (La. Ct. App. 1979).

[63]375 So. 2d 693 (La. Ct. App. 1979).

records. The court found that, because an adoptee could not learn about his or her pre-birth history, this did not mean that an adoptee could not learn about the first few years of his or her life. In *Kirsch,* the court permitted access to the adoption records.

Rights of Natural Parents

In *In re Christine,*[64] the natural mother of an adoptee petitioned the court with the hope of contacting her 11-year-old daughter's adoptive parents and then seeing her daughter. The mother wanted to see what type of child she had turned out to be, how she acted, what she looked like, and how her voice sounded. The court held that this did not constitute sufficient good cause to lift the seal of confidentiality from the records.

Conversely, in *Humphers v. First Interstate Bank,*[65] a natural mother sued the physician who delivered her daughter, whom the mother had placed for adoption. The adoptee, who was attempting to find her mother, went to the physician and enlisted his aid in gaining access to her medical records. The physician disclosed her mother's name and wrote a false letter stating that he had administered a medication named diethylstilbestrol to her mother and, because of the side effects, it was important that the adoptee contact her mother. The natural mother sued the physician for outrageous conduct, professional negligence, breach of a confidential relationship, invasion of privacy, and breach of contract. The trial court dismissed all of these counts. The Oregon Court of Appeals reversed the dismissal of the breach of a confidential relationship and invasion of privacy claims and affirmed the dismissal of the other three counts. The court held that "reasonable persons could not differ that the conduct alleged in plaintiff's complaint was not so extreme and outrageous that it exceeded any reasonable limit of social toleration. . . ." The professional negligence claim was dismissed because the court found that the physician's action in revealing the plaintiff's name did not constitute the practice of medicine. Thus, a medical malpractice claim was inappropriate. The court held that the plaintiff had not adequately alleged damages, and consequently it did not even have to decide if an implied contract existed. The case was remanded to the lower court for consideration of the breach of a confidential relationship and invasion of privacy counts.

Guidelines for Medical Record Practitioners

The balancing-of-interests analysis applied by most courts in these cases suggests an approach for medical records practitioners in responding to requests to

---

[64]121 R.I. 203, 397 A. 2d 511 (1979).

[65]68 Or. App. 573, 684 P.2d 581 *review granted* 297 Or. 781, 687 P.2d 795 (1984).

inspect the birth records of adoptees. Obviously such requests will be rare, primarily because adoptees and their adopting parents seldom possess the information that would be necessary to locate the adoptee's birth record. Circumstances will arise, however, in which the adoptee or the adoptive parent possesses sufficient information to permit medical records practitioners to locate the adoptee's birth records. When confronted with such a request, the medical records practitioner should consider the following guidelines, which should be subject to any applicable statutes and regulations.

Natural Parents

Natural parents of a child placed for adoption relinquish their right to inspect their child's medical record after the child has been adopted, because all parental rights with respect to that child have been terminated.

Adopting Parents

Adopting parents acquire all parental rights with respect to the adoptee following formal adoption; this includes, in most states, the right to inspect the adoptee's medical records until the adoptee attains the age of majority. Adopting parents, however, should not be permitted to inspect any information in the adoptee's birth record, for example, that contains information identifying the adoptee's natural parents, in deference to the natural parents' legitimate privacy interests. Medical records practitioners should exclude all such identifying information pertaining to the natural parents prior to making the adoptee's medical record available to the adopting parents for inspection.

Adoptee

The adoptee has the right to inspect his or her medical records on reaching the age of majority, subject to the same limitations with respect to identifying information relating to the adoptee's natural parents set forth in the preceding paragraph addressing the inspection rights of adopting parents.

Chapter 4

Access to Medical Records Information

The hospital owns the physical medical record subject to the patient's interest in the information in it. It is generally accepted that the medical record is a confidential document and that access to it should be limited to the patient, the patient's authorized representative and attending physician, and hospital staff members who have a legitimate interest in the record. There are several exceptions to this general rule, however, each of which permits other individuals to review the medical record. The exceptions include disclosures that are made pursuant to the federal Freedom of Information Act (FOIA); those required by the federal and state reimbursement regulations; those necessary to meet Peer Review Organization (PRO) requirements, as well as other review and state statutory reporting requirements; and those made to law enforcement agencies or other government agencies for appropriate purposes. Each of these disclosure exceptions is discussed later in this chapter. Furthermore, access to certain types of records is more restricted than the general rule would allow. For example, alcohol and drug abuse patient records may not be disclosed except as specifically authorized by the applicable federal regulations, and access to the records of mental health patients is severely limited in some states. Regardless of the applicable access rules in the state, hospitals must devise effective record security procedures that will protect and preserve the patient's confidentiality and the hospital's medical record. Hospitals that have converted all or part of their medical records to computer media should be especially careful to establish adequate record security measures.

Hospitals often receive numerous forms of legal process, such as subpoenas or court orders, that require them to provide patient record information. They must be prepared to respond appropriately to subpoenas, court orders, and other process served upon the institution which involve medical record information disclosure. The hospital's response procedure should be based on a careful review of the relevant state and federal requirements.

Hospitals can be held liable to their patients for the improper or unauthorized disclosure of medical record information. Aside from statutory penalties established in some jurisdictions, hospitals and practitioners may be liable for defamation, invasion of privacy, betrayal of professional secrets, and breach of contract for such disclosures. (Liability for improper disclosure of records is discussed in detail in Chapter 6.)

OWNERSHIP OF THE MEDICAL RECORD

It is a generally accepted rule that the medical record is owned by the hospital, subject to the patient's interest in the information contained in the record.[1] This rule is established by statute in some states. The Mississippi statute, for example, states that:

> [h]ospital records are and shall remain the property of the various hospitals, subject however to reasonable access to the information contained therein upon good cause shown by the patient, his personal representatives or heirs, his attending medical personnel and his duly authorized nominees, and upon payment of any reasonable charges for such service.[2]

Most states that have specific rules on record ownership include these provisions in their state hospital-licensing regulations. The Pennsylvania regulation is quite specific, "Medical records are the property of the hospital, and they shall not be removed from the hospital premises, except for court purposes."[3]

A few courts have held that a medical record is hospital property in which the patient has a limited property right. In *Pyramid Life Insurance Co. v. Masonic Hospital Association of Payne County*,[4] the patient's health insurer sought to enjoin the hospital from preventing the company from inspecting the patient's hospital records for purposes of settling an insurance claim even though the patient had authorized disclosure. The court stated first that the "records maintained by [the] hospital pertaining to care and treatment of patients and to expenses incurred by patients . . . [were] the property of the hospital."[5] Then, in granting the injunction, the court stated,

---

[1]JOINT COMMISSION ON ACCREDITATION OF HOSPITALS, ACCREDITATION MANUALS FOR HOSPITALS 83 (1984).

[2]Miss. Code Ann. §41–9–65 (1972). *See also* Tenn. Code Ann. §68–11–304 (1983).

[3]Pa. Regulations on General and Special Hospitals §115.28, 7 Pa.B. 3657 (1977). *See also* Kan. Hosp. Regulations, §28–34–9 (1974); Ky. Hosp. Regulations §3(11)(c) (1983); S.C. Minimum Standards for Licensing Hospitals §601.4 (1982); Tenn. Minimum Standards and Regulations for Hospitals, ch. 1200–8–3.05(1)(c) (1974); Utah Hosp. Rules and Regulations §V.A.8.a.1(a) (1977).

[4]191 F. Supp. 51 (W.D. Okla. 1961).

[5]*Id.* at 54.

[t]he patient has a property right in the information appearing or portrayed on the records and he, or those authorized by him, including an insurance company representative armed with authorization signed by the patient, is entitled to make such inspection and/or to copy such records without resort to litigation.[6]

The court in *Bishop Clarkson Memorial Hospital v. Reserve Life Insurance Company*[7] approached the issue of a patient's right to access to his record in another way, stating,

[t]he issue is not one of inconvenience [to the hospital], but whether the patient-policyholder has a sufficient interest in the records to waive the privilege which protects such records from inspection, and to authorize the insurer, which has the right to determine its liability for asserted claims, to inspect such records.[8]

This court qualified the patient's right to waive his privacy protection, holding that the patient's doctor could prevent the records from being released on the grounds that disclosure is not in the patient's best interests.[9] Some courts have held that a physician also has a definable legal interest in the record,[10] although it is unlikely that the physician's interest would take precedence over the patient's right of access to the record.

Although patients may have an interest in information contained in their medical records based on state statutes, it has been held that patients do not have a constitutional right to such information. In *Gotkin v. Miller*,[11] the plaintiff was a former mental patient who was denied access to her medical records and who could not establish a sufficient property interest in her medical records under the then applicable New York law. The patient sued the hospital, alleging that it had

---

[6]*Id. See also* Bishop Clarkson Memorial Hospital v. Reserve Life Insurance Co., 350 F. 2d 1006 (8th Cir. 1965); Rabens v. Jackson Park Hospital Foundation, 40 Ill. App. 3d 113, 351 N.E. 2d 276 (1976); Falum v. Medical Arts Center Hosp., 160 N.Y. Law J.2 (1968); Wallace v. University Hospitals of Cleveland, 171 Ohio St. 487, 172 N.E. 2d 459 (1961).

[7]350 F.2d 1006 (8th Cir. 1965).

[8]*Id.* at 1012.

[9]*Id.*

[10]Hampton Clinic v. District Court of Franklin County, 231 Iowa 65, 300 N.W. 646 (1941); McGarry v. J.A. Mercier Co., 272 Mich. 501, 262 N.W. 296 (1935). However, in Application of Kabes, 11 Misc. 2d 698, 175 N.Y.S. 2d 83 (N.Y. Sup. Ct., 1958), the hospital sought to vacate a motion for examination of its record librarian on the ground, among others, that the records belong to the hospital and the physicians. The court, in allowing the examination, did not discuss this point.

[11]379 F. Supp. 859 (E.D.N.Y. 1974).

violated her federal constitutional rights. The court held that the hospital's with-holding of information in this case did not constitute a violation of the patient's rights of free speech, privacy, and protection against unreasonable searches and seizures, or deprivation of property without due process.

When questions of medical records ownership arise, the hospital attorney should be aware that although the hospital owns the record, patients generally have a right to review their medical records unless a state or federal statute qualifies that right. State and federal statutes governing hospital licensure, mental health patients, and specific programs (such as alcoholism and drug abuse treatment centers), as well as licensing regulations applicable to hospitals and special programs, and relevant court decisions must be reviewed before questions regard-ing a specific case can be answered.

ACCESS TO THE MEDICAL RECORD BY OR ON BEHALF OF THE PATIENT

In the past, hospitals in many states could deny access to the medical record to patients themselves, who thereafter usually chose not to challenge the hospital's refusal to release record information. In recent years, however, the trend has been toward greater accessibility for the patient so that most jurisdictions now grant the patient or the patient's representative the right to examine and copy the medical record. Today, the general rule governing access by the patient may be stated as follows: the medical record is a confidential document, access to which should be restricted to the patient, to the patient's authorized representative, and to the attending physician and hospital staff members with a legitimate need for such access.

The broad confidentiality of the record has been established in some states by statute or regulation. Some statutes and regulations simply state that medical records are confidential and may not be disclosed except under the circumstances stated in the statute or regulation.[12] Other statutes are more specific and prohibit release or transfer of records without the consent of the patient or the patient's authorized representative.[13] The Joint Commission on Accreditation of Hospitals (JCAH) imposes strict standards of medical records confidentiality upon accredited hospitals.[14]

---

[12]*See, e.g.*, Iowa Code Ann. §68A. 7–2 (West 1973); Minn. Stat. Ann. §144.69 (West 1970); N.H. Rev. Stat. Ann. §126–A:4–a (1978); N.M. Stat. Ann. §14–6–1 (1978); N.Y. Pub. Health Law §2805–g(3) (McKinney Supp. 1983–84); N.D. Cent. Code §23–16–09 (1978).

[13]*See, e.g.*, Cal. Civ. Code §§56.10–56.11 (West 1982); Md. Health-Gen. Code Ann. §4–301 (1982).

[14]JCAH, ACCREDITATION MANUAL FOR HOSPITALS 83–84 (1984).

The courts in some jurisdictions have recognized a hospital's duty to maintain the confidentiality of its patient records. In *Cannell v. Medical and Surgical Clinic*,[15] the court found that physicians and hospitals have a duty, arising from the confidential nature of their relationship with the patient, to protect the patient's records from extrajudicial disclosure.

The Colorado medical records law, one of the most detailed of such enactments, allows the patient or the patient's designated representative to inspect the medical record at reasonable times and upon reasonable notice, but exempts from patient inspection records pertaining to the patient's psychiatric or psychological conditions, if, in the opinion of an independent, third party psychiatrist, such access would have significant negative impact upon the health of the patient. It further provides that a summary of the psychiatric records and notes, however, may be made available to the patient or the patient's designated representative after the termination of the treatment program upon written request of the patient. The law also requires the hospital to post in conspicuous public places notices of the availability of records for patient inspection, and to note the time and date of patients' requests for record inspection, and the time and date of the inspection. The patient must acknowledge the record inspection by signing and dating the file. The Colorado statute does not limit any right to inspect patient records that has been otherwise granted by statute.[16]

The Illinois statute illustrates the more common enactment that gives patients an unrestricted right of access to their medical records.

> Every private and public hospital shall, upon the request of any patient who has been treated in such hospital and after his or her discharge therefrom, permit the patient, his or her physician or authorized attorney to examine the hospital records, including but not limited to the history, bedside notes, charts, pictures and plates, kept in connection with the treatment of such patient, and permit copies of such records to be made by him or her or his or her physician or authorized attorney. A request for examination of the records shall be in writing and shall be delivered to the administrator of such hospital.[17]

The courts in many states have recognized the right of patients or their authorized agents to have access to their medical records, even in the absence of

---

[15]21 Ill. App. 3d 383, 315 N.E. 2d 278 (1974). *See also* Parkson v. Central DuPage Hospital, 105 Ill. App. 3d 850, 435 N.E. 2d 140 (1982); Rabens v. Jackson Park Hosp. Foundation, 40 Ill. App. 3d 113, 351 N.E. 2d 276 (1976).

[16]Colo. Rev. Stat. §25–1–801. *See also* Hawaii Rev. Stat. §622–57 (1976).

[17]Ill. Rev. Stat. ch. 110, §8–2001 (1984). *See also* Fla. Stat. Ann. §395.017 (West Supp. 1983); Idaho Code §39–1392d (1977); Me. Rev. Stat. Ann. tit. 22, §1711 (1980); Minn. Stat. Ann. §144.335–2 (West Supp. 1984); Okla. Stat. Ann. tit. 76, §19 (West Supp. 1983–84).

statutory authority. In *Wallace v. University Hospitals of Cleveland,*[18] a former patient was granted a mandatory injunction ordering the hospital to allow the patient's counsel to examine her hospital record. The lower court required the hospital to allow the attorney to inspect any and all records in the hospital pertaining to the hospital stay and treatment of the patient and to furnish a complete photostatic copy of the record to the patient. However, the appellate court modified the order so that the patient's attorney was required to inspect the records under the supervision of the hospital and was allowed to have photostatic copies made only of those parts of the record that the hospital considered proper under the circumstances of the case, bearing in mind the beneficial interest of the patient in the records and the general purpose for which the records were maintained. The patient appealed this order, but, between the filing of the appeal and the argument before the Supreme Court of Ohio, the hospital sent a complete copy of the patient's records to the attorney and granted permission to the attorney to examine and inspect any records pertaining to the patient's stay. A motion to dismiss on the ground that the case had become moot was therefore granted by the Ohio Supreme Court.

Thus, in *Musmann v. Methodist Hospital,*[19] it was determined that a patient was entitled to see his record despite a hospital ruling that the attending physician's consent was required. In *Application of Weiss,*[20] in which a former patient brought a special proceeding to compel a hospital to submit to an examination of its records to enable the patient to ascertain, for the purpose of instituting a malpractice action, the names of the physicians who had operated on him, the court held that the hospital was not entitled to withhold the records from the patient in order to conceal the identity of the physician. Rather, the court found that the patient had a right of access to his own records.

The numerous New York decisions involving pretrial discovery and examination proceedings that indicate judicial recognition of patients' right to view their records must be taken in context.[21] Pretrial discovery and examination are

---

[18]164 N.E. 2d 917 (Common Pleas Ct., Ohio, 1959), *aff'd and modified,* 170 N.E. 2d 261 (Ohio Ct. App. 1960), *motion to dismiss granted,* 171 Ohio St. 487, 172 N.E. 2d 459 (1961). *See also* Pyramid Life Ins. Co. v. Masonic Hosp. Assn., 191 F. Supp. 51 (W.D. Okla. 1961).

[19]Unreported case, No. C–2051, Superior Court, Marion Cty., Indiana, June 29, 1956.

[20]208 Misc. 1010, 147 N.Y.S. 2d 455 (1955).

[21]Gotkin v. Miller, 379 F. Supp. 859 (E.D.N.Y. 1974) (applying New York law); New York City Health and Hosp. Corp. v. Parker, 102 Misc. 2d 433, 423 N.Y. S. 2d 442 (1980); Jacobs v. City of New York, 35 Misc. 2d 120, 231 N.Y. 2d 855 (1962); Young v. Forest Hills General Hosp., 216 N.Y.S. 2d 101 (N.Y. Sup. Ct., 1961); Glazer v. Dept. of Hosp. of the City of New York, 2 Misc. 2d 207, 155 N.Y.S. 2d 414 (1956); Romano v. Mt. Sinai Hosp. 150 N.Y. S. 2d 246 (N.Y. Sup. Ct., 1956). *But cf.* Lipsey v. 940 St. Nicholas Ave. Corp., 12 Ad. 2d 414, 212 N.Y.S. 2d 205 (1961) (inspection of medical records not allowed under statute when hospital not a party); Jaffe v. City of New York, 196 Misc. 710, 94 N.Y.S. 2d 60 (1949); Petition of Cenci, 185 Misc. 479, 57 N.Y.S. 2d 231 (1945).

procedural remedies and do not create an absolute right for patients to see their records at any time. Such a right to pretrial discovery and examination is defined by the applicable statute or rule and is not recognized in the absence of pending or threatened litigation.[22]

In *Hutchins v. Texas Rehabilitation Commission*,[23] a Texas court of civil appeals ruled that a former patient of a rehabilitation center had a common law right to gain access to her records. The common law right, the court noted, overcomes "the presumption of confidentiality and prohibition of record disclosure in Section 30.47 of the Texas Education Code." Similarly, in *Rabens v. Jackson Park Hospital Foundation*,[24] the court found that a hospital had breached its common law duty to disclose a patient's medical data to him or his agent upon request. It also concluded that the hospital's conduct violated the state statute that further directs hospitals to allow a patient's attorney or physician to examine and copy hospital records.[25]

In some instances, a question may arise as to who is the patient's representative. In *Emmett v. Eastern Dispensary and Casualty Hospital*,[26] for example, when the son of a deceased patient requested access to his father's medical record for purposes of bringing a negligence action against the hospital, the hospital refused to release the records on the grounds that the son was not the father's administrator and therefore not the father's legal representative. The court held that the fiduciary relationship between the hospital and the patient requires disclosure of medical record information to the patient and that this duty of disclosure extends after the patient's death to the patient's next of kin.

In 1972, the American Hospital Association (AHA) published *A Patient's Bill of Rights*, which was intended to be used by hospitals and practitioners as a guide. However, the document received considerable national attention and, in at least one instance, was incorporated into a state statute.[27] As a result, some hospitals adopted this bill of rights as institutional policy and thereby became obliged to enforce it on behalf of their patients. (For a discussion of a hospital's legal standard of care, see Chapter 10.) Although the 1972 document does not state specifically that patients may inspect their charts, it establishes that patients shall receive complete information concerning their treatment in the hospital. In these hospitals, institutional policy may be interpreted as creating a right for patients to review

[22]Gotkin v. Miller, 379 F. Supp. 859 (E.D.N.Y. 1974) (applying New York Law).

[23]544 S.W. 2d 802 (Tex. Civ. App. 1976).

[24]40 Ill. App. 3d 113, 351 N.E. 2d 276 (1976); *see also* Thurman v. Crawford 652 S.W. 2d 240 (Mo. Ct. App. 1983).

[25]Ill. Rev. Stat. ch. 110, §8–2001 (1984).

[26]396 F.2d 931 (D.C. Cir. 1967).

[27]Minn Stat. Ann. §144.651 (West Supp. 1984).

their charts, even in the absence of a state statute or regulation creating such a right.

Several of the statutes that authorize the patient or the patient's representative to inspect records do not permit inspection of records until after the patient has been discharged from the hospital.[28] The question is frequently raised as to whether the hospital must allow patients to examine their records while they are still hospitalized. In the absence of a statutory or common law right of access during hospitalization, the hospital is not obligated to permit its patients to inspect their records on the hospital's patient care units. However, hospitals should consider whether a refusal to permit such an inspection will create unnecessary problems for the institution and its staff. A patient who is not allowed to examine his or her chart in the hospital may become hostile and more difficult to treat and may file a claim against the hospital if treatment ends in a poor result. Therefore, unless the patient's attending physician can establish a reasonable basis for an opinion that disclosure of the inpatient medical record would be harmful to the patient, the hospital should allow the patient to review the record. In some instances, a record review, coordinated by the patient's attending physician, can be used as a beneficial teaching device. If inpatients are allowed to examine their records, the hospital should employ its customary record security procedures. (Record security is discussed later in this chapter.)

Psychiatric Records

In some states, the rules governing access to the medical records of mental health patients differ from those applicable to medical records generally. In the past, mental health patients were not granted access to their medical records, even in states that granted a right of access to nonmental-health patients. It was widely believed that authorizing such patients to review their records would be injurious to their health. Today, however, mental health patients in some states have the same right to inspect their records as do other patients. In Illinois, for example, the Mental Health and Developmental Disabilities Confidentiality Act enables patients 12 years of age or older to inspect and copy their records.[29] The Act establishes a high level of confidentiality in mental health patient records and, apart from the patient and other persons specified, narrowly limits access to and disclosure of such records, even in judicial proceedings.

---

[28]*See, e.g.*, Fla. Stat. Ann. §395.017 (West Supp. 1983); Ill. Rev. Stat. ch. 110 §8–2001 (1983).
[29]Ill. Rev. Stat. ch. 91-1/2, §804 (1983).

Recent court decisions have recognized the right of mental health patients or their representatives to review their medical records.[30] In *Doe v. Commissioner of Mental Health*,[31] the Supreme Judicial Court of Massachusetts construed a statutory provision as requiring that a patient's medical record be released to her attorney if the proper procedures had been followed and the proper consent forms executed. The court found that the statutory provision pertaining to attorney access created an explicit mandatory exception to the general rule permitting non-disclosure. Under this section, the court concluded, the state has no discretion under the Massachusetts statute, and any attorney who meets its requirements must be given the records.

In *Sullivan v. State*,[32] a Florida state hospital adhered to its policy of denying patient access to medical records and rejected a mental patient's request to obtain a copy of his own record. Interpreting a state statute that confers upon a patient the right to designate the persons who may have access to his or her medical records, a Florida appeals court recognized—as had the legislature—that the patient could not properly exercise this right unless he or she had access to his or her records.

However, in *In the Matter of the Application for the Commitment of J.C.G. to Trenton Psychiatric Hospital*,[33] the mother of a minor who was involuntarily committed to a psychiatric hospital sought to have certain records pertaining to her daughter's treatment released to her. She alleged that decisions were being made by the hospital without her consent and that such decisions were not in the best interest of her daughter. The court, however, noted the mother's failure to produce sufficient evidence that the hospital had not been acting in the best interest of her daughter. Accordingly, the court stated, any information about the daughter must come from the daughter's court-appointed guardian, who, it observed, had argued that disclosure of hospital records would not be in the child's best interest. Although one purpose of appointing a guardian is to protect the minor against parental efforts to terminate treatment for reasons other than those that serve the best interest of the child, the court concluded that the mother was not precluded from requesting and receiving periodic reports of her daughter's treatment even if she could not receive the medical records.

Records of Minors

The law provides little specific guidance concerning who may have access to or authorize the release of the records of minor patients. In the absence of statutory or

---

[30]*See, e.g.*, Cynthia B. v. New Rochelle Hosp. Med. Center, 60 N.Y. 2d 452, 458 N.E. 2d 363, 470 N.Y.S. 2d 122 (1983) involving a hospital whose policy barred disclosure of sensitive psychiatric records even when authorized by a former patient.

[31]372 Mass. 534, 362 N.E. 2d 920 (1977).

[32]352 So. 2d 1212 (Fla. Dist. Ct. App. 1977).

[33]144 N.J. Super. 579, 366 A. 2d 733 (1976).

common law authority on this point, the generally accepted rule is that a hospital may disclose the medical record of a minor patient only upon the authorization of one of the patient's parents, unless a legal guardian has been appointed for the minor, and that a minor's parents may be allowed access to such records on behalf of the patient.

A number of state statutes governing access to medical records include specific directions concerning disclosure of a minor patient's records. A few states have statutes that permit the release of such records with the consent of either the patient's parent or the patient. The Mississippi statute governing disclosure of a minor's records is illustrative.

> Any person authorized and empowered to consent to surgical or medical treatment or procedures for himself or another may also waive the medical privilege for himself or the other person and consent to the disclosure of medical information and the making and delivery of copies of medical or hospital records. . . .[34]

Under the Mississippi statute, it is clear that a parent's consent is sufficient to authorize release of hospital records. It is not clear, however, whether a minor's consent alone is enough to authorize release of the records. No cases that interpret this provision have been reported, but an argument can be made that, where the controlling statute empowers the patient to authorize release of records but does not make the parent's consent mandatory, the consent of the minor alone is sufficient to authorize release of the records.

The applicable California statute allows the release of a minor's medical records on the parent's authorization only in certain specified situations.

> An authorization for the release of medical information by a provider of health care shall be valid if it:
>
> (a) Is handwritten by the person who signs it or is in typeface no smaller than eight-point type.
> (b) Is clearly separate from any other language present on the same page and is executed by a signature which serves no other purpose than to execute the authorization.
> (c) Is signed and dated by one of the following:
>   (1) The patient. A patient who is a minor may only sign an authorization for the release of medical information obtained by a provider of health care in the course of furnishing services to

---

[34]Miss. Code Ann. §41–41–11 (1972). *See also* Minn. Stat. Ann. §144.335 (1980).

which the minor could lawfully have consented under Part 1 (commencing with Section 25) or Part 2.7 (commencing with Section 60) of Division 1 of the Civil Code.

(2) The legal representative of the patient, if the patient is a minor or an incompetent. However, authorization may not be given under this subdivision for the disclosure of medical information obtained by the provider of health care in the course of furnishing services to which a minor patient could lawfully have consented under Part 1 (commencing with Section 25) or Part 2.7 (commencing with Section 60) of Division 1 of the Civil Code.

(3) The spouse of the patient or the person financially responsible for the patient, where the medical information is being sought for the sole purpose of processing an application for health insurance or for enrollment in a nonprofit hospital plan, a health care service plan, or an employee benefit plan, and where the patient is to be enrolled spouse or dependent under the policy or plan.[35]

The statute also implies that an authorization by a parent concerning matters for which a minor can consent is not valid. The authorization of the minor would appear to be sufficient to release his or her hospital records for any purpose for which a minor can lawfully consent.

The New York statute clearly requires authorization by one of the parents before the minor's hospital records can be released to a hospital or health care provider, even though records concerning abortion or treatment of venereal disease can never be released to the parent or guardians. The New York statute states,

[u]pon the written request of any competent patient, parent or guardian of an infant, committee for an incompetent, or conservator of a conservatee, an examining, consulting or treating physician or hospital must release and deliver, exclusive of personal notes of the said physician or hospital, copies of all x-rays, medical records and test records including all laboratory tests regarding that patient to any other designated physician or hospital, provided however, that such records concerning the treatment of an infant patient for venereal disease or the performance of an abortion operation upon such infant patient shall not

---

[35]Cal. Civ. Code §56.11 (West 1982).

be released or in any manner be made available to the parent or guardian of such infant.[36]

The statutes of other states simply are not clear on the question of parental control of access to a minor's records. Most statutes permit access to records with the consent of "the patient"[37] or "the person."[38] In these states, hospitals should follow the general rule and obtain the authorization of the patient's parent before disclosing records to third parties. In some situations, state statutes authorize certain categories of minors (such as emancipated minors or those who are pregnant, parents, married, or suffering from drug abuse) to consent to their own medical care. (For a further discussion of consent by a minor, see Chapter 7.) It is a logical extension of these statutory rules to allow such minors to consent to disclosure of their medical records, but there is little clear authority for such a position. Hospitals should use caution when disclosing the medical records of these special types of minor patients.

Record Duplication Fees

Although hospitals may have a duty to permit a patient and his or her representative to inspect and copy the patient's medical record, hospitals are not obligated to do so free of charge. In *Young v. Madison General Hospital,*[39] the court held that the hospital properly refused to reproduce and release voluminous patient records when it received only a form request and an offer to pay for "reasonable access." The court also held that it would be appropriate for the hospital to allow the requester to review personally the original record and indicate what parts of it he or she wanted to have copied at the requester's expense. In *Rabens v. Jackson Park Hospital Foundation,*[40] the court held that a hospital obligated to disclose record information to the patient could charge a reasonable fee for reproduction of the record. Fees charged by hospitals for reproduction of medical records should be based on the hospital's actual cost in removing the record from the record library and duplicating the portions requested.

---

[36]N.Y. Pub. Health §17 (McKinney Supp. 1984). *See also* Utah Code Ann. §78–25–25 (1977).

[37]*See, e.g.,* Colo. Rev. Stat. §25–1–801 (Supp. 1983); Ill. Rev. Stat. Ann. ch. 110, ¶ 8–2001 (1984); S.D. Codified Laws §34–12–15 (Supp. 1983).

[38]*See., e.g.,* Mont. Rev. Code Ann. §50–16–311 (1983); Okla. Stat. Ann., tit. 76, §19 (Supp. 1984); Wis. Stat. Ann. §804.10 (1977).

[39]337 So. 2d 931 (Miss. 1976).

[40]40 Ill. App. 3d 113, 351 N.E. 2d 276 (1976).

Record Security

It is essential that hospitals establish effective procedures for safeguarding medical records, not only to protect patient confidentiality, but also to prevent intentional alteration or falsification of records by hospital staff or by individuals who wish to file a personal injury claim against a practitioner or the hospital, or otherwise to use the records for an unlawful purpose. Some hospitals have learned to their misfortune that, given the opportunity, patients will occasionally remove important parts of their records or alter significant information in their records to improve their chances of bringing a successful professional negligence action. Hospitals have also found that, because medical records information can be useful to many people, some will do whatever is necessary to obtain it. In *People v. Home Insurance Co.*,[41] for example, insurance company agents surreptitiously procured hospital medical record information concerning two hospitalized insurance claimants. The district attorney unsuccessfully charged two insurance companies with theft, the court holding that such information did not constitute a "thing of value" within the meaning of the theft statutes.

To protect their medical records from such abuse, hospitals should adopt at least the following security precautions.

- Competent medical records or risk management personnel should review a record before it is examined by the patient or the patient's representative and should notify the appropriate hospital manager if the record is incomplete or otherwise defective, or if the record reveals a problem that could give rise to negligence liability in the hospital or its staff.
- An original medical record should not be permitted to be taken from the hospital's premises except pursuant to legal process (response to legal process is discussed later in this chapter), or pursuant to a defined hospital procedure allowing inpatients going to another facility for testing to take their medical record, if the patient is to return the same day and if the record is accompanied by a responsible hospital employee.
- Neither the patient, the patient's representative, nor any other person who is not an authorized hospital employee or staff member should ever be allowed to examine a medical record alone. The hospital should provide accommodations for people to inspect records in its medical records department or other location where proper surveillance is possible.

---

[41]197 Colo. 260, 591 P.2d 1036 (1979).

ACCESS BY OTHERS

There are exceptions to the general rule governing access to medical records. While certain types of medical records require a greater degree of confidentiality than others, there are also circumstances in which medical records information may be disclosed to third parties without the patient's authorization. It is important for those involved with release of medical information to understand the exceptions.

Alcohol and Drug Abuse Patient Records

In 1972, Congress passed Section 408 of the Drug Abuse Office and Treatment Act, which regulates the release of information from medical records relating to drug abuse patients.[42] Later, Congress amended the Comprehensive Alcohol Abuse and Alcoholism Prevention, Treatment, and Rehabilitation Act of 1970 to regulate the release of alcohol abuse patient records also.[43] The regulations accompanying these amendments are found in 42 C.F.R. Part 2 (1980) (the Rules). The Department of Health and Human Services is revising these regulations and expects to publish them in the near future. The general principle advocated by these rules is stated in Section 2.18: "Any disclosure made under this part, whether with or without the patient's consent, shall be limited to information necessary in the light of the need or purpose for the disclosure."

The coverage of the prohibition is broad. It applies to records of the identity, diagnosis, prognosis, or treatment of any patient, which are maintained in connection with the performance of any alcohol abuse or drug abuse prevention functions.[44] The term "records" is defined as inclusive of *any* information relating to a patient and acquired in connection with an alcohol or drug abuse program.[45]

Excluded from coverage are three types of communications, found in 42 C.F.R. §2.11(p). They are:

(1) communications among program personnel who need the information in connection with their duties
(2) communications in which the patient is not identified in any way
(3) communications between the hospital and an organization performing services such as data processing, dosage preparation, laboratory analysis, or legal, medical, accounting, or other professional services.

---

[42]*See* current version at 42 U.S.C. §290ee–3 (Supp. 1984).

[43]42 U.S.C. §290dd–3 (Supp. 1984).

[44]42 C.F.R. §2.12(a) (1983).

[45]*Id.* at §2.11(o).

Note, however, that in the third situation, the organization performing services for the hospital must have a written agreement with the program acknowledging that it is bound by the rules.[46]

Practically all programs will be covered by the Rules, because the federal government has asserted its jurisdiction broadly under the spending clause of the Constitution. Accordingly, 42 C.F.R. §2.12–1(c) states that, if a program receives a state or municipal grant, it falls within the federal jurisdiction if the state or local government in turn has been the recipient of *any* unrestricted grants or funds. Additionally, 42 C.F.R. §2.12–1(d) states that, if contributions to a program are deductible, the Rules provide that the program is regarded as receiving federal financial assistance. Few programs are totally privately funded, receive no tax deductions for contributions, and are neither licensed nor regulated by the federal government. Therefore, almost every drug or alcohol abuse program is governed by the Rules.

Hospitals must be wary of implicit disclosure of information. For example, if a drug or alcohol abuse patient is in a general care hospital, and the hospital fails to disclose information concerning him that it routinely discloses about other patients, the hospital could be liable for implicitly admitting that the patient was being treated for drug or alcohol abuse. Hospitals should, therefore, be advised to delete such patients from their registers unless the patients consent to their presence being acknowledged. This practice presents a host of potential problems for hospitals that maintain patient registers at their switchboards and information desks. Institutions must devise methods of identifying drug or alcohol abuse patients so that its personnel do not inadvertently release information in violation of the law.

An exception to the prohibition on disclosure occurs when a patient commits or threatens to commit a crime on the premises. The program personnel may then report the crime to authorities.[47] However, the suspect should not be identified as a program patient.[48]

The medical records of alcohol and drug abuse patients may be disclosed with the consent of the patient. This consent must be in writing and in accordance with 42 C.F.R. §2.31. The person releasing the medical records must notify the recipient of the fact that he in turn will also be bound by the Rules from further disclosure.[49] It is advisable to document this notice in writing. For example, the notice can be in the form of a routine form letter, sent to each recipient of alcohol and drug abuse patient records.

---

[46]*Id.* at §2.11(n).

[47]*Id.* at §2.13(d).

[48]*Id.*

[49]*Id.* at §2.32.

In general, minors may consent to the release of their drug and alcohol abuse records if they may also consent to treatment.[50] The Rules, however, adopt state law on the issue of a minor's ability to consent to treatment. As a result, the extent of a minor's ability to consent to the release of these records will vary from state to state.[51] The liberal handling of minors' records is tempered by the exception found in 42 C.F.R. §2.15(f), which states that a parent or guardian may be notified when a minor does not have the capacity to make a rational decision. The parent or guardian may be notified of relevant facts surrounding a situation that poses a substantial threat to the life or physical well-being of the minor or any other individual.

A patient may consent to the release of his records to his attorney,[52] family,[53] third party payers,[54] or others. However, an attorney is prohibited from further disclosure based on patient consent alone unless disclosure is authorized by other provision of the regulations; disclosure to family members is limited to the patient's past or current status; and disclosure to third party payers is limited to what is necessary for discharge of obligations with regard to paying for the services provided. The current regulations fail to describe what information is "necessary."

Disclosure without consent is permitted under limited circumstances. For example, disclosure to medical personnel may be made in a bona fide medical emergency.[55] A record must be made of the disclosure. There must be a written memorandum of:

- the patient's name or case number
- the date and time of the disclosure
- some indication of the nature of the emergency
- the information disclosed
- the name of the person to whom the information was disclosed and
- the name of the person who disclosed the information.[56]

Disclosure without consent may also be made for audit, inspection, or research purposes.[57] Those receiving the information must maintain strict administrative safeguards against further disclosure, which includes record security.[58]

---

[50]*Id.* at §2.15.
[51]*Id.*
[52]*Id.* at §2.35.
[53]*Id.* at §2.36.
[54]*Id.* at §2.37.
[55]*Id.* at §2.51.
[56]*Id.* at §2.51(e).
[57]*Id.* at §2.52.
[58]*Id.* at §2.52(a).

Certain governmental agencies may also receive information without the patient's consent.[59] However, the information should be limited to administrative and financial matters, with the clinical information being more closely guarded. Before disclosure to a governmental agency, the attorney general or other chief legal person of the state must furnish an opinion stating that the requirements of the Rules have been complied with.[60] It is not clear in the regulations whether this opinion must precede disclosure of both administrative and clinical information or just clinical information.

Disclosure without consent may also be made in response to a court order.[61] The procedure necessary to obtain a court order is described in the Rules. The patient's real name should not be used without his consent.[62] The person whose records are sought must be given notice and an opportunity to respond to the requested disclosure.[63] In addition, the scope of a court order is limited to "the facts or dates of enrollment, discharge, attendance, medication, and similar objective data, and may include only such objective data as is necessary to fulfill the purposes for which the order is issued."[64]

The Superior Court of the District of Columbia recently decided a case that highlights the impact of the Rules, *In the Matter of the Death of William Kennedy.*[65] An unidentified patient's body was found next to a drug treatment center, and no witnesses were available. The government therefore sought disclosure of the names of the center's patients. The court refused the court order, stating,

> [b]efore the patient is deprived of his anonymity, he has the right to be heard and tell the Court why, in his particular case, potential harm which would result from loss of confidentiality outweighs the gain to the United States which would be achieved by forced disclosure.

In the case of *United States v. Banks,*[66] a criminal defendant sought the testimony of a physician and psychiatrist concerning the treatment of a particular witness. The defendant hoped to show that the witness was using drugs that would have affected his mental clarity at the time of the trial. The court held that the

---

[59]*Id.* at §2.53.

[60]*Id.* at §2.53(d).

[61]*Id.* at §2.61.

[62]*Id.* at §2.64(a).

[63]*Id.* at §2.64(b).

[64]*Id.* at §2.63.

[65]No. SP–1724–80 (D.C. Super, Jan. 14, 1981).

[66]520 F. 2d 627 (7th Cir. 1975).

testimony was prohibited unless the witness waived his rights under the federal statute or the defendant acquired a court order.[67]

Another case exemplifying the practical impact of the laws and rules is *Raleigh Hills Hospital v. KUTV, Inc.*[68] A TV station conducting an investigation on local hospital practices was issued a restraining order forbidding it to obtain and use patients' medical records maintained by an alcohol treatment hospital unless it received the proper patient consent. The court noted that the Comprehensive Alcohol Abuse and Alcoholism Prevention, Treatment, and Rehabilitation Act distinguishes between information and records, with confidentiality clearly required only in regard to records. Nevertheless, the court ruled that until a hearing could be had on the requirements of the Act, the imposition of a limited restraint would not interfere unconstitutionally with the station's investigation. The court particularly noted that the station was free to interview willing persons and examine documents legally obtained that did not disclose patient names or other identifying information.

The language of the Act and Rules states that they preempt state law. This presents practical problems for hospitals faced with a state mandatory reporting statute, such as a child abuse reporting law, that conflicts with the Act and Rules. In one case in which such a conflict arose, the court upheld both statutes. In *State of Minnesota v. Andring,*[69] a state agency sought the patient's medical records held by a federally funded alcoholism treatment center. While undergoing treatment at the center, the patient reported to his therapist that he had had sexual contacts with his stepdaughter and a niece. The Minnesota Supreme Court held that the state statute was adopted to satisfy a federal child abuse statute that had been enacted by Congress the same year as the Comprehensive Alcohol Abuse and Alcoholism Prevention, Treatment, and Rehabilitation Act, and that Congress had not intended one to cancel out the other. However, the court limited the disclosure of record information to the identification of the allegedly abused children and of the parent or guardian, the nature of the children's injuries, and the identity of the person making the child abuse report. The center could not divulge the statements the patient made to his therapist about his conduct with the children.

At least one court has refused to imply a private cause of action under the Rules, in *Logan v. District of Columbia.*[70] Nevertheless, the Rules could be interpreted as creating a standard of care by which programs could be judged. Violation of such a standard could result in a claim for invasion of privacy.

---

[67]*Id.* at 631.

[68]No. C–81–0800 (D. Utah, Nov. 19, 1981).

[69]342, N.W. 2d 128 (Minn. 1984).

[70]447 F. Supp. 1328 (D.D.C. 1978).

Privacy Act Records

The Privacy Act of 1974[71] is designed to give private citizens control over any information collected by the federal government, in addition to control over how this information is used. It was enacted to stop widespread misuse of information in the government and prohibits the disclosure of records maintained on individuals by federal government agencies (including those agencies that operate hospitals) and by government contractors, except under the conditions and subject to the exceptions specified in the Privacy Act. The records governed by the Privacy Act may be disclosed if requested by or with the prior written consent of the individual to whom the records pertain. The Privacy Act not only permits an individual to gain access to information pertaining to himself or herself in federal agency records but also to have a copy made of all or any portion thereof and to correct or amend such records.[72] Such records may also be disclosed without such individual's consent to the persons and agencies set forth in the Act, including the following:

> [T]o those officers and employees of the agency which maintains the record who have a need for the record in the performance of their duties; . . . to a recipient who has provided the agency with advance adequate written assurance that the record will be used solely as a statistical research or reporting record, and the record is to be transferred in a form that is not individually identifiable; . . . to another agency or to an instrumentality of any governmental jurisdiction within or under the control of the United States for a civil or criminal law enforcement activity if the activity is authorized by law, and if the head of the agency or instrumentality has made a written request to the agency which maintains the record specifying the particular portion desired and the law enforcement activity for which the record is sought; . . . to a person pursuant to a showing of compelling circumstances affecting the health or safety of an individual if upon such disclosure notification is transmitted to the last known address of such individual; . . . pursuant to the order of a court of competent jurisdiction.[73]

The Privacy Act requires federal agencies to collect, maintain, use, or disseminate any record of identifiable personal information in a manner that ensures that

---

[71]5 U.S.C. §552a (1977).

[72]*Id.* §552a(d) (1977).

[73]*Id.* §552a(b) (1977).

such actions are for a necessary and lawful purpose, that the information is current and accurate for its intended use, and that adequate safeguards are provided to prevent misuse thereof.[74] Hospitals operated by the federal government are bound by the Privacy Act's requirements with respect to the disclosure of the medical records of their patients. Also, medical records maintained in a records system operated pursuant to a contract with a federal government agency are subject to the provisions of the Privacy Act.[75] For example, hospitals that maintain registers of cancer patients pursuant to a federal government contract or to federally funded health maintenance organizations are subject to the Privacy Act.[76]

Freedom of Information Act Records

The Freedom of Information Act (FOIA) was enacted by Congress in 1966. The purpose of the FOIA, which amends §3 of the Administrative Procedure Act, was "to provide a true Federal public records statute by requiring the availability, to any member of the public, of all of the executive branch records described in its requirements, except those involving matters which are within nine stated exemptions."[77] Medical records may be exempt from the FOIA requirements under specific circumstances.

The FOIA requires agencies of the federal government to make the following information available for public inspection and copying: final opinions, including concurring and dissenting opinions, as well as orders, made in the adjudication of cases;[78] those statements of policy and interpretations that have been adopted by the agency and are not published in the *Federal Register*;[79] and administrative staff manuals and instructions to staff that affect a member of the public,[80] unless the materials are promptly published and copies offered for sale.

The FOIA further provides that, to the extent required to prevent a clearly unwarranted invasion of an individual's personal privacy, an agency may delete identifying details when it makes available or publishes an opinion, statement of policy, interpretation, or staff manual or instruction. In each case, however, justification for the deletion must be fully explained in writing. Each agency is also required to maintain and make available a current index for public inspection and

---

[74]*Id.* §552a(f) (1977).

[75]*Id.* §552a(m) (1977).

[76]*Id.* §552 (1977 & Supp. 1980).

[77]H.R. Rep. No. 1497, prepared to accompany Senate Bill 1160, 89th Cong., 2d Sess., *reprinted in* 1966 U.S. CODE CONG. & AD. NEWS 2418.

[78]5 U.S.C. §552(a)(2)(A) (1977).

[79]*Id.* §552(a)(2)(B) (1977).

[80]*Id.* §552(a)(2)(C) (1977).

copying.[81] The index must provide identifying information as to matters covered by the FOIA. The FOIA also provides that, except as to records made available under its other provisions, records must be made promptly available to any person, on request, in accordance with published rules.[82]

Although the FOIA makes disclosure the general rule, it permits specifically exempted information to be withheld;[83] one specifically exempt category includes "personnel and medical files and similar files the disclosure of which would institute a clearly unwarranted invasion of personal privacy."[84]

There are three prerequisites for the application of this exception, commonly known as Exception 6: (1) the information must be contained in a personnel, medical, or similar file; (2) disclosure of the information must constitute an invasion of personal privacy; and (3) the severity of the invasion of personal privacy must outweigh the public's interest in the disclosure.[85] In determining whether information sought is within this exception, the relevant consideration is whether the privacy interests that arise from the information sought are similar to those arising from personnel or medical files and not whether the information is recorded in a manner similar to a personnel or medical record.[86]

In ruling on an Exception 6 claim, a court must determine de novo (1) whether the materials requested fall within the type of matter covered by the exemption, and if so, (2) whether the disclosure would constitute a clearly unwarranted invasion of personal privacy.[87] The courts have held that where there is an all important public interest in obtaining the information, the private interest in preventing disclosure must give way to the superior public interest, particularly where the invasion of privacy is minimal.[88]

The language, "clearly unwarranted invasion of personal privacy," has been interpreted by the courts as an expression of a congressional policy that favors disclosure and an instruction to the courts to tilt the balance in favor of disclosure.[89] The United States Supreme Court has held that there is no blanket

---

[81]*Id.* §552(a)(2) (1977).

[82]*Id.* §552(a)(3) (1977).

[83]Consumers Union of United States, Inc. v. Veterans Admin., 301 F. Supp. 796 (S.D.N.Y. 1969), *appeal dismissed as moot,* 436 F. 2d 1363 (2d Cir. 1971).

[84]5 U.S.C. §552(b)(6) (1977).

[85]Metropolitan Life Ins. Co. v. Usery, 426 F. Supp. 150 (D.D.C. 1976); De Planche v. Califano, 549 F. Supp. 685 (W.D. Mich. 1982).

[86]Harbolt v. Dept. of State, 616 F. 2d 772 (5th Cir.), *cert. denied,* 449 U.S. 856 (1980).

[87]Plain Dealer Publishing Co. v. U.S. Dept. of Labor, 471 F. Supp. 1023 (D.D.C. 1979).

[88]Campbell v. U.S. Civil Service Comm'n, 539 F. 2d 58 (10th Cir. 1976). *See also* Florida Medical Ass'n, Inc. v. U.S. Dept. of Health, Education and Welfare, 479 F. Supp. 1291 (M.D. Fla. 1979); Washington Post Co. v. U.S. Dept. of Health and Human Services, 690 F. 2d 252 (D.D.C. 1982).

[89]Ditlow v. Shultz, 517 F. 2d 166 (D.C. Cir. 1975); Celmins v. U.S. Dept. of Treasury, 457 F. Supp. 13 (D.D.C. 1977).

exemption for personnel files: nonconfidential information cannot be insulated from disclosure merely because it is stored by the agency in personnel files.[90] The exemption instead requires a balancing of the individual's right of privacy against the preservation of the public's right to governmental information.[91]

A file is considered similar to personnel and medical files if it contains intimate details of an individual's life, family relations, personal health, religious and philosophical beliefs, and other matters that, if revealed, would prove personally embarrassing to an individual of normal sensibilities.[92] Whether materials are similar files turns on whether the facts that would be revealed would infringe on some privacy interest as highly personal or as intimate in nature as that at stake in personnel and medical records; the court must then proceed to weigh this privacy interest against the public's interest in general disclosure.[93]

> If the balance favors the privacy element, the agency is justified in withholding the data; if the interests of the public in full revelation are stronger, the information must be released; and if the weights are approximately equal, the court must tilt the balance in favor of disclosure, the overriding policy of the Act.[94]

An agency is required to provide reasonably segregable nonexempt portions of an otherwise exempt record to any person requesting such record.[95] Agencies that maintain medical records or have obtained medical records legitimately from a hospital are required by the Privacy Act[96] and by this exemption to the FOIA to withhold disclosure of such records unless a court, in balancing individual and public interests in the information, orders disclosure or unless such records are requested by Congress.

Although medical records maintained by an agency need not be disclosed, disclosure may be required under the FOIA of any information taken from a hospital's medical records by medical researchers in connection with government-

---

[90]Dept. of the Air Force v. Rose, 425 U.S. 352 (1976).

[91]*Id.* at 380. *See also* Jaffee v. C.I.A., 573 F. Supp. 377 (D.D.C. 1983); New England Apple Council v. Donovan, 725 F. 2d 139 (1st Cir. 1984).

[92]Pacific Molasses Co. v. N.L.R.B. Regional Office 15, 577 F. 2d 1172 (5th Cir. 1978); Rural Housing Alliance v. U.S. Dept. of Agriculture, 498 F. 2d 73 (D.C. Cir. 1974); Sims v. C.I.A., 642 F. 2d (D.C. Cir. 1980).

[93]Board of Trade of City of Chicago v. Commodity Futures Trading Comm'n, 627 F. 2d 392 (D.C. Cir. 1980); Shaw v. U.S. Dept. of State, 559 F. Supp. 1053 (D.D.C. 1983); Public Citizen Health Research Group v. F.D.A. 704 F. 2d 1280 (D.D.C. 1983).

[94]627 F. 2d at 398.

[95]5 U.S.C. §552(b) (1977).

[96]*Id.* §552a (1977).

funded medical investigation and incorporated into research reports to a sponsoring agency. In *Forsham v. Harris*,[97] the United States Supreme Court held that information in such reports was not required to be disclosed under the FOIA but described circumstances that would require disclosure. There, a private organization of physicians sought to obtain the raw data underlying the report of the University Group Diabetes Program (UGDP), which had received substantial funding from the Department of Health, Education and Welfare (HEW) to conduct a long-term study of certain diabetes treatment regimens. When the UGDP refused to release the data, the physicians initiated a series of FOIA requests seeking access to the information and claiming that the UGDP data were agency records within the meaning of the act because (1) the UGDP received its funds from the federal government, (2) HEW had under its grant a right of access to the data, and (3) the information was the basis of reports on which the federal government took action in regulating drugs used in the treatment of diabetes. The United States Supreme Court rejected the petitioner's claims, holding that:

> written data generated, owned, and possessed by a privately controlled organization receiving federal study grants are not "agency records" within the meaning of the Act when copies of those data have not been obtained by a federal agency subject to the FOIA. Federal participation in the generation of the data by means of a grant from Department of Health, Education and Welfare (HEW) does not make the private organization a federal "agency" within the terms of the Act. Nor does this federal funding in combination with a federal right of access render the data "agency records" of HEW, which *is* a federal "agency" under the terms of the Act.[98]

The Court held that the grantee's data would become agency records if it could be shown that the agency directly controlled the day-to-day activities of the grantee.[99]

Hospitals that receive federal funds for purposes of medical research, therefore, can minimize the risk of disclosure of research data by avoiding extensive agency supervision of studies conducted by hospital staff and by obtaining the agency's acknowledgment that the data are confidential and will not be disclosed except as may be required by law.

Some states have adopted freedom of information acts. In *Baxter County Newspapers, Inc. v. Medical Staff of Baxter General Hospital,* the Supreme Court

---

[97]445 U.S. 169 (1980).

[98]*Id.* at 171.

[99]*Id.* at 180; *see also* Ciba-Geigy Corp. v. Mathews, 428 F. Supp. 523 (S.D.N.Y. 1977).

of Arkansas held that otherwise privileged information protected by statute may, under certain circumstances, be obtained under provisions of the Arkansas FOIA.[100] Although medical staff committee proceedings, for example, are absolutely privileged in Arkansas, the public cannot be excluded from committee meetings at county hospitals because of the "open meetings" requirement of the Arkansas FOIA. In this case, a newspaper reporter who was barred from a medical staff credentials committee meeting involving the question of whether a physician's staff privileges should be continued challenged the denial of access as a violation of the Arkansas FOIA. Despite the existence of a state statute granting absolute protection to medical review committee proceedings, the state supreme court ruled that, because the protective statute fails to create a specific exception to the Arkansas FOIA, the meetings must be open to the public. While mandating that the hearing of testimony by the credentials committee and the vote on the committee's recommendation by the medical staff must be in public session, the court tempered its decision by ruling that actual deliberation by committee members may be conducted in private.

Other states have taken a more protective position. In *Head v. Colloton*,[101] the court held that the Iowa FOIA does not compel disclosure of the identity of a potential bone marrow donor. Such a donor is a patient whose privacy rights should be protected. In *Short v. Board of Managers of The Nassau County Medical Center*,[102] a New York court held that its state FOIA does not require disclosure of the medical records of 29 abortions. The statute prohibited disclosure of records specifically exempted from disclosure under state or federal law. The plaintiff had argued that because personal identifying data had been or could be deleted, the records were no longer subject to the prohibition against disclosure. The court held that deletions do not cause documents to cease being medical records and, therefore, do not permit their disclosure.

PRO and PSRO Recordkeeping

PROs

The Tax Equity and Fiscal Responsibility Act of 1982[103] repealed the Professional Standards Review Organization (PSRO) program and replaced it with a similar one—the PRO (Peer Review Organization) program—that is likely to maintain much the same recordkeeping requirements as those currently imposed on PSROs. Federal regulations implementing the PRO program have yet to be

---

[100]622 S.W. 2d 495 (Ark. 1981).

[101]331 N.W. 2d 870 (Iowa 1983).

[102]57 N.Y. 2d 399 (1982).

[103]Pub. L. No. 97–248 (1982).

issued and consequently the specificity in disclosure requirements found in the PSRO regulations is still lacking in the PRO law. The PRO law does require, however, that PROs disclose, in accordance with procedures established by the federal Department of Health and Human Services (HHS), review information (1) to state or federal fraud and abuse agencies, (2) to federal and state agencies responsible for identifying cases involving risks to the public health, and (3) to state licensure or certification agencies.[104]

One very significant provision in the PRO law expressly specifies that a PRO is not to be considered a federal agency.[105] The intent of this provision is to preclude litigation similar to that experienced under the PSRO law, where attempts to declare PSROs federal agencies for purposes of FOIA requests led to conflicting court decisions.[106]

Although PSROs will gradually be phased out, existing ones will continue to be recognized until the successor program is established by the secretary of HHS and the new PROs are in place.[107] Current PSRO recordkeeping requirements must, therefore, continue to be observed.

PSROs

The PSRO program was created by a 1972 amendment to the Social Security Act.[108] The program was established to review health services provided to Medicare and Medicaid patients to determine whether these services (1) are medically necessary, (2) meet professional standards of care, and (3) are delivered in the least costly appropriate manner.[109] By statute,[110] a PSRO is required to hold patient information in confidence and is not to disclose it except for the purposes specified in the PSRO statute, for health care planning and fraud or abuse investigations, or as the secretary of the Department of Health and Human Services shall provide in the regulations. A PSRO may examine records pertinent to health care services provided to federal reimbursement program patients in any hospital in the PSRO area as may be necessary to:

---

[104]42 U.S.C. §1320c–9(b)(1)(1983).

[105]*Id.* §1320c–9(a).

[106]*See* notes 119 and 120, and accompanying text, *infra.*

[107]Pub. L. No. 97–248 §150, 1982 U.S. CODE CONG. & AD. NEWS (96 Stat.) 395.

[108]Pub. L. No. 92–603, tit. II, §249 F(b), 1972 U.S. CODE CONG. & AD. NEWS (*current version at* 42 U.S.C. §1320c (1983)).

[109]Pub. L. No. 92–603, tit. II, §249 F(b), 1972 U.S. CODE CONG. & AD. NEWS (*current version at* 42 U.S.C. §1320c–3(1) (1983)).

[110]Pub. L. No. 92–603, tit. II, §249 F(b), 1972 U.S. CODE CONG. & AD. NEWS (*current version at* 42 U.S.C. §1320c–9 (1983)).

(1) perform nondelegated review functions;
(2) evaluate cases which preadmission review, concurrent review, (medical care evaluation) studies, or profile analysis have shown to deviate from the PSRO norms, criteria, or standards;
(3) evaluate the capability of the hospital to assume delegated PSRO functions; or
(4) monitor the performance of a hospital that has assumed delegated PSRO functions.[111]

A PSRO may examine the medical records of patients whose care is not federally funded only if the hospital authorizes access to such records.[112] When examining medical records, a PSRO must restrict its examination of records to those necessary to achieve the aforementioned purposes, must cooperate with those agencies responsible for other examination functions under federal programs to minimize duplication of effort, must conduct its inspection of records during reasonable hours, must maintain written records of the examination in its principal office, and must provide copies of the written reports to hospital management.[113]

Hospitals that refuse to permit a PSRO to examine their patients' medical records in accordance with the applicable regulations may be held in violation of their obligations under Section 1160 of the Social Security Act[114] and may lose their eligibility to participate in federal reimbursement programs.

Another federal regulation requires hospitals, upon request, to supply copies of their patients' medical records to a PSRO.[115] This provision is inconsistent with the previously discussed regulations that merely permit a PSRO staff to examine the patients' medical records only at the hospital. This broader authority is likely to be reflected in future modification of agreements, commonly known as memoranda of understanding, between PSROs and hospitals concerning medical review.

In a recent decision, the United States Court of Appeals for the District of Columbia held that for purposes of the FOIA,[116] PSROs are not government agencies. *Public Citizen Health Research Group v. Department of Health, Education and Welfare* [117] was an action under the FOIA brought by the Public Citizen Health Research Group (Public Citizen) against HEW and the National Capital

---

[111]42 C.F.R. §466.4(a) (1983).
[112]*Id.* §466.4(b).
[113]*Id.* §466.4(c)
[114]42 U.S.C. §1320c-9(b) (1983).
[115]42 C.F.R. §474.1(a)(3) (1983).
[116]5 U.S.C. §552(e) (1982).
[117]668 F. 2d 537, 544 (D.C. Cir. 1981).

Medical Foundation, Inc. (the Foundation), which had been designated by HEW as the PSRO for Washington, D.C. The plaintiff sought disclosure of PSRO documents and alleged that the nondisclosure of these documents violated FOIA. In an earlier ruling, the district court held that information kept by a PSRO was disclosable under the FOIA if the patients to which the information pertained were not identifiable.[118]

The issue before the court of appeals was whether the Foundation as a PSRO was a government agency. The court compared the definition of the term "agency" in the Administrative Procedure Act[119] with that definition contained in the FOIA. The court also reviewed the legislative history of the PSRO program and stated:

> [w]e think these expressions demonstrate the fixed purpose of Congress that PSROs should be independent medical organizations operated by practicing physicians in the private sector, and not government agencies run by government employees. Government, said the committee, should not undertake to review the appropriateness and quality of medical services. A holding that the Foundation, an organization of private physicians, constitutes a government agency would be inconsistent with the congressional purpose.[120]

Among the factors that influenced the court's decision were that PSROs are organized under local law, not federal law, and that federal PSRO regulations were promulgated merely to ensure proper fund allocation rather than to impose day-to-day supervision on a PSRO, which would make it a government agency. That a PSRO makes final decisions is not of itself conclusive of agency status, the court continued, saying that such status can only be determined by examining each situation within its own context.

The court concluded by agreeing with the lower court that "the PSRO program will experience a severe setback, if not fatal blow, should PSRO records become generally available through the FOIA,"[121] but differed with the district court's conclusion that it was up to Congress to remedy the situation.[122]

In *St. Mary Hospital v. Philadelphia Professional Standards Review Organization*,[123] a federal district court, relying upon *Forsham v. Harris*[124] and legislative

---

[118]Public Citizen Health v. Dept. of Health, 477 F. Supp. 595, 601 (D.D.C. 1979).

[119]5 U.S.C. §551(1) (1982).

[120]668 F. 2d at 543 (D.C. Cir. 1981).

[121]*Id.* at 544.

[122]*Id.*

[123]No. 78–2943 (E.D. Pa., June 25, 1980).

[124]445 U.S. 169 (1980).

history, held that Congress intended for a PSRO to be a private, nongovernmental body; and that a PSRO is not an agency within the meaning of the FOIA. Subsequent to this case, Congress enacted a statute that provides that a PSRO shall not be required to release any records in response to an FOIA request until the later of (1) one year after the date of entry of a final order requiring that such records be made available, or (2) the last day of the session of Congress during which the court order was entered.[125]

Statutory Reporting and Other Disclosure Requirements

Many state statutes and regulations and a few federal regulations require hospitals to disclose confidential medical records information without the patient's authorization. Medical records, for example, may be released to the receiving facility when a patient is transferred to another health care facility,[126] when they are required by the state's board of medical examiners,[127] when state health department inspectors[128] or county medical examiners[129] request them, or when the hospital closes and must send its patient records to another institution.[130]

Disclosure of medical records information made pursuant to statutory or regulatory requirements does not subject a hospital or practitioner to liability, even if the disclosure is made against the patient's express wishes. As these statutory provisions authorizing release of medical records vary from state to state, hospitals should be aware of the special disclosure rules applicable in their jurisdictions.

Child Abuse

The child abuse reporting laws of most jurisdictions require hospitals and practitioners to report cases of actual or suspected child abuse. The statutes also protect persons making such reports in good faith from liability for improper disclosure of confidential information, even if the report is erroneous.[131] The Illinois statute is illustrative:

---

[125]Pub. L. No. 96–499 §928, 1980 U.S. CODE CONG. & AD. NEWS (94 Stat.) 2630, *amended by* 42 U.S.C. §1320c–9 (1983).

[126]Md. Health-Gen. Code Ann. §4–301 (1982).

[127]Nev. Rev. Stat. 629.061 (1983).

[128]N.Y. Mental Hygiene Law §31.09 (McKinney 1978).

[129]Cook County Ordinance, ch. 5, §36 (1980).

[130]Miss. Code Ann. §41–9–79 (1972).

[131]*See, e.g.,* Fla. Stat. Ann. §827.07(9) (West 1976); Mont. Code Ann. §41–3–203 (1983); Harris v. City of Montgomery, 435 So. 2d 1207 (Ala. 1983). For a thorough discussion of child abuse reporting, *see* Fraser, *A Glance at the Past, a Glance at the Present, a Glimpse of the Future: A Critical Analysis of the Development of Child Abuse Reporting Statutes,* CHICAGO-KENT L.R. 641 (1978).

Any physician, hospital, hospital administrator and personnel engaged in examination, care and treatment of persons, surgeon, dentist, osteopath, chiropractor, podiatrists, Christian Science practitioner, coroner, medical examiner, school personnel, truant officers, social services administrator, registered nurse, licensed practical nurse, director or staff assistant of a nursery school or a child day care center, law enforcement officer, registered psychologist, or field personnel of the Illinois Department of Public Aid or the Department of Public Health, Department of Mental Health and Development Disabilities, Department of Corrections, probation officer, or any other child care or foster care worker having reasonable cause to believe a child known to them in their professional or official capacity may be an abused child or a neglected child shall immediately report or cause a report to be made to the Department. Whenever such person is required to report under this Act in his capacity as a member of the staff of a medical or other public or private institution, school, facility or agency, he shall make [a] report immediately to the Department in accordance with the provisions of this Act and may also notify the person in charge of such institution, school, facility or agency or his designated agent that such report has been made. The privileged quality of communication between any professional person required to report and his patient or client shall not apply to situations involving abused or neglected children and shall not constitute grounds for failure to report as required by this Act.[132]

These reports frequently require the disclosure of information from hospital medical records, and such disclosures made in good faith without the authorization of the patient or the patient's parent or guardian does not subject the hospital to liability. Failure to make a report of child abuse by those required to do so can lead to liability in negligence for any additional injuries the child later sustains when discharged to a hostile home environment.[133] Reports and disclosures made subsequent to the initial report that are part of a government agency's continuing investigation are permissible. Hospitals should make a reasonable effort to determine the validity of the investigation before releasing information from the medical record.

Drug Abuse

Some states require physicians and others to identify patients who obtain drugs that are subject to abuse so that patient names and addresses can be entered into a

---

[132]Ill. Ann. Stat. ch. 23, §2054 (Smith-Hurd Supp. 1983–1984). *See also* Ill. Ann. Stat. ch. 23, §2059 (Smith-Hurd Supp. 1983–1984) for a grant of immunity from liability.

[133]*See* Landeros v. Flood, 17 Cal. 3d 399, 551 P. 2d 389, 131 Cal. Rptr. 69 (1976).

state registry.[134] Such was the case in *Whalen v. Roe,*[135] in which the United States Supreme Court held that the New York statute requiring physicians to make such reports was the product of an orderly and rational legislative decision and a reasonable exercise of the state's broad police powers, and that the statute neither infringed upon the patient's personal privacy rights nor impaired the right of physicians to prescribe the drugs subject to the reporting law.

Poison and Industrial Accidents

A few states require physicians to report illness or disease they believe was contracted in connection with employment.[136] The reports are made to the state's department of public health and usually include the name, address, occupation, and illness of the patient and the name and address of the patient's employer. The purpose of these statutes is to enable public health officials to investigate occupational diseases and to recommend methods for eliminating or preventing them.

Abortion

Several states require hospitals and practitioners to report abortions they perform[137] and any complications that may develop.[138] Other states require hospitals to report fetal deaths, including those resulting from abortions.[139] Courts have held these requirements to be rationally related to a compelling state interest in maternal health and not to be an infringement upon the physician-patient relationship, the right to an abortion, or any personal right of privacy.[140]

Cancer

A few states require disclosure of information from the medical records of cancer patients to central state or regional tumor registries.[141] These registries usually contain demographic, diagnostic, and treatment information about

---

[134]*See, e.g.,* Ill. Ann. Stat. ch. 56-1/2, §§1311, 1312(a); (Smith-Hurd Supp. 1984–1985) Cal. Health and Safety Code §11167 (West Supp. 1984).

[135]429 U.S. 589 (1977). *See also* Volkman v. Miller, which held valid the maintenance of computerized records on crisis center outpatients, 52 A.D. 2d 146, 383 N.Y.S. 2d 95 (1976). *But see* Commonwealth v. Donoghue, 4 Mass. App. Ct. 752, 358 N.E. 2d 465 (Mass. App. 1976). Reporting statute was held to be unconstitutionally vague.

[136]*See, e.g.,* Ga. Code Ann. §34–9–290 (1982); Minn. Stat. Ann. §144.34 (West Supp. 1984).

[137]Minn. Stat. Ann. §145.413 (West Supp. 1984).

[138]*See, e.g.,* Ill. Ann. Stat. ch. 38, §81–30.1 (Smith-Hurd Supp. 1983–1984).

[139]*See, e.g.,* N.Y. Pub. Health Law §4160 (McKinney 1977).

[140]*See, e.g.,* Schulman v. New York City Health and Hosp. Corp. 38 N.Y. 2d 234, 342, N.E. 2d 501, 379 N.Y.S. 2d 702 (1975).

[141]*See, e.g.,* Minn. Stat. Ann. §144.68 (West Supp. 1984).

patients who suffer from the same or similar diseases and are designed to provide raw data for studies concerning the incidence of a disease in the population; long-term prognosis of the disease; type, duration, and frequency of treatment rendered to patients with the disease; and other indicators of the health care industry's ability to manage the disease. Usually operated by statewide, tax-exempt organizations funded by federal grants, the registries rely to a large extent upon the cooperation of individual hospital registries and obtain patient information directly from participating hospitals pursuant to agreements between the hospitals and the registry.

In the absence of a state reporting statute or other statutory or regulatory authority for reporting patient information to a registry, disclosure of such information without the patient's authorization may subject the hospital to liability for improper release of confidential data. Hospitals that have chosen to participate in a cancer or other registry should seek statutory or regulatory authority for release of medical record information to such registries. If legislative action is impractical, participating hospitals should exercise care in drafting agreements with registries. Such contracts should contain safeguards against improper disclosure of confidential information by the registry and an indemnification of the hospitals for claims against them that may result from their release of data to the registry or from improper disclosure by the registry.

Communicable Diseases

Communicable disease reporting laws requiring hospitals and practitioners to inform public health authorities of infectious disease cases are among the oldest compulsory reporting statutes in many states. The statutes or regulations usually list diseases that should be reported and direct practitioners to give local public health officials the patient's name, age, sex, address, and identifying information, as well as the details of the patient's illness.[142] Hospitals should disclose only the information required by the statute.

Misadministration of Radioactive Materials and Blood Transfusion Reactions

Federal regulations require hospitals to report to the Nuclear Regulatory Commission any misadministration of radioactive materials. Misadministration is defined as the administration of a radiopharmaceutical or radiation other than the one intended, and of a radiopharmaceutical or radiation given to the wrong patient or administered to the right patient by a route other than that prescribed by the

---

[142]*See, e.g.,* Conn. Gen. Stat. Ann. §19a–215 (West Supp. 1984); N.Y. Pub. Health Law §201 (McKinney 1977).

physician.[143] Regulations also require hospitals to report to the director of the Bureau of Biologics of the federal Food and Drug Administration all fatalities resulting from collection or transfusion of blood.[144]

Access by Hospital Staff

Hospital policy generally allows members of its medical and nursing staff access to patient records, without patient consent, for certain authorized purposes. It is the hospital's responsibility, however, to safeguard both the record and its content against loss, defacement, and tampering, and from use by unauthorized individuals. These guidelines are generally set forth in hospital or medical staff bylaws, and less frequently, in state statutes or regulations.

The JCAH accreditation standards, as well as several state statutes, permit the release of confidential patient information to qualified personnel for the purpose of conducting scientific research, audits, program evaluations, official surveys, education, and quality control activities, without patient authorization.[145]

Some states, however, have more restrictive policies concerning access to hospital medical records by the hospital staff. Maryland, for example, only allows access to the patients' medical records to members of the medical staff performing medical or allied support services for or on behalf of the patient. Medical researchers may also only acquire access to patients' medical records pursuant to a protocol approved by an institutional review board.[146]

The JCAH interpretation of its accreditation standards also suggests that,

> [w]hen certain portions of the medical records are so confidential that extraordinary means are considered necessary to preserve their privacy, such as in the treatment of some psychiatric disorders, these portions may be stored separately, provided the complete record is readily available when required for current medical care or follow-up, for review functions, or for use in quality assessment activities.[147]

Alcohol and drug abuse patients' records are also basically treated in a more restrictive manner. Hospital policy may limit access to these records to a more limited group.

---

[143]45 Fed. Reg. §31701 (1950).

[144]21 C.F.R. §606.170(b) (1983).

[145]See, e.g., R.I. Gen. Laws §5–37.3–4 (Supp. 1983); Wyo. Ann. Stat. §35–2–601 (1977); JCAH, ACCREDITATION MANUAL FOR HOSPITALS 84 (1984); Ill. Ann. Stat. ch. 110 §§8–2101–2105 (Smith-Hurd Supp. 1983); (S.C. Health and Environmental Control Dept. R61–16 (1982)).

[146]Md. Health-Gen. Code Ann. §4–301(c)(5) (Supp. 1984).

[147]JCAH, ACCREDITATION MANUAL FOR HOSPITALS 84 (1984).

In the absence of state statutory law, the majority of hospitals allows access to a patient's medical record to those persons directly involved in the care of the patient. Patients' medical records may also be examined for required clinical and financial auditing purposes, for utilization review, and for other quality assurance activities. Records may also be available for research provided that all information that would identify the patient is deleted when the research data are tabulated and reported. Nontreating physicians, therefore, will generally not have automatic access to patients' medical records unless the records are used for the purposes previously discussed.

Hospital policies should include the procedures that medical and hospital staff members should follow to obtain access to medical records. These procedures may be incorporated in hospital or medical staff bylaws and regulations as well as in appropriate hospital policy manuals.

Disclosures for Medical Research

Many medical research projects involve the use of patients' medical records. These records are typically used to determine response to specific types of therapy, relationships between population characteristics and incidence of illness, or to obtain statistical information important to the development of more efficient treatment. Most states, therefore, have adopted the position that medical and nursing staff members may examine patient records for medical research purposes.[148] A minority of states also allows approved medical investigators access to patients' medical records.[149] Hospitals that permit their staffs to conduct medical research studies, however, should establish an Institutional Review Board (IRB) or other medical review committee to evaluate the risk to the patient and the potential benefits of the research.

Although the hospital has a duty to its patients to ensure that patients' records remain confidential, it also has a vested interest in medical research projects. The hospital must, therefore, balance the patients' rights to privacy and expectations of confidentiality against the researchers' interest in advancing medical science for the general welfare. It often becomes necessary for hospitals to impose controls and limitations on staff access to medical records for research purposes.

There is also a general consensus among hospitals that individuals who are not hospital employees should have limited access to patients' medical records.[150]

---

[148]*See, e.g.,* R.I. Gen. Laws §5–37.3–4 (Supp. 1983); Wyo. Ann. Stat. §35–2–601 (1977).

[149]*See, e.g.,* Pa. Dept. of Pub. Health Rules and Regulations for Hospitals §115.27. *See also* Kelsey, *Privacy and Confidentiality in Epidemiological Research Involving Patients,* IRB Rev. Hum. Subjects Research, Feb. 1981 at 1 (publication by the Hastings Center, Hastings-on-Hudson, N.Y.).

[150]*See* Melum, *Balancing Information and Privacy,* 58 Hosp. Prog. 68–69, 79 (1979). Gordis and Gold, *Privacy, Confidentiality, and the Use of Medical Records in Research,* 207 Science 153 (1980).

Some hospitals, therefore, are informing patients on admission that their records may be made available to approved investigators.[151] This practice informs potential subjects that their records may be used in a research project undertaken by one who is not a member of the hospital staff but whose project is approved by the IRB or medical committee of the hospital.

Research proposals involving human subjects must be reviewed and approved by the IRB or medical review committee of the hospital. Hospitals that are federal grantees or contractors and that conduct experimental medical research on human subjects are required by federal regulations to establish an IRB to evaluate proposed research protocol.[152] The IRB is responsible for determining whether the research would be beneficial to society, and whether adequate safeguards are available to protect the human subjects at risk.[153] Assurances must be given as part of the research protocol that the medical research projects will be subject to continuing review by the IRB.

Although written authorization by the patient granting access to medical records is usually desirable, it is often impractical to obtain patient consent for retrospective studies. In the absence of patient consent, the IRB, consistent with applicable federal regulations and state law, must implement safeguards to be followed by medical investigators who are granted access to patients' past medical records.

Although federal regulations generally recognize the need to obtain informed consent when medical research exposes individuals to potential harm, in limited circumstances the regulations allow access to patients' medical records without any prior authorization. One such circumstance is the disclosure for retrospective research or program evaluation of records relating to patients in federal drug or alcohol abuse treatment programs. The United States Public Health Service's regulations governing such disclosures state that:

> the . . . rationale for requiring informed consent does not apply to the same degree in situations involving the disclosure of clinical records for research in the form of follow-up or retrospective studies. Under these circumstances, the risk to the subject is that some disclosure or misuse of information from which he could be identified might result in embarrassment, lost opportunity, or other forms of psychological or social injury. While that possibility of harm could be reduced by requiring consent to every review of clinical records for research purposes, a

---

[151]See Kelsey, *supra* note 149.

[152]45 C.F.R. §46.103 (1983).

[153]See *id.* at §46.111. *See also* Univ. of Texas Health Sciences Center, *Conference on the Legal Aspects of Institutional Review Boards* (Sept. 26–27, 1980).

similar result can be achieved by the less restrictive method of limiting further disclosure of identifying information by the researcher.[154]

In addition, requirements that patient consent be obtained before any medical record is examined would severely hamper medical and epidemiological research.[155]

Although the federal regulations recognize the problems in obtaining patient authorization for retrospective studies, the burden is ultimately with the states or individual hospitals to determine whether access to patients' records should be granted.

While many states permit IRB-approved researchers to obtain patients' medical records without prior patient consent, such researchers usually must ensure that their findings will not disclose information that identifies a particular patient.[156]

Unfortunately, applicable statutes and regulations do not grant medical record access to a uniformly defined class of individuals. For example, the director of the Pennsylvania Health Standards and Quality Bureau has included within the group of authorized persons hospital staff members and parties that undertake studies with appropriate medical staff approval.[157] By contrast, Oregon's statutory treatment is more restrictive: it prohibits disclosure of patients' medical records to parties other than the patients' health care providers or insurers who are deemed to have a "need to know" such information.[158]

However, hospitals and researchers alike should realize that patients' records retain their essentially confidential nature even after their disclosure to approved researchers. For example, at least one federal court recently refused to force the founder of the University of Chicago's Registry for Hormonal Transplacental Carcinogenesis to disclose identifiable information gleaned from research participants' records to a diethylstilbestrol manufacturer who requested the information for use in defending a products liability lawsuit.[159] Even though the manufacturer offered to pay the researcher to delete all of the participants' names and addresses, the court believed that mere disclosure of the participants' unique factual circumstances could reveal their identities.[160] Therefore, the court concluded that the

---

[154]42 C.F.R. §2.52–1(i) (1979).

[155]*See supra* note 150.

[156]*See, e.g.,* R.I. Gen. Laws §5–37.3–4 (Supp. 1983). *See also* Gordis and Gold, *supra* note 150, at 153.

[157]*See* Hershey, *Using Patient Records for Research: The Response from Federal Agencies and the State of Pennsylvania,* IRB Rev. Hum. Subjects Research, Oct. 1981 at 8 (publication by The Hasting Center, Hastings-on-Hudson, N.Y.).

[158]Or. Rev. Stat. §192.525 (Supp. 1981).

[159]*See* Andrews v. Eli Lilly & Company, 97 F.R.D. 494 (N.D. Ill. 1983).

[160]*Id.* at 502.

manufacturer's need for the information outweighed neither the need to protect participants' privacy nor the possible negative effect such a disclosure would have upon all medical researchers' ability to locate willing research participants.[161]

In addition, the degree of record disclosure allowed may vary with the reason for the patient's hospitalization. Both federal and state statutes and regulations typically restrict the use of medical records concerning patients hospitalized for mental illness or alcohol and drug abuse.[162] One example is the Illinois Mental Health and Developmental Disabilities Confidentiality Act.[163] With a few limited exceptions, this statute requires parties who wish to inspect or use mental patients' medical records to obtain the consent of the patients or their guardians.[164] Since each state's requirements may vary, hospitals and health care lawyers should examine applicable statutes and regulations in their jurisdictions. Lacking explicit statutory authority, hospitals should be reluctant to disclose patients' records to anyone except their internal clinical or research personnel.

In the absence of state regulations establishing stricter standards for the disclosure of patients' medical records for use in conducting biomedical or epidemiological research, without patient authorization the IRB or research committee should require that the following safeguards be met before authorizing disclosure of these confidential records to medical investigators.

1. The information will be treated as confidential.
2. The information will be communicated only to qualified investigators pursuing an approved research program designed for the benefit of the health of the community.
3. Adequate safeguards to protect the record or information from unauthorized disclosure will be established.
4. The results of the investigation will be presented in a way that prevents identification of individual subjects.[165]

---

[161]*Id.* at 503. *See also* Farnsworth v. Proctor & Gamble Company, No. C83–2085A (N.D. Ga., Mar. 30, 1984) (available June 14, 1984, on LEXIS, Genfed library, Dist. file). The Farnsworth court refused to allow Proctor & Gamble to obtain names and addresses of participants in a Center for Disease Control study of Toxic Shock Syndrome (TSS), because the need to protect participants from embarrassment and to avoid impairing the CDC's research function outweighed Proctor & Gamble's interest as a private litigant. Farnsworth, slip op. at 4 (citing Andrews, *supra* note 159, at 500).

[162]*See generally* discussion of records of alcohol and drug abuse patients, *supra*.

[163]Ill. Ann. Stat. ch. 91-1/2, §§801 to 817 (Smith-Hurd Supp. 1983–84).

[164]*See id.* at §§805(a), 806 to 812.

[165]Melum, *supra* note 150, at 68–69, 79; Walters, *The Use of Medical Records for Research at Georgetown University,* IRB REV. HUM. SUBJECTS RESEARCH, March 1981, at 1 (publication by The Hastings Center, Hastings-on-Hudson, N.Y.).

Hospitals should prohibit access to medical records by investigators whose medical studies do not include at least these safeguards as determined by the IRB or other appropriate committee, barring statutory law to the contrary.

Utilization Review and Quality Assurance Activities

In addition to their uses in medical research, patients' records also play a critical role in the continuous effort to improve the quality of health care services and to increase the efficiency with which they are provided. Patients' records are necessarily one of the primary sources of data for such utilization reviews and other quality assurance activities. Therefore, health care providers and health law practitioners must be aware of the statutes, regulations, and judicial opinions in their jurisdictions that may affect their ability to use medical records for these purposes.

Federal legislation passed in 1982[166] requires HHS to enter contracts with PROs. Composed primarily of health care practitioners from a designated geographic area, these PROs perform quality assurance and utilization reviews of health care providers seeking reimbursement for their services through the Medicare program.[167] PROs will eventually replace PSROs, which have performed these same review functions for both the Medicare and Medicaid programs for several years.[168] Until HHS promulgates regulations implementing the PRO review program, however, PSROs will continue to function.[169]

Essentially, PSROs must review all federally funded health care services provided in a specified geographic area and must determine whether:

1. the services were medically required
2. the services met recognized standards of professional care, and

---

[166]*See* the Tax Equity and Fiscal Responsibility Act of 1982, Pub. L. No. 97–248 (hereinafter cited as TEFRA), §§141–150, 96 Stat. 324, 381–395 (current version at 42 U.S.C. §§1320c to 1320c–12 (Supp. 1983)).

[167]*See* 42 U.S.C. at §§1320c–2, 1320c–3.

[168]*See* the Social Security Amendments of 1972, tit. II, §249(F)(b) (hereinafter cited as Amendments of 1972), subsection 1155(2), 1972 U.S. CODE CONG. & AD. NEWS 1548, 1675–76 (currently codified at 42 U.S.C. §1320c–3(a) (Supp. 1983)).

[169]*See* TEFRA, *supra* note 166, at §150; 96 Stat., at 395. On October 17, 1983, the Department of Health and Human Services published an agenda of current and projected rulemakings, which indicated that the Health Care Financing Administration is currently developing regulations for the PRO review program. The agenda also indicated that HHS and HCFA have classified these rules as "priority regulations." *See* 48 Fed. Reg. 47340, 47347 (1983).

3. the services, if provided to inpatients, could have been furnished in a less costly facility or method.[170]

To fulfill these functions, current federal regulations give PSROs broad authority to inspect and use federal program patients' medical records.[171] However, PSROs do not have unlimited access to records. To examine records of non-federal-program patients, a PSRO must obtain authorization from the hospital.[172] Since patients' medical records are a critical data source for PSRO review, and since PRO functions will be virtually identical to those listed above,[173] the new record access regulations for PROs will probably contain a similarly broad grant of record access authority.

In addition to federal quality assurance requirements, the JCAH also requires all hospitals seeking accreditation to establish internal systems for quality assurance and utilization review.[174] The quality assurance plan focuses primarily upon identifying and eliminating specific patient care problems and must include at least the following general features.

1. identification of problems (both existing and potential)
2. assessment of the problems' cause and extent, as well as development of problem-solving priorities
3. implementation of actions needed to eliminate the problems
4. followup or monitoring to determine whether actions were effective, and
5. documentation to support the system's aggregate efficiency.[175]

The primary goal of utilization review, however, is to ensure that the hospital allocates all of its resources—staff, equipment, and supplies—so that it may render competent professional health care at the lowest possible cost.[176] This review may be conducted during the patient's hospitalization (called concurrent review) or after the patient's discharge (called retrospective review); however, either form of review will examine the complete duration of the patient's care, from the admission decision to discharge planning.[177] The hospital must put both

---

[170]Amendments of 1972, *supra* note 168, at subsection 1155(a)(1)(A)–(C), 1972 U.S. CODE CONG. & AD. NEWS at 1675–76.

[171]42 C.F.R. §466.4(a) (1983).

[172]*Id.* at §466.4(b).

[173]*See* 42 U.S.C. §1320c–3(a)(1) (1983).

[174]JCAH, ACCREDITATION MANUAL FOR HOSPITALS 147–79, 193–94 (1984).

[175]*Id.* at 147–48.

[176]*Id.* at 193. *See also* K. WATERS & G. MURPHY, MEDICAL RECORDS IN HEALTH INFORMATION 626 (1979).

[177]K. WATERS & G. MURPHY, *supra* note 176, at 416.

its utilization review and quality assurance plans in writing, must reevaluate and revise them at least annually, and must document their use and efficacy.[178]

Although these plans rely upon many data sources,[179] the most valuable sources are clearly patients' confidential medical records. Many states have recognized the need for this sensitive information and have enacted statutes that expressly authorize hospitals to disclose patient records to staff quality control committees.[180] One example is found in the California Code.

> (c) A provider of health care may disclose medical information as follows:
>
> . . . .
>
> (4) The information may be disclosed to organized committees and agents . . . medical staffs of licensed hospitals . . . if the committees, agents, organizations, or persons are engaged in reviewing . . . health care services with respect to medical necessity, level of care, quality of care, or justification of charges.[181]

However, not all states specifically allow such disclosures. For example, the Tennessee Code contains several provisions known collectively as the Medical Records Act of 1974,[182] but none of these provisions specifically authorizes disclosure of patient records to hospital quality control committees. Instead, the statute states simply that "hospital records shall not constitute public records, and nothing in [the Act] shall be deemed to impair any privilege of confidentiality conferred by law on patients, their personal representatives, or heirs."[183] Tennessee hospitals, therefore, are left to assume that their quality assurance committees may obtain access to medical records for appropriate quality assurance purposes. Given the almost universal approval of such functions, this is a safe assumption.

Some states without statutes specifically granting record access to quality control committees may have case law that permits disclosures. In a 1975 Missouri

---

[178]*See* JCAH, Accreditation Manual for Hospitals, at 147–48, 193–94 (1984).

[179]*See id.* at 148, 194.

[180]*See, e.g.,* Ariz. Rev. Stat. Ann. §36–445.02 (Supp. 1983–84); Cal. Civ. Code §56.10(c)(4) (West Supp. 1984); Iowa Code Ann. §135.40 (West 1972); La. Rev. Stat. Ann. §44.7(D) (West 1982); Mich. Comp. Laws Ann. §333.2633 (1980); Minn. Stat. Ann. §145.62 (West Supp. 1984); Miss. Code Ann. §41–63–3 (Supp. 1984); Ohio Rev. Code Ann. §2305.24 (Page Supp. 1983); R.I. Gen. Laws §5–37.3–4(b)(2) (Supp. 1983); Tex. Civ. Code Ann. §4447(d)(1) (Vernon 1976).

[181]Cal. Civ. Code §56.10(c)(4) (West Supp. 1984).

[182]Tenn. Code Ann. §§68–11–301 to 68–11–311 (1983).

[183]*Id.* at §68–11–304(c).

appellate case,[184] for example, a staff physician sought to prevent the disclosure of his patients' records to a hospital committee that was investigating his qualifications and competency. Missouri had a physician-patient privilege statute that rendered a physician incompetent to testify regarding any information received during a professional consultation with a patient.[185] The physician argued that the privilege should prevent the use of patient records in a competency determination because their use would constitute a type of testimony at what basically was a hearing. The court reviewed the privilege's history and noted that no state had ever treated the privilege as an absolute prohibition against a physician's disclosure.[186] After balancing the parties' opposing interests, the court concluded the privilege was inapplicable because "[t]he public's interest in the disclosure of the information to the internal staff of the hospital and in assuring proper medical and hospital care outweigh[ed] the patient's interest in concealment."[187]

The differing postures of Missouri, Tennessee, and California illustrate the potential for variation in the law from state to state. Hospital administrators and health law practitioners should, therefore, consult the statutes, regulations, and common law in their jurisdictions before authorizing the use of patients' medical records for purposes of quality assurance and utilization review.

Government Agencies

Health care facilities have a strong interest in the privacy of their medical records, and as a general rule the hospital may refuse to release records to government officials. However, such government officials are entitled to search and seize medical records if they first obtain a judicially issued search warrant. Because a search warrant requires the approval of a neutral magistrate and must specifically state the place to be searched, the objects to be seized, and the reason for the search, it effectively denies general "fishing expeditions" by the government. Nevertheless, in some instances government officials are entitled to access to medical records even in the absence of a search warrant.

The Fourth Amendment to the United States Constitution is the source of the search warrant requirement, to protect persons and their houses, papers, and effects from unreasonable searches and seizures. The amendment is thus designed "to safeguard the privacy and security of individuals against arbitrary invasions by governmental officials."[188] Although the amendment was intended to apply

---

[184]Klinge v. Lutheran Medical Center of St. Louis, 518 S.W. 2d 157 (Mo. App. 1975).

[185]*See* Mo. Ann. Stat. §491.060(5) (Vernon 1952) (currently in force).

[186]518 S.W. 2d at 164.

[187]*Id.* at 166.

[188]Camara v. Municipal Court, 387 U.S. 523, 528 (1967).

primarily to private residences, its proscription of warrantless searches as presumptively unreasonable applies to commercial premises as well.[189] Generally, therefore, government access to medical records without a search warrant is presumptively unreasonable and violates the Fourth Amendment.

Although the search warrant requirement has been almost exclusively associated with criminal investigations, the Supreme Court of the United States has specifically stated that administrative or regulatory searches also come within the Fourth Amendment's scope.[190] Whether a court will impose a warrant requirement on an administrative search, however, depends on whether the search is designed to enforce a general regulatory scheme or is aimed at specific licensed industries. The Supreme Court has imposed a warrant requirement when an administrative search is conducted pursuant to general regulatory legislation that applies to all residences, structures, or employers within a given jurisdiction. For example, the Court has required a warrant in situations involving a residential search pursuant to a municipal housing code,[191] a commercial search of a locked warehouse to enforce a municipal fire code,[192] and routine commercial inspections of business premises not open to the public under the Occupational Safety and Health Act of 1970.[193]

Courts have treated searches of specific licensed industries differently, however. In *Colonnade Catering Corp. v. United States*,[194] the Supreme Court upheld a statute providing for warrantless inspection of the business records of licensed liquor dealers. The court refused to adhere to cases like *Camara* and others that impose a warrant requirement on searches conducted pursuant to general regulatory laws.[195] Instead, because the liquor industry is an industry long subject to stringent government regulation, the Court deferred to congressional standards of reasonableness for this warrantless regulatory search.[196]

Similarly, in *United States v. Biswell*,[197] the Court upheld a statute authorizing warrantless inspections of the business premises of federally licensed firearms dealers. Although the firearms industry did not share the liquor industry's long history of regulation, the Court nonetheless deemed it essential to federal and state law enforcement efforts to closely scrutinize interstate firearms traffic. More

---

[189]*See* Marshall v. Barlow's, Inc., 436 U.S. 307, 312 (1978).

[190]*See* See v. City of Seattle, 387 U.S. 541, 545 (1967). *See also* Camara, *supra* note 188, at 535.

[191]Camara, *supra* note 188, at 540.

[192]*See supra* note 190, at 545–46.

[193]Marshall, *supra* note 189, at 315.

[194]397 U.S. 72 (1970).

[195]*Id.* at 77.

[196]*Id.*

[197]406 U.S. 311 (1972).

importantly, the Court examined the privacy interests of a firearms dealer and concluded that:

> inspections for compliance with the Gun Control Act pose only limited threats to the dealer's justifiable expectations of privacy. When a dealer chooses to engage in the pervasively regulated business and to accept a federal license, he does so with the knowledge that his business records, firearms, and ammunition will be subject to effective inspection.[198]

The Supreme Court has therefore given only general consideration to the issue of warrantless administrative searches, stating that a warrant may not be required for searches that protect very strong national interests, or for searches of businesses that either are federally licensed or have a long history of supervision and pervasive regulation. Recent state and lower federal court decisions also recognize these two basic types of administrative searches, concerning both general regulatory schemes and specific licensed industries, and have analyzed situations involving government access to health care facilities generally and medical records specifically.

Nursing Homes and Pharmacies

The courts of California and New York have, in recent years, authorized warrantless searches of medical facilities, but only in certain narrowly defined situations. The seminal case is *People v. Firstenberg*,[199] a 1979 California decision that upheld a warrantless inspection of the business records of a skilled nursing facility. In *Firstenberg*, a county health inspector routinely inspected the facility's records, without a search warrant, and discovered that the defendant, a licensee of the facility, had commingled patients' funds with his own. The court rejected the defendant's challenge to the warrantless search on the grounds that the health care industry in California had been pervasively regulated and that the state's interest in regulating the industry outweighed the facility's privacy interest.[200]

Two factors serve to distinguish the *Firstenberg* decision from situations involving searches of a hospital's medical records. First, the California legislature has subjected not only the general health care industry, but long-term health facilities in particular, to a thorough regulatory scheme. Such intense regulation is similar to the regulation of alcohol and firearms on the federal level, which was the

---

[198]*Id.* at 316.

[199]92 Cal. App. 3d 570, 155 Cal. Rptr. 80 (Cal. Ct. App. 1979), *cert. denied*, 444 U.S. 1012 (1980).

[200]*Id.* at 580–81, 155 Cal. Rptr. at 85–86.

key in the *Colonnade* and *Biswell* decisions. In states that do not regulate the health care industry to the same extent that California does, that part of *Firstenberg's* rationale fails.

The second distinguishable characteristic of *Firstenberg* lies in the nature of "skilled nursing facilities." In that regard the court stated:

> It is, of course, obvious that [frequent and unannounced] inspections are crucial to the effective oversight of the physical well-being of patients, to assure that they are not neglected or even abused. Frequent, unannounced inspections are also essential to effective protection of patients' financial welfare. Financial records can easily be concealed or even falsified. Patients are helpless to protect themselves. . . . [Most] nursing home patients are neither aware of, nor capable of protesting misuse of their funds. The knowledge that records can be examined without prior notice is the surest guarantee that nursing home licensees will fulfill their fiduciary responsibilities toward their patients. Such inspections are also the most effective method of assuring that those who fail to fulfill these responsibilities are identified so that their conduct can be corrected or their licenses revoked. The necessity for unannounced warrantless inspections in the long-term health care industry is just as great as in the firearms industry and such inspections are, therefore, reasonable within the meaning of the Fourth Amendment.[201]

Although the court's rationale in *Firstenberg* of patient welfare could conceivably be stretched to apply also to hospitals, the court's decision expressly applied only to searches of long-term health care facilities. California courts had previously used the same rationale of patient welfare to ratify warrantless searches of licensed *convalescent* hospitals.[202] Using language analogous to that found in *Firstenberg*, one court stated that "if no inspection without a warrant may be made of a hospital, once it begins operations, to secure the health, safety, even the lives of the helpless and the aged or infirm, we should be told expressly, rather than by implication."[203] Although the court spoke broadly of the right to search convalescent hospitals without a warrant because of the need to protect helpless patients, it is important to note that the actual inspection conducted did not extend to medical records.

---

[201]*Id.*

[202]People v. White, 259 Cal. App. 2d Supp. 936, 65 Cal. Rptr. 923 (Cal. App. Dept. Super. Ct. 1968).

[203]*Id.* at 940, 65 Cal. Rptr. at 926.

New York courts have, in two decisions, authorized warrantless searches of pharmacy records and licensed nursing homes. *People v. Curco Drugs, Inc.*,[204] involved the warrantless search of pharmacy records by state health inspectors, pursuant to statute. The court found that pharmacy records in New York are subject to inspection without warning because the pharmacist accepts a state license subject to the right of warrantless inspection. Thus, the court refused to impose a warrant requirement even though health inspectors had time and opportunity to procure a warrant.[205]

A second New York case, *Uzzilia v. Commissioner of Health*,[206] upheld a state statute that authorized thorough warrantless inspections of "hospitals and home health agencies," a term that includes nursing homes.[207] The court emphasized, as did the California court in *Firstenberg*, the need to protect the interests of "elderly and infirm persons entrusted to nursing homes."[208] Because of the overriding interest of the state in protecting nursing home residents, and because of the thorough regulation of nursing homes in New York, the court concluded that such warrantless searches did not violate the Fourth Amendment.[209]

Day Care Centers and Abortion Clinics

Although the New York and California decisions appear to authorize broad warrantless searches by state health authorities, recent federal court decisions put definite limits on that power, particularly when the medical facility involved is a public health clinic. The most recent case, however, rejected warrantless searches of licensed family day care centers. In *Rush v. Obledo*,[210] a California district court distinguished the *Firstenberg* decision, stating that:

> *Firstenberg* relied in part on the longstanding heavily regulated nature of institutions giving medical care to the aged and infirm, and on the fact that skilled nursing homes are part of the health industry, a pervasively regulated field that also includes hospitals and similar institutions. . . . The regulation of *health* care, as opposed to part-time *custodial* care of well children, has a somewhat longer history and is far more extensive."[211]

---

[204]76 Misc. 2d 222, 350 N.Y.S. 2d 74 (N.Y. Crim. Ct. 1973).

[205]*Id.* at 229–32, 350 N.Y.S. 2d at 82–84.

[206]47 A.D. 2d 492, 367 N.Y.S. 2d 795 (1975).

[207]*See* N.Y. Pub. Health Law §§2801(1), 2803(1)(a) (McKinney Supp. 1983–84).

[208]47 A.D. 2d at 497, 367 N.Y.S. 2d at 801.

[209]*Id.* at 498, 367 N.Y.S. 2d at 802.

[210]517 F. Supp. 905 (N.D. Cal. 1981).

[211]*Id.* at 911.

The court in *Rush,* after rejecting the comparison of day care centers to the thorough regulation of nursing homes, food and drug dealers, mining activities, and shipping, next examined whether any government interest in warrantless searches outweighed the privacy interests of the day care centers. Because of the potential misdemeanor convictions for certain regulatory violations, and because day care centers are more like private residences than skilled nursing facilities, the court concluded that the centers had a very strong privacy interest. On the other hand, the government's interest in conducting warrantless searches was speculative and minor. Any government need for surprise inspections would be protected, for a court may issue search warrants without notice to the party whose premises are to be searched. Furthermore, violations are detectable without entrance to the center, because children are released back to their parents' care daily and presumably could be questioned concerning the condition of the day care center.

Although family day care centers are substantially unlike hospitals, two district courts have invalidated statutes allowing warrantless searches of health facilities that perform abortions. In *Akron Center for Reproductive Health, Inc. v. City of Akron,*[212] an Ohio district court rejected the city's contention that health care facilities are a pervasively regulated business or an industry long subject to close inspection. Thus, hospitals and clinics were entitled to the detached judgment of a neutral magistrate as required by the warrant procedure.

In a case almost identical to *Akron,* a Louisiana district court in *Margaret S. v. Edwards*[213] also denied that hospitals and clinics that perform abortions are a pervasively regulated business. Rather, the medical profession has "a history of respect towards the recognized need for privacy in the doctor-patient relationship."[214]

The court in *Edwards* determined that the strong privacy interest of the medical profession far outweighed the minimal state interest. First, a state interest in sanitary conditions and properly trained personnel does not imply a need to make an unannounced search of hospital records. Second, the need for surprise inspections can be preserved by the warrant procedure, as the California district court in *Rush* noted, since a search warrant can be issued without notice to the medical facility. The court in *Edwards* concluded that "[t]he State has a legitimate interest in reviewing records or in inspecting facilities, [b]ut the decision to enter and inspect [should] not be the product of the unreviewed discretion of the enforcement officer in the field."[215]

---

[212]479 F. Supp. 1172 (N.D. Ohio 1979).

[213]488 F. Supp. 181 (E.D. La. 1980). .

[214]*Id.* at 216.

[215]*Id.* (quoting See v. City of Seattle, 387 U.S. 541, 545 (1967)).

Judicial Approach to the Problem

Courts that have dealt with the problem of government access to medical records have generally followed a two-step analysis. Initially, a court determines whether the medical facility is, under that state's law, a pervasively regulated business, or an industry with a long history of close supervision. If the hospital is characterized as such, which could well be the case in California, that court will either authorize a warrantless search of the facility or uphold a statute that provides for warrantless inspections.

Nursing homes and the pharmaceutical industry are examples of heavily regulated industries that are, as a result, subject to warrantless inspections. On the other hand, depending on state law, hospitals, clinics, and day care centers are generally distinguished from other industries subject to thorough regulation, such as liquor and firearms.

After making the inquiry into the thoroughness of regulation and determining that the medical facility is not a pervasively regulated business, a court balances the privacy interest of the facility against the government interest to determine if a warrantless search would nevertheless be reasonable. In striking such a balance, the government's need for surprise is not a factor. The California court in *Firstenberg* emphasized the need for surprise as a factor in its decision to authorize warrantless searches of skilled nursing facilities; however, the district courts in both *Rush* and *Edwards* pointed out that the government can obtain a warrant without notifying the medical facility. Therefore, the government's need for surprise inspection, if it exists at all, should not be a factor in the balancing process.

In balancing privacy against government interest, the key issue is not whether a search or inspection shall be conducted, but whether it may be made without a search warrant. Although it may be difficult to assert that the government has no interest whatsoever in medical records, a hospital is on firmer ground in insisting that government officials stay within the limits established by the warrant-obtaining procedure. Whether a court will require a warrant depends somewhat on whether the burden of getting a warrant will negate the purpose of making the search. Medical facilities should assert that requiring the government to obtain a search warrant secretly will not in any way diminish the opportunity or effect of inspecting medical records. In sum, there are simply no exigent circumstances that compel warrantless inspection.

That a state statute authorizes warrantless searches of medical records does not affect the foregoing two-step analysis. A court must nevertheless determine if the statute violates the Fourth Amendment by analyzing the extent of medical facility regulation and by striking the privacy interest balance. A statute that broadly allows inspections of all aspects of medical facilities, including medical records, will generally be determined to violate the Fourth Amendment because the statute's terms are too broad. The Washington Supreme Court, in *Washington Massage Foundation v. Nelson,*[216] rejected a statute that authorized any state or local law enforcement officer to "visit and inspect the premises of each massage business establishment."[217] The court emphasized that a statute empowering warrantless searches must at least sufficiently state the scope, time, and place of inspection, and that the authorized inspection must be relevant to the statute's purposes. Statutes authorizing broad warrantless inspections of medical facilities are subject to the same judicial rejection.

If the government does obtain a search warrant, a medical facility could nevertheless be subject to a government "fishing expedition" if the warrant is not sufficiently detailed. The warrant must state with particularity the scope and place to be searched. A court cannot properly issue a warrant based on a government assertion of valid public interest; rather, the government must state specifically why it requires a search of specific medical records. The object of the warrant procedure is to take away from the government the unfettered discretion to inspect and seize any medical records. Thus, a medical records practitioner who believes that a search warrant is indeed insufficiently particular should affirmatively withhold consent to the search, for consent to an administrative search can be easily implied. On the other hand, a search warrant that states in detail the time and place of the search, and the specific records to be searched, must be obeyed.

Law Enforcement Agencies

As a general rule, hospitals should not release medical records or other patient information to law enforcement personnel without the patient's authorization. In the absence of statutory authority or legal process, a police agency has no authority to examine a medical record. (Release of medical record information to government agencies is discussed earlier in this chapter.) If, however, a law enforcement official provides the facility with a valid court order or subpoena, the hospital, upon the advice of its attorney, should provide the information requested.

Upon the advice of its attorney, the hospital may determine that it would be in the community's best interest to release specific medical record information to law enforcement personnel. To do so, the hospital may rely upon the doctrine of qualified privilege. (For an elaboration of this and other principles of the law of defamation, see Chapter 6.) This common law doctrine permits a party (i.e., the hospital) with a duty or a legitimate interest in conveying the information to make communications to a second party (i.e., the law enforcement agency) with a corresponding interest in receiving the particular information. The data transferred

---

[216]687 Wash. 2d 948, 558 P. 2d 231 (1976).
[217]Wash. Rev. Code Ann. §18.108.180 (1975).

must be made in good faith, given without malice, and be based upon reasonable grounds.[218] Thus, the doctrine of qualified privilege protects the hospital only if the law enforcement officer who receives the medical record information acts under the authority of law. Before releasing such information, hospital personnel should determine that there is a basis for the request and that the officer requesting it is performing official duties. The information released should be only that which is appropriate to the purpose for which the particular request is made; a hospital should not release a patient's record in whole unless there are reasonable grounds for doing so. For example, if the law enforcement officer is requesting the results of a blood alcohol test, the hospital should not release information concerning the patient's unrelated prior hospitalization for a fractured leg.

In addition to the doctrine of qualified privilege and cases involving court subpoenas, there are statutory exceptions to the general rule requiring hospitals to refrain from releasing patient information to law enforcement agencies in the absence of patient consent. State law varies widely concerning the release to government agencies of medical record information without patient authorization. In South Carolina, for example, the medical records confidentiality statute allows disclosure of medical record information without a patient's consent only in certain instances, including when "[d]isclosure is necessary in cooperating with law enforcement agencies. . . ."[219]

Thus, some patient records, such as those concerning victims of crime or carriers of contagious disease not specifically designated by statute, may be revealed to government officials without the patient's consent in the course of routine police investigations or public health inquiries. Such disclosures, however, should only be made pursuant to the state statute's confidentiality restrictions. In these situations, the hospital should demonstrate respect for the patient's privacy rights by seeking disclosure consent from the patient, preferably during the hospital admissions process.

State law also varies widely as to a hospital's duty to report certain kinds of information, such as cases involving gunshot or knife wounds,[220] child abuse,[221]

---

[218]See Tarasoff v. Regents of the University of California, 17 Cal. 3d 425, 551 P. 2d 334, 131 Cal. Rptr. 14 (1976), where the court held that the physician or the hospital had an affirmative duty to report a patient to law enforcement agencies because the patient's medical or psychological condition represented a foreseeable risk to third persons. The physician or hospital in this situation should have disclosed information that the patient had threatened to kill the eventual victim since the physician and hospital are protected by the doctrine of qualified privilege. See also Hicks v. U.S., 357 F. Supp. 434 (D.D.C. 1973), aff'd 511 F. 2d 407 (D.C. Cir. 1975).

[219]S.C. Code Ann. §44–23–1090 (Law Co-op. 1976).

[220]See, e.g., N.Y. Penal Law §265.25 (McKinney 1982); Cal. Penal Code, §11160 (West 1982).

[221]See Landeros v. Flood, 17 Cal. 3d 399, 551 P. 2d 389, 131 Cal. Rptr. 69 (1976). See generally M. Paulsen, Child Abuse Reporting Laws: The Shape of the Legislation, 67 COLUM. L. REV. 1 (1967).

and disorders affecting a motorist's ability to drive safely.[222] In states having these types of reporting statutes, a patient's consent is not required in order to release the record. In fact, under some statutes hospitals may be guilty of criminal misdemeanor if they do not report certain cases.[223] Statutory reporting requirements are discussed earlier in this chapter.

Although there is no clearly defined constitutional doctrine outlining government access to medical records, Supreme Court decisions have mandated a constitutional right to privacy in cases of abortion[224] and birth control.[225] The construction of a general right to privacy restricting government access to medical records, however, remains undeveloped. In a 1973 federal district court case,[226] a school program designed to identify eighth grade potential drug abusers by psychological testing was declared unconstitutional. Among other things, the court noted that the aim of the program was to create a massive data bank[227] available to the school bureaucracy on a widespread basis. Rather than scrutinizing the privacy of the information in the medical records that were being compiled as a result of the program, however, the court found that there was a constitutional shield against the questionnaire's intrusion into family privacy interests. The court's lack of emphasis on the intimacy of the medical record information probed by the test and its focus instead on family interests may limit the applicability of this case to law enforcement agencies and similar governmental bureaus where there are no family privacy interests at issue. This case demonstrates the willingness of some courts to emphasize more developed constitutional principles instead of discussing principles of medical records confidentiality. However, it is important for medical records practitioners to recognize that established constitutional terms of privacy are available to protect medical records under the broad shield granted to family matters and will likely be expanded by the courts or Congress in the future to apply specifically to medical records.

In a 1974 New York appellate court case,[228] the statistical and informational purposes of a city ordinance requiring that abortion patients' names and addresses be reported on abortion certificates and the compilation of that information in a central data bank were held to outweigh the privacy interests of the plaintiffs' doctors and patients. The court found valid the compelling state interests of the

---

[222]*See, e.g.,* Cal. Health and Safety Code §410 (West 1982).

[223]*See* Cal. Penal Code §11160–62 (West 1982).

[224]Roe v. Wade, 410 U.S. 113 (1973); Doe v. Bolton, 410 U.S. 179 (1973).

[225]Griswold v. Connecticut, 381 U.S. 479 (1965).

[226]Merriken v. Cressman, 364 F. Supp. 913 (E.D. Pa. 1973).

[227]*Id.* at 916.

[228]Schulman v. New York City Health and Hosp. Corp., 44 A.D. 2d 482, 355 N.Y.S. 2d 781 (1st Dept. 1974).

government in acquiring for counseling purposes statistics on women who have had multiple abortions. In light of this case, the constitutional prohibition against a law enforcement agency's access to medical records is weak. Under the New York rationale, the privacy interests of patients are not important where a law enforcement agency seeks to collect records for statistical or advisory purposes. Hospitals, however, should avoid litigation in this area by refusing law enforcement agencies' access to medical records in the absence of a statutory or court mandate. The undefined constitutional standard concerning law enforcement agencies' access to medical records could serve as a litigious trap for hospitals that too easily release a patient's medical record information to law enforcement agencies.[229]

Computerized Medical Records

Hospitals that use computers to collect, store, and retrieve patient medical information must achieve a delicate balance between the patient's privacy rights concerning the contents, ownership, accuracy, and release of the information and the hospital's need to have efficient information systems. The ease with which third parties, such as insurance companies, obtain and duplicate computerized records threatens the confidential relationship between doctor and patient.[230]

The benefits of computerized recordkeeping to a hospital can be far-reaching. Besides permitting space-efficient, current, and legible records, computer systems can facilitate a hospital's obtaining a complete and accurate medical history of a new patient within seconds. Computerized medical records can also improve hospital management's ability to make decisions concerning utilization, physician practices, staffing, etc. Appropriate use of computer systems can also prevent misuse and misplacement of medical records information. At least one court has held that a private hospital has an affirmative duty to exercise reasonable care in maintaining medical records. In *Fox v. Cohen*,[231] the Illinois appellate court referred to regulations of state and national health care organizations to define this common law duty of hospitals. Although the court reserved the questions of the length of time and manner in which records are kept as determinable on a case by case basis, computerized medical records systems can enhance a hospital's ability to meet its duty of reasonable care.

---

[229]*See generally*, California Bankers Ass'n v. Schultz, 416 U.S. 21 (1974), involving a challenge to the constitutionality of Title II of the Bank Secrecy Act which requires the reporting to the federal government of certain foreign and domestic financial transactions of bank customers.

[230]*See, e.g.*, Hammonds v. Aetna Cas. & Sur. Co., 243 F. Supp. 793 (N.D. Ohio 1965), describing the physician's duty to maintain confidentiality concerning a patient's medical information. *See also* comment, *Medical Data Privacy*, 25 BUFFALO L. REV. 491, 497 (1976). At least one commentator has noted, however, that there is no generally applicable duty of confidentiality on the part of the data system comparable to the physician's duty of confidentiality.

[231]84 Ill. App. 3d 744, 406 N.E.2d 178 (1980).

The concerns hospitals express in using computerized medical records have been categorized by one observer as being largely fourfold.[232] First, physicians and nurses doubt the legal acceptability of the medical record as a substitute for handwritten medical records. The use of automated data systems to maintain medical records, however, has not been questioned by the courts or restricted by statute in many states. This is especially true because many medical records have been produced by computer since the first use of computers in medical testing and monitoring in intensive care units and laboratories, etc.

Second, physicians are concerned that an increase in malpractice lawsuits may result from the ease with which computers allow patients to obtain access to their records. Although suits concerning the patient's right to medical record privacy are bound to occur, it appears that the use of computers concerning the same information previously recorded by hand will have no substantial effect on professional liability for malpractice.

Third, hospitals have expressed interest in knowing if the computer must be run at the hospital site, or whether computer facilities may be off site and shared by other facilities. As long as the computer is programmed to ensure the privacy of patient medical records, hospitals may share facilities with other institutions in the absence of state law to the contrary. The need for confidentiality in computer programming rather than the location of the computerized medical records was outlined in an HHS report examining the use of computers. The report also supported the patient's right to correct misinformation in the medical record and to consent to uses beyond the original purposes of the data compilation. No recommendation was made with regard to the ability of hospitals to share computer facilities and provisions for separate record access and storage.[233]

Finally, hospitals using computerized systems should be alerted to problems stemming from possible abuse of medical records by third parties, such as insurers. The use by these third parties of the patient's highly confidential information can, for example, be devastating to individuals seeking insurance coverage. This is especially true because once a third party has gained access to the information there is no traditional privileged communications statute directly pertaining to computerized medical records.[234] At least one court, however, has held that where a plaintiff-patient signed authorization of release to an insurance company, the insurance company was not liable for invasion of privacy in

---

[232]*See* N. Wynstra, *Computerized Medical Records: Legal Problems and Implications*, 2 TOPICS IN HEALTH RECORD MANAGEMENT 75 (Dec. 1981).

[233]*See* HEW, *Records, Computers and the Rights of Citizens*, XX–XXI, Report of the Secretary's Advisory Committee on Automated Personal Data Systems, U.S. Dept. of Health, Education and Welfare, July 1973.

[234]*See supra* note 230.

divulging the information to a third party with an interest in the patient's health.[235] Following this ruling, the entire computer industry gained some authority for the widespread dissemination of medical record information, possibly free of any duty to ascertain the truth of the information exchanged.

Even in the absence of state law defining proper use of computerized medical records, hospitals should have a medical record confidentiality policy encompassing both manual and computerized records. Hospitals should have security devices and security programs to prevent unauthorized access to stored data. One problem hospitals with automated systems face is their lack of control over computer access codes given to hospital personnel. The hospital's medical records policy, employment policy, and medical staff bylaws should establish severe sanctions for the disclosure by hospital medical, nursing, and other staff members of their computer access codes. Some hospitals require staff members to sign a statement acknowledging that disclosure of their computer access codes is justification for the immediate termination of their employment or medical staff privileges. Hospital computer data banks and storage media should be secure from authorized access through other computer or electronic facilities, and the hospital should conduct periodic systems security checks to determine whether record confidentiality can be breached. Hospitals that contract with outside computer service bureaus for automated record storage should include in their service contracts carefully drawn provisions governing the confidentiality of patient data, storage security, and indemnification of the hospital by the bureau for costs and judgments arising from the unauthorized disclosure of confidential information by the bureau.

RESPONSE TO LEGAL PROCESS

Hospitals may be required to release medical record information pursuant to legal process that they may receive. The term "legal process" generally refers to all of the writs that may be issued by a court during the course of a legal action, or by an attorney in the name of the court but without court review. Hospitals are generally concerned with two types of legal process: the subpoena and the court order.

Subpoenas

Hospitals customarily receive two types of subpoenas: (1) a subpoena *ad testificandum,* which is a written order commanding a person to appear and to give testimony at a trial or other judicial or investigative proceeding; and (2) a subpoena *duces tecum,* which is a written order commanding a person to appear, give

---

[235]Senogles v. Security Benefit Life Ins. Co., 217 Kan. 438, 536 P. 2d 1358 (Kan. 1975).

testimony, and bring all documents, papers, books, and records described in the subpoena. These devices are used to obtain documents during pretrial discovery and to obtain testimony during trial.

Those authorized to issue subpoenas vary from state to state. In most states, judges, clerks of the court, justices of the peace, and other officials are so authorized.[236] In federal courts, only the clerks of the courts are so authorized.[237] The form of the subpoena is prescribed by statute in certain states, such as in New York,[238] and by rule of court in others.[239]

A valid subpoena usually contains the following information.

1. name of the court (or other official body in which the proceeding is being held)
2. names of the plaintiff and the defendant
3. docket number of the case
4. date, time, and place of the requested appearance
5. specific documents sought (if the subpoena is a subpoena *duces tecum*)
6. name and telephone number of the attorney who caused the subpoena to be issued, and
7. signature or stamp and seal of the official empowered to issue the subpoena.

For federal courts, subpoenas are generally served in person by United States marshals. For state courts, they are generally served by sheriffs. However, many state statutes provide that any competent person of not less than 18 years of age may serve subpoenas.[240] The manner of service varies from state to state: in some, the subpoena may be served by mail or delivery,[241] and in others it must be read or physically handed to the person by the server.[242]

Usually, subpoenas must be served within a specified period of time prior to the required appearance. In several states, statutes establish this period with specific reference to medical records. An example of such a statute is that of Connecticut.

A subpoena directing production of such hospital record shall be served not less than twenty-four hours before the time for production, provided such subpoena shall be valid if served less than twenty-four hours before

---

[236]*See, e.g.,* Me. Rev. Stat. Ann., tit. 16, §101 (1964).

[237]Fed. R. Civ. P. 45(a).

[238]*See* N.Y. Civ. Prac. Law §2306 (Consol. 1978).

[239]*See, e.g.,* Conn. Gen. Stat. Ann. §4–104 (West 1969).

[240]*See, e.g.,* Kan. Stat. Ann. §60–245d (1983).

[241]*See, e.g.,* Ill. Rev. Stat. ch. 110, §2–1101 (Smith-Hurd 1983).

[242]*See, e.g.,* Mo. Ann. Stat. §491.120 (Vernon 1952).

the time of production if written notice of intent to serve such subpoena has been delivered to the person in charge of the record room of such hospital not less than twenty-four hours more than two weeks before such time for production.[243]

In most states, subpoenas must be accompanied by a fee to reimburse the person subpoenaed for his time and for travel expenses.

Several cases have addressed the legitimacy of disclosing certain medical records in response to a grand jury subpoena. The Illinois Supreme Court has ruled that disclosure to a grand jury of the identities of abortion clinic patients does not violate the physician-patient privilege or the patients' constitutional right of privacy.[244] Refusing to comply with a grand jury subpoena for the names of clinic patients who receive public aid, the clinic's president claimed that because the facility renders only abortion-related services, disclosure of the women's identities would necessarily reveal the privileged information that they terminated their pregnancies. The Illinois high court balanced the patients' interests in maintaining confidentiality with the public's interest in maintaining the breadth of the grand jury's investigative powers in criminal matters and decided that under the circumstances of this case, the public's interest was greater. Because the information requested was very limited, would be kept secret by the grand jury, and did not involve disclosure of confidential medical records, the Illinois court explained that the names must be revealed. Moreover, the court added, nondisclosure of the names would enhance the physician's opportunity to conceal his or her own misconduct. Addressing the possible infringement of the women's constitutional right to privacy, the court stated that any intrusion would be minimal, noting again that the information sought was limited to the patients' names and would be revealed only to the grand jury.

Similarly, a grand jury may gain access to information that psychiatric patients have consented to release from their medical records to insurers for reimbursement purposes, a federal appeals court in Illinois has ruled, because such consent constitutes a waiver of any physician or psychotherapist privilege that may exist, given the patients' "expectation that the confidential character of the records would necessarily be compromised pursuant to the reimbursement process."[245] In a federal investigation of possible criminal misconduct by a psychotherapist, a grand jury subpoenaed records that contained patient names, their diagnoses, and a listing of their visits, which had been submitted to an insurer for reimbursement. Although the doctor and the insurer claimed that releasing the records would

---

[243]Conn. Gen. Stat. Ann. §4–104 (West 1969).

[244]People v. Florendo, 95 Ill. 2d 155, 477 N.E. 2d 282 (1983).

[245]In re Pebsworth, 705 F. 2d 261, 262 (7th Cir. 1983).

violate Illinois' psychotherapist-patient privilege, the federal court ruled that it was not bound by a state-created privilege. Therefore, the court continued, even though Illinois law prevents insurance companies from disclosing without the patients' written consent the kind of information the grand jury sought, and further provides that any agreement purporting to waive this requirement is void, in a federal court these state prohibitions are superseded by federal law. The court further noted that when the patients consented to disclosure of their records for insurance purposes, it was "easily anticipatable" that the records would be sought for an investigation such as this. If this were a civil matter or if the records sought contained detailed psychological patient profiles, the court stated that it might have found the records confidential. Because this was a criminal investigation, however, and the nature of the records was administrative rather than substantive, the court ordered the records released.

Court Orders

Occasionally, a state or federal court, or a state commission, orders a hospital to release medical records or other confidential patient information or to produce patient records in court. Written court orders are usually served upon hospitals in a manner similar to that of subpoenas, but court orders may also be issued verbally in court to the hospital's attorney. Provided the court order does not violate a statute or regulation, the hospital should make every effort to comply with it. A hospital can contest a court order and present its case to the court before any sanctions for failure to comply are imposed. Failure to comply with a final, valid court order subjects either the person ordered to act or hospital corporate officers, if the corporation has been ordered to act, to a contempt-of-court citation. Hospital corporate officers are liable if a hospital fails to follow the order even if a hospital department head is the person who actually fails to act.

A court order requiring the disclosure of medical records will not violate the statutory physician-patient privilege if "sufficient steps" are taken to safeguard the identity of the patients involved, the Arizona Court of Appeals has ruled.[246] Although the state supreme court had previously ruled that a trial court's order requiring physicians to disclose the names, addresses, and the means of contacting patients they had treated undermined the purpose and intent of the physician-patient privilege, the question remained as to whether the removal of all information in medical records that tended to identify the patients would render the records discoverable. In this case, the appeals court, noting that the Arizona Supreme Court had objected only to identification of the patients, ruled that the disclosure of anonymous records is permissible.

---

[246]Ziegler v. Superior Court of County of Pima, 134 Ariz. 390, 656 P. 2d 1251 (1982).

Compliance

A hospital should comply with valid legal process, properly served upon it, in the manner prescribed by its state's statutes. In recent years, many states have enacted statutes establishing compliance procedure with specific reference to subpoenas of medical records.[247] Other states have not enacted such statutes and thus treat subpoenas of medical records like any other subpoenas.[248] Hospital administrators should be aware of current developments in their own states in this rapidly changing area of the law. Failure to comply correctly with a subpoena, without reasonable justification, is punishable as contempt of court.

The time permitted for compliance with subpoenas of medical records varies from state to state. For example, in California, the statutory period is 5 days in criminal cases and 15 days in civil cases,[249] and in Virginia it is 20 days.[250] Generally, the records must be sealed, then enclosed in an envelope, and may be opened only with the court's authorization. Most states expressly permit copies to be submitted in lieu of the original documents. A few states, including Alabama,[251] specify that the court may subpoena the originals if the copies are illegible or if their authenticity is in dispute.

In several states, records furnished in compliance with legal process must be accompanied by an affidavit from the hospital's record custodian. The purpose of this affidavit is to certify the records' genuineness. Mississippi requires that the affidavit state:

  (a) that the affiant is a duly authorized custodian of the records; and has authority to certify such records,
  (b) that the copy is a true copy of all records described in the subpoena,
  (c) that the records were prepared by personnel of the hospital, staff physicians, or persons acting under the control of either, in the ordinary course of hospital business at or near the time of the act, condition, or event reported therein, and

---

[247]See, e.g., Ala. Code §12–21–6 (1975); Ark. Stat. Ann. §28–937 (Supp. 1983); Conn. Gen. Stat. Ann. §4–104 (West 1969); Ky. Rev. Stat. §422.305 (Supp. 1982); Miss. Code Ann. §41–9–103 (1972); Nev. Rev. Stat. §52.325 (1979); N.Y. Civ. Prac. Law §C2306:1 (Consol. 1978); Or. R. Civ. P. 55(H); Tenn. Code Ann. §68–11–402 (1983); Va. Code §8–01–413 (Supp. 1982).

[248]See, e.g., Cal. Evid. Code §1560 (West Supp. 1985).

[249]Id.

[250]See Va. Code §8–01–413 (1977).

[251]See Ala. Code §12–21–6 (1975).

(d) certifying the amount of the reasonable charges of the hospital for furnishing such copies of the records.[252]

The statutes of Arkansas, California, Nevada, Oregon, Tennessee, and other states contain substantially similar provisions.[253] These statutes provide, in addition, that if the hospital possesses none, or only part, of the records described in the subpoena, the custodian must so certify in the affidavit. The custodian may be required to attend the proceeding if the subpoena orders him to do so.

Very few states define the term "custodian." However, the statutes of Nevada and Tennessee indicate that a physician, nurse, therapist, or any hospital employee who has care of a patient's records may be subject to subpoena of these records.[254]

A hospital is not expected to respond to requirements that would be considered unreasonable. If a hospital receives a subpoena after the date upon which it is required by statute to be served, the hospital has no obligation to respond. Certainly if the subpoena arrives the day after the designated response date that appears on the document, the hospital need not respond. The hospital cannot reasonably respond to a subpoena that commands presentation of records so voluminous or old that they cannot be reproduced by the return date given. Finally, a hospital is not expected to comply with a subpoena that commands production of records that are not in the hospital's possession. For these cases, the administrator, with the advice of counsel, should develop responses for the hospital to subpoenas and court orders. If the attorney or official who initiated the subpoenas becomes unreasonable, the hospital should refer the matter to its legal counsel. If the subpoena was initiated by a plaintiff in an action against the hospital, the institution should not comply with the subpoena, but should require the plaintiff to file a motion to produce the records so that, if appropriate, the hospital will have an opportunity to argue against disclosure. If a subpoena is invalid or improper, the hospital may file a motion to quash it. The court or other issuing authority will determine after a hearing on the motion whether to enforce, modify, or quash the subpoena.

Hospital attorneys can serve as important advisors to their clients in connection with the receipt and response to legal process. The attorney not only should assist hospital administration and medical records practitioners in designing a procedure for processing subpoenas and court orders, but also should be available to advise the hospital when it receives unusual subpoenas or subpoenas that demand records that may not be released in response to a subpoena. The hospital's attorney is often

---

[252]*See* Miss. Code Ann. §41–9–109 (1972).

[253]*See* Ark. Stat. Ann. §28–937 (Supp. 1983); Cal. Evid. §1560 (West Supp. 1985); Nev. Rev. Stat. §52.325 (1979); Or. R. Civ. P. 55(H); Tenn. Code Ann. §68–11–402 (1983).

[254]*See, e.g.,* Nev. Rev. Stat. §52.325 (1979); Tenn. Code Ann. §68–11–402 (1983).

the best person to deal with other attorneys who have made unreasonable demands for records from the hospital.

The hospital staff member most frequently served with subpoenas is the person with custody of the medical records. In most cases this is the director of the medical records department; however, for the purpose of the statutes of Nevada, Tennessee, and other states, the custodian may be any person who prepares records, such as a physician, nurse, or therapist, or anyone entrusted with the care of the records.[255] The person assigned to process subpoenas of medical records should respond in accordance with a procedure established by the hospital and approved by the hospital's attorney. The procedure should include at least the following steps:

- Examine the record subject to subpoena to make certain it is complete, that signatures and initials are legible, and that each page identifies the patient and the patient's hospital number.
- Read the record to determine whether the case forms the basis for a possible negligence action against the hospital and, if so, notify the appropriate administrator. (In some hospitals, the medical records department performs this function in coordination with the risk management or legal department.)
- Remove any material that may not properly be obtained in the jurisdiction by subpoena, such as, in some states, notes referring to psychiatric care, or copies of records from other facilities, and correspondence.
- Number each page of the medical record, and write the total number of pages on the record jacket.
- Prepare a list of the medical record contents to be used as a receipt for the record if the record must be left with the court or an attorney. (Most medical records departments use a standard form for this purpose.)
- Whenever possible, use a photocopy of the record rather than the original in responding to legal process.

Rather than send original medical records to a court or an attorney through the mail, hospitals should designate a person to deliver records in person. Hospitals lose all control over their records once they are placed in the mail, and the loss of an original medical record may be a serious problem for a hospital defendant in a negligence action for a patient who may require future hospitalization.

---

[255]*See* Nev. Rev. Stat. §52.325 (1979); Tenn. Code Ann. §68–11–401 (1983).

Chapter 5

Courtroom Disclosures of Medical Records Information

In recent years, medical records have become increasingly important in the prosecution and defense of legal actions at trial and in administrative proceedings before government regulatory agencies. Success in a workers' compensation claim, personal injury action, or professional negligence suit often depends upon the information contained in these records. Consequently, patients and other parties in the litigation seek every record that may be relevant to their controversy and demand access to patient medical records, hospital and medical staff quality assurance and other committee records, and hospital incident reports. Whether these records are discoverable or admissible may significantly affect the outcome of the legal action. The manner in which these records are created and maintained will significantly affect their value as legal documents and their discoverability and admissibility.

At the outset, it is important to distinguish between the discoverability and admissibility of evidence. Discoverability involves access to documents or witnesses; admissibility concerns whether documents, objects, or testimony may formally be admitted into evidence in a trial. Something may be discoverable but, under the applicable rules of evidence, may not be admissible into evidence. In many jurisdictions, discoverability is not dependent upon admissibility. The court or administrative hearing officer or panel, applying applicable evidentiary rules, will determine whether a record is discoverable or admissible. Since these rules vary from state to state, it is extremely important for hospitals to refer questions on this subject to their legal counsel. The institutions' counsel will interpret applicable rules and help the hospital prepare an appropriate argument for or against discoverability or admissibility.

MEDICAL RECORDS

Although there is diversity of opinion as to the admissibility of medical records in judicial and quasi-judicial proceedings, and although the decisions may vary based on the particular facts, the applicable rules of evidence, the type of proceeding, and numerous other factors,[1] many modern decisions generally hold medical records to be admissible.[2] Whether medical records are admissible is of primary importance to the hospital in its own defense, since such records may contain information damaging to the hospital. For example, if the hospital is a defendant in a medical malpractice lawsuit, a medical record that clearly shows that a hospital nurse incorrectly administered a medication would be damaging to the hospital's defense. The record might also show that the physician improperly prescribed the medication, a fact that might help the hospital's case. Whether such a record is discoverable and admissible, therefore, will be significant to the hospital. The admission of records in proceedings in which the hospital is not a party should be of less concern to the hospital, provided that it obeys applicable law and properly discloses the medical records sought in such proceedings.

Hearsay and the Business Records Exception

Under traditional rules of evidence, a patient care record is hearsay in that it is a statement made out of court, introduced into a court proceeding for the purpose of proving the truth of the facts asserted in that statement.[3] Generally, hearsay is not admissible into evidence. The primary rationale underlying this rule is that, if hearsay is admitted, the right to cross-examine the declarant is lost. Consider, for example, the situation in which a nurse has made an entry regarding the patient's blood pressure. The following problems may result if the record is admitted into evidence as proof of the patient's blood pressure: first, the opposing side cannot ask the nurse about mistakes he or she may have made in transcribing the record; second, the jury cannot observe the nurse's demeanor and judge the nurse's veracity; third, the jury will be unable to check the records as it would if the record were part of the nurse's testimony in the courtroom. Because hearsay is not admissible into evidence unless it falls within one of the exceptions discussed below, medical records have historically been inadmissible.[4] However, today medical records may be admitted into evidence on a variety of other grounds.

In states that have enacted the Uniform Rules of Evidence or the Uniform Business Records as Evidence Act, medical records are admissible where it can be

---

[1]*See generally* Annots. 10 A.L.R. 4th 552 (1981); 69 A.L.R. 3d 104 (1976); 69 A.L.R. 3d 22 (1976); 10 A.L.R. Fed. 858 (1972); 44 A.L.R. 2d 553 (1955); 38 A.L.R. 2d 778 (1954); 175 A.L.R. 274, 286 (1948); 120 A.L.R. 1124 (1939); 75 A.L.R. 378 (1931); *see also* 6 WIGMORE, EVIDENCE §1707 (Chadbourn rev. 1976).

[2]*See* 40 AM. JUR. 2d *Hospitals and Asylums* §43 (1968).

[3]*See* McCORMICK, EVIDENCE §313 (2d ed. 1972).

[4]*See* Chernov v. Blakeslee, 95 Conn. 617, 111 A. 908 (1921); Jordan v. Apter, 93 Conn. 302, 105 A. 620 (1919); Piccarreto v. Rochester Gen. Hosp., 279 A.D. 625, 108 N.Y.S. 2d 717 (1951); Sauer v. Weidel, 218 A.D. 805, 218 N.Y.S. 888 (1926); A.A. v. State, 43 Misc. 2d 1004, 252 N.Y.S. 2d 800 (1964).

shown that they qualify as business records, which are documents that are made in the regular course of business at or within a reasonable time after the event recorded occurred and under circumstances that reasonably might be assumed to reflect the actual event accurately.[5] Further, documents that summarize hospital records and are kept in the regular course of business, such as discharge summaries and record extracts, may also be admitted into evidence as business records.[6]

In federal courts, medical records may be admissible as business records under Rule 803(6) of the Federal Rules of Evidence. Rule 803(6) allows the admission of a record of an event made at or near the time of the event by a person with knowledge of the event, if the record is made in the regular course of business, and if it is the regular practice of the business to keep such a record. In addition, the method or circumstances of preparation must not indicate a lack of trust-worthiness. The trial court is given great latitude in determining the circumstances that indicate trustworthy or untrustworthy preparation.[7] Improper alteration of a record is illustrative of circumstances that suggest a lack of trustworthiness.[8] Courts generally favor the admission of evidence under Rule 803(6).[9]

Application of the business records exception to the hearsay rule is not unlimited, however. Information in the medical record may be inadmissible as a business record to the extent that it is not germane to the patient's diagnosis or treatment. For example, in *Mikel v. Flatbush General Hospital,*[10] a New York appeals court held that a statement by an unidentified person as to how a patient's accident occurred did not qualify as part of a business record.[11]

Thus, a medical record may be held inadmissible because it contains objection-able conclusions or opinions. While hospital records "may of necessity contain some basic conclusions, there is a point at which opinion evidence and expert opinions as to how accidents occurred will be objectionable."[12] Observations in a

---

[5]*See, e.g.,* Fla. Stat. Ann. §§90.101–90.958 (West 1979); N.D. Cent. Code §31–08–01 (1976); Okla. Stat. Ann. tit. 12, §§2101–3103 (West 1980); McCormick, Evidence §313 (2d ed. 1972).

[6]Sandegren v. State, 397 So. 2d 657 (Fla. 1981).

[7]Mississippi River Grain Elevator v. Bartlett & Co. Grain, 659 F. 2d 1314, 1315 (5th Cir. 1981).

[8]Hiatt v. Groce, 215 Kan. 14, 523 P. 2d 320 (1974).

[9]*See* Matter of Ollag Constr. Equip. Corporation, 665 F. 2d 43 (2d Cir. 1981).

[10]49 A.D. 2d 581, 370 N.Y.S. 2d 162 (1975). *See also* Davies v. Butler, 95 Nev. 763, 602 P. 2d 605 (1979), unattributed statement in medical record regarding source of liquid on patient's clothing held inadmissible.

[11]Mikel v. Flatbush Gen. Hosp., 49 A.D. 2d 581, 370 N.Y.S. 2d 162 (1975).

[12]Skogen v. Dow Chemical Co., 375 F. 2d 692, 704 (8th Cir. 1967). "Opinion evidence" is evidence of what the witness thinks, believes, or infers in regard to facts in dispute, as distinguished from his or her personal knowledge of the facts themselves. Black's Law Dictionary 985 (5th ed. 1979). An "expert opinion" is the opinion evidence of some person who possesses special skill or knowledge in some science, profession or business which is not common to the average person and which is learned only through special study or experience. *Id.* at 519.

patient care record that physicians are trained to make and that they routinely make in the course of treating patients may be admissible. For example, the observation by a physician that the plaintiff-patient was intoxicated upon arrival at the hospital was held admissibie.[13] However, it is clear that a record that stated that the patient was injured by a car that ran a red light would not be admissible to prove the color of the traffic light. In *Skogen v. Dow Chemical Co.*,[14] the court held that a medical record that concluded that a patient's injuries were caused by inhalation of insect poisoning was inadmissible. The court of appeals in *Skogen* held that "this conclusion of causation is not one that all persons skilled in the art would likely reach. . . . It is a conclusion not based upon directly observable fact or well-known tests."[15]

Even if not found to be a business record, a medical record may be admissible if it qualifies under some other exception to the hearsay rule. For example, declarations against interest, spontaneous exclamations, dying declarations, and admissions of a party may all be admissible as exceptions to the hearsay rule if recorded by a person with personal knowledge.[16] These statements by their nature are generally free of the untrustworthiness and inaccuracy that underlie most untested assertions by a third party, and, where the persons making the statements are unavailable to testify in court (because of death or other causes), courts will admit their statements into evidence. For example, if a person makes a statement of facts that is against his interest, it is assumed the statement is true. Statements made in a moment of surprise or in immediate response to an unexpected event are usually considered trustworthy because the declarant had no time to fabricate a false statement.

A wide variety of statutes provides for the admission of hospital records into evidence based on the fact that such records are public or official records. This is especially true in jurisdictions in which statutes require records to be kept by public hospitals. The rationale is that the requirement that the record be kept ensures that the information in the record will be reliable. Hospital records may also be admissible under workers' compensation laws. Under Illinois law, for example, medical records, certified as true by a hospital officer and showing medical treatment given an employee in the hospital, are admissible as evidence of the medical status of the workmen's compensation claimant.[17]

Under the hospital lien laws of most states, the defendant against whom a suit for damages has been filed is permitted to examine the hospital records pertaining

---

[13]Rivers v. Union Carbide Corp., 426 F. 2d 633, 637 (3d Cir. 1970).

[14]Skogen v. Dow Chemical Co., 375 F. 2d 692, 704 (8th Cir. 1967).

[15]*Id.* at 705.

[16]Skillern & Sons, Inc. v. Rosen, 359 S.W. 2d 298 (Tex. 1962); *see also* 5 WIGMORE, EVIDENCE, ch. 48 (Chadbourn rev. 1974).

[17]Ill. Ann. Stat. ch. 48, §138.16 (Smith-Hurd Supp. 1984–1985).

to the treatment of the injured plaintiff if the hospital claims a lien. The Illinois lien law, for example, also requires any hospital claiming a lien under the act to furnish any party to an action in court or the clerk of the court a written statement of the injuries and treatment of the plaintiff as shown by the hospital records.[18]

Before a hospital record may be admitted in evidence under an exception to the hearsay rule, it must meet the usual evidentiary tests of relevancy, materiality, and competency. Although these three terms are often used as synonyms, they have distinct meanings.[19] Relevancy refers to the logical relationship between the proposed evidence and a fact to be established.[20] Materiality refers to whether a fact or proposition is at issue in the particular dispute.[21] Competency refers to what the very nature of the thing to be proved requires as fit and appropriate proof in the circumstances.[22] Evidence must be relevant, material, and competent before it can be admitted.

The Concept of Privileged Communications

Although medical records may be admissible by reason of an exception to the hearsay rule, the introduction of records may still be objected to on the ground that the information contained in them is subject to a physician-patient confidential communication statute. Such statutes protect the communications made between a patient and a physician from disclosure in judicial or quasi-judicial proceedings under circumstances specified in the statute. The purpose of this privilege is to protect the confidentiality of the physician-patient relationship in order to encourage the patient to tell the physician all the information necessary for treatment, no matter how embarrassing.[23] Statutory provisions vary as to the scope and extent of the patient's privilege to prevent disclosure by the physician, the extent to which the physician may exercise the patient's privilege, and the nature of the proceeding in which the privilege may be raised.[24]

Several concepts must be kept in mind in applying the patient-physician privilege. First, since the courts historically have not recognized this privilege, with a few exceptions discussed later in this chapter, no privilege will exist in the absence of statute.[25] Second, where the privilege does exist by virtue of a statute,

---

[18]Ill. Ann. Stat. ch. 82, §99 (Smith-Hurd 1966).

[19]Am. Jur. 2d *Evidence* §251 (1967).

[20]*Id.* at §252.

[21]*Id.*

[22]*Id.* at §257.

[23]*See* Annot. 10 A.L.R. 4th 552, at 557.

[24]*See, e.g.,* Ill. Ann. Stat. ch. 110, §8-802 (Smith-Hurd Supp. 1982); N.J. Stat. Ann. §2A: 84A-22.2 (West 1976); Osterman v. Ehrenworth, 106 N.J. Super. 515, 256 A. 2d 123 (1969).

[25]Am. Jur. 2d *Witnesses* §230 (1976).

it will generally apply only to statements made to licensed physicians,[26] obtained in order for the physician to treat, cure, or alleviate that patient's condition[27] and will not apply to matters that fall outside the physician-patient relationship.[28] Third, the privilege is created in order to protect the patient's privacy, and not the physician's.[29] Finally, when the patient puts his or her health in issue (e.g., by suing for injuries sustained in the course of treatment) or otherwise consents to disclosure, the privilege will generally be waived.[30]

Illinois law prohibits any physician or surgeon from disclosing information acquired while attending to a patient in a professional relationship necessary to enable the physician to treat the patient.[31] This statute limits the application of the privilege in a number of situations, including homicide trials, civil or criminal malpractice actions, and patient consent. When the patient brings an action in which his or her physical or mental condition is at issue, the court may find that the patient implied consent to the admission of the record.

The Oklahoma privilege statute provides that a communication is confidential if it is not intended to be disclosed to third persons, except persons present to further the interest of the patient in the examination, persons reasonably necessary to transmit the communication, or persons who are participating in the treatment under the direction of the physician, including the patient's family.[32] Exceptions to this privilege in Oklahoma include communications made pursuant to a court-ordered examination of a patient when the communication relates to the purpose for which the examination was ordered. Also excepted from the privilege are communications that are relevant to the physical, mental, or emotional condition of a patient in any proceeding in which the patient relies upon that condition as an element of his or her claim or defense.

Virginia's privilege statute protects the information a physician acquires in treating a patient in a professional capacity if the information is necessary to treat the patient.[33] The Virginia statute states, however, that when the physical or mental condition of a patient is at issue, or when the court decides disclosure is necessary "to the proper administration of justice," the information will not be privileged.

The patient may waive his or her privilege expressly or by failing to assert it. Courts often disagree on what constitutes a waiver and what is the extent of such a

---

[26]*Id.* at §237.

[27]*Id.* at §§241, 249.

[28]*Id.* at §§239, 250.

[29]*Id.* at §231; People v. Bickham, 89 Ill. 2d 1, 431 N.E. 2d 365 (1982).

[30]81 AM. JUR. 2d *Witnesses* §§264, 268, 270 (1976).

[31]Ill. Ann. Stat. ch. 110, §8–802 (Smith-Hurd Supp. 1982).

[32]Okla. Stat. Ann. tit. 12, §2503 (West Supp. 1983).

[33]Va. Code §8.01–399 (1977).

waiver.[34] Most courts hold that the act of bringing a suit that places the party's physical or mental health in issue constitutes an implied waiver of the privilege.[35] For example, in *McCluskey v. United States*,[36] a wrongful death action brought on behalf of the deceased, an issue arose as to the pecuniary loss to the deceased's mother. The court held that the medical records of the mother's kidney treatment were relevant in determining her life expectancy, reasoning that she had waived any privilege by bringing her suit and putting her health into issue. Further, many confidential communications statutes expressly provide that the privilege is waived if the injured party brings a suit in which his or her physical condition is at issue.[37] However, the mere fact that a trial involves an issue of the patient's physical condition does not result in a waiver of the privilege. For example, in *State of Arizona v. Santeyan*,[38] results of a urinalysis were held inadmissible in a prosecution for drunk driving. The tests were not performed at the police's request, and the court held that the patient had not waived his privilege.

On the other hand, a growing minority of courts has construed privilege statutes liberally in favor of the patient and do not find a waiver of the privilege unless it is evident that the patient intended to waive it. The South Dakota Supreme Court, for example, places the burden of establishing that the patient has waived the privilege on the party asserting the claim of waiver.[39] Similarly, some courts have held that to waive the privilege requires a clear, unequivocal act showing such waiver. In *State ex rel. Gonzenbach v. Eberwein*,[40] the court held that the patient had not waived his privilege by turning his records over to his insurer because that act was not so unequivocal as to demonstrate an intention to abandon the privilege. Rather, it was an act consistent with the intention to reveal confidential information only to the extent necessary to obtain treatment and payment.

Although confidential communications statutes have been held to apply to confidential matters appearing in patient care records, they affect the hospital directly only in those cases in which the hospital is a litigant. In suits between the patient and others, it is not the hospital's concern or right to assert the privilege, or to oppose the records subpoena. The court may, however, order the hospital to permit examination of medical records without disclosing confidential communications.[41] For example, in *Application of Larchmont Gables*,[42] a hospital was

---

[34]*See generally* 10 A.L.R. 4th 552, at 558.

[35]Carr v. Schmid, 105 Misc. 2d 645, 432 N.Y.S. 2d 807 (1980).

[36]562 F. Supp. 515 (S.D.N.Y. 1983).

[37]*See, e.g.*, Ill. Ann. Stat. ch. 110, §8.802 (Smith-Hurd Supp. 1982).

[38]136 Ariz. 108, 664 P. 2d 652 (1983).

[39]Schaffer v. Spicer, 88 S.D. 36, 215 N.W. 2d 134 (1974).

[40]655 S.W. 2d 794 (Mo. Ct. App. 1983).

[41]*See* In re D.M.C., R.L.R., Jr., 331 N.W. 2d 236 (Minn. 1983); Application of Larchmont Gables, Inc., 188 Misc. 164, 64 N.Y.S. 2d 623 (1946).

[42]188 Misc. at 164, 64 N.Y.S. 2d at 623.

ordered to furnish all information on the treatment, care, and maintenance of the injured person to a party liable for a hospital lien. This information was necessary to evaluate the reasonableness of the hospital's charges yet did not disclose confidential communications concerning the diagnosis and treatment of the patient. In general, however, whether the privilege should be asserted and whether it will be applied are issues for the courts and the parties litigant.

In suits in which the hospital is a party but neither the patient nor the physician is a party, the hospital may be able to assert the physician-patient privilege on behalf of the patient. While the effectiveness of the hospital's nonparty assertion depends on the requirements of the applicable statute, several court decisions have permitted a party litigant to assert the privilege on behalf of a patient who was not a party to the action.

The Pennsylvania Supreme Court in *In re The June 1979 Allegheny County Investigating Grand Jury*[43] held that the West Allegheny Hospital properly asserted the physician-patient privilege on behalf of a patient in refusing to submit the original records of certain tissue specimens. A hospital may assert this privilege when the personal nature of the records results in an obligation on the part of the hospital to maintain the confidentiality of the information by limiting access to the records to authorized personnel. More generally, a hospital that asserts the privilege for a patient who is not a party to the action is acting consistently with its interest in protecting its patient's confidentiality, and the court will decide when the privilege applies. Unless the applicable law requires the hospital to disclose medical records information in these circumstances, hospitals should attempt to assert the confidential communications privilege on behalf of the patient, if the patient is not a party to the lawsuit.

Some courts have held that the physician-patient privilege may give way to an overriding public interest.[44] For example, when dealing with a child care or custody case, courts often find that the interest of the child outweighs the parents' interest in keeping medical records confidential.[45] The Illinois confidential communications statute specifically provides that the privilege does not apply in civil or criminal actions arising out of the filing of a report under Illinois' Abused and Neglected Child Reporting Act.[46] In this situation, a court may protect the physician-patient privilege, in part, by allowing a private examination of medical records by the court and other interested parties.

---

[43]490 Pa. 143, 415 A. 2d 73 (1980); *see also* Parkson v. Central DuPage Hospital, 105 Ill. App. 3d 850, 435 N.E. 2d 140 (1982).

[44]People v. Doe, 107 Misc. 2d 605, 607, 435 N.Y.S. 2d 656, 658 (1981).

[45]*See, e.g.,* Bieluch v. Bieluch, 190 Conn. 813, 462 A. 2d 1060 (1983); In re Baby X, 97 Mich. App. 111, 293 N.W. 2d 736 (1980); In re Doe Children, 93 Misc. 2d 479, 402 N.Y.S. 2d 958 (1978); *but see* In re Adoption of H.Y.T., 436 So. 2d 251 (Fla. Dist. Ct. App. 1983).

[46]Ill. Ann. Stat. ch. 110, §8.802(7) (Smith-Hurd Supp. 1982).

The interest of the state in a grand jury investigation may also override the physician-patient privilege. In *People v. Doe*,[47] a New York trial court ruled that a hospital under investigation for Medicare violations was required to turn over the billing and medical records of 96 former patients to the grand jury. Noting that "the privilege was never intended to prevent disclosure of evidence of a crime," the court refused to grant the hospital's request to quash the grand jury's subpoenas.[48]

While the physician-patient privilege is a creation of statute, a few courts in jurisdictions in which no statutory privilege exists have by court decision created such a privilege and have extended it to hospital records.[49] Federal courts have declined to create a privilege in the absence of congressional legislation.[50] A federal court may also decline to apply the state's physician-patient privilege statute. In *Memorial Hospital for McHenry County v. Shadur*,[51] a United States court of appeals held that Illinois' privilege statute did not apply in a federal civil action under the Sherman Antitrust Act.

In some cases, the privilege may be defeated. In negligence actions against health care providers, it is a general rule, sometimes referred to as the other transaction rule, that evidence of similar acts or omissions is not admissible. However, if the admission of such evidence is sought to prove a fact of the case on trial—for example, to show prior knowledge of a defect or to rebut a contention that it was impossible for the accident to happen in the manner claimed—the evidence will be admissible.[52] Under these exceptions, the medical records of persons other than the plaintiff may be admitted into evidence. For example, in *Gunthorpe v. Daniels*,[53] the court of appeals of Georgia allowed the introduction of evidence as to orthodontic treatment rendered by the dentist defendant to patients other than the plaintiff. Here, the court stated that in addition to these exceptions, the evidence was admissible on the question of malice or wanton misconduct in the plaintiff's claim for punitive damages and to contradict any possible testimony by the defendant that in similar cases, similar treatment had not resulted in the same unfortunate results.

---

[47]107 Misc. 2d 605, 435 N.Y.S. 2d 656 (1981).

[48]*Id.* at 608, 435 N.Y.S. 2d at 658. *See also* In re Pebsworth, 705 F. 2d 261 (7th Cir. 1983).

[49]*See, e.g.*, Ex parte Day, 378 So. 2d 1159 (Ala. 1979); Horne v. Patton, 291 Ala. 701, 287 So. 2d 824 (1973); 10 A.L.R. 4th 552.

[50]General Motors Corp. v. Director of Nat'l Inst. for Occupational Safety & Health, 636 F. 2d 163 (6th Cir. 1980).

[51]664 F. 2d 1058 (7th Cir. 1981).

[52]Chastain v. Fuqua Indus., Inc., 156 Ga. App. 719, 275 S.E. 2d 679 (1980); Gunthorpe v. Daniels, 150 Ga. App. 113, 257 S.E. 2d 199 (1979).

[53]150 Ga. App. 113, 257 S.E. 2d 199 (1979).

Discoverability of medical records is governed generally by the rules pertaining to access to such records. In most jurisdictions, medical records are discoverable. (For a discussion of this topic, see Chapter 4.)

HOSPITAL AND MEDICAL STAFF RECORDS

Hospitals are required by a variety of authorities to establish and maintain programs to monitor and improve the quality of the patient care they provide. Included in these quality assurance programs are certain committees of the medical staff, each of which may collect data and generate records concerning the performance of individual physicians practicing in the hospital or the treatment provided to particular patients in the hospital. Counsel representing plaintiffs in professional negligence actions against practitioners and hospitals have shown an increasing interest in the proceedings, records, and reports of these committees as a source of important evidence. Peer review committees have the responsibility of monitoring and evaluating the quality of care provided by a particular hospital. Typically, a hospital will have at least the following committees: (1) the executive committee; (2) the credentials committee; (3) the medical audit committee; (4) the tissue committee; and (5) the utilization review committee.[54] Each of these entities generates documents and information that could be quite damaging to a doctor charged with malpractice.

The executive committee establishes, implements, and enforces the standards of medical care for the hospital. It receives reports from the other hospital committees and makes recommendations regarding reduction or termination of staff privileges and the granting or denial of admission to the medical staff. It also keeps records of its deliberations and correspondence between the committee and various staff members.[55]

The credentials committee evaluates all applications for staff privileges by new physicians. This committee should keep extensive records. It typically would have a file for each member on the staff, possibly containing:

> an application form, medical school transcripts, letters of reference from previous employers or institutions containing an evaluation of the physician's professional competence, licensure date, and information regarding any previous disciplinary action or reduction in staff privileges. If the credentials committee is evaluating a staff member with the

---

[54]Holbrook and Dunn, *Medical Malpractice Litigation: The Discoverability and Use of Hospital Quality Assurance Committee Records*, 16 WASHBURN L.J. 54 (1976).

[55]*Id.*

idea of reducing his privileges, the file may also contain complaints from other staff members.[56]

The medical audit committee evaluates the quality of medical care. Documents generated by this committee might include records of meetings, information received from various hospital departments, and the standards used.[57]

The tissue committee supervises the quality of surgery. It maintains criteria used in evaluating the need for surgery, produces minutes or reports of the review of any surgery, and reports to the executive committee where surgery is continuously and flagrantly unnecessary.[58]

Finally, the utilization review committee inquires into the necessity of a patient's length of stay in the hospital. Its deliberations are usually recorded and its correspondence with a particular doctor would also be kept on file.[59]

The potential value of such records to the plaintiff in a negligence action is clear, and the demand for access to them has created a substantial body of statutory and common law. A hospital should be familiar with the applicable statutory provisions and relevant court decisions in its state before it establishes procedures for creating and maintaining hospital and medical staff committee records. (For a discussion of the rules applicable in each state, see Appendix C.)

Discoverability of Committee Records

Authorities do not agree on whether hospital and medical staff committee records should be discoverable. Some courts hold that, if quality assurance programs are to work properly, they must be conducted confidentially, and that the records of such are not discoverable. Other courts give greater weight to the plaintiff's need for information vital to his or her case than to policy considerations in favor of confidential committee proceedings. In response to the decisions declaring those records to be discoverable, many state legislatures have enacted statutes protecting the records from discovery to varying degrees.

Numerous states have enacted statutes that protect hospital and medical staff review committee records from discovery, although the extent of protection varies. Some statutes provide that such records generally are not subject to subpoena, discovery, or disclosure; other statutes state specifically that such committee records, proceedings, and reports are not discoverable or describe such material as confidential or privileged. A common exception to nondiscovery

---

[56]*Id.* at 60.

[57]*Id.*

[58]*Id.*

[59]*Id.*

statutes allows physicians to discover records of staff privilege committees when contesting the termination, suspension or limitation of their staff privileges. Nondiscovery statutes also typically provide that the statute is not to be construed as protecting from discovery information, documents, and records that are otherwise available from original sources. Further, persons who testify before committees are not immune from discovery, but they may not be asked about their testimony before the committee. (For a discussion of statutes applicable in each state, see Appendix C.) The California nondiscovery statute is typical.

> Neither the proceedings nor the records of organized committees of medical [or] medical-dental staffs in hospitals having the responsibility of evaluation and improvement of the quality of care rendered in the hospital or medical . . . review . . . committees of local medical . . . societies shall be subject to discovery. . . . [No] person in attendance at a meeting of any such committee shall be required to testify as to what transpired thereat.[60]

Although most statutes provide protection only to medical staff committee activities and records, a few statutes are broad enough to include other hospital review committees.[61] The Tennessee statute, for example, defines "medical review committee" as,

> any committee of a state or local professional association or society, or a committee of any licensed health care institution, or the medical staff thereof, or any committee of a medical care foundation or health maintenance organization, the function of which, or one of the functions of which, is to evaluate and improve the quality of health care rendered by providers of health care service or to determine that health care services rendered were professionally indicated or were performed in compliance with the applicable standard of care or that the cost of health care rendered was considered reasonable by the providers of professional health care services in the area and shall include a committee functioning as a utilization review committee under the provisions of Public Law 89–97 . . . (Medical Law) or as a utilization and quality control peer review organization under the provisions of the Peer Review Improvement Act of 1982, Public Law 97–248 . . . or a similar committee or a committee of similar purpose, to evaluate or review the

---

[60]Cal. Evid. Code §1157 (West Supp. 1984). *See also* West Covina Hosp. v. Superior Court, 153 Cal. App. 3d 134, 200 Cal. Rptr. 162 (1984).

[61]*See* Statutes of Idaho, Louisiana, Minnesota, Tennessee, and Texas discussed in the state-by-state analysis, Appendix C.

diagnosis or treatment or the performance or rendition of medical or hospital services which are performed under public medical programs of either state or federal design.[62]

Federal statutes governing Professional Standards Review Organizations prohibit disclosure of any data or information acquired by any PSRO in the exercise of its duties, except under circumstances provided for by regulation or to federal or state agencies in connection with authorized health planning activities or investigations of fraud or abuse.[63] (For a discussion of the confidentiality of PSRO and PRO records, see Chapter 4.)

Courts of numerous jurisdictions have construed nondiscovery statutes with varying results. In *Young v. Gersten*,[64] an Ohio court found that the state's protective statute did not violate the plaintiff's right to equal protection. The Ohio court held that the legislature's intent to encourage unfettered discussion before medical quality assurance committees was reasonable according to the attendant circumstances and, therefore, not constitutionally offensive.

The courts that have prohibited discovery of hospital and medical staff committee records have found an overwhelming public interest in holding hospital quality assurance committee meetings on a confidential basis. In *Bredice v. Doctor's Hospitals, Inc.*,[65] a professional negligence action in which the patient's estate sought the minutes and reports of staff committees concerning the patient's death in the hospital, the court reasoned that constructive professional criticism cannot occur when committee members fear that their comments might be used against a colleague in a malpractice suit. The *Bredice* court held that, absent a showing of extraordinary circumstances, the minutes and records of staff committees are privileged.[66] The court did not elaborate on what would constitute extraordinary circumstances.

Several courts that have construed state nondiscovery statutes that prohibit access to committee records have followed the *Bredice* public policy rationale. In *Mennes v. South Chicago Community Hospital*,[67] an Illinois appellate court, citing *Bredice*, held that the Illinois nondiscovery statute shields records relating to the granting of physicians' staff privileges and their reappointments from discovery in a malpractice case. The *Mennes* court noted the public policy rationale discussed in the *Bredice* case to support its refusal to construe Illinois'

---

[62]Tenn. Code Ann. §63–6–2191(a) (Supp. 1983).

[63]Pub. L. No. 92–603, tit. II, §249 F(b), 1972 U.S. Cong. & Ad. News (*Current version* at 42 U.S.C. §1320c–9 (1983).

[64]56 Ohio Misc. 1, 381 N.E. 2d 353 (1978).

[65]50 F.R.D. 249 (D.D.C. 1970).

[66]*Id.* at 251.

[67]100 Ill. App. 3d 1029, 427 N.E. 2d 952 (1981).

nondiscovery statute narrowly.[68] In *Jenkins v. Wu*,[69] the Illinois Supreme Court also relied on the *Bredice* rationale to uphold the constitutionality of the Illinois nondiscovery statute.

Several courts have recognized that there are public policy considerations in favor of confidential committee proceedings especially where nondiscovery is mandated by statute, and therefore, these courts will construe nondiscovery statutes to promote the legislative intent. In *Posey v. District Court*,[70] the Colorado Supreme Court interpreted a nondiscovery statute that prohibited the subpoena of review committee records "in any suit against the physician" to prohibit the subpoena of records in any civil suit, including a suit against a hospital. In interpreting the same statute in another case, that court also denied discovery of review committee records by a physician seeking damages due to the suspension of staff privileges.[71] The Georgia Supreme Court, in *Hollowell v. Jove*,[72] held that the Georgia statute that prohibited the discovery of the "proceedings and records" of review committees included the records of a medical review committee relating to care of patients other than the plaintiff or decedent represented by the plaintiff. The *Hollowell* court also found that the discovery of whether any medical review committee meetings relating to the care of the decedent were held and who attended the meetings would be an "intrusion into the 'proceedings' of the committee" and that therefore such information was nondiscoverable.[73] In *Morse v. Gerity*,[74] U.S. district court, interpreting the Connecticut peer review statute, found that the statute was intended to cover all peer review proceedings and not just those proceedings relating to the patient-plaintiff. In ruling against discovery, the court in *Morse* said "[t]he overriding importance of these review committees to the medical profession and the public requires that doctors have unfettered freedom to evaluate their peers in an atmosphere of complete confidentiality. No chilling effect can be tolerated if the committees are to function effectively."[75]

It is important to consider how broadly the courts will construe the protection of the relevant nondiscovery statute. In *Kappas v. Chestnut Lodge, Inc.*,[76] the court

---

[68]*Id.* at 1032, 427 N.E. 2d at 954. *See also* Posey v. District Court, 196 Colo. 396, 586 P. 2d 36 (1978); Oviatt v. Archbishop Bergan Mercy Hosp., 191 Neb. 224, 214 N.W. 2d 490 (1974); Texarkana Mem. Hosp. Inc. v. Jones, 551 S.W. 2d 33 (Tex. 1977).

[69]Jenkins v. Wu, 102 Ill. 2d 468, 468 N.E. 2d 1162 (1984); *see also* Kappas v. Chestnut Lodge, Inc. 709 F. 2d 878 (4th Cir. 1983).

[70]196 Colo. 396, 586 P. 2d 36 (1978).

[71]Franco v. District Court, 641 P. 2d 922 (Colo. 1982).

[72]247 Ga. 678, 279 S.E. 2d 430 (1981).

[73]*Id.* at 682, 279 S.E. 2d at 434.

[74]520 F. Supp. 470 (D. Conn. 1981).

[75]*Id.* at 472.

[76]709 F. 2d 878 (4th Cir. 1983).

construed the statute broadly. In that case, a malpractice action, the plaintiff sought to discover the transcripts of staff conferences concerning the patients' care and treatment. The plaintiff claimed that the statute protected only medical review committees in the area of peer review and disciplinary review. The applicable Maryland statute provided that "[t]he proceedings, records, and files of a medical review committee are neither discoverable nor admissible into evidence in any civil action arising out of matters which are being reviewed and evaluated by the committee."[77] The statute defines medical review committees generally as committees formed and approved by the hospital's governing board, whose function was to evaluate the performance and quality of health care. The court observed that staff conferences are roundtable discussions concerning individual cases, attended by a cross-section of hospital staff and personnel. Although these conferences do not involve formal peer evaluation or discipline, they provide a less structured method of reviewing the care being provided at the hospital. Based on this observation, the court found that the staff conferences fell within Maryland's broad definition of a medical review committee whose proceedings are protected from discovery by the statute.[78] Similarly, in *Murphy v. Wood*,[79] an Idaho court interpreted the Idaho statute to protect the proceedings of the hospital's tumor committee.

However, other courts have construed more narrowly the scope of the non-discovery statutes and have permitted the discovery of hospital and medical staff records that fell outside the scope. For example, a California court of appeals in *Matchett v. Superior Court for County of Yuba*[80] held that while credentials committee records may be statutorily privileged, hospitals' administration records were not covered by California's nondiscovery law. Further, where the applicable statute protected only the records of a specific hospital committee, such as the utilization review or peer review committee, the records of other hospital or staff committees were held discoverable.[81] A statute that protects information "collected for or by individuals or committees assigned [a quality] review function" does not protect data obtained by physicians on their own initiative and later presented to a review committee.[82] The Arizona Supreme Court, construing a state statute that allowed the trial judge to determine what may be disclosed, held that:

---

[77]*Id.* at 880.

[78]*Id.*

[79]105 Idaho 180, 667 P. 2d 859 (Idaho App. 1983).

[80]40 Cal. App. 3d 623, 115 Cal. Rptr. 317 (1974).

[81]*Id; see also* Davidson v. Light, 79 F.R.D. 137 (D. Colo. 1978); Young v. King, 136 N.J. Super., 127, 344 A. 2d 792 (1975); Coburn v. Seda, 101 Wash. 2d 270, 677 P. 2d 173 (1984) (*en banc*).

[82]Marchand v. Henry Ford Hosp., 398 Mich. 163, 247 N.W. 2d 280 (1976).

the proper demarcation is between purely factual, investigative matters and materials which are the product of reflective deliberation or policymaking processes. Statements and information considered by the committee are subject to subpoena for the determination of the trial judge, but the reports and minutes of the medical review committees are not.[83]

The courts are likely to find committee records discoverable if they fall within a statutory exception to a nondiscovery rule[84] or if they are sought by persons not specifically prohibited from access to such records.[85] Moreover, some courts have prohibited inquiry of review committee members concerning the proceedings, records, actions, and recommendations of the committee but have construed protective statutes as allowing committee members to be called as expert witnesses and asked hypothetical questions based on facts in evidence that are obtained from nonprivileged sources.[86]

In federal cases, state-enacted statutory privileges may not apply. Rule 501 of the Federal Rules of Evidence provides that, in federal court cases, the court must apply the federal common law of privilege with respect to discovery questions, except where state law supplies the rule of decision, as in diversity cases.[87] In *Robinson v. Magovern*,[88] a federal antitrust action brought by a physician who had been denied privileges at one of the defendant hospitals, the U.S. district court held that the need for relevant evidence outweighed the need for confidentiality in hospital staff committees. Therefore, the plaintiff could discover hospital medical staff committee records, even though such records were privileged under the Pennsylvania Peer Review Protection Act.

The U.S. Court of Appeals for the Seventh Circuit applied Rule 501 and allowed discovery in a federal antitrust case brought by a physician who alleged restraint of trade by a group of competing physicians who misused a hospital's committee apparatus to exclude him from the medical staff. The court in *Memorial Hospital for McHenry County v. Shadur*[89] explained that Illinois confidentiality

---

[83]Tucson Medical Center, Inc. v. Misevch, 113 Ariz. 34, 37, 545 P. 2d 958, 961 (1976).

[84]Roseville Community Hosp. v. Superior Court for Placer County, 70 Cal. App. 3d 809, 139 Cal. Rptr. 170 (1977); Auld v. Holly, 418 So. 2d 1020 (Fla. Dist. Ct. App. 1982), *quashed in part*, 450 So. 2d 217 (Fla. 1984); Good Samaritan Hosp. Ass'n v. Simon, 370 So. 2d 1174 (Fla. Dist. Ct. App. 1979).

[85]*See* Unnamed Physician v. Commission on Medical Discipline of Md., 285 Md. 1, 400 A. 2d 396, *cert. denied*, 444 U.S. 868, 100 S.Ct. 142, 62 L.Ed. 92 (1979), statute prohibiting discovery of committee records "by any person" does not prevent review by a state agency.

[86]Eubanks v. Ferrier, 245 Ga. 763, 267 S.E. 2d 230 (1980).

[87]Fed. R. Evid. 501.

[88]83 F.R.D. 79 (W.D. Pa. 1979).

[89]664 F. 2d 1058 (7th Cir. 1981).

law was not binding because the case was brought under federal law. Further, even though the federal courts should consider the state's interest in granting confidentiality, this interest did not outweigh the "public interest in private enforcement of federal antitrust law."[90] The court in *Memorial Hospital* was influenced by the fact that denying the physician access to the requested documents would prevent him from bringing his action altogether, since his complaint centered upon the proceedings of the committee.[91]

Further, some federal courts have permitted discovery of peer review committee records when violation of a federal constitutional right is alleged. For example, in *Dorsten v. Lapeer County General Hospital*,[92] when a female physician requested access to peer review records to prove that a hospital had violated federal law by sexual discrimination, the U.S. District Court for Eastern Michigan allowed access despite a state law mandating absolute confidentiality of peer review records. The female physician alleged that a hospital had denied her staff privileges because of her sex. Although the court had already granted her access to her own peer review materials, the physician claimed she needed access to peer review reports of male physicians applying for staff privileges to compare the standards used in the decision-making process. Pointing out that a federal court need not follow state law when a constitutional violation is involved, the court ruled that the federal interest in protecting citizens from unconstitutionally disparate treatment takes precedence over the state statute's policy of promoting candid and conscientious evaluations of clinical practices. The court observed that the physician's sexual discrimination charge would be extremely difficult to argue without access to the male physicians' records.[93] Besides, the court concluded, the state's interests could be adequately preserved by an appropriate protective order over the documents.[94]

A federal court in Kentucky has also ruled that the peer review committee records may be discoverable, even though a state statute specifically prohibited discovery of such records. In *Ott v. St. Luke Hospital of Campbell County, Inc.*,[95] a physician claimed that a public hospital denied him due process in the rejection of his application for staff privileges. He contended that peer review committee meetings were held without giving him notice or the opportunity to be heard, and that the committee employed constitutionally improper considerations and ulterior motives in denying him staff privileges. Although the federal court recognized that

---

[90]*Id.* at 1063.

[91]*Id.*

[92]88 F.R.D. 583 (E.D. Mich. 1980).

[93]*Id.* at 586.

[94]*Id.*

[95]522 F. Supp. 706 (E.D. Ky. 1981).

a state statute specifically granted peer review committee records privileged status, it noted that it was not bound by state law in deciding a federal question, and therefore declined to rule on the basis of the statute. Instead, the court found that although the peer review committee probably understood that their communication would not be disclosed, and although the relationship among the members of the committee is one to be fostered, there was no evidence that the committee's functions would be substantially impaired by a denial of privilege. "Indeed," the court ruled, "the true efficiency of such committees may be fostered by an atmosphere of openness, in that they may be less likely to rely on hearsay or information tainted by bias or prejudice in making their decisions. . . ."[96] Further, the court believed that it would not be able to evaluate effectively the plaintiff's constitutional claims if the records were kept confidential.[97]

The courts that have permitted discovery of committee records in the absence of nondiscovery statutes have emphasized the benefit to the litigation process of liberal discovery rules. In *Kenney v. Superior Court,*[98] a California court of appeals found that records of the hospital's prior disciplinary proceedings against a defendant physician on the hospital staff may assist the plaintiff in preparation for trial and held that such records should be available to the plaintiff. Pointing to the court's responsibility to balance the legitimate needs of plaintiffs to ascertain relevant facts against possible interference with a litigant's request of privacy, the court stated that the party seeking the information must show good cause for obtaining it.[99] The court will determine whether such party's reason for seeking the information constitutes good cause. In apparent response to the *Kenney* decision, the California legislature in 1968 enacted a nondiscovery statute, considered below, that now protects such committee records.[100]

In *Nazareth Literary and Benevolent Institution v. Stephenson,*[101] a 1973 Kentucky court of appeals followed the reasoning in *Kenney* and specifically rejected qualified privilege for committee records accorded by the court in *Bredice.* The court found no public policy in favor of protecting such records from discovery where it could be shown that the information sought was "relevant to the subject matter involved in the pending action" and held that confidentiality of staff committee proceedings must give way to discovery of truth.[102] Moreover, the court refused to protect committee records under the attorney's work product

---

[96]*Id.* at 711.

[97]*Id.*

[98]255 Cal. App. 2d 106, 63 Cal. Rptr. 84 (1967).

[99]*Id.* at 113, 63 Cal. Rptr. at 88.

[100]Cal. Evid. Code §1157 (West Supp. 1980). *See also* Matchett v. Superior Court for County of Yuba, 40 Cal. App. 3d 623, 629, 115 Cal. Rptr. 317, 320 (1974).

[101]503 S.W. 2d 177 (Ky. 1973).

[102]*Id.* at 179.

rule, which protects from discovery information in an attorney's file developed in anticipation of litigation. The *Stephenson* court found that the reports of medical staff members concerning the defendant physician's qualifications for staff membership were not part of such a file.[103]

The Wisconsin Supreme Court has also expressed doubt as to whether the public interest in maintaining the confidentiality of committee records was compelling enough to warrant the judicial creation of a nondiscovery rule. In *Davison v. St. Paul Fire & Marine Ins. Co.*,[104] the Wisconsin court refused to apply retroactively Wisconsin's nondiscovery statute, to find a privilege at common law, or to extend the statutory privilege granted to records that are required by law to be kept, to hospital committee records. In *Shibilski v. St. Joseph's Hospital of Marshfield, Inc.*,[105] a Wisconsin hospital asserted a privilege founded upon the attorney's work product rule on the ground that its attorney exercised control and direction over the statements, committee minutes, and investigative reports sought by plaintiff. The court held that, although the information sought was properly within the attorney's work product, the plaintiff had shown sufficient cause for discovery to overcome the privilege.

Admissibility of Committee Records

While courts generally adhere to liberal rules of discovery in the absence of nondiscovery statutes, they are inclined to find hospital and medical staff quality assurance committee records inadmissible as hearsay. Unlike medical records, committee minutes and reports often do not meet the formal requirements of the business records exception to the hearsay rule. Hospital committees do not generate records at or reasonably soon after the time at which the events discussed occurred. Moreover, committee records usually contain conclusions or opinions that are generally inadmissible. In a few states, statutes specifically declare these records to be inadmissible.[106] However such records may be admitted under other exceptions to the hearsay rule, such as declarations against interest, admissions of a party, and spontaneous exclamations.

A party who is unable to overcome these barriers to admissibility may still be able to have committee records admitted into evidence under Federal Rule of Evidence 703, which allows an expert witness to express an opinion based, in part, upon information "perceived by or made known to him at or before hearing."[107]

[103]*Id.* at 178.

[104]75 Wis. 2d 190, 248 N.W. 2d 433 (1977).

[105]83 Wis. 2d 459, 266 N.W. 2d 264 (1978).

[106]*See, e.g.*, Florida, Minnesota, Montana, and Oregon statutes in the state-by-state analysis, Appendix C.

[107]Fed. R. Evid. 703.

If counsel succeeds in obtaining the records and allows the expert witness to review them before trial, the expert witness may be able to testify concerning the content of the records. Further, an expert witness may be able to testify concerning the contents of medical records even though the records are found to have been improperly admitted.[108]

HOSPITAL POLICIES GOVERNING COMMITTEE RECORDS

Since state statutes and court decisions concerning protection of peer review and quality assurance activities from discovery vary considerably, hospitals should carefully review and understand thoroughly the applicable law. Institutions should organize and operate peer review and quality assurance activities in a manner designed to obtain the greatest possible protection available under applicable law. While arguments may be made in support of the discoverability of committee records, hospitals generally can operate with greater flexibility and efficiency and with less risk if peer review and quality assurance records carry some degree of protection.

Once the hospital has developed its policies concerning committee records, all hospital and medical staff personnel involved in committee activities should be educated as to the importance of following policies meticulously. Peer review and quality assurance activities should be identified as such and documented in a manner that reinforce their official peer review status and thereby will likely qualify them for maximum protection under state law.

All peer review committee minutes and reports should be carefully prepared and should demonstrate that the hospital performed an objective, considered review. In most states, committee minutes should document primarily actions taken on the matter discussed and not the details of the actual discussion or personal comments made by committee members. The hospital should limit distribution of and access to committee minutes and reports to as few individuals and files as possible.

In all matters relating to developing policies governing the creation and use of peer review and quality assurance materials, hospitals should consult with their legal counsel, especially in states in which rules of discoverability are ambiguous or in which courts have narrowly construed protection statutes. Hospitals should instruct their legal counsel to advise them of changes in applicable law as they occur and to review these policies at least annually.

---

[108]*See, e.g.,* Wilson v. Clark, 84 Ill. 2d 186, 417 N.E. 2d 1322 *cert. denied,* 454 U.S. 836, 102 S.Ct. 140, 70 L.Ed. 2d 117 (1981).

HOSPITAL INCIDENT REPORTS

An incident is ". . . any happening which is not consistent with the routine operation of the hospital or the routine care of a particular patient. It may be an accident or a situation which might result in an accident."[109] A hospital generates incident reports in order to document promptly the circumstances surrounding an incident, to alert its insurer or defense counsel to a potential liability situation, and to create data with which to monitor the number and type of incidents occurring in the institution. Incident reports are an essential part of good hospital risk and claims management programs and, like other hospital records, can be a fertile source of information for parties in litigation involving hospitals.

In many states, incident reports are protected from discovery primarily under the attorney-client privilege and the attorney's work product rule.[110] Where legal advice is sought from an attorney acting as such, communications between the attorney and the client relating to such advice are privileged and therefore may not be disclosed by the attorney unless the client waives the privilege.[111] Therefore, an incident report made to an attorney for purposes of obtaining legal advice based thereon may not be discovered.[112] Incident reports made by hospital staff to the hospital's insurer in connection with anticipated settlement or defense of a negligence action are protected by the attorney's work product rule and are not discoverable,[113] unless the party seeking the reports can demonstrate to the court that the information sought is or might lead to admissible evidence, is material to the trial preparation, or is for some other reason necessary to promote the ends of justice.[114] However, in *Bernardi v. Community Hospital Association*,[115] the court held that incident reports not prepared exclusively for the hospital's attorney were not protected by the attorney-client privilege. In that case, the nurse who allegedly

---

[109]AHA AND NATIONAL SAFETY COUNCIL, SAFETY GUIDE FOR HEALTH CARE INSTITUTIONS 33 (1972).

[110]*But see* In re Application To Quash Subpoena Duces Tecum in Grand Jury Proceedings, 86 A.D. 2d 672, 446 N.Y.S. 2d 382 (N.Y. App. Div. 1982).

[111]*See* McCORMICK, EVIDENCE §§87–93 (2d ed. 1972).

[112]*See* Sierra Vista Hosp. v. Superior Court for San Luis Obispo County, 248 Cal. App. 2d 359, 56 Cal. Rptr. 387 (1967).

[113]*See* Sligar v. Tucker, 267 So. 2d 54 (Fla. Dist. Ct. App. 1972); Verini v. Bochetto, 49 A.D. 2d 752, 372 N.Y.S. 2d 690 (1975). *But see* Kay Laboratories, Inc. v. District Court for Pueblo County, 653 P. 2d 721 (Colo. 1982); Shibilski v. St. Joseph's Hosp. of Marshfield, Inc., 83 Wis. 2d 459, 266 N.W. 2d 264 (1978).

[114]*See* Peters v. Gaggos, 72 Mich. App. 138, 249 N.W. 2d 327 (1976).

[115]166 Colo. 280, 443 P. 2d 708 (1968).

was negligent completed the reports, placed a copy in the patient's medical record, and gave copies to the hospital administrator and director of nursing.

In *Wiener v. Memorial Hospital for Cancer and Allied Diseases*,[116] a New York court would not extend the state's statute to prohibit discovery of postincident investigation reports. In *Wiener*, the plaintiff was misdiagnosed as having cancer. In her suit against the hospital, she attempted to discover statements and records relating to a retrospective investigation of her case. The court found that the reports were not protected from discovery within the New York statute prohibiting disclosure of "proceedings [and] records relating to performance of medical review functions."[117] Although peer review investigations are clearly not discoverable within the statute, the hospital could not establish that the incident reports constituted a medical review function and, therefore, was ordered to produce the records.[118]

Since incident reports constitute hearsay, they are inadmissible in evidence unless they fall into one of the exceptions to the hearsay rule.[119] The hearsay exception most frequently cited for the purpose of admitting incident reports into evidence is the business records exception, particularly where the party seeking the reports can show that the report was made in the routine course of business at or near the time of the occurrence reported under circumstances that would indicate a high degree of trustworthiness.[120] Although some courts have interpreted "business" narrowly, the trend is toward admitting incident reports that meet the requirements of the business record exception.[121]

Although it is becoming difficult in some jurisdictions to prevent discovery and admission of incident reports, a hospital that has established incident-reporting procedures should take the following action to protect its reports.

1. Treat incident reports as confidential documents, clearly marked as such.
2. Strictly limit the number of copies made and the distribution of the reports in the institution.
3. Do not place a copy of the report in the patient's medical record or in a file on the patient care unit. Copies may be retained with other quality assurance records, however.

---

[116]114 Misc. 2d 1013, 453 N.Y.S. 2d 142 (1982).

[117]*Id.*

[118]*Id.* at 1015, 453 N.Y.S. 2d at 144.

[119]McCORMICK, EVIDENCE §§246, 306 (2d ed. 1972).

[120]*See* Fagan v. Newark, 78 N.J. Super. 294, 188 A. 2d 427 (1963); Burt v. St. John's Episcopal Hosp., N.Y.L.J., Oct. 30, 1981, at 15, col. 1 (N.Y. Sup. Ct., Oct. 29, 1981).

[121]*See* Comment, *Hospital Accident Reports: Admissibility and Privilege*, 79 DICK. L. REV. 493 (1974).

4. Limit the content of the report to facts, not conclusions or assignment of blame. Analyses of the cause of an incident should be placed in a separate document.
5. Address the report and any separate analysis of an incident to the hospital's attorney or claims manager by name.
6. Train hospital personnel to complete incident reports with the same care used in completing a medical record.
7. Generally treat incident reports as quality assurance records and subject them to the same stringent policies as are applied to other quality assurance records.

Chapter 6

Liability for Improper Disclosure of Medical Records

A release of medical records information that has not been authorized by the patient or that has not been made pursuant to statutory, regulatory, or other legal authority may subject the hospital and its staff to civil and criminal liability. Three possible civil liability actions are available to patients who show injury as a result of a disclosure of information in their medical records by hospitals or physicians: defamation, invasion of privacy, and breach of contract. In addition, the state may impose criminal or professional disciplinary sanctions for violation of statutory confidentiality requirements.

STATUTORY PENALTIES

In a few states, the disclosure of medical records information in a manner or to persons not authorized by state statute constitutes a criminal offense. The Tennessee statute, for example, states that:

> willful violation of the provisions of [the Medical Records Act] shall constitute a misdemeanor and shall be punishable as provided for by law. No hospital, its officers, employees, or medical and nursing personnel practicing therein, shall be civilly liable for violation of [the Medical Records Act] except to the extent of liability for actual damages in a civil action for willful or reckless or wanton acts or commissions constituting such violation. Such liability shall be subject, however, to any immunities or limitations or liability or damages provided by law.[1]

The provisions of the Illinois Mental Health and Developmental Disabilities Confidentiality Act are more specific as to civil remedies available to the patient.

---

[1]Tenn. Code Ann. §68–11–311 (1983). *See also* Hawaii Rev. Stat. §324–34 (Supp. 1983).

Any person aggrieved by a violation of this Act may sue for damages, an injunction, or other appropriate relief. Reasonable attorney's fees and costs may be awarded to the successful plaintiff in any action under this Act.[2]

Such statutory sanctions do not exist where the state has executed a statute prohibiting improper release of medical records.

DEFAMATION

Defamation may be defined as a written or oral communication to someone other than the person defamed of matters that concern a living person and tend to injure that person's reputation.[3] Traditionally, libel is a written form of defamation, while slander is oral. Libel is actionable without proof of actual damages, although special damages would ordinarily have to be shown in order for oral publications to be actionable. Medical records may contain information that is inaccurate and that, if published, would tend to affect a person's reputation in the community adversely. Thus, conceivably, disclosure by a hospital to an unauthorized person would result in an action for defamation.[4]

However, the possibility of a patient's obtaining a recovery against the hospital for defamation for release of medical records information is slight. Medical records entries are ordinarily true, and, as a general rule, truth of the published statement is an absolute defense to a civil cause of action for libel or slander, irrespective of the publisher's motive. Although the rule has been modified in some states to allow application of the defense only where the publisher's motive was good, the traditional rule, even as modified, provides substantial protection for hospitals.

Moreover, the law recognizes two privileges that permit publication of even false statements that are injurious to the subject's reputation. These are absolute privilege and qualified privilege. Publications made in legislative, judicial, and administrative proceedings are absolutely privileged, and thus do not give rise to a cause of action in defamation. Disclosure of defamatory medical records information in a court would, therefore, not be actionable. In *Gilson v. Knickerbocker Hospital,*[5] for example, plaintiff sued the hospital for libel, claiming that, by

---

[2]Ill. Ann. Stat. ch. 91 1/2, §815 (Supp. 1984–85); *See also* Fla. Stat. §395.018 (1983).

[3]W. PROSSER, LAW OF TORTS 739–744 (4th Ed. 1971).

[4]*But see* Collins v. Walters, No. 82 Civ. 6014, slip op. (S.D.N.Y. Oct. 28, 1983). Comments made to fellow employees about the plaintiff might not constitute public disclosure.

[5]280 App. Div. 690, 116 N.Y.S. 2d 745 (1952).

complying with a lawful subpoena, the hospital had maliciously allowed the publication of false and defamatory matter contained in the medical record. The record contained an observation that plaintiff was under the influence of alcohol. The court granted the hospital's motion for summary judgment, stating that the defendant's act was absolutely privileged in that it was acting pursuant to lawful judicial process.

A qualified privilege exists as to

> communication made in good faith, without actual malice, with reasonable or probable grounds for believing them to be true, on a subject matter in which the author of the communication has an interest, or in respect to which he has a duty, public, personal or private, either legal, judicial, political, moral, or social, made to a person having a corresponding interest or duty.[6]

Where a hospital is serving its own interests, as in its efforts to procure payment from a third party, there can be no doubt that communications are privileged, since the hospital may be considered an interested party.[7] Also, in those instances in which a public interest is being served, such as protecting the community from highly contagious diseases, it would be proper to inform those persons interested in the relevant facts. For example, in *Simonsen v. Swensen*,[8] the Nebraska Supreme Court, ruling upon the question of whether a physician had violated a statute that prohibited out-of-court disclosure of confidential communications, held the physician not liable for disclosing to the owner of a boardinghouse the fact that his patient had a venereal disease. Despite intimating that the diagnosis was incorrect, the court reasoned that the rules of qualified privilege, under the law of defamation, would govern this case. The physician was held to have had a moral or legal duty to disclose his diagnosis to those persons who might be endangered by this contagious disease. While this case involved an action for violation of a professional confidence, the court used the same standard that is used in measuring a qualified privilege in an action for defamation. In *Quarles v. Sutherland*,[9] a customer sued a store owner for injuries sustained inside the store. The store's physician examined the injured customer and gave the medical report to the store's attorney. The court held that the release of this report was a true communication made in good faith to an interested party and, as such, was subject to a qualified privilege.

---

[6]53 C.J.S. *Libel and Slander* §89 (1948 and Supp. 1984).

[7]Patton v. Jacobs, 118 Ind. App. 358, 78 N.E. 2d 789 (1948).

[8]104 Neb. 224, 177 N.W. 831 (1920). *See also* Shoemaker v. Friedburg, 80 Cal. App. 2d 911, 183 P. 2d 318 (1947).

[9]215 Tenn. 651, 389 S.W. 2d 249 (1965).

In some cases, it is important for health care practitioners to record their suspicions in the medical record. If a practitioner suspects child abuse, or drug abuse, or venereal disease, he or she may need to order tests to confirm its existence or to rule it out as a diagnosis. This kind of statement, if made in a proper manner and without malice, will likely be protected under the theory of qualified privilege. The record, however, should be complete, so that if the suspected condition did not actually exist, the record reflects the fact it did not exist.

A person who has knowingly signed forms consenting to the release of medical records is barred from bringing a defamation suit when those records are subsequently released, according to a federal court in Minnesota.[10] At the request of his employer, a pilot submitted to a chemical dependency evaluation, the results of which indicated that he was an alcoholic. Prior to the analysis, the pilot signed a number of forms including consent forms for the release of information relating to his evaluation and treatment. The records, which contained the diagnosis of alcoholism, were released to the pilot's employer and the employer's insurance company. When the pilot was subsequently grounded, and then fired (apparently for an unrelated reason), he brought suit against the facility where the test was performed and the chemical dependency counselor, alleging that they defamed him with their diagnosis of episodic excessive drinking and acute and chronic chemical dependency, and that their diagnosis of early stages of alcoholism had an inadequate factual basis and resulted from a lack of diligence in ascertaining the truth. Although the pilot admitted that he signed release forms, he contended that he did not consent to the release of the defamatory statements because either they were not in existence or their contents were not known to him at the time he signed the forms. The court, however, found that there was no indication that the pilot did not know the implications of the forms that he signed, and that there was no evidence of fraud or malice on the part of those who prepared the reports contained in the released records. Citing the principle that "one who agrees to submit his conduct to investigation knowing that its results will be published consents to the publication of the honest finding of the investigators," the court concluded that the pilot could not sue for defamation.

If the disclosure of the record exceeds the scope of the authorization given by the patient or other appropriate person, the disclosure will be unauthorized and will subject the person releasing the information to liability. (For a discussion of access to medical records, see Chapter 4.)

A more difficult question is presented when neither the interest of the hospital nor that of the general public is directly involved. Such cases may arise when insurance companies, litigating parties, newspapers, etc., request permission to

---

[10]Williamson v. Stocker, No. 4–79–335 slip op. (D. Minn. Dec. 21, 1982).

examine or obtain information from the medical records. It is conceivable that, in answering a private and confidential inquiry, depending upon the facts of the situation, the hospital is acting in the discharge of a legal, moral, or social duty, and its answer may thus be privileged. This assumption is based on the principle that when an apparently interested party makes a request for information concerning the general business character or credit of an individual, it creates a moral justification for disclosure because, under ordinary social standards, a reasonable person would feel called upon to speak.[11] By analogy, one could argue that disclosure of data in medical records to an insurance company or to a litigating party is qualifiedly privileged, since the interest of the community in securing justice would create a moral duty in the hospital to comply with such a request. For example, an insurance company made a qualifiedly privileged disclosure concerning a person's health when it caused certain information, adverse to the plaintiff's interest, to be recorded with an agency subscribed to by other life insurance companies.[12] The extent of the qualified privilege is uncertain and impossible to reduce to a formula. The disclosure must be justified by the importance of the interest served, and it must be called for by a legal or moral duty, or by generally accepted standards of decent conduct. In any action brought for defamation, the court will determine whether the prerequisites of qualified privilege have been met.

In these cases, the hospital is well advised to take the conservative approach and withhold medical records information unless it finds an exceptionally good reason to disclose it. What the hospital considers appropriate reasons should be developed with the help of the institution's legal counsel and should be set forth in its medical records policies. Should it do so under the circumstances described earlier, the theories of qualified privilege may provide a defense to an action by the patient in defamation. The possibility of establishing a qualified privilege should not in itself justify disclosure of medical records information, however.

---

[11]Porterfield v. Burger King Corp., 540 F. 2d 398 (8th Cir. 1976); Estes v. Lawton-Byrne-Bruner Ins. Agency Co., 437 S.W. 2d 685 (Mo. Ct. App. 1969); Melcher v. Beeler, 48 Colo. 233, 110 P. 181 (1916); Froslee v. Lund's State Bank, 131 Minn. 435, 155 N.W. 619 (1915); Richardson v. Gunby, 88 Kan. 47, 127 P. 533 (1912); Posnett v. Marble, 62 Vt. 481, 20 A. 813 (1890). *But see* Aku v. Lewis, 52 Hawaii 366, 477 P. 2d 162 (1970).

[12]Mayer v. Northern Life Ins. Co., 119 F. Supp. 536 (N.D. Cal. 1953). *See also* Hutchinson v. New England Telephone and Telegraph Co., 350 Mass. 188, 214 N.E. 2d 57 (1966), which held that qualified privilege existed when operator erroneously identified plaintiff as one who telephoned a bomb threat; Doane v. Grew, 220 Mass. 171, 107 N.E. 620 (1915), which held that a qualified privilege attached to the response of an employer concerning a former servant with respect to an inquiry made by a prospective employer of the servant; Rude v. Nass, 79 Wis. 321, 48 N.W. 555 (1891), which held that a qualified privilege existed where the defendant answered a letter about a nun written in the interests of a father whose daughter had been associating with the nun, despite the apparent lack of concern in the matter by the defendant.

A request for information by a totally disinterested party can never create a situation of qualified privilege. For a disclosure to be privileged, the party to whom it is made always must have a valid interest in obtaining the information. Whether or not the information was requested or volunteered will help to determine whether the publisher acted in good faith or had a moral duty to communicate. Moreover, it is important to remember that the qualified privilege can be lost if it is abused or if the publication is found to be malicious.[13]

In general, however, disclosure of information or permitted examination of hospital records does not lead to liability for defamation.

INVASION OF PRIVACY

Releasing patient information to news media in some cases may make a hospital liable to the patient for an invasion of privacy. An invasion of an individual's right of privacy is a civil wrong that has been defined as an unwarranted appropriation or exploitation of that individual's personality, the publication of his or her private concerns in which the public has no legitimate interest, or a wrongful intrusion into his or her private activities. To give rise to an action for damages, this exploitation, publication, or intrusion must be done in a way that would cause outrage or mental suffering, shame, or humiliation to a person of ordinary sensibilities.[14]

There is some overlap between the theories of defamation and invasion of privacy: an unauthorized disclosure of medical information may give rise to an action under both theories. Several factors distinguish the two causes of action. First, truth of the information published is often a defense to an allegation of defamation; it is not a defense to an invasion of privacy. Thus, an unauthorized disclosure even of accurate medical information could subject a hospital to liability for invasion of a patient's privacy. Second, to recover for defamation, the plaintiff must often prove special damages; that is, that the disclosure actually harmed him or her. The plaintiff need not prove special damages to recover for an invasion of privacy. Third, the two theories provide redress for different types of injury arising from the unauthorized disclosure of personal information. A cause of action for invasion of privacy looks to the harm a disclosure has caused to the plaintiff's feelings.[15] Thus, a plaintiff in an action for invasion of privacy may recover even for the disclosure of favorable information. Defamation, on the other hand, focuses on the injury to the plaintiff's reputation. Fourth, the law of defamation normally requires publication to a second person; although an action

---

[13]PROSSER, LAW OF TORTS 792–796 (4th ed. 1971).

[14]*Id.* at 802–818.

[15]*Id.*

for invasion of privacy often involves publication, it is not a necessary element for recovery. Thus a single human agency can invade an individual's privacy.

Defamation and invasion of privacy resemble one another in that the public interest places similar restrictions on the right to recover for both causes of action. Thus, a disclosure entitled to protection by the qualified privilege in a defamation action cannot be the basis for recovery for invasion of privacy.

A right of privacy is personal to the individual whose privacy has been invaded. The right does not extend to members of the individual's family. The individual cannot assign his or her right to privacy. An action for invasion of privacy cannot arise from a publication concerning one who has died unless the state's statutes establish such a cause of action. Corporations and partnerships have no right to privacy.

The plaintiff in a suit for invasion of privacy need not prove that the invasion caused him or her economic loss, but may recover monetary or other damages that he or she can prove resulted from the invasion.

One commentator has divided invasion of privacy into four categories: (1) appropriation of plaintiff's name or likeness for the defendant's benefit; (2) intrusion upon the plaintiff's solitude or private concerns; (3) public disclosure of embarrassing private facts; and (4) publicity that places the plaintiff in a false light in the public eye. Because medical records are highly personal, improper disclosure of patient information can easily constitute invasion of privacy, as the following court decisions illustrate.

Courts have found an improper appropriation of the plaintiff's likeness for the defendant's benefit primarily where defendant exploited the plaintiff for commercial benefit. However, some courts have applied invasion of privacy theories to situations where the defendant used the plaintiff's name or likeness for the defendant's noncommercial benefit. In *Clayman v. Bernstein*,[16] for example, the court prohibited a physician from using photographs of the plaintiff patient's facial development in connection with medical instruction. The court found that even taking the plaintiff's picture without her express consent was an invasion of privacy; it was not necessary to show that the physician had improperly used the photographs or shown them to others to establish liability. Further, having a second individual develop the pictures would constitute publication, even if the negative had never been printed. The court reached a similar conclusion in *Estate of Berthiaume v. Pratt*.[17] There, a physician photographed a terminally ill patient shortly before his death. The physician had taken other photographs of the patient in the course of his treatment. The court found evidence, however, that the patient had objected to being photographed on the occasion giving rise to the lawsuit.

---

[16]38 D.&C. Pa. 543 (1940).

[17]365 A. 2d 792 (Me. 1976). For a discussion of taking unauthorized photographs as invasion of privacy in this and other contexts, see Annot., 86 A.L.R. 3d 365 (1978).

Further, the court noted that the final picture had not been related to the patient's treatment; the patient was not even under the defendant physician's care when the picture was taken. The court rejected the physician's argument that his scientific interest in having a full photographic record of the patient's case justified taking the picture.

Taking a picture for scientific purposes should be distinguished from publishing an individual's name or likeness in connection with a newsworthy event. In the latter case, the individual does not have an action for invasion of privacy.

Hospital medical records policies should establish the circumstances under which the institution will permit the patient to be photographed for any reason. Photographs taken in connection with scientific research should be part of a research protocol approved by appropriate committees of the medical staff. All other photographs of patients should be taken in accordance with hospital policy. In general, these policies should require approval of such photography by an appropriate hospital representative.

Courts have found an unwarranted intrusion upon the plaintiff's solitude or private concerns where the defendant bugged the plaintiff's telephone or bedroom, invaded the plaintiff's house, or in other ways intruded in an objectionable manner into the plaintiff's concerns.[18] Monitoring a patient's telephone conversations from the hospital may subject an institution not only to liability for invasion of privacy, but also to liability under federal statutes prohibiting the interception of private communications.[19] Also, when nonmedical personnel are allowed to witness medical procedures or to examine the patient without the patient's consent, the invasion of the patient's privacy may be actionable.[20]

Publication of private facts that causes embarrassment to the plaintiff or that places the plaintiff in a false light in the public eye gives rise to an action for invasion of privacy if the publication exceeds generally accepted standards of decent conduct. However, such a publication may not be actionable if it is in the community's interest or required to protect the publisher's freedom of speech. The leading case in the hospital industry is *Bazemore v. Savannah Hospital*.[21] This case recognizes a hospital's duty to prevent unauthorized persons from invading its patients' privacy. There, parents brought a petition against a hospital, a photographer, and a newspaper to recover damages and to enjoin the unauthorized publication of pictures of their deceased, malformed child. The parents claimed

---

[18]PROSSER, LAW OF TORTS 802–818 (4th ed. 1971).

[19]Gerrard v. Blackman, 401 F. Supp. 1189 (N.D. Ill. 1975).

[20]*See* Byfield v. Candler, 33 Ga. App. 275, 125 S.E. 905 (1924); DeMay v. Roberts, 46 Mich. 160, 9 N.W. 146 (1881). *See also* Knight v. Penobscot Bay Medical Center, 420 A. 2d 915 (Me. 1980). The viewing of plaintiff's delivery of child by nurse's husband was found, under the circumstances, not to be an invasion of privacy.

[21]171 Ga. 257, 155 S.E. 194 (1930).

that this publication constituted an invasion of privacy. Defendant argued that any right to an action for invasion of privacy lay in the child, not its parents, and that, since the child died, publication of its picture invaded no one's privacy. On appeal, the Supreme Court of Georgia rejected this argument and found that the plaintiffs' petition stated a cause of action for invasion of privacy against the hospital where the child was cared for as well as against the photographer and newspaper responsible for publishing its picture. The petition specifically alleged a duty on the part of the hospital,

> upon the arrival of said child, to properly care for and administer to it such skill, comforts, and protection as would safely protect it . . . from an invasion of an unauthorized person or persons, whereby its monstrosity and nude condition would be likely to be exposed to any person, and particularly to the general public. . . .[22]

Thus, the court recognized that the hospital had a duty to protect the privacy of its patients. Although *Bazemore* dealt with the practice of photographing patients, its holding is broadly applicable. A hospital also could be liable for an invasion of privacy if it improperly discloses information in its patients' medical records.

The right of privacy, however, is not an absolute right. The purpose of the right is to protect the citizen from mass dissemination of information concerning private, personal matters. An individual's actions or situation may become of such public interest that publication alone of personal information about him or her is no longer an invasion of privacy. Moreover, courts have held that an oral publication alone cannot constitute an invasion of privacy.[23] Further, publication of information to an extent reasonably calculated to serve the legitimate interests of the publisher cannot constitute an invasion of privacy.[24] This restriction is similar to the qualified privilege in defamation actions. Thus, release or disclosure of information in the medical record to private individuals, such as attorneys, insurance company representatives, or family members, for purposes of reimbursement, litigation, etc., would not ordinarily constitute an invasion of the right

---

[22]*Id.*

[23]Pangallo v. Murphy, 243 S.W. 2d 496 (Ky. Ct. App. 1951); Melvin v. Reid, 112 Cal. App. 285, 297 P. 91 (1931); Brents v. Morgan, 221 Ky. 765, 299 S.W. 967 (1927); Warren & Brandeis, *The Right to Privacy*, 4 HARV. L. REV. 193 (1890).

[24]Kaletha v. Bortz Elevator Co., Inc., 178 Ind. App. 654, 383 N.E. 2d 1071 (1978); Voneye v. Turner, 240 S.W. 2d 588 (Ky. Ct. App. 1951); Patton v. Jacobs, 118 Ind. App. 358, 78 N.E. 2d 789 (1948); Lewis v. Physicians & Dentists Credit Bureau, 27 Wash. 2d 267, 177 P. 2d 896 (1947). *But see* Brents v. Morgan, 221 Ky. 765, 299 S.W. 967 (1927) and Trammell v. Citizens News Co., 285 Ky. 529, 148 S.W. 2d 708 (1941). Publishing a notice in a newspaper that the plaintiff owed money to a creditor was too broad to serve the legitimate interests of the publishers; this information was not of any public interest.

of privacy.[25] Further, in order to constitute an invasion of privacy, the release, disclosure, or publication must be of such a nature as to outrage or cause mental suffering, shame, or humiliation to a person of ordinary sensibilities.[26]

Where the patient expressly consents orally or in writing to disclosure of private information, the patient cannot later be heard to complain that the disclosure was an invasion of privacy. The patient's consent protects the hospital if the patient wanted the information disclosed for his or her benefit and the hospital disclosed the information in the manner the patient authorized.[27] Therefore, hospitals should endeavor to obtain the patient's written consent to the disclosure of information. If a patient authorizes a disclosure but refuses to sign an authorization form, hospital personnel should note the patient's consent on the form, properly sign and date the note and insert the form in the patient's medical record. Teaching hospitals, especially, should be certain their patients understand that they will be participating in the education and training of medical, nursing, and other students who may observe or assist in the patients' treatment. Hospitals should establish and enforce strict rules against permitting lay persons to observe patient treatment without express patient consent. Hospital policy should include safeguards against the use of patient-authorized photographs or videotape in an unauthorized manner or for an unauthorized purpose. The policy should require that patient authorization include specific language describing permitted uses of the materials and should prohibit uses not authorized by the patient. The hospital should also be careful not to draft a policy on confidentiality that is too vague.[28]

Perhaps the hospital practice most likely to give rise to questions of the invasion of privacy is the release of information concerning patients to news agencies. A hospital has no legal obligation whatsoever to disclose medical records information to news media. However, hospitals may, as a matter of local policy, release such information under certain circumstances. While the right of privacy does not

---

[25]Curry v. Corn, 52 Misc. 2d 1035, 277 N.Y.S. 2d 470 (1966). Doctor's disclosure of a woman's medical status to her prospective husband was not an invasion of her privacy. Pennison v. Provident Life & Accident Ins. Co., 154 So. 2d 617 (La. Ct. App. 1963). Disclosure to plaintiff's insurance company not an invasion of privacy; Mikel v. Abrams, 541 F. Supp. 591 (W.D. Mo. 1982) aff'd, 716 F. 2d 907 (8th Cir. 1983). Disclosure of husband's medical records to wife was not an invasion of the husband's privacy; Inverson v. Frandsen, 237 F. 2d 898 (10th Cir. 1956). Disclosure to psychiatrist treating plaintiff and officials at plaintiff's school protected by qualified privilege; therefore apparently not an invasion of privacy.

[26]See Annot., 138 A.L.R. 22 (1938), 14 A.L.R. 2d 750 (1950). See also 62 AM. JUR. Privacy §1 (1972); Reed v. Real Detective Publishing Co., 63 Ariz. 294, 162 P. 2d 133 (1945); Cason v. Baskin, 159 Fla. 31, 30 So. 2d 635 (1947); Davis v. General Finance & Thrift Corp., 80 Ga. App. 708, 57 S.E. 2d 225 (1950); Warren & Brandeis, The Right to Privacy, 4 HARV. L. REV. 193, 216 (1890).

[27]See, e.g., Clark v. Geraci, 29 Misc. 2d 791, 208 N.Y.S. 2d 564 (Sup. Ct. 1960). Plaintiff patient had authorized defendant physician to disclose incomplete information about his illness; plaintiff was therefore estopped from claiming that he had not consented to the defendant's disclosure of the underlying cause of the illness, alcoholism.

[28]See, e.g., Group Health Plan, Inc. v. Lopez, 341 N.W. 2d 294 (Minn. Ct. App. 1983).

prohibit publications that are of public or general interest, the extent of publication is still a matter to be weighed carefully by the hospital in each case. Announcements simply of patient admissions, discharges, or births ordinarily pose no problem, unless the hospital specializes in the care of patients with specific diseases that are considered shameful in the public mind. To publicize the fact that Mrs. Jones gave birth to a normal healthy boy could not ordinarily be considered overstepping the bounds of propriety, but to publicize the fact that Mrs. Jones gave birth to a stillborn monstrosity or that Miss Brown had a child might be actionable.

If the patient is a public figure, his or her prominence, in itself, makes virtually all of the patient's doings of interest to the public.[29] Relatively obscure people may voluntarily take certain actions that bring them before the public, or they may be victims of occurrences that are newsworthy, such as accidents, crimes, etc., thus making them of interest to the public. The latitude extended to the publication of the personal matters, names, photographs, etc., of public figures varies. Public figures may not complain if their lives are given some publicity, and this may be true long after they have ceased to be in the public eye. For example, in *Estate of Hemingway v. Random House, Inc.*,[30] Ernest Hemingway's widow was unable to recover for invasion of privacy against a young author who had written a memoir describing her personal feelings and relationship with her husband. As the widow of a major literary figure and author of magazine articles on her relationship with her husband, she was a public figure. Even ordinary citizens who voluntarily adopt a course of action that is newsworthy or are involuntarily involved in a newsworthy event cannot complain if the event is reported along with their names and pictures. In *Bernstein v. National Broadcasting Co.*,[31] the court held that a former

---

[29]Cason v. Baskin, 159 Fla. 31, 30 So. 2d 635 (1947). *See also* Firestone v. Time, 271 So. 2d 745 (Fla. 1972).

[30]23 N.Y. 2d 341, 244 N.E. 2d 250, 296 N.Y.S. 2d 771 (1968). *See also* Martin v. Dorton, 210 Miss. 668, 50 So. 2d 391 (1951). Local sheriff was public officer whose right to privacy was limited; Cohen v. Marx, 94 Cal. App. 2d 704, 211 P.2d 320 (1950). Plaintiff waived his right to privacy by becoming a professional prizefighter. *See also* Cason v. Baskin, 159 Fla. 31, 30 So. 2d 635 (1947); Sidis v. F.R. Pub. Corporation, 113 F.2d 806 (2d Cir. 1940). Plaintiff, who had been a famous child prodigy and a public figure, was still of legitimate interest to the public; magazine story on his life after he faded from public view was therefore not an invasion of his privacy. Flake v. Greensboro News Co., 212 N.C. 780, 195 S.E. 55 (1937). For a collection of cases discussing waiver and loss of the right to privacy, *see* Annot., 57 A.L.R. 3d 16 (1974). *See also* Dennis v. Adcock, 138 Ga. App. 425, 226 S.E. 2d 292 (1976), where the court held that the plaintiff, by failing to object to the introduction of damaging hospital records by defendants in plaintiff's previous personal injury suit, had waived his right to privacy regarding them. The court indicated that a disclosure protected by the qualified privilege in a suit for libel could not be the basis for a suit for invasion of privacy.

[31]129 F. Supp. 817 (D.D.C. 1955), *aff'd*, 232 F. 2d 369, *cert. denied*, 352 U.S. 945 (1956). *See also* Blount v. T.D. Pub. Co., 77 N.M. 384, 423 P. 2d 421 (1967). Whether the account of a man's murder, 10 months after its occurrence, invades the privacy of his widow, depended in part on whether the jury found that the account was newsworthy. Langford v. Vanderbilt Univ., 199 Tenn. 389, 287 S.W. 2d 32

defendant in a criminal case could not prevent a later dramatization of the case that did not name him. In such cases, individual rights give way before the public interest in being informed and in freedom of the press. A strange illness or an accident is often a newsworthy event. Thus, a hospital that discloses the identity and medical condition of a patient in connection with such an event often would not be liable for an invasion of privacy. However, as time passes, the identity of the participant in such an event loses importance and action for invasion of the right of privacy may then be allowable.[32]

Moreover, the name and photograph of the victim of a circumstance that is itself newsworthy may be published.[33] However, in *Barber v. Time, Inc.*,[34] the court found that a magazine could be liable for invasion of privacy when it published the name and picture of the plaintiff in a story concerning a strange ailment for which she was being treated. Defendant's employees had obtained the plaintiff's picture by surreptitious means and over her express objections. In holding that the plaintiff was entitled to recover, the court said:

> certainly if there is any right of privacy at all, it should include the right to obtain medical treatment at home or in a hospital for an individual personal condition (at least if it is not contagious or dangerous to others) without personal publications. . . . Whatever the limits of the right of

(1956), filing an action is a matter of public record. Smith v. Doss, 251 Ala. 250, 37 So. 2d 118 (1948). Daughters of man, thought to have been murdered, who abandoned family and reappeared 25 years later could not complain when radio station broadcasted the account of his disappearance; decedent's actions made him a public figure and his story a part of the community's history. Berg v. Minneapolis Star & Tribune Co., 79 F.Supp. 957 (D. Minn 1948). Litigation over child custody is newsworthy and publication related to this litigation is not an invasion of privacy. Metter v. Los Angeles Examiner, 35 Cal. App. 2d 304, 95 P.2d 491 (1939). Suicide of someone's wife is a newsworthy event; the husband could not prevent publication of her picture.

[32]Bernstein v. National Broadcasting Co., 129 F. Supp. 817 (D.D.C. 1955); Montesano v. Donrey Media Group, 94 Nev. 644, 668 P. 2d 1081, 1086 (1983), *cert. denied,* 104 S. Ct. 2172 (1984). Passage of time is a relevant factor in determining whether a publication involves a matter of legitimate public concern; Mau v. Rio Grande Oil Inc., 28 F. Supp. 845 (N.D. Cal. 1939), plaintiff, victim of an armed robbery, could sue for invasion of privacy a broadcasting company that named plaintiff in a dramatization of the robbery 18 months after it occurred; Melvin v. Reid, 112 Cal. App. 285, 297 P. 91 (1931). Plaintiff, former prostitute who had married and led a quiet life for seven years, had an action for invasion of privacy against the producers of a movie which depicted her life and used her maiden name. *But cf.* Smith v. Doss, *supra,* note 31.

[33]Bremmer v. Journal-Tribune Pub. Co., 247 Iowa 817, 76 N.W. 2d 762 (1956), publication of mutilated dead boy's picture; Kelley v. Post Publishing Co., 327 Mass. 275, 98 N.E. 2d 286 (1951), publication of automobile accident victim's picture; Themo v. New England Newspaper Pub. Co., 306 Mass. 54, 27 N.E. 2d 753 (1940), plaintiff had no absolute right to prevent newspaper from publishing his picture without his consent; Jones v. Herald Post Co., 230 Ky. 227, 18 S.W. 2d 972 (1929), publication of picture of murder victim's wife who had struggled with her husband's assailants. *See also* Annot., 30 A.L.R. 3d 203 (1970), invasion of privacy by use of plaintiff's name or likeness for nonadvertising purposes.

[34]348 Mo. 1199, 159 S.W. 2d 291 (1942).

privacy may be, it seems clear that it must include the right to have information given to or gained by a physician in the treatment of an individual's personal ailment kept from publication which would state his name in connection therewith without such person's consent.[35]

The court found that while the plaintiff's ailment was of some interest to the public, her identity was not. Publishing her name and picture, which conveyed no medical information, was thus an invasion of her privacy.

While it may be argued that the reasoning of the Missouri court in the *Barber* case is applicable only to illnesses, as distinguished from accidents or catastrophes, the illness was at least as newsworthy as any physical harm that may have occurred in an accident. The *Barber* case appears to conflict with the majority view discussed above. However, the case may be distinguished because publication in the national magazine was in a section devoted to medical news. Public interest was not keyed to the identity of the victim, but rather to the disease or illness. Consequently, the use of the victim's name and picture was not necessary; and, because the illness was so degrading in nature, she was allowed to recover. In the case of newsworthy occurrences reported in the daily newspapers, motion pictures, radio, or television, the identity of the participants or victims is as much a part of the news as the facts concerning their misfortune.

Although a hospital should be reluctant to release patient information to the news media, the institution may determine in some cases that release of information of legitimate news value may be appropriate. In such circumstances, risk of liability is dependent on the specific nature of the disclosure; in some instances, the liability risk would be at a minimum. Merely releasing the status of the patient's condition generally does not create liability exposure, but disclosing more detailed information or a photograph without the patient's consent should be avoided. While the patient's participation in a newsworthy event may protect the hospital that releases specific information about the patient from an invasion of privacy action, the best policy the hospital can adopt is to refuse to release any information (other than status of the patient) without the patient's consent. The fact that the patient is newsworthy does not *require* the hospital to disclose information; it may simply protect the hospital if it *chooses* to disclose the information. The best approach is to protect the patient's confidentiality, if possible.

BETRAYAL OF PROFESSIONAL SECRETS

One school of thought with regard to the role of the physician is that the release or disclosure of information in the medical record might give rise to liability

[35]*Id.* at 1207, S.W. 2d at 295.

because it constitutes a breach of the physician's duty to keep such information in confidence.[36]

In *Simonsen v. Swensen*,[37] the plaintiff's physician informed the plaintiff's landlady that the plaintiff was suffering from a contagious venereal disease. The landlady immediately forced the plaintiff to vacate the premises. The plaintiff sued the physician on the theory that a confidential communication had been revealed. The court held that the statute pertaining to confidential communication applied only to courtroom testimony but construed the statute relating to unprofessional conduct of physicians more broadly. This statute provides that the betrayal of professional secrets to the detriment of the patient is cause for revocation of the physician's license. The court stated that this provision imposed a duty on the physician to keep secret confidences entrusted to him or her by a patient. However, although the court concluded that an action would lie for damages flowing from breach of this duty, it found the act of the physician in this case to be qualifiedly privileged, since the physician also had a duty to disclose the existence of the contagious disease to persons likely to be affected. The court found that, although the physician generally had a duty to keep the patient's information confidential, his disclosure to the landlady in this case was privileged, and he was held not liable to the patient.

Several other courts have similarly concluded that the public policy underlying state testimonial privilege and unprofessional conduct statutes requires that the physician-patient relationship be a confidential one, and accordingly that a physician's breach of confidentiality is actionable.[38] The only recent decision refusing to recognize a cause of action for unauthorized disclosure of information obtained through the physician-patient relationship arose in a jurisdiction that apparently had no professional conduct statute, and the court based its decision in part on the sufficiency of the redress available to the patient through an action for invasion of privacy.[39]

Courts that have recognized that physicians have a legal duty to maintain their patients' confidentiality have also indicated that two defenses are available to the

---

[36]Anker v. Brodnitz, 98 Misc. 2d 148, 413 N.Y.S. 2d 582, *aff'd*, 73 A.D. 2d 589, 422 N.Y.S. 2d 887 (1979), *appeal dismissed*, 51 N.Y. 2d 743, 411 N.E. 2d 789, 432 N.Y.S. 2d 364 (1980). A cause of action exists against a doctor who without authority discloses his patient's confidences.

[37]104 Neb. 224, 177 N.W. 831 (1920).

[38]Geisberger v. Willuhn, 72 Ill. App. 3d 435, 390 N.E. 2d 945 (1979); Schaffer v. Spicer, 88 S.D. 36, 215 N.W. 2d 134 (1974); Horne v. Patton, 291 Ala. 701, 287 So. 2d 824 (1973); Hammonds v. Aetna Casualty and Surety Company, 243 F. Supp. 793 (N.D. Ohio 1965); Hague v. Williams, 37 N.J. 328, 181 A. 2d 345 (1962); Clark v. Geraci, 29 Misc. 2d 791, 208 N.Y.S. 2d 564 (Sup. Ct. 1960); Berry v. Moench, 8 Utah 2d 191, 331 P. 2d 814 (1958).

[39]Logan v. District of Columbia, 447 F. Supp. 1328 (D.D.C. 1978). *Cf.* Quarles v. Sutherland, 215 Tenn. 651, 389 S.W. 2d 249 (1965). Medical licensing statute is merely administrative and creates no cause of action in favor of patient.

physician charged with breaching that duty: privilege and waiver. Privilege will arise where failure to disclose information about the patient would jeopardize the health or safety of third persons or of the patient.[40]

There is less agreement about the scope of the defense of waiver. In *Hague v. Williams*,[41] the plaintiffs had filed a death claim under a policy insuring their deceased daughter. In response to the insurance company's inquiries, the defendant's physician disclosed that the child had a congenital heart defect. Armed with this information, the insurer settled the claim at a steep discount. While recognizing the physician's duty of confidentiality, the court found that the claim itself put the patient's health in issue, and hence amounted to a waiver of confidentiality.

A much narrower view of the waiver defense was adopted by the court in *Schaffer v. Spicer*.[42] The defendant's psychiatrist disclosed extensive information concerning the plaintiff's state of health to her husband's attorney in the course of lengthy divorce and custody proceedings, during which the plaintiff herself had testified that she had consulted a psychiatrist. The plaintiff's testimony indicated that she had only consulted and been diagnosed by the psychiatrist. The testimony did not relate to the nature and extent of her illness or treatment, nor did it relate to any communications with the psychiatrist. As a result, the court found that the plaintiff's testimony did not amount to a waiver of the confidential relationship. Furthermore, even if the plaintiff's statement consituted a waiver of the testimonial privilege, it did not completely release the doctor from his duty of secrecy and loyalty to his patient. A dissenting opinion, however, suggested that the interest of the children in the custody proceedings was an interest sufficient to justify the physician's disclosures.[43]

If the defenses of privilege and waiver are unavailable to the defendant, what damages may the plaintiff recover for breach of confidentiality? It appears that the action lies in tort, and accordingly consequential damages would be recoverable. This is the view adopted by the court in *MacDonald v. Clinger*,[44] in which the defendant psychiatrist divulged intimate matters concerning the plaintiff patient to the patient's wife. The court found that the defendant was in breach of a fiduciary responsibility implicit in the physician-patient relationship and allowed the plaintiff to recover damages for the deterioration of his marriage, the loss of his job, and emotional distress.

The *MacDonald* court's concept of fiduciary responsibility, which mirrors the characterization of disclosures in the *Simonsen* case as betrayal of professional

---

[40]*See, e.g.*, Horne v. Patton, 287 So. 2d at 830.

[41]37 N.J. 328, 181 A. 2d 345 (1962).

[42]88 S.D. 36, 215 N.W. 2d 134 (1974).

[43]Schaffer v. Spicer, 215 N.W. 2d at 140.

[44]84 A.D. 2d 482, 446 N.Y.S. 2d 801 (1982).

secrets, raises a further question: what is the standard to which the physician will be held in case of breach of this duty of confidentiality? Although no reported decision has analyzed this issue, a concurring opinion in *MacDonald* suggested that characterizing the physician as a fiduciary creates a presumption that disclosure is unjustified and may have the effect of imposing a more rigorous standard of care on physicians in disclosure actions than in medical malpractice actions.[45]

In theory, if a licensing statute or regulation affecting hospitals were to prohibit the disclosure of confidential information concerning patients, a hospital making such a disclosure could be liable civilly.[46] The hospital's liability would presumably share the features and be subject to the exceptions previously identified for disclosures made by a physician. Moreover, if a hospital improperly disclosed medical records information, it could be subject to penalties imposed for violations of conditions of participation in federal reimbursement programs.[47] There are no reported cases imposing liability or penalties under these theories, however.

BREACH OF CONTRACT

Recently, courts have demonstrated a willingness to apply the ethical standards of the medical profession to compel physicians to maintain the confidentiality of information they obtain in the course of treating their patients. The ethical standards of the American Medical Association (AMA) prohibit physicians in most situations from revealing a confidence entrusted to them by a patient during treatment.[48] Moreover, the medical practice acts of many states require physicians to maintain the confidentiality of their patients' medical information, and the AMA has published standards of hospital conduct that require hospitals to protect their patients' privacy.[49] Some courts now appear willing to enforce these standards as part of the contractual relationship between physicians and their patients.

For example, in *Hammonds v. Aetna Casualty and Surety Co.*,[50] the court held that a physician breached an implied condition of his physician-patient contract when he disclosed medical information to a hospital's insurer without the patient's consent. The court emphasized the rights of patients to rely on the ethical standards of confidentiality as on an express warranty. Having announced a contractual cause of action, however, the court also adopted an invasion of privacy theory and

---

[45]446 N.Y.S. 2d at 806 (Simmons, J. concurring).

[46]*See, e.g.*, Rules and Regulations for the Licensure of General and Special Hospitals in Virginia §208.7 (1977).

[47]*See* 42 C.F.R. §405.1026(a) (1983).

[48]Current Opinions of the Judicial Council of the AMA, 5.05 (1984).

[49]American Medical Association, *A Patient's Bill of Rights* (1972).

[50]237 F. Supp. 96 (N.D. Ohio 1965) and 243 F. Supp. 793 (N.D. Ohio 1965).

concluded that a physician's unauthorized disclosure of communications made in the course of treatment is tortious conduct.

Similarly, in *Doe v. Roe*,[51] which involved publication by the defendant's psychiatrist of a book including extensive transcripts of statements made by the plaintiff patient during treatment, the court found both breach of a contractual covenant to keep statements in confidence and a tortious invasion of privacy, and proceeded to award consequential damages for suffering and humiliation. Also in *MacDonald* (discussed earlier in this chapter) the court announced that although the duty of confidentiality has its origin in the contractual relations between physician and patient, breach of that duty is tortious, and accordingly consequential damages are recoverable.[52] This statement is especially significant because the *MacDonald* court denied that there was a cause of action for invasion of privacy but reached the same result as the *Doe v. Roe* court in terms of recoverable damages.[53]

The breach of contract theory seems to have gained a foothold in the more recent decisions. However, it tends to be approved as one of a number of related theories of liability rather than as the sole theory upon which a plaintiff relies. It is particularly closely linked with the breach of confidentiality theory; the main difference between the two is that the former implies a duty under the contract while the latter imposes a duty as an implication of statutory policy.[54] Furthermore, the courts seem willing to award tort damages whether the theory of liability is, strictly speaking, based on tort or contract. It is therefore possible that patients who cannot succeed against a hospital or practitioner under traditional tort theories of defamation and invasion of privacy may nonetheless be able to recover in full for breach of an implied contract on which they relied where the hospital or physician has disclosed medical information without patient consent and in violation of ethical standards.

---

[51]93 Misc. 2d 201, 400 N.Y.S. 2d 668 (Sup. Ct. 1977).

[52]MacDonald v. Clinger, 446 N.Y.S. 2d at 804.

[53]*Id.* at 803.

[54]The court in Geisberger v. Willuhn, 72 Ill. App. 3d 435, 390 N.E. 2d 945, 948 (1979) referred to the two causes of action as "probably co-extensive."

Chapter 7

Documentation of Patient Consent in the Medical Record

Health care providers must secure proper authorization before performing diagnostic or therapeutic procedures on a patient. In most circumstances, the express or implied consent of the patient or the patient's representative constitutes authorization to diagnose or treat. In most instances the law requires that the patient or patient's representative be given sufficient information concerning the nature and risks of the recommended and alternative treatments so that the consent given is an informed consent. If the patient or patient's representative decides not to consent, usually the examination or procedure cannot be performed. However, in several limited circumstances, the law overrides the patient's decision and provides authorization for involuntary treatment, such as in emergencies and in civil commitment for some mental illness and substance abuse. Consent, however, can never be sufficient authorization for procedures that are prohibited by law.

Physicians and other independent practitioners have the primary responsibility for obtaining informed consent or other authorization for treatment. Hospitals are generally not liable for the physician's failure to secure authorization, unless the physician is an employee or agent of the hospital. However, the hospital frequently assists members of its medical staff to secure written confirmation of the patient's consent when the physician is unable to do so. Thus, hospital administrators, medical records administrators, and individual health care providers must be familiar with the legal principles governing patient consent and the proper documentation of consent.

The requirements of consent and informed consent, the decision-making roles of patients and their representatives, the exceptions to the consent requirement, and the function of the medical record in the patient consent process are discussed in this chapter.

THE DISTINCTION BETWEEN CONSENT AND INFORMED CONSENT

The common law has long recognized the right of persons to be free from harmful or offensive touching. The intentional harmful or offensive touching of another person without authorization is called battery. The earliest medical consent lawsuits arose in England in the eighteenth century when surgery was done without consent or other authorization. In these early cases, the courts found the surgeons liable for battery. When there is no consent or other authorization for a procedure, modern courts still find the physician liable for battery.

Another series of cases involves situations in which the patient consents to a procedure without having sufficient information to make an informed decision. Finding that the physician has a legal duty to disclose sufficient information to the patient, the courts in the past ruled that providing incorrect or insufficient information invalidated the consent and rendered the physician liable for battery. Today, nearly all courts have adopted the position that failure to disclose the necessary information does not invalidate consent. As a result, a procedure performed without adequate disclosure is not considered battery. However, failure to disclose sufficient information is a separate wrong for which there can be liability based on negligence.

Thus, consent alone protects the health care provider from liability for battery, while informed consent is necessary to protect the health care provider from liability for negligence.

In California, the courts have extended the informed consent doctrine to require informed refusal. In *Truman v. Thomas*,[1] the court ruled that a physician could be liable for a patient's death from cancer of the cervix based on the physician's failure to inform the patient of the risks of not consenting to a recommended Pap smear. The Pap smear would probably have led to discovery of the patient's cancer in time to begin treatment that would have extended her life.

Express and Implied Consent

Consent may be either express or implied. Express consent is consent that is given by direct words, either orally or in writing. There are a few procedures, particularly procedures involving reproduction, for which some states require written consent. With the exception of these procedures, either oral or written consent can be legally sufficient authorization where express consent is necessary. However, because it is often difficult to prove oral consent, providers should seek written consent.

---

[1]27 Cal. 3d 285, 611 P. 2d 902 (1980).

Implied consent includes consent that is inferred from the patient's conduct and consent that is presumed in certain emergencies. When a patient voluntarily submits to a procedure with apparent knowledge of the nature of the procedure, the courts will usually find implied consent. For example, in *O'Brien v. Cunard S.S. Co.*,[2] the court found that a woman had given her implied consent to being vaccinated by extending her arm and accepting the vaccination without objection. Consent is also presumed to exist in medical emergencies, unless the health care provider has reason to believe that consent would be refused.[3] This emergency exception to the consent requirement clearly applies when there is an immediate threat to life or health. In *Jackovach v. Yocom*,[4] the court found implied consent to the removal of a patient's mangled limb that had been run over in a train accident. The court accepted the physician's determination that the amputation was necessary to save the patient's life. Courts have disagreed on whether pain is enough justification to find implied consent. In *Sullivan v. Montgomery*,[5] the court found pain to be a significant factor in establishing a finding of implied consent, while in *Cunningham v. Yankton Clinic*,[6] the court found pain not to be a sufficient emergency because the danger to the patient's health was not immediate and the patient was conscious and able to make an informed decision.

Some courts have found implied consent to extensions or modifications of surgical procedures beyond the scope specifically authorized when unexpected conditions arise, and when the extension or modification is necessary to preserve the patient's life. Many surgical consent forms include explicit authorization of extensions or modifications to preserve the patient's life or health. These provisions minimize disagreements over the scope of authorization by providing an opportunity for the patient to forbid specific extensions or modifications.

Both express consent and implied consent must be obtained voluntarily. While there are no reported cases dealing with this issue outside of the medical research context, a consent secured through coercion or undue inducement would likely be void if challenged.

There are some exceptions to the requirement of consent in which the law authorizes treatment despite the refusal of the patient or the patient's representative. These exceptions are discussed later in this chapter.

Informed Consent

The courts have developed two standards for determining the adequacy of the information given the patient by the physician in order to obtain the patient's

---

[2]154 Mass. 272, 28 N.E. 266 (1891).

[3]If the patient previously refused treatment, consent could not be implied by an emergency requiring such treatment.

[4]212 Iowa 914, 237 N.W. 444 (1931).

[5]155 Misc. 448, 279 N.Y.S. 575 (N.Y. City Ct. 1935).

[6]262 N.W. 2d 508 (S.D. 1978).

consent: (1) the professional or reasonable physician standard, and (2) the materiality or reasonable patient standard. In states using the first standard, the physician has a duty to provide the information that a reasonable medical practitioner would provide under the same or similar circumstances.[7]

The second standard has been adopted by an increasing number of states. Under the materiality standard, the extent of the physician's duty to provide information is determined by the information needs of the patient, rather than by professional practice. Information that is material to the decision must be disclosed. In *Canterbury v. Spence,*[8] the court defined a risk to be material "when a reasonable person, in what the physician knows or should know to be the patient's position, would be likely to attach significance to the risk or cluster of risks in deciding whether or not to forego the proposed therapy."

Under the second standard, the elements of an adequate explanation include disclosure of the patient's medical condition, the nature and purpose of the proposed procedure, the consequences and risks of the procedure, the feasible alternatives, and the consequences of refusing all treatment. Nearly all courts recognize that not all risks can be disclosed. The physician must disclose only risks that he or she knows or should know could occur without any intervening negligence. One useful guideline in providing adequate information is for physicians to describe the risks that could result in the most severe consequences and the risks that have a large probability of occurring.

In *Hales v. Pittman,*[9] the patient told the physician that preserving his ability to work was crucial in determining a course of treatment. The court ruled that the physician should have informed him of the risks that could affect his ability to work. This case illustrates that when the patient indicates the need for additional information, there may be a duty to provide it.

The most difficult element for the patient to prove in an informed consent case is causation. The plaintiff must prove that deviation from the acceptable consent standard caused the injury. Thus, the plaintiff must prove that consent would not have been given if the risk that occurred had been disclosed. The courts have developed two standards for this proof. Some jurisdictions apply an objective standard to determine what a prudent person in the patient's position would have decided if the patient had been informed of the risk.[10] Other courts apply a subjective standard, which requires the plaintiff to prove that he or she would have refused to consent to the procedure if informed of the risk.[11] Either of these stand-

---

[7]Natanson v. Kline, 186 Kan. 393, 350 P. 2d 1093, 1106 (Kan. 1960).

[8]464 F. 2d 772, 787 (D.C. Cir.), *cert. denied,* 409 U.S. 1064 (1972).

[9]118 Ariz. 305, 576 P. 2d 493 (1978).

[10]Canterbury v. Spence, 464 F. 2d 772 (D.C. Cir.), *cert. denied,* 409 U.S. 1064 (1972).

[11]Wilkinson v. Vesey, 110 R.I. 606, 295 A. 2d 676 (R.I. 1972).

ards provides substantial protection for the conscientious physician who discloses the major risks, and whose patient suffers from a more remote risk. A patient who consents to a procedure knowing of the risk of death and paralysis will find it difficult to convince a court that knowledge of a minor risk would have led to refusal.

Exceptions to the Informed Consent Requirement

The courts have recognized four situations in which consent is required, but informed consent, i.e., adequate disclosure, is not necessarily required: emergencies, the therapeutic privilege, patient waiver, and prior patient knowledge.

In emergencies in which consent is implied, there is a corollary modification of the disclosure requirement. When there is no time to secure consent, there is clearly no time to provide the information required for an informed consent. In *Crouch v. Most,*[12] the patient suffered from a snake bite that required immediate treatment. The court recognized that even when there is time to secure consent, certain emergency situations may allow only an abbreviated disclosure of information about the required treatment.

Most courts recognize an exception to the informed consent doctrine, called therapeutic privilege, when disclosure of information poses a significant threat of detriment to the patient. Courts have carefully limited the therapeutic privilege by making it inapplicable when the physician fears only that the information might lead the patient to forego needed therapy. Thus, physicians should rely on this privilege only when they can document that a patient's anxiety is significantly above the norm. In *Lester v. Aetna Casualty and Surety Co.,*[13] the court ruled that when the therapeutic privilege is applied to prevent the patient from receiving information, the information must be disclosed to a relative. Before the procedure can be performed, the informed relative must concur with the patient's consent to the procedure. Most courts addressing the issue have adopted this position. One case to the contrary, however, is *Nishi v. Hartwell,*[14] in which the court ruled that no disclosure to relatives was required because the duty to make full disclosure arises from the physician-patient relationship and is owed only to the patient.

Some cases have indicated that a patient can waive the right to be informed prior to giving consent.[15] However, it is doubtful that courts will accept a waiver initiated by a treating physician. A prudent physician should not suggest a waiver but instead should encourage reluctant patients to be informed. If the patient

---

[12]432 P. 2d 250, 254 (N.M. 1967).

[13]240 F. 2d 676 (5th Cir.), *cert. denied,* 354 U.S. 923 (1957).

[14]473 P. 2d 116, 112 (Hawaii 1970).

[15]Putensen v. Clay Adams, Inc., 12 Cal. App. 3d 1062, 91 Cal. Rptr. 319, 333 (1970).

persists, the waiver should be documented in the patient's medical record and carefully witnessed. The documentation should describe the patient's waiver and the physician's effort properly to inform the patient.

No liability arises for nondisclosure of risks that are accepted as common knowledge or that the patient has experienced previously. The physician should be reasonably certain that the patient would reasonably understand commonly known risks.

One state eliminated the requirement of disclosure of risks by statute. Georgia Code §31–9–6 (1981) states that the physician need only disclose "in general terms the treatment or course of treatment to obtain an informed consent." In *Young v. Yarn,*[16] the court interpreted this statute to eliminate the requirement that risks be disclosed. As a result, the Georgia courts no longer base liability on failure to disclose risks.

WHO CAN GIVE CONSENT

The person who makes the consent decision must be legally and actually competent to make the decision and must be informed, unless one of the exceptions applies. Competent adults and some mature minors make decisions regarding their own care. Someone else must make the decisions for incompetent adults and other minors.

Competent Adults

The age of majority is established by the legislature of each state. In most states, legal majority is now 18 years of age. In some states, a person can be considered an adult before the statutory age of majority by taking certain actions, such as by getting married or serving in the armed forces.

An adult is competent if (1) a court has not declared him or her incompetent, and (2) he or she is generally capable of understanding the consequences of alternatives, weighing the alternatives by the degree they promote his or her desires, and choosing and acting accordingly. There is a strong legal presumption of continued competence. For example, in the case of *In re Yetter,*[17] the court found a woman competent to refuse a breast biopsy even though she was committed to a mental institution with a diagnosis of chronic schizophrenia and two of her three reasons for refusal were delusional. In *Lane v. Candura,*[18] the court found a

---

[16]136 Ga. App. 737, 222 S.E. 2d 113 (Ga. Ct. App. 1975).

[17]62 Pa. D. & C. 2d 169 (Pa. C. Pl., Northampton Co. 1973).

[18]6 Mass. App. 377, 376 N.E. 2d 1232 (1978).

woman competent to refuse the amputation of her gangrenous leg even though her train of thought sometimes wandered, her conception of time was distorted, and she was confused on some matters. The fact that her decision was medically irrational and would lead to her death did not demonstrate incompetence. The court believed she understood the alternatives and the consequences of her decision.

Competence is not necessarily determined by psychiatrists. A practical assessment of competence should be made by the physician who obtains the consent or accepts the refusal. When it is difficult to assess competence, consultation of a specialist should be considered. If the physician suspects underlying mental retardation, mental illness, or disorders that affect brain function, the consultant should be a psychiatrist or other appropriate specialist.

Incompetent Adults

The patient's guardian or, if no guardian exists, the representative of the incompetent adult patient makes consent decisions on the patient's behalf. Representatives of patients, such as family members or friends, have a narrower range of permissible choices regarding that patient than they would have concerning their own care. In addition, the known wishes of the patient should be considered in reaching decisions about treatment.

When a court rules that a person is incompetent, the court designates a person to be the incompetent person's guardian. The guardian has the legal authority to make most of the decisions regarding the incompetent person's care.

Because some patients who are actually incompetent have never been determined to be incompetent by a court, they have no legal guardians. When decisions must be made concerning the care of these patients, it is common practice to seek a decision from the next of kin or others who have assumed supervision of the patient. In many states, statutes[19] or court decisions support this practice.[20]

If the incompetence is temporary, the medical procedure should be postponed until the patient is competent and capable of making his or her own decision, unless the postponement presents a substantial risk to the patient's life or health, in which case consent will be implied from the emergency.

When a patient expresses wishes concerning treatment before becoming incompetent, the patient's wishes should be seriously considered in choosing a course of treatment. If a patient was aware of his or her condition and available treatment alternatives when he or she expressed those wishes, the wishes should usually be followed. When there is significant unanticipated change in the patient's condition

---

[19]Miss. Code Ann. §§41–41–3 and 41–41–5 (1972).
[20]Farber v. Olkon, 40 Cal. 2d 503, 254 P. 2d 520 (1953).

or in available treatments, there is more latitude for the patient's representative or guardian to reach a decision that departs from the patient's wishes.

Any person acting on behalf of an incompetent adult or a minor has a responsibility to act in the best interests of the adult or minor. There are two procedures—organ donation and sterilization—that cannot be authorized by persons making decisions on behalf of incompetent adults or minors without prior court approval. In some states, courts will not approve kidney donations by incompetents[21] and minors without court approval. Furthermore, in those states the guardian may not give consent because the best interests of the minor or the incompetent are not served by the procedure.[22] Courts in other states that have upheld the right of a guardian to authorize kidney donations[23] based their approval on the close relationship between the donor and the proposed recipient, the emotional injury to the donor if the recipient were to die, and the reasonable motivations of the patient and the patient's parent or guardian.

Minors

Parental or guardian consent should be obtained before treatment is given to a minor, unless (1) the patient requires emergency treatment, (2) the situation is one in which the consent of the minor has been statutorily declared to be sufficient, or (3) treatment has been ordered by a court or other legal authority.

Emergency Care

As with adults, consent for treatment of a minor is implied in medical emergencies when an immediate threat to the patient's life or health exists. If the health care provider believes that the patient's parents would refuse consent to emergency treatment and if time permits, the health care provider should seek court authorization for treatment or notify the appropriate government agency responsible for seeking court authorization. If the patient requires immediate treatment, the provider in most cases should treat the minor, even if the parents object. The hospital, with the help of its legal counsel, should establish policies for responding to these situations.

Emancipated Minors

Emancipated minors may consent to their own medical care. Minors are considered emancipated when they are married or otherwise no longer subject to

---

[21]In re Guardianship of Pescinski, 67 Wis. 2d 4, 226 N.W. 2d 180 (1975).

[22]In re Richardson, 284 So. 2d 185 (La. Ct. App. 1973).

[23]Strunk v. Strunk, 445 S.W. 2d 145 (Ky. 1969); Hart v. Brown, 29 Conn. Super. 368, 289 A. 2d 386 (1972).

parental control or regulation and are not supported by their parents. The specific factors necessary to establish emancipation are usually set forth in a statute and vary from state to state. Some states require that the parent and child agree on the emancipation, so that a minor cannot become emancipated in those states simply by running away from home. In some states, the doctrine of emancipation is established by the courts, and no statutory definition of emancipation exists. Because the doctrine of emancipation is unsettled in many states, hospitals should try to find another basis upon which to treat a minor without parental or guardian consent. A hospital policy established with the advice of legal counsel will help guide practitioners confronted with this issue.

Mature Minors

Mature minors may consent to some medical care under common law and constitutional principles and under the statutes of some states. Many states have treatment of minors statutes that authorize older minors to consent to any medical treatment. The age limits and scope of treatments to which a minor may consent vary from state to state. Many states have special laws concerning minors' consent to venereal disease and substance abuse treatment without regard to age. In states that do not have an applicable consent statute for minors, there are minimal risks associated with providing necessary treatment to mature minors with only parental consent. The oldest minor who was treated solely on his own consent and who won a reported lawsuit based on lack of parental consent was 15 years old. In that case, the minor consented to removal of some skin for a donation to another person for a skin graft operation. The court found, however, that the procedure was not necessary, and that parental consent should have been obtained.[24]

The right of privacy in the United States Constitution restricts the state's authority to mandate parental involvement in certain decisions concerning reproduction, such as termination of pregnancy. When treating any minor, however, it is prudent to urge that the minor involve his or her parents in making consent decisions. When a mature minor refuses to permit parental involvement, the health care provider can give the necessary care without substantial risk based on the minor's consent alone, unless there is likelihood of harm to the minor or others that can only be avoided through parental involvement. When the likelihood of such harm arises, parents should usually be involved, unless state law forbids notification of the parents.

Parental or Guardian Consent

Either parent can give legally effective consent for treatment of a minor child, except when the parents are legally separated or divorced. While it is not necessary

---

[24]Bonner v. Moran, 126 F. 2d 121 (D.C. Cir. 1941).

to determine the wishes of both parents, if a provider knows or suspects that one parent objects, the provider should use caution and seek the advice of its legal counsel. In the case of *In re Rotkowitz*,[25] the court authorized surgical correction of a child's deformity when the parents disagreed. When the parents are legally separated or divorced, usually only the consent of the custodial parent must be obtained unless there is an agreement between the parents that both must agree. The provider should rely upon the parent or parents to provide information that substantiates the authority of one or both of them to consent to the minor's care.

RESPONSIBILITY FOR SECURING CONSENT

It is the physician's responsibility to provide the necessary information to the patient concerning his or her condition and proposed treatment and to obtain informed consent before proceeding with diagnostic and therapeutic procedures. Other independent practitioners who order procedures have a similar responsibility concerning those procedures. The hospital is generally not liable for the failure of the physician or other independent practitioner to secure informed consent, unless the physician is an employee or otherwise acting on behalf of the hospital.[26] Some states have codified this principle in their statutes. For example, Ohio Rev. Code Ann. §2317.54 states "[a] hospital shall not be held liable for a physician's failure to obtain an informed consent from his patient prior to a surgical or medical procedure, unless the physician is an employee of the hospital."

One of the earliest court decisions addressing physician liability for operating without consent, *Schloendorff v. Society of New York Hospital*,[27] observed that while the hospital is generally not liable for operations without consent by physicians who are independent contractors, the hospital may be liable for failing to intervene when it has actual knowledge that the procedure is being performed without required informed consent. Some attorneys believe that this could be extended to situations in which the hospital should have known there was no authorization.

In *Magana v. Elie*,[28] an Illinois court suggested that a hospital may be liable for an independent physician's failure to obtain informed consent based on the concept of corporate negligence. This case not only breaks with precedent in a number of states but also appears to be the broadest extension to date of the scope of legal duties owed directly by hospitals to patients. While the case may be an aberration, a medical records practitioner in a state in which the corporate

---

[25]175 Misc. 948, 25 N.Y.S. 2d 624 (Dom. Rel. Ct. 1941).

[26]Fiorentino v. Wenger, 19 N.Y. 2d 407, 227 N.E. 2d 296 (1967).

[27]211 N.Y. 125, 105 N.E. 92 (1914).

[28]108 Ill. App. 3d 1028, 439 N.E. 2d 1319 (1982).

negligence doctrine has been expanding should ensure that a procedure is in place to monitor physicians' efforts to obtain informed consent from patients treated in the hospital and for taking corrective action when appropriate consent is not obtained. (For a discussion of corporate negligence theories, see Chapter 10.)

Medical records practitioners can determine that documentation is in the patient's medical record substantiating informed consent; they cannot judge the adequacy of the consent. Hospital administration and medical staff officers should make certain that medical staff bylaws clearly place the responsibility of obtaining informed consent on the treating physician. Hospital employees (e.g., nurses and resident physicians) should assist the physician in accordance with a carefully prepared institutional policy. It is generally recognized that it is not feasible for the hospital to be responsible for the adequacy of information a physician gives his or her patient in order for the patient to make an informed decision. The monitoring necessary to enforce such a rule could destroy the physician-patient relationship. However, the hospital can be held liable for failing to intervene if it knew the physician's disclosure was not adequate.

There is disagreement concerning the appropriate role of hospital employees in the consent process. Some hospitals permit nurses to obtain the required signature of the patient on the consent form once the physician has informed the patient of proposed procedures and obtained the patient's verbal authority to proceed with treatment. Other hospitals permit nurses to provide some or all of the information necessary for the patient to give an informed consent. Although both of these approaches provide the patient with some or all of the information necessary for an informed consent, they could impair the physician-patient relationship by reducing the opportunity for adequate communication and negotiation. These practices could also shift the liability for inadequacies of the information the patient receives to the hospital as the employer of the nurse. To avoid these adverse consequences, some hospitals prohibit nurses from securing consents. In hospitals where this limitation on the nurses' role is not practical, nurses who secure signatures on consent forms should not attempt to answer patient questions concerning the procedure. If the patient seeks additional information or expresses reluctance to consent, the nurse should contact the physician rather than attempting to convince the patient to sign the form.

Although participation of hospital nurses in the consent process is permissible under the law of most states, hospitals should use caution in establishing consent procedures that involve nurses. The soundest approach is to require the person recommending the treatment to provide the patient sufficient information to make an informed decision but to permit nurses to document the physician's consent conference with the patient by obtaining the patient's signature on the hospital's consent form.

The routine use of a standard consent form before performing certain procedures may protect the hospital from the risk of liability based on lack of consent.

A battery consent form described later in this chapter will fulfill this purpose. The purpose of the standard consent form, therefore, is twofold: (1) to document that the physician discussed the information required by state law for informed consent, and (2) to protect the hospital from an action in battery for treating without consent.

The role of hospital employees in completing a consent form should be limited to (1) screening for completion of the form or alternative authorization to ascertain that the hospital has documented the patient's consent in accordance with established hospital policy, and (2) informing the responsible physician when the patient has concerns or questions about the consent form, seems to be confused about the proposed treatment, or has withdrawn or retracted consent previously given. The patient may withdraw his or her consent at any time, even if the patient has already signed a consent form. If the physician does not respond appropriately, medical staff and hospital officials should be notified in order to determine whether intervention is necessary.

DOCUMENTATION

Consent is not merely a form, despite common belief to the contrary. The patient and all involved with providing health care services should understand clearly that obtaining the patient's consent means obtaining the patient's authorization for diagnosis and treatment. Once the patient has authorized the proposed care, it is important to document that authorization in the patient's medical record. Most attorneys who represent physicians and hospitals agree that the best way to document informed consent is to secure the signature of the patient or the patient's representative on an appropriate form. If there is a proper form signed by the appropriate person, the courts usually accept the form as proof of consent, unless the plaintiff can prove that special circumstances require that the form be disregarded. A few attorneys disagree with the desirability of a form signed by the patient and recommend that the physician write a note in the medical record concerning the discussion of consent with the patient or the patient's representative. These attorneys are concerned that courts will view a consent form as all the information given to the patient and not believe the physician's testimony that he or she gave additional information. Hospitals using consent forms should indicate that the form does not contain all the information provided by the physician.

The Joint Commission on Accreditation of Hospitals (JCAH) accreditation standards concerning medical records require "evidence of appropriate informed consent" for procedures or treatments for which it is required by hospital policy.[29]

---

[29]JOINT COMMISSION ON ACCREDITATION OF HOSPITALS, ACCREDITATION MANUAL FOR HOSPITALS, 81 (1984).

The JCAH does not specify the procedures or treatments and does not require the consent to be documented by the signature of the patient or the patient's representative. Although several accredited hospitals do not require the patient's signature on a progress note or consent form, the more prudent practice is for the hospital or its medical staff to require the appropriate practitioner to obtain a consent on a standard form or in a progress note signed by the patient prior to performing certain procedures or treatments.

A hospital's consent policy should require that the patient or the patient's representative provide a signed consent for certain types of procedures, including (1) major or minor invasive surgery, (2) all procedures that involve more than a slight risk of harm, (3) all forms of radiological therapy, (4) electroconvulsive therapy, (5) all experimental procedures, and (6) all procedures for which consent forms are required by statute or regulation. The hospital and its medical staff should outline more specifically in hospital policy the treatments for which a signed consent is required.

In developing or applying a policy concerning the use of consent forms, hospitals should be aware that the actual process of providing information to the person giving consent and of determining the person's decision is more important than the consent form. The form is only evidence of the consent process and is not a substitute for the consent process. Hospitals should designate a senior administrator or medical staff officer to determine that actual consent exists even when the form has been lost or inadvertently not signed prior to treatment, or when other circumstances make it difficult to secure the necessary signature. In all cases, the information on a consent form must be consistent with the information given the patient by the physician. If the physician gives information different from that on the standard consent form, he or she should revise the form before the patient signs it.

CONSENT FORMS

There are three basic types of consent forms: (1) the blanket consent form, (2) the battery consent form, and (3) the detailed consent form.

Blanket Consent Forms

In the past, many hospitals provided consent forms that authorized any procedure the physician wished to perform. In cases such as *Rogers v. Lumbermens Mutual Casualty Co.*,[30] courts have ruled that these blanket consent forms are not evidence of consent to major procedures because the procedure is not specified on

---

[30]119 So. 2d 649 (La. Ct. App. 1960).

the form. While some attorneys recommend the continued use of a blanket admission consent form to cover the procedures for which individual special consent is not sought, most attorneys believe these admission forms provide no more protection than the implied consent that is inferred from admission and submission to minor procedures. Moreover, because they show a failure to document proper consent for major procedures, blanket admission consent forms used for such procedures can be harmful to the hospital's and physician's positions in defense of a malpractice lawsuit arising from such procedures.

Battery Consent Forms

For major procedures, most hospitals now utilize consent forms that provide space for the name and description of the specific procedure. In addition, the form states that (1) the person signing has been told about the medical condition, consequences, risks, and alternative treatments; and (2) all the person's questions have been answered to his or her satisfaction. This type of consent form will usually defeat a claim of battery if the proper person signs the form and the procedures described in the form are the ones performed on the patient. Following the procedures concerning the use of the form provides strong support for the hospital's position that the person who signed was adequately informed. It also provides support for the physician's assertion that the patient was informed. However, it is still possible that the person who signed a battery consent form could convince a court that he or she did not receive information concerning consequences, risks, and alternatives to the treatment, especially if someone other than the physician obtained the patient's signature.

Detailed Consent Forms

Some physicians use forms that include written detail describing the medical condition, procedure, consequences, risks, alternatives to treatment, and alternative treatments. Such forms have been mandated for federally funded sterilizations and research involving human subjects. It is much more difficult for the patient to prove that the information included in the form was not disclosed. However, detailed consent forms can be costly and time consuming to prepare for each individual procedure, and the risks and alternatives they describe change so that the forms can become obsolete. Thus, some physicians who use detailed consent forms use them only for procedures such as cosmetic surgery for which there is a higher risk of misunderstanding and unsatisfactory results.

Challenges to Consent Forms

Although consent forms are strong evidence of informed consent, they are usually not conclusive. The person challenging the adequacy of the consent process will have an opportunity to convince the court that informed consent was not actually obtained. For example, the person who signed the form may prove he or she was not competent due to the effects of medication. Thus, it is important that the explanation be given and the signature be obtained at a time when the consenting party is capable of understanding the decision he or she is making. Consent forms may also be challenged on the basis that the wording was too technical or that the form was written in a language the patient could not understand. Although persons are presumed to have read and understood documents they have signed, courts will not apply this presumption when the document is too technical or is written in a language not understood by the patient. As a result, it is important that forms are understood by the person signing them. If the person has difficulty understanding English, someone, preferably a hospital employee capable of understanding the technical information, should translate the form. It is usually not necessary to have forms in other languages, although it is advisable to have forms in the primary languages used by a substantial portion of the patients served by the hospital. It is usually sufficient to have the form orally translated and have the translator certify that the form and discussion of the procedure have been orally translated for the person signing the form. If a patient refuses to sign a consent form but is willing to give oral consent after receiving an adequate explanation of the procedures, the fact of oral consent and the reason for the patient's refusal to sign should be documented on the consent form, along with the witnessed signature of the person obtaining the verbal consent.

A consent form may also be challenged on the grounds that the signature was not voluntary. Because the person signing would have to prove that there had been some threat or undue inducement to prove that the signature was coerced, it is difficult to prove coercion. However, if a physician misrepresents the probability of death or injury involved in refusing to undergo the proposed procedure, the patient or the patient's representative might be successful in showing coercion and thereby invalidate the patient's prior consent.

Exculpatory Clauses

Some providers have included exculpatory clauses in their consent forms stating that the person signing the form waives the right to sue for injuries or agrees to limit any claims to not more than a specified amount. Courts will not enforce exculpatory clauses in lawsuits brought by patients against health care providers.

For example, in *Tatham v. Hoke*,[31] the court refused to enforce a $15,000 limit on liability in an agreement the patient signed before surgery. Moreover, courts may invalidate the entire consent form together with such clauses. Courts are hostile to exculpatory language, especially where it is imposed on an individual by a large organization.

Period of Validity of Consent Forms and Withdrawal of Consent

There is no absolute limit on the period of validity of a consent or the documentation of that consent by a signature on a consent form. If the patient's condition or the available treatments change significantly, the earlier consent is no longer valid, and a new consent should be obtained. Otherwise, the consent is valid until it is withdrawn.

Whenever a patient refuses to consent to or withdraws consent for treatment, the attending physician should be notified, and written acknowledgment of the refusal or withdrawal should be obtained after the physician has discussed the implications of the refusal or withdrawal with the patient. These steps generally will protect the hospital from liability. If the patient refuses to sign a form releasing the hospital from responsibility for the consequences of refusal or withdrawal of consent, these facts should be thoroughly documented in the medical record.

Because a claim that consent was withdrawn becomes more credible as time passes, some hospitals obtain a new consent each time the patient is admitted. The consent may be obtained in the physician's office prior to the admission, provided that the time between the consent and the admission is not too long. Some hospitals use a guideline that consent forms should be signed no more than 30 days before the procedure; others require new consents periodically, especially in outpatient treatment settings. Carefully prepared hospital policy should establish guidelines governing the validity of patient consent.

Impact of Statutes

Some states have passed statutes concerning consent forms that must be considered when developing consent forms for use in those states. Several statutes provide that, if the consent form contains certain information and is signed by the appropriate person, it is conclusive evidence of informed consent[32] or creates a presumption of informed consent.[33] Such statutes indicate how the courts will treat forms containing only the information specified in the statute. The statutes do

---

[31]469 F. Supp. 914 (W.D.N.C. 1979), *aff'd*, 622 F. 2d 584, 622 F. 2d 587 (1980).

[32]Nev. Rev. Stat. §41A.110 (1981).

[33]Iowa Code §147.137 (1981).

not apply to forms containing different information. Although it is not a violation of these statutes to use a form that contains different information or to forego the use of a form completely in states that make certain forms conclusive evidence of informed consent, hospitals should be sure that a decision to use forms that do not meet the statutory requirements is based on careful consideration of the risks. In any case, hospitals should not adopt such forms without the advice of their legal counsel.

SUPPLEMENTS TO DOCUMENTATION

Some physicians are now supplementing their explanations to patients of proposed treatment with other educational materials, such as booklets and movies. For example, some physicians are making audiovisual recordings of the consent process to supplement or even substitute for written consent. In addition, some physicians give their patients tests or have their patients write their own consent forms to determine and document the level of understanding. None of these steps is legally required today, but they should be given serious consideration whenever controversial procedures are proposed.

The hospital should adopt policies governing the use of these supplemental materials and should specify how these materials became part of the patient's medical record. If these materials and procedures are used in the hospital, the institution should require that a copy of them be made available to the hospital and, if possible, be made a part of the patient's permanent medical record.

INSTITUTIONAL POLICY ON CONSENT

Hospital administration can do several things to make sure the consent process works to the advantage of the patient, the physician, and the hospital. First, the hospital administrative staff can develop adequate policies that explain consent: what it is, when it is necessary, who must obtain it and when, and in what manner it should be documented. At the same time, administration should make certain such policies are reviewed and updated routinely, with particular attention paid to:

- identifying policies that are not being followed so that appropriate action can be taken
- recognizing when changes in the law, regulations, and licensing and accreditation requirements necessitate a change in policies
- reviewing consent forms to be sure they conform to current requirements and that forms that include preprinted descriptions of risks of or alternatives to the proposed procedures are consistent with current medical knowledge. When

the risks or alternatives change, so should the forms. The review of consent forms should include a review of the procedures and instructions for their use to make sure they are adequate and accurate.

Second, as procedures are developed to implement consent policy, care should be taken to make hospital procedures conducive to patient understanding of the consent he or she is being asked to give and the patient's right to refuse to give consent and to obtain answers to questions prior to giving consent or to signing a consent form. This means that employees involved in obtaining a patient's signature on a consent form must be educated in current consent concepts and in the manner in which to carry out their responsibilities. Of particular concern should be the attitude the employees project to the patient when carrying out this function, since this attitude will reflect positively or negatively on the organization and its approach to the consent process.

Third, a single person should be assigned primary responsibility within the organization to obtain timely and helpful responses to questions concerning consent. If the facility has in-house legal counsel, an attorney may be that person. Otherwise, it should be an individual who has the ability to determine when a situation is such that an attorney's assistance is needed and who can then translate the advice obtained into appropriate action within the facility.

Chapter 8

Medical Records and Hospital Risk Management

Hospital risk management programs depend in large measure upon medical records and medical records practitioners for information necessary to identify potential risks. Medical records practitioners, therefore, can contribute significantly to the success of a risk management program, but to do so, they must have a good working knowledge of risk management principles, program objectives, and how medical records information affects management of potential risk.

This chapter will discuss generally the relationship between hospital quality assurance programs and risk management, the definition of risk management and components of hospital risk management programs, and the use of medical records in risk management, including the role of medical records departments in risk management programs.

NATURE AND PURPOSE OF A HOSPITAL RISK MANAGEMENT PROGRAM

While large industrial corporations, the insurance industry, and other industries have had substantial experience developing and implementing risk management and quality control programs, the hospital industry's experience with risk management principles and techniques is relatively new. Hospitals were slow to recognize the importance of risk management partly because the doctrine of charitable immunity[1] protected the hospital industry in many states from negligence liability actions. With the abolition of the doctrine, the exposure to medical malpractice claims of hospitals expanded enormously. Other developments have also fostered this recognition of risk management, including the malpractice crisis of the mid 1970s, and the imposition of the requirement, beginning in 1980 and continuing to

---

[1]For a discussion of the doctrine of charitable immunity, see Chapter 10.

the present, that all hospitals accredited by the JCAH have in place comprehensive quality assurance programs.[2] Despite this delayed recognition, the "hospital industry's familiarity with risk management principles and applications has increased dramatically in the last 10 years."[3]

THE RELATIONSHIP BETWEEN QUALITY ASSURANCE AND RISK MANAGEMENT

Although the purposes of hospital risk management programs and quality assurance programs are often viewed as complementary to one another, "the [conceptual and functional] separation of risk management and quality assurance into different activities is an artifact of their historical development."[4] Recently, however, hospitals have begun to recognize the importance of integrating risk management with quality assurance, as the sources of data relied on by each of these two disciplines are substantially similar, and the data may be obtained in a more cost-effective manner if properly coordinated. Nevertheless, quality assurance and risk management differ in at least one significant respect related to the perspective each brings to the analysis of data. Quality assurance generally approaches the identification and analysis of patient care problems and issues from the perspective with regard to goals of what should occur in the hospital, whereas risk management tends to approach these tasks from the perspective of what should not occur in the hospital. Quality assurance often looks at patterns of activity, while risk management often concentrates on specific incidents.

Quality assurance, therefore, has a more global perspective reflected in the 1984 JCAH *Accreditation Manual for Hospitals,* which states, with respect to quality assurance, that

> [t]he hospital shall demonstrate a consistent endeavor to deliver patient care that is optimal within available resources and consistent with achievable goals. A major component in the application of this principle is the operation of a quality assurance program.[5]

---

[2]*See, e.g.,* JOINT COMMISSION ON ACCREDITATION OF HOSPITALS, ACCREDITATION MANUAL FOR HOSPITALS 147–149 (1984).

[3]Schmitt, *Risk Management—It's More Than Just Insurance,* HEALTH CARE FINANCIAL MANAGEMENT (March 1983), at 10.

[4]E. RICHARDS III & K. RATHBUN, MEDICAL RISK MANAGEMENT (1983) 51 [herein cited as RICHARDS & RATHBUN].

[5]JCAH, ACCREDITATION MANUAL FOR HOSPITALS 147 (1984).

The JCAH standards consider the following components to be essential to a sound quality assurance program:

- Identification of important or potential problems, or related concerns, in the care of patients.
- Objective assessment of the cause and scope of problems or concerns, including the determination of priorities for both investigating and resolving problems. Ordinarily, priorities shall be related to the degree of impact on patient care that can be expected if the problem remains unresolved.
- Implementation, by appropriate individuals or through designated mechanisms, of decisions or actions that are designed to eliminate, insofar as possible, identified problems.
- Monitoring activities designed to ensure that the desired result is achieved and sustained.
- Documentation that reasonably substantiates the effectiveness of the overall program to enhance patient care and to ensure sound clinical performance.[6]

DEFINITION OF RISK MANAGEMENT

Some confusion exists over the proper definition of risk management in the hospital industry because the term is not self-defining.[7] Nevertheless, if a risk is defined as "an exposure to the chance of injury or financial loss,"[8] then the management of risk in a hospital is the process of identifying, evaluating, and treating the risk of financial loss to the hospital. Exposure to financial loss or risk is generated by the hospital's property, personnel, and activities. At least one commentator has noted that

> as these organizational elements interact, an unlimited number of circumstances arise that present a possibility of loss, even if a loss does not actually occur. As a result, hospital risk management is not limited to direct patient care activities.[9]

Whether a risk management program can effectively undertake prevention of all preventable financial risks, however, is questionable. In practice, hospital risk

---

[6]*Id.* at 147–148.

[7]Schmitt, *Risk Management—It's More Than Just Insurance,* HEALTH CARE FINANCIAL MANAGEMENT (March 1983), at 11.

[8]RICHARDS & RATHBUN, *supra* note 4, at 21.

[9]Schmitt, *Risk Management—It's More Than Just Insurance,* HEALTH CARE FINANCIAL MANAGEMENT (March 1983), at 11.

managers seldom take responsibility for the financial risk associated with a business failure, which is more likely within the responsibility of the institution's chief financial officer. Risk management programs, like other hospital activities, must exist in the complex political structure of the hospital. If the program takes on more than it can manage or more than institutional politics will tolerate, the program's effectiveness will suffer.

Moreover, although an ideal risk management program would eventually eliminate all risks and all possibility of exposure to financial loss, this goal is impossible for hospitals to achieve, as the rendering of medical care is unavoidably accompanied by the potential for injury. Thus, the definition of risk management must be tempered by reality; the cost to prevent risks must not exceed the cost of the risk itself.

THE RISK MANAGEMENT PROCESS AND THE COMPONENTS OF A HOSPITAL RISK MANAGEMENT PROGRAM

Understanding and appreciating the elements of loss exposure is essential to comprehending the scope and depth of the risk management process. Risk management theory states that any given loss exposure has three elements:

1. The subject of a loss includes assets or any tangible owned thing of value, as well as the income produced therefrom.
2. The cause of a loss includes natural, human, and economic forces causing losses, such as, for example, fire, theft, medical malpractice, unemployment, etc.
3. The value of a loss includes the relative financial effect on the organization, such as, for example, the percentage of hospital assets lost or committed to payment for the loss.[10]

Consequently, hospital risk management programs should be designed to permit monitoring of all of the hospital's financial resources as well as any actual or potential threats to those resources.[11] This does not mean, however, that the risk management program should take responsibility for the institution's financial and personnel departments. It means that information concerning these areas should be available to the risk manager, and all departments of the hospital should coordinate their efforts to reduce loss risks.

---

[10]*Id.*
[11]*Id.*

The structural process that most hospitals have designed to identify and minimize the economic threats arising from these loss exposures typically includes six identifiable components:

1. identification
2. evaluation
3. elimination
4. reduction
5. transfer of liability
6. insurance

Prospective, concurrent, and retrospective identification of loss exposure is the most important component of any hospital risk management program and the most difficult element for any risk manager to master. Tools that help identify loss exposure include checklists or inventories of assets and important resources, operational flow charts and financial statements, patient incident or unusual occurrence reports, medical audits, interdisciplinary risk management or quality assurance committees, and constant communication among hospital staff and physicians about patient complaints and problems.

After a loss exposure has been identified, efforts are focused on an evaluation of the loss exposure to determine its economic threat to the hospital. Evaluation of loss exposure is based on three predictive factors:

1. loss frequency, or the number of times the incidence giving rise to the loss is likely to occur
2. loss severity, or the estimated dollar loss of each individual incident
3. loss dispersion, or the range in estimated dollar losses for similar incidents[12]

Individuals responsible for risk management in hospitals, using these three factors, rely on hospital-specific and industrywide data of documented past experience with identified incidents to evaluate the loss exposure. Included in this process is the use of probability theory, both formal (using the laws and principles of probability theory) and informal (using the experience and judgment of the risk manager with respect to past hospital experience and community standards).

Emerging from and included within the evaluation process is a risk classification system, based on the economic consequences of the occurrence of specific individual risks. Classification systems vary, but they generally break down into the following categories:

---

[12]*Id.* at 16.

1. Prevented risks: These are risks whose cost of occurrence is higher than their cost of management and whose occurrence may result in the assessment of additional legal sanctions (e.g., punitive damages) against the hospital. Included within this class are intentional torts and injuries determined to have been caused by gross negligence.
2. Normally prevented risks: These are risks whose cost of occurrence is greater than the cost of their management but whose occurrence will be considered to be the result of negligent conduct. Included within this class are most negligent injuries (e.g., medical malpractice) and most types of product liability actions.
3. Managed risks: These are risks whose cost of occurrence is only slightly greater than their cost of management. Injuries that occur as the result of a risk within this class usually require the injured party to prove that the defendant owed a special duty to the injured party, a duty that was breached by the defendant.
4. Unprevented risks: These are risks whose cost of occurrence is less than their cost of management.
5. Unpreventable risks: These are risks whose occurrence is unmanageable.[13]

Proper and accurate classification of a risk or loss exposure into one of these classes is difficult but very important, as the class of a risk determines how much effort must be expended to prevent the risk from occurring.[14] Misclassification of a risk can result in large financial losses to an institution. Consequently, classifications of risks should be periodically reviewed to "determine if the cost of the risk-taking behavior has changed, thereby altering the classification."[15]

The remaining four components of the risk management process are essentially loss control techniques that are designed to "change loss exposures by reducing the frequency, financial seriousness, or variation of losses."[16] The technique used depends, in substantial part, on the class to which the risk or loss exposure has been assigned.

Elimination of a loss exposure or risk, once it has been identified and evaluated, is mandatory for prevented risks and may be appropriate for certain normally prevented risks. For example, a hospital may choose to avoid a risk altogether by not recruiting physicians whose practice is associated with very high risk surgical procedures because the hospital does not consider it prudent to invite such exposure to potential loss.

---

[13]RICHARDS & RATHBUN, *supra* note 4, at 25.

[14]*Id.*

[15]*Id.*

[16]Schmitt, *Risk Management—It's More Than Just Insurance*, HEALTH CARE FINANCIAL MANAGEMENT (March 1983), at 17.

Risks that cannot be eliminated should be reduced and include normally prevented risks and many managed risks. A substantial amount of a risk manager's time and effort is typically devoted to reducing normally prevented risks and many managed risks. It is clear that the legal liability that arises from a normally prevented risk is inextricably linked with the risk management efforts devoted to preventing such risks.[17] That is, the greater and the clearer the legal liability associated with a normally prevented risk, the greater the risk manager's effort to prevent its occurrence. Many of the precautions commonly thought of as forming the standard of care, e.g., sterile technique, sponge counts, and proper diagnostic tests and workups, are part of the risk management prevention strategy, and "the explicit description and documentation of the precautions taken can prevent many malpractice suits from being filed."[18]

The fifth component of the risk management process, transfer of liability, does not change the actual loss exposure, as is true with efforts directed toward eliminating or reducing risks. Rather, a transfer of liability is a loss financing technique designed to provide funds for paying losses incurred as the result of some normally prevented risks, managed risks, and a few unprevented risks. Exculpatory agreements limiting legal liability are the primary tools used to transfer liability. Examples include having patients sign an agreement releasing the hospital from liability and responsibility for theft of personal property not left in the hospital's safe,[19] and the use of warranties and hold harmless and indemnification agreements with manufacturers and suppliers of drugs, equipment, and services to the hospital.

The last component of the risk management process is utilized for unpreventable risks and for all the other classes of risk as a safeguard against both anticipated and unanticipated losses. Insurance is another loss financing technique that does not alter the actual loss exposure but simply funds the losses that occur as a result of the risk. Insurance utilized by hospitals is not just limited to malpractice insurance. It includes general liability insurance, fire insurance, business interruption insurance, officers and directors liability insurance, and other types of insurance. In addition to commercial insurance, many hospitals have established planned programs of funded risk retention (or self-insurance) as a more cost-effective method for insuring against loss than commercial insurance.

The importance of hospital risk management programs to the effective delivery of quality medical care has been acknowledged by the federal government [20] and

---

[17]RICHARDS & RATHBUN, *supra* note 4, at 29.

[18]*Id.*

[19]Schmitt, *Risk Management—It's More Than Just Insurance*, HEALTH CARE FINANCIAL MANAGEMENT (March 1983), at 20.

[20]MEDICARE AND MEDICAID GUIDE (CCH) ¶5999x–32 (1983). This section provides that a provider must have an adequate risk management program to examine the cause of losses and to take action to reduce the frequency and severity of losses in order to be reimbursed for self-insurance.

more than half the states that have either malpractice statutes or hospital licensing statutes requiring hospitals to have risk management programs.[21] Many of the state statutes establish minimum requirements for such risk management programs, which are similar to those discussed. The Rhode Island statute is typical.

Every hospital licensed in this state and its insurance carrier shall cooperatively, as part of their administrative functions, establish an internal risk management program which shall include at least the following components:

(1) an in-hospital grievance or complaint mechanism designed to process and resolve as promptly and effectively as possible grievances by patients or their representatives related to incidents, billing, inadequacies in treatment, and other factors known to influence medical malpractice claims and suits. Such mechanism shall include appointment of a representative accountable to the hospital administration who shall anticipate and monitor on a day-to-day basis such grievances and administer said mechanism;

(2) the continuous collection of data by each hospital with respect to its negative health care outcomes (whether or not they give rise to claims), patient grievances, claims suits, professional liability premiums, settlements, awards, allocated and administrative costs of claims handling, costs of patient injury prevention and safety engineering activities, and other relevant statistics and information;

(3) medical care evaluation mechanisms, which shall include but not be limited to tissue committees or medical audit committees, to review the appropriateness of procedures performed, to periodically assess the quality of medical care being provided at an institution, and to pass on the necessity of surgery;

(4) education programs for the hospital's staff personnel engaged in patient care activities dealing with patient safety, medical injury prevention, the legal aspects of patient care, problems of communication and rapport with patients, and other relevant factors known to influence malpractice claims and suits.[22]

---

[21]Schmitt, *Risk Management—It's More Than Just Insurance*, HEALTH CARE FINANCIAL MANAGEMENT (March 1983), at 10.

[22]R.I. Gen. Laws §23–17–24 (1979).

It is evident that medical records form an essential part of the data used in risk management, and that the medical records department in all hospitals is an integral part of the risk management and quality assurance process.[23]

THE USE OF MEDICAL RECORDS IN RISK MANAGEMENT

The medical record is the basic document for all quality assurance and risk management activities.[24] The JCAH minimum requirements for a medical record are discussed in Chapter 1 and will not be reviewed at length in this chapter.[25] Nevertheless, certain JCAH requirements that are important from the perspective of quality assurance and risk management will be highlighted here. Particular attention shall be given to reviewing potential problems in record management, some of the various uses of medical records in quality assurance audits, and recommendations for a simple risk management program within a medical records department itself.

The medical records department and its personnel occupy an important position in ensuring that hospital staff members who have either the authority to make entries in the medical record or the right to examine the record do so in accordance with applicable laws, regulations, and accreditation standards. For JCAH-accredited hospitals, the accreditation standards recognize five basic purposes for maintaining medical records, which are also important to the proper functioning of a risk management and quality assurance program.[26]

The first purpose is "to serve as a basis for planning patient care and for continuity in the evaluation of the patient's condition and treatment."[27] In this instance, the purpose of the medical record as an ongoing record of care on which medical treatment decisions are based and justified is consistent with the hospital's responsibility, as part of its quality assurance functions, to audit and evaluate the care rendered a patient at any particular time. This is extremely important to the management of risk where a patient is cared for "by several physicians who must coordinate their different treatment plans."[28]

The second purpose identified by JCAH for which medical records are maintained is "to furnish documentary evidence of the course of the patient's medical evaluation, treatment, and change in condition during the hospital stay, during an ambulatory care or emergency visit to the hospital, or while being followed in a

---

[23]JCAH, ACCREDITATION MANUAL FOR HOSPITALS 86–87 (1984).

[24]RICHARDS & RATHBUN *supra* note 4, at 151.

[25]*See* Chapter 1.

[26]JCAH, ACCREDITATION MANUAL FOR HOSPITALS 79 (1984).

[27]*Id.*

[28]RICHARDS & RATHBUN *supra* note 4, at 152.

hospital-administered home care program."[29] This is important for both the medical needs of the patient and the management of risk in the hospital.[30] For example, planning a patient's future treatment depends on the patient's response to treatment, while from the risk management perspective, the record presumably permits the hospital to demonstrate, in the event a claim is made against the hospital, that the patient was cared for in accordance with the applicable standard of care.[31]

The third purpose is "to document communication between the responsible practitioner and any other health professional who contributed to the patient's care."[32] Some experts have noted that this "is a legally important and often overlooked purpose of the medical record. The different sections of the medical record do not exist in isolation. Someone caring for the patient must be familiar with the patient as a whole."[33] Inconsistencies within a particular patient's medical record are not difficult to identify through a medical care audit. A medical records department, through the hospital's medical care audit function, should periodically review nursing notes, physicians' progress notes, consultants' reports, and laboratory test results for inconsistencies. Periodic audits of this kind are helpful not only to the effective management of risk, but also for the purpose of determining whether the medical record satisfies the standard of "documenting that there was communication among the members of the health care team."[34]

The fourth purpose identified by JCAH is "to assist in protecting the legal interest of the patient, the hospital and the responsible practitioner,"[35] while the fifth purpose is "to provide data for use in continuing education and in research."[36] The significance of each of these to risk management and to quality assurance and control is evident.

Other JCAH standards that are important to a hospital's risk management program include the requirements that a hospital use the unit record system;[37] that all medical records be confidential, secure, current, authenticated, legible and complete;[38] and that "the role of medical record personnel in the overall hospital quality assurance program and in committee functions . . . be defined."[39]

---

[29]JCAH, ACCREDITATION MANUAL FOR HOSPITALS 79 (1984).

[30]RICHARDS & RATHBUN *supra* note 4, at 153.

[31]*Id.*

[32]JCAH, ACCREDITATION MANUAL FOR HOSPITALS 79 (1984).

[33]RICHARDS & RATHBUN *supra* note 4, at 153.

[34]*Id.* at 154.

[35]JCAH, ACCREDITATION MANUAL FOR HOSPITALS 79 (1984).

[36]*Id.*

[37]*Id.* at 80.

[38]*Id.* at 83.

[39]*Id.* at 86.

Thus, the medical records department's role in the risk management program of each hospital should include the following components:

- Supervision of data gathering, with documentation of the data produced at all levels.
- Training of clerical personnel engaged in locating the most useful sources of required information.
- Determination of the incidence of relevant data requested for the use of committees and individuals.
- Screening of medical records for compliance with established clinical criteria and designated exceptions or equivalents as established by the medical staff.
- Participation in the selection and design of forms used in the medical record, and in the determination of the sequence and format of the contents of the medical record.
- Suggesting to the professional staffs methods of improving the primary source data that will facilitate their retrieval, analysis, tabulation, and display.
- Performing ongoing informational surveillance of practice indicators or monitors for medical staff review.
- Ensuring the provision of a mechanism to protect the privacy of patients and practitioners whose records are involved in quality assessment activities.[40]
- Reviewing all requests for access to or copies of medical records by patients and third parties to determine their validity under applicable state law.[41]
- Reviewing all medical records for which requests for access to or copies of medical records have been received from, in particular, patients, attorneys, and court orders or subpoenas, to determine whether it is apparent from the medical record whether the hospital has potential exposure to liability. Medical records personnel should confer closely with the hospital's risk manager and legal counsel in this function, as the early identification of potential claims against a hospital can greatly enhance and facilitate the hospital's defense to any claim that may be brought against it.

Each of these components of a risk management program within the medical records department should be evaluated within the needs of the institution and available personnel and resources, so that the most effective risk management program may be implemented within the hospital.

---

[40]*Id.* at 87.

[41]For a thorough discussion of the legal requirements governing access to medical records, *see supra* Chapter 4.

Chapter 9

Introduction to the
American Legal System

The law affects many of the judgments that health record administrators, health professionals, and technical staff must make each day. The decisions they make may have significant potential legal consequences. Since it is impractical, if not impossible, to secure professional legal advice before making every decision, medical records administrators must develop an understanding of the medical records law so they will be able to exercise judgment consistent with applicable law and to identify problems that require expert legal counsel.

The purpose of this chapter is to set forth general information about law, including the mechanics of the American legal system and the roles of the branches of government in creating, administering, and enforcing the law

THE NATURE OF LAW

According to most definitions, law is, in essence, a system of principles and processes by which people who live in a society deal with their disputes and problems, seeking to solve or settle them without resort to force. Law governs the relationships among private individuals, organizations, and government. Through law, society establishes standards of behavior and the means to enforce those standards. Law that deals with the relationships between private parties is called private law, whereas public law deals with the relationships between private parties and government. The increasing complexity of society and life in the United States has been accompanied by a broadening of the scope of public law, and the regulation of private persons and institutions has become more pervasive.

Private law is concerned with the recognition and enforcement of the rights and duties of private individuals and organizations. Legal actions between private parties are of two types: tort and contract. In a tort action, one party asserts that wrongful conduct on the part of the other party has caused harm and seeks compensation for the harm suffered. In a contract action, one party asserts that, in failing to fulfill an obligation, the other party has breached the contract, and the party seeks either compensation or performance of the obligations as a remedy.

An important part of public law is criminal law, which proscribes conduct considered injurious to the public order and provides for punishment of those found to have engaged in proscribed conduct. Public law consists also of an enormous variety of regulations designed to advance societal objectives by requiring private individuals and organizations to follow specified courses of action in connection with their activities. While there are criminal penalties for those who do not abide by the regulations, the purpose of public law is to secure compliance with and attain the goals of the law, not to punish offenders.

The formulation of public policy concerning health care has thrust hospitals into the arena of legislative debate about health planning, containment of health care costs, quality of clinical laboratory operations, medical device safety, research with human subjects, confidentiality of patient information, labor relations, employment policies, facility safety, and other important topics. The object of public law at both the federal and state level is to deal with societal problems of a broad nature.

Law serves as a guide to conduct. Most disputes or controversies that are covered by legal principles or rules are resolved without resort to the courts. Thus, each party's awareness of the law and of the relative likelihood of success in court affects its willingness to modify its original position and reach a compromise acceptable to both sides.

SOURCES OF LAW

The four primary sources of law are federal and state constitutions, federal and state statutes, the decisions and rules of administrative agencies, and the decisions of the courts.

The Constitution

The Constitution of the United States is the supreme law of the land. It establishes the general organization of the federal government, grants certain powers to the federal government, and places certain limits on what the federal and state governments may do.

The Constitution establishes and grants certain powers to the three branches of the federal government—the legislative, executive, and judicial branches. The Constitution is also a grant of power from the states to the federal government. The federal government has only the powers granted to it by the Constitution. These powers are both express and implied. The express powers include, for example, the power to collect taxes, declare war, and regulate interstate commerce. The Constitution also grants the federal government broad implied powers to enact laws "necessary and proper" for exercising its other powers. When the federal government establishes law, within the scope of its powers, that law is supreme. All conflicting state and local laws are invalid.

The Constitution also places certain limits on what the federal and state governments may do. The most famous limits on federal power are the first ten amendments to the Constitution, the Bill of Rights. The basic rights protected by the Bill of Rights include the right to free speech, free exercise of religion, freedom from unreasonable searches and seizures, trial by jury, and the right not to be deprived of life, liberty, or property without due process of law. State powers are limited by the Fourteenth Amendment, as follows: ". . . nor shall any state deprive any person of life, liberty or property, without due process of law; nor deny to any person within its jurisdiction the equal protection of the laws." These clauses of the Fourteenth Amendment are frequently referred to as the due process clause and the equal protection clause. The right of privacy is another constitutional limitation on both state and federal governmental power that frequently affects hospitals and health care professionals.

Due Process of Law

The due process clause imposes restrictions and duties only on state action, not on private action. Actions by state and local governmental agencies, including public hospitals, are considered to be state actions and must comply with due process requirements. Actions by private individuals at the behest of the state can also be subject to the requirements. In the past, private hospitals were considered to be engaged in state action when they were regulated or partially funded by governmental agencies. Today it is rare for private hospitals to be considered engaged in state action on this basis.

The due process clause applies to state actions that deprive a person of "life, liberty or property." In this context, a position or a particular status can be considered property. For example, a physician's appointment to the medical staff of a public hospital and a hospital's institutional licensure from the state are considered property rights. Thus, in the first example, the public hospital must provide due process to the medical staff applicant, while in the second situation the state and local governmental agencies provide due process to the hospital.

The process that is due varies somewhat depending on the situation. Due process consists primarily of two elements: (1) the rules being applied must be reasonable and not vague or arbitrary; and (2) fair procedures must be followed in enforcing the rules. Two fundamental procedural protections must be offered: (1) notice of the proposed action; and (2) an opportunity to present evidence as to why the disputed action should not be taken. The phrase "due process" in the

Fourteenth Amendment also has been interpreted by the United States Supreme Court to include nearly all of the rights in the Bill of Rights. Thus, state governments may not infringe on those rights.

Equal Protection of the Laws

The equal protection clause also restricts state action. The concept of equal protection is intended to ensure that like persons are treated in a like fashion. As a result, the equal protection clause is concerned with the legitimacy of the classification used to distinguish persons for various legal purposes. The determination of whether a particular difference between persons can justify a particular difference in rules or procedures can be difficult. In general, courts require that the government agency justify the difference with a rational reason. The major exception to this standard is the strict scrutiny courts apply to distinctions based on particular "suspect classifications," such as race.

Right of Privacy

In *Griswold v. Connecticut,*[1] the United States Supreme Court recognized a constitutional right of privacy. The Supreme Court has ruled that the right of privacy limits governmental authority to regulate contraception, abortion, and other decisions affecting reproduction. Several state courts have ruled that the right of privacy permits terminally ill patients and those acting on their behalf to choose to withhold or withdraw medical treatment.[2]

State Constitutions

Each state also has its own constitution. The state constitution establishes the organization of the state government, grants certain powers to the state government, and places certain limits on what the state government may do.

Statutes

Another major source of law is statutory law, which is the law enacted by a legislature. Legislative bodies include the United States Congress, state legislatures, and local legislative bodies, such as city councils and county boards of supervisors. Congress has only the powers delegated by the Constitution, but those powers have been broadly interpreted. State legislatures have all powers not denied by the United States Constitution, by federal laws enacted within the authority of the federal government, or by the state constitution. Local legislative

---

[1]381 U.S. 479 (1965).

[2]*See, e.g.,* Satz v. Perlmutter, 379 So. 2d 359 (Fla. 1980).

bodies have only those powers granted by the state. Through statutes or constitutional amendments, some states have granted local governments broad powers authorizing home rule.

When federal and state law conflict, valid federal law supersedes. In some cases, federal law may preempt an entire area of law, so that state law is superseded even if it is not in direct conflict. In some law, such as the bankruptcy law, Congress explicitly preempts dual state regulation. In other areas of the law, the courts find that preemption is implied from the aim and pervasiveness of the federal scheme, the need for uniformity, and the likelihood that state regulation would obstruct the full goals of the federal action. Preemption is not always implied, especially when the state is exercising its police power to protect the public health. In *Huron Portland Cement Co. v. Detroit,*[3] the United States Supreme Court ruled that the extensive federal regulation and licensure of shipping did not preempt a city ordinance concerning smoke emissions. Therefore, a federally licensed vessel could be prosecuted for violating the ordinance.

When state law and local government rules conflict, valid state law supersedes. In some cases, state law may preempt an entire area of law, so that local law is superseded even if it is not in direct conflict. For example, in *Robin v. Incorporated Village of Hempstead,*[4] the court ruled that New York had preempted the regulation of abortions. Therefore, additional regulation by local authorities was prohibited.

Decisions and Rules of Administrative Agencies

The decisions and rules of administrative agencies are other sources of law. Legislatures have delegated to numerous administrative agencies the responsibility and power to implement various laws. The delegated powers include the quasi-legislative power to adopt regulations and the quasi-judicial powers to decide how the statutes and regulations apply to individual situations. The legislature has delegated these powers because it does not have the time or expertise to address the complex issues involved in many areas that the legislature believes need to be regulated. Examples of administrative agencies that have been delegated these powers include the Food and Drug Administration (FDA), the National Labor Relations Board (NLRB), and the Internal Revenue Service (IRS).

The FDA has the power to promulgate regulations and apply them to individual determinations concerning the manufacture, marketing, and advertising of foods, drugs, cosmetics, and medical devices. The NLRB has the power to decide how national labor law applies to individual disputes, and the IRS has the power to

---

[3] 362 U.S. 440 (1960).

[4] 285 N.E. 2d 285 (N.Y. 1972).

promulgate regulations and apply them to individual disputes concerning federal taxation. Many administrative agencies, such as the NLRB, seek to achieve some consistency in their decisions by following the position they adopted in previous cases involving similar matters. This is similar to the way the courts develop the common law, discussed later in this chapter. When dealing with these agencies, it is important to review the body of law that has evolved from their previous decisions.

Administrative rules and regulations are valid only to the extent that they are within the scope of the authority granted by legislation to the agency that has promulgated them. The Constitution also limits delegation by the legislature. The legislature must retain ultimate responsibility and authority by specifying what regulations the administrative body may make. In the past, courts often declared delegations to be unconstitutional unless there was considerable specificity. Today the courts interpret the Constitution to permit much broader delegation, but the general area of law must still be specified.

The Congress and many state legislatures have passed administrative procedure acts. These laws specify the procedures administrative agencies must follow in promulgating rules or reaching decisions in contested cases, unless another law specifies different procedures for the agency to follow. Generally, these laws provide that most proposed rules be published to allow individuals an opportunity to comment before the rules are finalized. Many federal agencies must publish both proposed and final rules in the *Federal Register*. Many states have comparable publications of the proposed and final rules of state agencies. Those involved with hospitals should monitor proposed and final rules through these publications, their professional or hospital associations, or other publications. Administrative agencies often rely on the public and the industries regulated by the agencies to alert agency personnel to the potential implications of agency proposals through this comment process.

Court Decisions

The judicial decision is the fourth source of law. In the process of deciding individual cases, the courts interpret statutes and regulations, determine whether specific statutes and regulations are permitted by state or federal constitution, and create the common law when deciding cases not controlled by statutes, regulations, or a constitution.

Disagreements over the application of statutes or regulations to specific situations frequently arise. In some situations, an administrative agency has the initial authority to decide how they shall be applied. The decision of the administrative agency can usually then be appealed to the courts. However, courts generally defer to the decisions of administrative agencies in discretionary matters and limit their review to whether the delegation to the agency was constitutional and whether the agency acted within its authority, followed proper procedures, had a substantial basis for its decision, and acted without arbitrariness or discrimination. Whether or not an administrative agency is involved, the court may still have to interpret the statute or regulation or decide which of two or more conflicting statutes or regulations apply. Courts have developed several rules for interpretation of statutes. In some states, a statute specifies rules of interpretation. These rules or statutes are designed to help determine the intent of the legislature in passing the law.

The courts also determine whether specific statutes or regulations violate the Constitution. All legislation and regulations must be consistent with the Constitution. The case of *Marbury v. Madison*[5] established the power of the courts to declare legislation invalid when it is unconstitutional.

Many of the legal principles and rules applied by the courts in the United States are the product of the common law developed in England and, subsequently, in the United States. The term "common law" is applied to the body of principles that evolves from court decisions resolving controversies. Common law is continually being adapted and expanded. During the colonial period, English common law applied uniformly. After the American Revolution, each state provided for the adoption of part or all of the then existing English common law. All subsequent common law in the United States has been developed on a state basis, so common law may differ from state to state. Statutory law has been enacted to restate many legal rules and principles that initially were established by the courts as part of the common law. However, many issues, especially those pertaining to disputes in private law, are still decided according to common law. Common law in a state may be changed by enactment of legislation modifying it or by later court decisions that establish new and different common law.

In deciding specific controversies, courts for the most part adhere to the doctrine of *stare decisis*, which is frequently described as following precedent. By referring to similar cases previously decided and applying the same rules and principles, a court arrives at the same ruling in the current case as in the preceding one. However, slight differences in the situations presented may provide a basis for recognizing distinctions between precedent and the current case. Even when such differences are absent, a court may conclude that a particular common law rule is no longer in accord with the needs of society and may depart from precedent. One clear example of this departure from precedent in the law affecting hospitals was the reconsideration and elimination in nearly every state of the principle of charitable immunity, which had provided nonprofit hospitals with virtual freedom from liability for harm to patients resulting from wrongful conduct. In state after state over a period of 30 years, courts found justification to overrule precedents that had provided immunity and, thereby, allow suits against nonprofit hospitals.

---

[5] U.S. 137 (1803) (1 Cranch).

Another doctrine that courts follow to avoid duplicative litigation and conflicting decisions is *res judicata*, which means a thing or matter settled by judgment. When a legal controversy has been decided by a court and there are no more appeals available, those involved in the suit may not take the same matters to court again. This is different from *stare decisis* in that *res judicata* only applies to those parties involved in the prior suit and the issues decided in that suit. The application of the doctrine of *res judicata* can be complicated by disagreements over whether specific matters were actually decided in the prior case.

GOVERNMENTAL ORGANIZATION AND FUNCTION

This section focuses on the structure of the three branches of government—the legislative, executive, and judicial branches—and the manner in which the functions of the three branches interrelate. In a simplified summary of the functions of the three branches, the legislature makes the laws, the executive branch enforces the laws, and the judiciary branch interprets the laws. The three branches of government exist under a vital concept in the constitutional framework of the United States government and of the various state governments: the separation of powers. Essentially, separation of powers means that no one of the three branches of government is clearly dominant over the other two; however, in the exercise of its functions, each may affect and limit the activities, functions, and powers of the others.

The concept of separation of powers—which may be referred to as a system of checks and balances—is illustrated by the involvement of the three branches in the federal legislative process. Specifically, when a bill to create a statute is enacted by Congress and signed by the president, a representative of the executive branch, it becomes law. If the president should veto the bill, a two-thirds vote of each house of Congress can override the veto. Finally, the president can prevent a bill from becoming law by not taking any action while Congress is in session. Thus, by his veto the president can prevent a bill from becoming law temporarily and possibly prevent it from becoming law at all if later sessions of Congress do not act favorably on it. A bill that has become law may ultimately be declared invalid by the United States Supreme Court, an agency of the judicial branch of government, if the Court decides that the law is in violation of the Constitution.

Another example of the relationship between the branches of government involves the selection of federal court judges. Individuals nominated by the president for appointment to the federal judiciary, including the United States Supreme Court, must be approved by the United States Senate. Thus, over time, both the executive and legislative branches can affect the composition of the judicial branch of government.

In addition, while a Supreme Court decision may be final with regard to the specific controversy before the Court, Congress and the president may generate revised legislation to replace the law previously held unconstitutional. The processes for amending the Constitution, while complex and often time-consuming, can also serve as a method for offsetting or overriding a Supreme Court decision.

Each of the three branches of government has a different primary function. The function of the legislative branch is to enact laws. This process may involve creating new legislation or amending or repealing existing legislation. It is the legislature's responsibility to determine the nature and extent of the need for new laws and for changes in existing legislation. By means of a committee system, legislative proposals are assigned or referred for study to committees with specific areas of concern or interest. The committees conduct investigations and hold hearings, at which interested persons may present their views, in order to assist the committee members in their consideration of the bills. Some bills eventually reach the full legislative body where after consideration and debate they may be either approved or rejected. The Congress and every state legislature except Nebraska consist of two houses. (Nebraska has only one house.) Both houses must pass identical versions of a legislative proposal before it can be brought to the chief executive.

The primary function of the executive branch is to enforce and administer the law. However, the chief executive, either the governor of a state or the president of the United States, has a role in the creation of law through his or her power either to approve or veto a legislative proposal. The exception is North Carolina, where the governor has no veto power. If the chief executive accepts the bill through the constitutionally established process, it becomes a statute, a part of the enacted law. If the chief executive vetoes the bill, it can only become law if the process for overriding the veto by the legislature is successful.

The executive branch of government is organized into departments. The departments have responsibilities for different areas of public affairs and each enforces the law within its assigned area of responsibility. Much of the federal law affecting or pertaining to hospitals is administered by the Department of Health and Human Services. In most states there are separate departments with responsibility over health and welfare matters, and these departments administer and enforce most laws pertaining to hospitals. Other departments and government agencies also affect hospital affairs, however. On the federal level, for example, laws relating to wages and hours of employment are enforced by the Department of Labor.

The judicial branch of government is responsible for adjudicating and resolving disputes in accordance with law. Many types of disputes involving hospitals come before the courts. For example, suits against hospitals by patients seeking compensation for harm allegedly suffered as the result of wrongful conduct by hospital personnel are decided by the courts. Hospitals resort to the courts to challenge exercises of authority by government agencies and departments, to have legislation concerning hospitals declared invalid, to collect unpaid hospital bills, and to enforce contracts.

Although many disputes and controversies are resolved without resort to the courts, in many situations there is no way to end a controversy without submitting to the adjudicatory process of the courts. A dispute brought before a court is decided in accordance with the applicable law; this application of the law is the essence of the judicial process.

ORGANIZATION OF THE COURT SYSTEM

It is necessary to understand the structure of the court system to understand the effect of court decisions as precedents and understand the judicial branch of government. There are over 50 court systems in the United States, including the federal court system, each state's court system, the District of Columbia court system, and the court systems of Puerto Rico and the territories. These courts do not all reach the same decisions concerning specific issues. Frequently, a majority approach and several minority approaches exist on each issue. Thus, careful review is necessary to determine which court's decisions apply to an individual hospital and, if no court decisions are specifically applicable, to predict which approach the courts are likely to adopt.

The federal court system and many state court systems have three levels of courts—trial courts, intermediate courts of appeal, and a supreme court. Some states have no intermediate courts of appeal.

State Court System

The trial courts in some states are divided into special courts that deal with specific issues, such as family courts, juvenile courts, probate courts, and limited courts that deal only with lesser crimes, such as misdemeanors, or with civil cases involving limited amounts of money. Each state has trial courts of general jurisdiction that may decide all disputes not assigned to other courts or those disputes barred from the courts by valid federal or state law.

At the trial court level, the applicable law is determined and the evidence is assessed to determine the facts. The applicable law is then applied to those facts. It is the judge's role to determine what the law is. If there is a jury, the judge instructs the jury as to the law, and the jury determines the facts and applies the law. If there is no jury, the judge also determines the facts. In either case, the determination of the facts must be based on the evidence properly admitted during the trial, so the facts may not necessarily be what actually happened.

In some cases, everyone agrees on the facts, and the only issues presented to the court concern what the law is. In other cases, everyone agrees what the law is, but there is disagreement over the facts. To determine the facts for purposes of deciding the case, the credibility of the witnesses and the weight to be given other evidence must be determined. Many cases involve both questions of law and questions of fact. The judge has significant control over the trial even when a jury is involved. If the judge finds that insufficient evidence has been presented to establish a factual issue for the jury to resolve, the judge can dismiss the case or, in civil cases, direct the jury to decide the case in a specific way. In civil cases, even after the jury has decided, the judge can decide in favor of the other side.

Most state court systems have an intermediate appellate court. Usually, this court only decides appeals from trial court decisions. In some states, there are a few issues that can be taken directly to the intermediate appellate court. When an appellate court decides an appeal, it does not accept additional evidence. It uses the evidence presented in the record from the trial court. Appellate courts almost always accept the determination of the facts by the jury or judge in the trial court because the jury and judge saw the witnesses and, therefore, can more accurately judge their credibility. Usually, the appellate court bases its decision on whether proper procedures were followed in the trial court and whether the trial court properly interpreted the law. However, an appellate court will occasionally find that a jury verdict is so clearly contrary to the evidence that it will either reverse the decision or order a new trial.

Each state has a single court at the highest level, usually called the supreme court. In some states the name is different. For example, in New York the highest court is called the Court of Appeals, while trial courts are called supreme courts. The highest level court in each state decides appeals from the intermediate appellate courts or, in states without intermediate appellate courts, from trial courts. The highest level court frequently has other duties, including adopting rules of procedure for the state court system and determining who may practice law in the state, which includes disciplining lawyers for improper conduct.

Federal Court System

The federal court system has a structure similar to state court systems. The federal trial courts are the United States district courts and special purpose courts, such as the Court of Claims, which hears certain claims against the United States. Federal trial courts are fundamentally different from state trial courts because the federal courts have limited jurisdiction. A federal suit either must involve a question of federal law or must concern a dispute between citizens of different states. In many cases, the controversy must involve at least $10,000. Federal questions include cases involving possible violations of federal law or of rights under the United States Constitution. When a federal trial court decides a controversy between citizens of different states, it is acting under what is called its diversity jurisdiction, using federal court procedures but applying the law of the applicable state. Sometimes federal trial courts will decline to decide state law questions until they have been decided by a state court. This is called abstention. It is designed to leave state issues for state courts and to minimize the workload of the federal courts. Federal courts will generally not abstain when there are also important federal questions not affected by the state law question. Some states have procedures by which the federal courts can directly ask a state court to decide a particular question of state law when it is important to the decision of a case before the federal court.

Appeals from the federal trial courts go to a United States court of appeals. The United States is divided into 12 areas, called circuits, numbered 1 through 11, plus the District of Columbia circuit court.

The highest court in the United States is the United States Supreme Court, which decides appeals from the United States court of appeals. Decisions of the highest state courts may also be appealed to the United States Supreme Court if they involve federal laws or the United States Constitution. When the courts of appeals or the highest state courts decline to review a lower court decision, the decision sometimes can be directly appealed to the United States Supreme Court.

The United States Supreme Court has the authority to decline to review most cases. With only a few exceptions, a request for review is made by filing a petition for a *writ of certiorari*. If the Supreme Court grants the *writ of certiorari*, the record for the lower court decision is transmitted to the Supreme Court for review. In most cases, the Supreme Court denies the *writ of certiorari*. Such a denial does not indicate approval of the lower court decision; it merely means the Supreme Court declines to review the decision.

Stare Decisis

The preceding description illustrates the complexity of the court system in the United States. When a court is confronted with an issue, it is bound by the doctrine of *stare decisis* to follow the precedents of higher courts in the same court system that have jurisdiction over the geographic area where the court is located. Each appellate court, including the highest court, is generally also bound to follow the precedents of its own decisions, unless it decides to overrule the precedent due to changing conditions. Thus, decisions from equal or lower courts or from courts in other court systems do not have to be followed. One exception occurs when a federal court decides a controversy between citizens of different states and must follow the state law as determined by the highest court of the state. Another exception is when a state court decides a controversy involving a federal law or constitutional question and must follow the decisions of the United States Supreme Court. Another situation that may force a court to change its prior position is a change in the applicable statutes or regulations by the legislature or an administrative agency.

When a court is confronted with a question that is not answered by applicable statutes or regulations and the question has not been addressed by its court system, the court will usually examine the judicial solutions reached in the other systems to decide the new issue. When a court decides to reexamine its position on an issue it has addressed, the court will often examine the judicial decisions of the other systems to decide whether to overrule its position. A clear trend in decisions across the country can form a basis for a reasonable legal assessment of how to act even when the courts in a particular area have not decided the issue. However, a court is not bound by the decisions from other systems, and it may reach a different conclusion.

Thus, there can be a majority approach to a certain issue that many state court systems follow and several minority approaches that other states follow. State courts show more consistency on some issues than others. For example, nearly all state courts have completely eliminated charitable immunity. However, while nearly all states require informed consent to medical procedures, many states determine the information that must be provided to patients by reference to what a patient needs to know, while several states make the determination by reference to what other physicians would disclose. A few states have not yet decided what reference to use.

Differences in applicable statutes and regulations between states may force courts in different states to reach different conclusions regarding certain questions. For example, numerous states have enacted statutes that protect hospital and medical staff review committee records from discovery, although the extent of protection varies. Some statutes provide that such records generally are subject to subpoena, discovery, or disclosure; other statutes state specifically that such committee records, proceedings, and reports are not discoverable or describe such material as confidential or privileged. There are also common exceptions to the nondiscovery statutes, allowing physicians to discover records of staff privilege committees when contesting the termination, suspension, or limitation of their staff privileges. As a result of these variations, courts throughout the country have construed nondiscovery statutes with varying results.

In summary, while it is important to be aware of trends in court decisions across the country, legal advice should be sought before taking actions based on decisions from court systems that have no jurisdiction over the geographic area in which the hospital is located.

Chapter 10

Principles of Hospital Liability

Since the abolition of the doctrine of charitable immunity in the mid 1960s, hospitals have been confronted with significant increases in the number of malpractice lawsuits brought against them for alleged instances of negligent treatment of patients. In contrast, for well over 100 years physicians have voiced their concern at the increase in the number of malpractice claims brought against them. For example, in 1847, one surgeon wrote: "Legal prosecutions for malpractice in surgery occur so often that even a respectable surgeon may well fear for the results of his surgical practice."[1] While the perception that malpractice lawsuits are continuing to escalate at an uncontrolled rate is fairly universal and is of concern to all individuals involved in delivering health care services, it is nevertheless true that a malpractice suit remains an infrequent occurrence. In 1975, at the beginning of the malpractice crisis, when professional liability insurance premiums increased so dramatically, one commentator noted that "[s]tatistically, only about one out of every 226,000 patient visits to doctors results in a malpractice action, and the majority of hospitals, no matter how large, go through an entire year without having a single claim filed against them."[2] Still, when a medical malpractice lawsuit is brought against a hospital, the role of the medical records practitioner and the medical record of the patient are of great importance, because the medical record becomes a legal document and evidence of the care that was provided, which may or may not demonstrate that the medical care given was negligent. Moreover, the ability of the patient to bring a lawsuit against a hospital

---

[1]Annas, *The Rights of Hospital Patients* 198 (1975), *quoting* Burns, *Malpractice Suits in American Medicine before the Civil War*, 43 BULL. HIST. MED. 41, 52 (1969) [hereinafter cited as Annas].

[2]Annas, *supra* note 1, at 199, *citing* MEDICAL MALPRACTICE: REPORT OF THE SECRETARY'S COMMISSION ON MEDICAL MALPRACTICE, U.S. Department of Health, Education & Welfare, DHEW Pub. No. (OS) 73–88 (U.S. Government Printing Office, Stock #1700 00114) (1973), at 12.

within the time allowed by law has a significant bearing on the record retention policies developed by each medical records practitioner.

Chapter 9, in introducing the nature and services of law and the structure of the American legal system, distinguished between public law, which is concerned primarily with regulating and enforcing individual conduct (principally criminal law), and private law, which is concerned either with the enforcement of agreements among individuals (contract law) or the enforcement of duties and rights between and among individuals in their conduct toward one another (tort law). This chapter reviews the principles of private law, specifically tort law, that govern the circumstances under which, and the determination of when, hospitals, through the conduct of their employees, agents, or medical staff, will be held liable for the payment of money damages to individuals who claim to have suffered an injury as the result of their conduct. This chapter does not address the principles underlying hospital violations of criminal law, nor does it specifically review instances in which hospitals have been held liable for the actions or conduct of their medical records personnel, as that is the subject of Chapter 6. Rather, the purpose of this chapter is to provide a foundation for understanding the circumstances under which the courts will impose liability on hospitals for the negligent conduct of their employees, agents, or medical staff.[3]

NEGLIGENCE DEFINED

Defining negligence in theory is relatively simple, and the legal literature has propounded many definitions,[4] but most definitions of negligence essentially state that it is "a matter of risk—that is to say, of recognizable danger of injury. . . . Against this probability, and gravity of the risk, must be balanced in every case the utility of the conduct in question."[5] Stated another way, negligence is conduct society considers unreasonably dangerous and is classified as such because "first, the [individual] did foresee or should have *foreseen* that it would subject another or

---

[3]This chapter illustrates the principles of hospital liability by discussing conduct considered by courts to be negligent; that is, conduct which is considered to be not as safe as society is entitled to expect from individuals under the circumstances. Intentional torts, for example, invasion of privacy, defamation of character, false imprisonment, etc., are not specifically considered, as several other chapters in the book consider and discuss such causes of action. Moreover, if one understands negligence theory and its principles, the analysis of intentional torts is conceptually not difficult to understand and appreciate.

[4]Posner, *A Theory of Negligence*, 1 J. LEGAL STUDIES 29 (1972); RESTATEMENT (SECOND) OF TORTS §282 (1965); Terry, *Negligence*, 19 Harv. L. Rev. 40 (1915).

[5]*See* W. PROSSER, HANDBOOK OF THE LAW OF TORTS 145–49 (4th ed. 1971).

others to an appreciable risk of harm, and second, the magnitude of the perceivable risk was such that the [individual] should have acted in a safer manner."[6]

In practice, however, defining negligence can be much more difficult, because such theoretical definitions of negligence do not offer a standard of care by which conduct may be evaluated and determined to be unreasonably dangerous. This has led to the adoption of the reasonable person standard, which asks a jury, for example, to evaluate the conduct of the parties involved in a lawsuit in light of the general experience and background of each member of the jury. Thus, there is no special knowledge required to determine whether a driver who failed to stop at a stop sign and injured another party was negligent. Professional liability cases are different in this respect because the average jury member typically does not possess the special knowledge that would be needed to determine whether the professional against whom a lawsuit was brought used the skill and care required of him or her. This is particularly true, for example, in claims brought against hospitals for medical malpractice, because the perceivable danger that should have been avoided (that is to say, the risk or hazard related to the delivery of medical treatment) typically is not commonly known or understood.

> Consequently, the standard by which a professional is to be judged in determining the amount of danger that he should have perceived from alternative [courses] of action must be one that takes into account that the [individual] has held himself out as possessing technical skill and knowledge above that which is commonly known. . . .[7]

PRINCIPLES OF HOSPITAL LIABILITY

The Doctrine of Charitable Immunity

It is important to realize that not-for-profit hospitals have only recently been held liable for the negligent conduct of their employees. Prior to the late 1950s and early 1960s, many not-for-profit hospitals were held by courts to be immune from liability for the negligent conduct of their employees under the doctrine of charitable immunity. The doctrine of charitable immunity was premised on the assumption that not-for-profit institutions, like hospitals, depend solely on the income from their property and the endowments and gifts of benevolent persons for funds to carry out the charitable purposes for which they were organized. The funds and property thus acquired, stated one court:

---

[6]Keeton, *Medical Negligence—The Standard of Care*, SPECIALTY LAW DIGEST: HEALTH CARE (March 1980), at 3.

[7]*Id.* at 5.

are held in trust and cannot be diverted to the purpose of paying damages for injuries caused by the negligent or wrongful acts of its servants and employees to persons who are enjoying the benefit of the charity. An institution of this character, doing charitable work of great benefit to the public without profit, and depending upon gifts, donations, legacies and bequests made by charitable persons for the successful accomplishment of its beneficial purposes, is not to be hampered in the acquisition of property and funds from those wishing to contribute and assist in the charitable work, by any doubt that might arise in the minds of such intending donors as to whether the funds supplied by them will be applied to the purposes for which they intended to devote them, or diverted to the entirely different purpose of satisfying judgments recovered against the donee because of the negligent acts of those employed to carry the beneficent purpose into execution.[8]

Over time, however, the impracticality of the doctrine of charitable immunity was recognized, and exceptions to its blanket exemption from liability were created. For example, in *Moore v. Moyle*,[9] the Illinois Supreme Court held that "the sole object of the doctrine . . . was to protect the trust funds of charities from depletion through the tortious conduct of their employees and agents"[10] and concluded that "the exemption or immunity which has been afforded a charitable institution should go no further than to protect its trust funds from being taken to satisfy its liability for the tortious acts of its agents or servants."[11] Subsequently, in a decision of national importance, the Illinois Supreme Court held, in the case of *Darling v. Charleston Community Memorial Hospital*, that

the doctrine of charitable immunity can no longer stand. . . . [A] doctrine which limits the liability of charitable corporations to the amount of liability insurance that they see fit to carry permits them to determine whether or not they will be liable for their torts and the amount of that liability, if any. Whether or not particular assets of a charitable corporation are subject to exemption from execution in order to satisfy a judgment does not determine liability. No such issue arises until liability has been determined.[12]

---

[8]Parks v. Northwestern University, 218 Ill. 381, 385, 75 N.E. 991, 993 (1905), *overruled in Darling v. Charleston Community Memorial Hospital, infra* note 12.

[9]405 Ill. 555, 92 N.E. 2d 81 (1950), *overruled in Darling v. Charleston Community Memorial Hospital, infra* note 12.

[10]*Id.* at 559–60, 92 N.E. 2d at 84.

[11]*Id.* at 565, 92 N.E. 2d at 86.

[12]33 Ill. 2d 326, 337–38, 211 N.E. 2d 253 (1965), *cert. denied*, 383 U.S. 946 (1966).

With the doctrine of charitable immunity thus cast aside, the exposure of hospitals to liability claims increased dramatically, based on a number of legal theories.

Elements of a Negligence Claim against a Hospital[13]

For an individual to prevail in a suit alleging the negligence of a hospital, one must prove the existence of four elements. First, it must be proven that the hospital had a duty to act in accordance with a standard of reasonable care so as to prevent injury to a patient. Second, it must be demonstrated that the defendant's conduct failed to conform to the applicable standard of care. This element is referred to as the breach of duty. Third, the plaintiff must prove that the defendant's breach of duty proximately caused the plaintiff's injury. Proximate cause is a factual determination typically decided by a jury based on the evidence introduced and accepted at trial and is not discussed at length herein. One should not conclude, however, that proximate cause is a simplistic issue not worthy of further study. Determining whether an event or action proximately caused the event or action that led to the plaintiff's injury has challenged the thinking of some of the foremost jurists of the United States, as they have struggled with the problems of "intervening events," "transferred negligence," and "foreseeability."[14] Last, the plaintiff must show that he or she suffered actual harm or injury as a result of the defendant's negligent conduct, for which the plaintiff may request money damages. Damages may be recovered for all physical pain and suffering caused by the negligent act, as well as for any emotional distress accompanying the injury. In addition, the plaintiff may seek compensation for any reduction in the quality of life, such as loss of consortium. Out-of-pocket costs, past and future medical costs, and past and future wage losses are all compensable as actual damages. Recovery of these damages may be limited, or even barred, by the doctrines of comparative negligence or contributory negligence, discussed later in this chapter.

Two different theories of negligence are generally used in support of liability actions against hospitals for alleged negligent conduct. Under the more traditional and older theory, the hospital, as a separate entity that can be sued in its own right, is recognized as an entity that can act or function only through the individuals it employs. As a result, the negligent actions of the hospital's employees over whom it has control are imputed to the hospital under the doctrine of *respondeat superior*, or the doctrine of agency.

---

[13]For an excellent and lengthy discussion of the principle of hospital liability, *see* Hospital Law Manual, *Principles of Hospital Liability*, Attorney's Volume 11 B (Aspen Systems Corporation, March 1984) [hereinafter cited as Aspen Hospital Law Manual].

[14]*See, e.g.,* Justice Cardozo's opinion in Palsgraf v. Long Island R.R. Co., 248 N.Y. 339, 162 N.E. 99, *rehearing denied* 249 N.Y. 511, 164 N.E. 564 (1928).

The second theory, more recent in origin, holds the hospital liable for its own independent acts of negligence. This theory, known as corporate negligence, imposes on the hospital the responsibility for monitoring the activities of the independent and nonemployed individuals functioning within its facilities. The doctrine of corporate negligence has had a significant effect on hospital-medical staff relationships, since its application to hospitals can and does result in hospital liability for the negligent conduct of physicians on its medical staff. Under either theory, the four elements of a negligence action, discussed previously, must be proven.

The Hospital's Duty

Upon the initiation of treatment or the admission of the patient to the hospital, the duty arises to render patient care services in accordance with the applicable standard of care. The scope of the hospital's duty with respect to the quality of treatment rendered has been expanded greatly under recent court decisions through reliance on the doctrine of *respondeat superior* and on the theory of liability premised on corporate negligence. Correspondingly, the standard of care against which a hospital's conduct will be measured has become more demanding, and hospitals have been held more directly responsible for the quality of medical care provided by its independent staff physicians, who are not employees of the hospital.

Unquestionably, the leading court decision in this area is *Darling v. Charleston Community Memorial Hospital*,[15] an Illinois Supreme Court decision, which is significant in three respects. First, it abolished the doctrine of charitable immunity in Illinois, consistent with the nationwide trend to abrogate that doctrine.[16] Second, the court held, in a proposition subsequently adopted by courts in several other states,[17] that state licensing requirements for hospitals, standards of the Joint Commission on the Accreditation of Hospitals and the hospital's own bylaws, policies, rules, and regulations could be introduced as evidence of the duty or standard of care the hospital owed to its patients. Third, the *Darling* decision has been frequently cited as authority for imposing an independent legal duty on a hospital to monitor and provide overall surveillance of the quality of patient care

[15]33 Ill. 2d 326, 211 N.E. 2d 253 (1965), *cert. denied,* 383 U.S. 946 (1966) [hereinafter cited as Darling].

[16]President and Directors of Georgetown College v. Hughes, 130 F. 2d 810 (D.C. Cir. 1942); Bell v. Presbytery of Boise, 91 Idaho 374, 421 P. 2d 745 (1966); Adkins v. St. Francis Hospital, 149 W. Va. 705, 143 S.E. 2d 154 (1965).

[17]Lucy Webb Hayes Nat'l Training School v. Perotti, 419 F. 2d 704 (D.C. Cir. 1969); Niblack v. U.S., 438 F. Supp. 383 (D. Colo. 1977); Johnson v. Misericordia Community Hospital, 99 Wis. 2d 708, 301 N.W. 2d 156 (1981).

seivices provided in its facility and to intervene when inadequate or inappropriate medical care is rendered to a patient. The patient in the *Darling* case suffered immediate complications and the eventual amputation of his leg following the negligent application of a leg cast by a Dr. Alexander, who was on duty in the emergency department of the hospital. Although it is not known from the court's opinion whether Dr. Alexander was an employee of the hospital or an independent nonemployed physician on the medical staff of the hospital, the court concluded:

> The conception that the hospital does not undertake to treat the patient, does not undertake to act through its doctors and nurses, but undertakes instead simply to procure them to act upon their own responsibility, no longer reflects the fact. Present-day hospitals, as their manner of operation plainly demonstrates, do far more than furnish facilities for treatment. They regularly employ on a salary basis a large staff of physicians, nurses and interns, as well as administrative and manual workers, and they charge patients for medical care and treatment, collecting for such services, if necessary, by legal action. Certainly, the person who avails himself of "hospital facilities" expects that the hospital will attempt to cure him, not that its nurses or other employees will act on their own responsibility.[18]
>
> . . . [O]n the basis of the evidence before it the jury could reasonably have concluded that the nurses did not test for circulation in the leg as frequently as necessary, that skilled nurses would have promptly recognized the conditions that signalled a dangerous impairment of circulation in the plaintiff's leg, and would have known that the condition would become irreversible in a matter of hours. At that point it became the nurses' duty to inform the attending physician, and if he failed to act, to advise the hospital authorities so that appropriate action might be taken. As to consultation, there is no dispute that the hospital failed to review Dr. Alexander's work or require a consultation; the only issue is whether its failure to do so was negligence. On the evidence before it the jury could reasonably have found it was.[19]

Subsequent Illinois court decisions[20] interpreting the *Darling* decision have concluded that *Darling* was not meant as new law to be generally used to impose

---

[18]Darling, 33 Ill. 2d 326, 332, 211 N.E. 2d, 253, 257, *citing* Bing v. Thunig, 2 N.Y. 2d 656, 666, 143 N.E. 2d 3, 8 (1957).

[19]Darling, 33 Ill. 2d 326, 333, 211 N.E. 2d 253, 258.

[20]Lundahl v. Rockford Memorial Hospital Ass'n, 93 Ill. App. 2d 461, 235 N.E. 2d 671 (1968); Collins v. Westlake Community Hospital, 12 Ill. App. 3d 847, 299 N.E. 2d 326 (1973), *rev'd on other grounds*, 57 Ill. 2d 388, 312 N.E. 2d 614 (1974).

liability upon hospitals for all negligent treatment rendered by an attending physician. Other courts, however, citing the *Darling* case, have significantly expanded the scope of the hospital's duty to check properly a physician's credentials upon application to the medical staff,[21] or to obtain information concerning prior negligent conduct of an applicant to the hospital's medical staff.[22] Nevertheless, *Darling* at the very least supports the proposition, with respect to the hospital's obligation to a patient concerning the treatment rendered by an attending physician, that where a patient received negligently administered treatment in the hospital and the hospital knew or reasonably should have known that the treatment was negligent, the hospital is negligent for failing to intervene to require further review or consideration of the treatment rendered. Other courts have similarly interpreted *Darling*, holding that a hospital is liable for injuries caused by the negligence of a staff physician where it can be shown that the hospital had actual or constructive notice of the physician's prior incompetent efforts at performing a comparable medical task,[23] or that the hospital, through the exercise of reasonable care, could have acquired such knowledge and acted on it to prevent the patient's injury but failed to do so.[24]

Breach of Duty

After the standard of care or the hospital's duty has been established, evidence must be offered to prove the hospital's conduct amounted to a breach of that duty. Generally, the standard of care required of a hospital depends on the circumstances of the particular case. The most common means for determining the standard of care for hospitals typically has involved the testimony of experts. However, as the *Darling* case demonstrated, the standard of care may be determined by examining the criteria outlined in statutes, regulations, accreditation standards, and hospital bylaws, rules, regulations, and policies. The importance of this statement to medical records practitioners cannot be overlooked, because it suggests a cautious and realistic approach to drafting hospital policies, rules, and regulations, and, moreover, demands that the medical records practitioner be generally familiar with applicable laws, regulations, and court decisions governing the creation, maintenance, and security of medical records. Following is a review of each of the

---

[21]*See, e.g.,* Johnson v. Misericordia Community Hospital, 99 Wis. 2d 708, 301 N.W. 2d 156 (1981).

[22]*See, e.g.,* Elam v. College Park Hospital, 132 Cal. 3d 332 (1982); Joiner v. Mitchell County Hospital Authority, 125 Ga. App. 1, 186 S.E. 2d 307 (1971), *aff'd,* 229 Ga. 140, 189 S.E. 2d 412 (1972).

[23]*See, e.g.,* Purcell v. Zimbelman, 18 Ariz. App. 75, 500 P. 2d 335 (1972).

[24]*See, e.g.,* Gonzales v. Nork, Cal. Super. App. Dep't. Court Mem. of Dec. No. 228566 (Nov. 19, 1973), *retransferred to Ct. App. on other grounds,* 20 Cal. 3d 500, 143 Cal. Rptr. 240, 573 P. 2d 458 (1978).

more frequently employed means of proving the standard of care and ascertaining whether it was breached.

Community Standards

Perhaps the most common method of establishing the applicable standard of care in a particular case and demonstrating a breach of that duty is by showing a violation of community standards. Expert testimony is typically required to establish the standard of care recognized in medical and hospital communities.[25] Certain exceptions to this rule are recognized where, for example, the reasonableness of the hospital's conduct may be evaluated on the basis of the common knowledge and experience of a lay person.[26] For example, in *Stepien v. Bay Memorial Medical Center*,[27] a Florida court held that expert testimony was not required when a confused patient fell from a bed with no siderails. A related issue to proving liability based on a showing of a violation of community standards is whether the community is a local, state, or national community. The traditional rule, favorable to hospitals, required that a hospital's conduct conform to the standards of other hospitals in the same locality.[28] This rule was subsequently altered to include practices common to hospitals in the same or similar communities,[29] and the modern trend has been for courts to evaluate a hospital's conduct against a standard that is not necessarily the same as for that of the other hospitals in the area in which the hospital in question is located.[30]

Statutes and Regulations

Statutes and regulations may be used as evidence of common practice. Alternatively, under certain circumstances, courts will consider a statute or regulation as establishing a standard of care, the violation of which will result in hospital liability to the patient if the patient and the injury suffered fall within the class of persons and harms the statute or regulation was designed to safeguard and the injuries it was designed to prevent.[31] Similarly, accreditation standards, particularly those of the JCAH, strongly suggest the standard of care required of a

---

[25]*See, e.g.*, Walker v. North Dakota Eye Clinic, Ltd., 415 F. Supp. 891 (D.N.D. 1976); Krause v. Bridgeport Hosp., 169 Conn. 1, 362 A. 2d 802 (1975).

[26]*See, e.g.*, Newhall v. Central Vermont Hospital, Inc., 133 Vt. 572, 349 A. 2d 890 (1975). Stepien v. Bay Memorial Medical Center, 397 So. 2d 333 (Fla. Dist. Ct. App., *petition dismissed* 402 So. 2d 607 (Fla. 1981).

[27]397 So. 2d 333 (Fla. Dist. Ct. App. 1981).

[28]*See, e.g.*, Mason v. Geddes, 258 Mass. 40, 154 N.E. 519 (1926).

[29]*See, e.g.*, Wood v. Miller, 158 Or. 444, 76 P. 2d 963 (1938); Weintraub v. Rosen, 93 F. 2d 544 (7th Cir. 1937).

[30]*See, e.g.*, Chandler v. Neosho Memorial Hosp., 223 Kan. 1, 574 P. 2d 136 (1977).

[31]Darling, *supra* note 12.

hospital.[32] Consequently, medical records practitioners, in particular, should recognize the liability risk that is inherent in the violation of these standards.

Hospital Policies

A hospital's internal rules, as contained in protocols, policies, procedure manuals, and bylaws, can be and are frequently used as evidence of the standard of care required in a particular case.[33] Many times a hospital's rules simply embody a standard of conduct already imposed on the hospital by other regulatory or accrediting bodies. All too frequently, however, hospitals establish rules that establish an internal standard of care greater and more demanding than that required by regulatory or accrediting standards, or even that expected in the community. An example is the case of *Johnson v. St. Bernard Hospital*,[34] an Illinois appellate court decision.

In *Johnson,* the court held that the requisite standard of care applicable to the hospital included a self-imposed obligation to assist staff members in obtaining consultations. The court examined two provisions of the hospital's bylaws, one of which provided that "urgent consultation shall be answered within 24 hours from the time requested and all other consultations shall be answered within 48 hours. After 48 hours, if consultation is not answered, administration shall be notified."[35] The other bylaw provision authorized the hospital to take corrective action against staff physicians whenever necessary to enforce the standards of the medical staff or "in the best interests of patient care."[36] Rejecting the hospital's claim that obtaining a consultation was a medical decision solely within the province of the attending physician, the court stated:

> we believe that the hospital bylaws impose a duty upon the hospital to use reasonable efforts to assist physicians or its staff in obtaining consultations from other staff physicians. This conclusion does not require the hospital administration to engage in the practice of medicine.
> . . . It requires not medical expertise, but administrative expertise, to enforce rules and regulations which were adopted by the hospital to insure a smoothly run hospital, routine and adequate care, and under which the physicians have agreed to operate.[37]

---

[32]Darling, *supra* note 12.
[33]Darling, *supra* note 12.
[34]79 Ill. App. 3d 709, 399 N.E. 2d 198 (1979) [hereinafter cited as Johnson].
[35]*Id.* at 711, 399 N.E. 2d at 201.
[36]*Id.* at 717, 399 N.E. 2d at 205.
[37]*Id.*

The message of this case is clear. For anyone likely to be involved in drafting hospital bylaws or rules and policies, "care should be taken to avoid creating a self-imposed standard of conduct that is either impossible to satisfy or infeasible because of practical constraints."[38] Certainly, each hospital's risk management and quality assurance programs should include procedures for identifying hospital policies that are not being followed so that careful evaluation of the need for the policy can be conducted. Obviously, out-of-date or inappropriate policies should be revised. (For a general discussion of hospital risk management and quality assurance programs and activities, see Chapter 8.)

Res Ipsa Loquitur

An exception to the general principle that a plaintiff must prove negligence in order to establish the defendant's liability is the doctrine of *res ipsa loquitur*. This doctrine is applicable where a court determines, as a matter of law, that "the occurrence is such as in the ordinary course of things would not have happened if the party exercising control or management had exercised proper care."[39]

The elements that must be established for the doctrine to apply are the following: (1) the defendant must have had exclusive control over the thing that produced the injury, (2) the injurious occurrence ordinarily would not have occurred in the absence of the defendant's negligence, (3) the injury must have been one that could not have occurred from any voluntary action by the plaintiff, and, in some states, (4) the defendant must have had superior knowledge of the course of the accident.[40]

For example, in *Burke v. Washington Hospital Center*,[41] the plaintiff underwent abdominal surgery, and following the operation, the plaintiff's evidence showed she still had a surgical sponge inside her abdominal cavity. The court held that there was evidence that the physician's initial surgery caused the problem[42] (i.e., the physician had had exclusive control over the devices that caused the injury); that the condition would not normally have occurred in the absence of negligence,[43] and that the injury did not occur as a result of any voluntary action by the plaintiff, as she was under anesthesia.

[38]Aspen Hospital Law Manual, *supra* note 13, at 17.

[39]Walker v. Rumer, 72 Ill. 2d 495, 502, 381 N.E. 2d 689, 691 (1978). For a statutory recodification of the doctrine of *res ipsa loquitur, see* Ill. Rev. Stat. ch. 110, §2–1113 (Smith-Hurd 1983).

[40]*Id.*

[41]475 F. 2d 364 (D.C. Cir. 1973).

[42]*Id.* at 365.

[43]*Id.*

Contributory and Comparative Negligence

Proof of hospital negligence does not mean the hospital is exclusively liable for the plaintiff's injuries. Two related doctrines of negligence law, contributory negligence and comparative negligence, operate to reduce or eliminate a hospital defendant's ultimate liability to the plaintiff who has established the hospital's negligence.

Contributory negligence is an absolute bar or defense to a plaintiff's claim for damages. Specifically, if a defendant whose negligence has been established can prove that the plaintiff's conduct breached his or her duty of self-protection and contributed to the injury, the plaintiff's claim for damages will be denied. Essentially, the elements that a defendant must establish to prove the plaintiff's negligence parallel those the plaintiff must prove to establish the negligence of the defendant.[44]

Under the comparative negligence doctrine, the fault of the plaintiff is compared with that of the defendant in determining the amount of damages to be awarded to the plaintiff. In practice, a percentage is assigned to the respective negligence of each party, which is thereafter used to reduce the plaintiff's recovery according to the plaintiff's relative degree of fault. Varying forms of comparative negligence have been adopted. The pure form of comparative negligence permits the plaintiff to recover damages for the portion of the injury attributable to the defendant's negligence, irrespective of which party was at greater fault.[45] Under the approach used in a majority of the states that have adopted the doctrine of comparative negligence, a modified comparative negligence is applied, and the plaintiff whose negligence is determined to have exceeded that of the defendant's is barred from recovering any damages.[46]

Statutes of Limitation

State statutes, commonly referred to as statutes of limitation, are an important limitation upon the liability of hospitals. As a matter of public policy, all states have established prescribed periods of time after which a plaintiff may not sue a defendant, so that a defendant does not face unending exposure to liability for his or her actions.

Typically, claims against hospitals for injuries caused by the negligence of the hospital or its employees have been classified as personal injury actions. Usually the statute of limitation applicable to such claims is two years; that is, a plaintiff

---

[44]*See, e.g.,* Borus v. Yellow Cab Co., 52 Ill. App. 3d 194, 367 N.E. 2d 277 (1977).

[45]*See, e.g.,* Alvis v. Ribar, 85 Ill. 2d 1, 421 N.E. 2d 886 (1981).

[46]*See, e.g.,* Wis. Stat. §895.045 (1983 and West Supp. 1983–1984).

has two years from the date of his injury in which to sue the defendant for the injuries the plaintiff sustained as a consequence of the defendant's alleged negligent conduct. Failure to file suit within the prescribed time period bars the plaintiff from suing the defendant for that injury.

A growing number of jurisdictions has specific statutes of limitation applicable to medical malpractice actions, which supersede the more common and traditional personal injury time period.[47] These statutes vary with respect to the period of limitation and the types of health care providers that are affected by the statute. The two primary issues in this area of the law of concern to medical records practitioners and all other health care professionals are (1) the computation of the statutory time period, and (2) the general circumstances in which the beginning of the statutory time period during which a plaintiff has to file suit is deferred or tolled by law for reasons of public policy.

Ordinarily, the statutes of limitation applicable to negligence actions begin to run when the injury occurs.[48] Claims against hospitals, however, often involve considerations, not found in common personal injury negligence claims, that affect the ability of the plaintiff to know when he or she was injured. The classic example, of course, is the foreign object left inside the patient after surgery. The plaintiff usually does not learn of the problem until some time after the injury occurred. Under traditional statutes of limitation rules, the time period would begin to run from the date of the injury, whether or not the plaintiff knew he or she was injured, thereby seriously jeopardizing and possibly even barring the plaintiff's right to file a claim against the person who injured the plaintiff. In many states, rules have been adopted to mitigate the harshness of this general principle. The most straightforward of these rules is known as the discovery rule, which states that the statute of limitation does not begin to run until the wrongful act was or reasonably should have been discovered.[49] In an effort to minimize any undue prejudice to hospital defendants that could result from the application of the discovery rule, several states have limited its applicability solely to claims arising from foreign objects left in the body.[50]

Extensive application of the discovery rule has greatly increased hospital and physician exposure to liability and has resulted in a concomitant inability of professional liability insurers to predict accurately their potential financial obligations. This, together with the proliferation of medical malpractice claims in the 1970s, has resulted in huge increases in medical malpractice insurance premiums. In an effort to balance the interests of plaintiffs and defendants in these circum-

---

[47]*See, e.g.*, Ill. Rev. Stat. ch. 110, §13–212 (1984).

[48]*See, e.g.*, Hawks v. DeHart, 206 Va. 810, 146 S.E. 2d 187 (1966).

[49]*See* W. PROSSER, HANDBOOK OF THE LAW OF TORTS, 144 (4th ed. 1971); Oliver v. Kaiser Community Health Foundation, 5 Ohio St. 3d Ill, 449 N.E. 2d 438 (1983).

[50]*See, e.g.*, Ga. Code Ann. §9–3–72 (1982); Mo. Rev. Stat. §516.105 (Supp. 1984).

stances, many states have adopted another limitation on the discovery rule, known as the double time limit. This statute permits an action to be brought within a prescribed time period after discovery, but it also sets a maximum time period for action, dating from the cause of the injury, that bars any claim irrespective of when discovery of the injury occurs. In Illinois, for example, a plaintiff may bring a medical malpractice lawsuit two years after he or she discovers the injury but no more than four years after the event that caused the injury.[51]

A final departure from the discovery rule is the continuous treatment rule. Under this rule, the time of injury and the time of discovery are immaterial. The rule is premised on the theory that patients will not change their physician or hospital unless and until they become aware that they are being negligently treated. The statutes of limitation begin to run when the relationship between the hospital, or the physician, and the patient terminates.[52] The practical effect of such a rule is potentially to extend indefinitely the period of time during which a patient can bring a malpractice action. Consequently, it has been adopted in few states.

The last issue of importance to determining when the statute of limitation period begins to run involves the circumstances under which, by law and for reasons of public policy, the statute of limitation period does not start when it would otherwise normally begin to run. This is known as an event that tolls the running of the statute of limitation.

A majority of jurisdictions provides that, in the event of a patient's mental incompetence or minority, the limitation period will not begin to run until the patient is declared competent or reaches the age of majority.[53] The rationale underlying these rules is that mental incompetence and minority are legal disabilities affecting the individual's ability to know of the existence of an injury and a corresponding right to sue for damages.

In some states, the statutes of limitation may also be tolled where a fiduciary relationship (e.g., the existence of a guardian of a disabled person, the trustee of a trust, etc.) is determined to exist between the hospital and the injured party. Fraud, constructive fraud, and fraudulent concealment are encompassed within such circumstances, and courts may find that the hospital had a duty to disclose information and that it breached that duty.[54] A good example of fraudulent concealment is a hospital's refusing to give patients access to their medical

---

[51]Ill. Rev. Stat. ch. 110, §13–212 (1984). *See also* Ariz. Rev. Stat. Ann. §12–542 (1982 and West Supp. 1983–1984), two years after discovery but no more than six years after date of injury.

[52]*See, e.g.*, Mich. Comp. Laws §600.5838 (West Supp. 1983–1984).

[53]*See, e.g.*, Ariz. Rev. Stat. Ann. §12–502 (1982); Cal. Civ. Pro. Code §352 (1983); Mich. Comp. Laws §600.5851 (1981).

[54]*See, e.g.*, Nutty v. The Universal Engineering Corp., 564 F.Supp. 1459 (S.D. Ill. 1983); Garcia v. Presbyterian Hospital Center, 92 N.M. 652, 593 P. 2d 487 (1979).

records. In *Waits v. United States*,[55] for example, the plaintiff alleged that his leg had to be amputated because of the failure of physicians at a Veterans Administration hospital to order certain tests and followup laboratory reports reasonably promptly and to administer proper antibiotics for control of the infection. He argued that he should not be barred by the statute of limitations because the hospital failed to give him access to his medical records, thereby delaying his ability to discover the acts of negligence causing his injury and precluding him from bringing his cause of action within the statutory time period. The court agreed, holding that his claim was not barred by the statute of limitation.[56]

---

[55]611 F. 2d 550 (5th Cir. 1980).

[56]*Id*. at 553; *see also* Emmett v. Eastern Dispensary and Casualty Hospital, 396 F. 2d 931 (D.C. Cir. 1967); Harrison v. United States, 708 F. 2d 1023 (5th Cir. 1983).

List of Statutes Concerning Medical Records

This appendix contains a list of state statutes concerning medical records that are cited in this book. Some states publish statutes in more than one form. As a result, the citations found here are from the publications following the name of each state. Since state legislatures revise their statutes constantly, laws not listed here may appear from time to time. Therefore, this appendix should be used as a general guide to the statutory treatment of medical records in the various states.

Alabama:

Alabama Code Annotated

§12–21–5.	Copy of hospital records, admissibility.
§12–21–6.	Same, Subpoena duces tecum; inspection; form; weight; cost.
§22–8A–4.	Written declaration, requirements, form.
§22–9–11.	Records and reports of inmates and births and deaths in institutions.
§22–9–71.	Certification of medical data.
§22–16–12.	Record of consultation or treatment.
§22–50–9.	Same, Powers generally.
§22–50–10.	Same, Transfer of authority to board from existing agencies.
§22–50–11.	Same—Additional and cumulative powers.
§26–10–5.	Recordation, inspection, etc., of petition, orders, etc., in adoption proceedings; effect of final order of adoption as to legal rights, obligations, etc., of natural parents, adopting parents, and child generally; visitation rights of natural grandparents; annulment, avoidance, etc., of final adoption order.
§34–24–58.	Decisions, opinions, etc., of utilization review committee privileges.
§38–7–13	Records to be kept by child care facility; use and disclosure information.

Alaska:

Alaska Statutes

§18.20.085.	Hospital records retention.
§18.20.090.	Information confidential.
§18.23.030.	Confidentiality of records of review organization.
§18.23.065.	Patient access to records.
§47.30.130.	Right to humane care and treatment and consent to surgery, certain psychiatric therapies, and autopsies.
§47.30.140.	Mechanical restraints.
§47.30.150.	Rights of patients.

Arizona:

Arizona Revised Statutes Annotated

Ch. 5, §12–542.	Injury to person, injury when death ensues, injury to property, conversion of property, forcible entry and forcible detainer, two-year limitation.
Ch. 13, §12–2235.	Doctor and patient.
Ch. 1, §36–151.	Definitions.
Ch. 3, §36–339.	Reproduction of records.
Ch. 3, §36–340.	Disclosure of records, violations.
Ch. 3, §36–341.	Copies of and data from vital records.
Ch. 3, §36–343.	Persons required to keep records.
Ch. 4, §36–445.01.	Information relating to review of certain medical practices inadmissible as evidence not subject to discovery, participants not required to testify, medical-legal panel.
Ch. 4, §36–445.02.	Immunity for serving on or furnishing information to review committees.
Ch. 5, §36–509.	Confidential records.

Arkansas:

Arkansas Statutes Annotated

§16–501.	Reproduction of business records and public records by photograph, microfilm, or photostat, certificate as to original.
§28–937.	Furnishing copies of records in compliance with subpoenas.
§82–357.	Records available for medical research, immunity from damage, liability for publication of findings, identity of patient confidential, privileged communications.
§82–530.	Fees for copies and searches, criminal penalties.
§82–531.	Records required to be kept.
§82–532.	Duty to furnish information relative to vital events.
§82–533.	Penalties.
§§82–3801–3804.	Death with dignity.

Uniform Rules of Evidence

§28–101, Rule 503.	Physician- and psychotherapist-patient privilege.

California:

California Evidence Code Annotated

§994.	Physician-patient privilege.
§1158.	Presentation of authorization of inspection and copying of patient's records, failure to comply, costs.

§1156.	Records of medical study of in-hospital staff committee.
§1156.1	Records of medical or psychiatric studies of quality assurance committees.
§1157.	Proceedings and records of medical, medical-dental, podiatric, registered dietician, or veterinary staff review committees, local medical, dental, dental hygienist, podiatric, dietetic, veterinary, or chiropractic society review committees.
§1157.5.	Organized committee of nonprofit medical care foundation or professional standards review organization, proceedings and records.
§1157.6.	Proceedings and records of quality assurance committees for county health facilities.
§1157.7.	Application of section 1157, discovery or testimony, prohibitions, application of public records or meetings provisions.
§1550.	Photographic copies made of business records.
§1560.	Compliance with subpoena duces tecum for business records.

Business and Professions Code

| §2282. | Practice in hospital with staff of five or more physicians and surgeons without adoption of certain rules. |
| §2283. | Practice in hospital with staff of less than five physicians and surgeons without adoption of certain rules. |

California Civil Code

| §56.10. | Authorizations necessity, exceptions. |
| §56.11. | Authorization, form and content. |

California Penal Code

§11160.	Injuries by deadly weapon or criminal act, report by hospital or pharmacy, contents of report.
§11161.	Injuries by deadly weapon or criminal act, report by physician or surgeon.
§11162.	Violation; offense; punishment.

California Health and Safety Code

§410.	Authority of department to define disorders; reports for use of department of motor vehicles
§§7185–7193.	Natural Death Act.
§11167.	Epidemics, accidents or calamities, oral prescriptions for Schedule II controlled substances, use of other than official form for written prescriptions, record.

Colorado: *Colorado Revised Statutes*

§12–43.5–102.	Establishment of review committee, function.
§13–90–107.	Who may not testify without consent.
§25–3–204.	Records not public.
§25–4–508.	Inspection of records.

§25–1–801.	Patient records in custody of health care facility.
§27–10–120.	Records.

Connecticut: *Connecticut General Statutes Annotated*

§4–104.	Inspection and subpoena of hospital records.
§4–105.	Procedure where right to inspect records is denied.
§38–19a.	Peer review: definitions, immunity, discovery permissible re proceedings.

Delaware: *Delaware Code Annotated*

Tit. 10, §8116.	Savings for infants or persons under disability.
Tit. 19, §2321.	Minimum duration of incapacity.
Tit. 19, §2322.	Medical and other services and supplies as furnished by employer.
Tit. 19, §2323.	Selection of physician, surgeon, dentist, optometrist, or chiropractor by employee.
Tit. 24, §1768.	Immunity of persons reviewing medical records, medical care, and physicians' work.
Tit. 25, §4301.	Liens in favor of charitable hospitals.
Tit. 25, §4302.	Establishment of lien, notice of claim.
Tit. 25, §4303.	Attachment of lien to judgment.
Tit. 25, §4304.	Release as effective, liability of person making payment, limitation.
Tit. 25, §4305.	Recording of liens, fees.
Tit. 25, §4306.	Examination of hospital records.
Tit. 29, §7202.	Records.

Delaware Rules of Evidence

§503.	Confidential communications statute.

Dist. of Columbia: *District of Columbia Code Encyclopedia Annotated*

§6–2422.	Declaration: execution, form.
§14–307.	Confidential communications statute.

Florida: *Florida Statute Annotated*

§63.162.	Hearings and records in adoption proceedings, confidential nature.
§§90.101–90.958.	Florida Evidence Code.
§395.016.	Patient records, form and content.
§395.017.	Patient records, copies, examination.
§395.018.	Criminal and administrative penalties, injunctions, emergency orders, moratoriums.
§395.202.	Patient records, copies, examination.
§395.25.	Examinations for cancer of the cervix and breast.
§768.40.	Medical review committee, immunity from liability.
§827.07(9).	Abuse of children, immunity.

Georgia: *Georgia Code Annotated*

§31–9–4.	Care and treatment of mentally ill.
§31–9–5.	Same, abortion and sterilization procedures.

§66–345.	Mechanical restraints.
§66–346.	Right to communication and visitation, exercise of civil rights.
§66–347.	Writ of habeas corpus.
§66–348.	Disclosure of information.
§66–349.	Penalty for violation.
§66–350.	Detention pending judicial determination.
§66–351.	Repayment of money found on discharge of patient.
§66–352	Money found on mentally ill persons, disposition.

Illinois:

Illinois Annotated Statutes

Ch. 4, §§9.1–18.	[Adoption] records confidential.
Ch. 23, §§2051–2061.7.	Abused and Neglected Child Reporting Act.
Ch. 23, §2053.	Definitions.
Ch. 23, §2054.	Persons required to report, medical personnel, privileged communications, transmitting false report.
Ch. 23, §2059.	Immunity from liability, presumption.
Ch. 23, §2060.	Testimony by person making report.
Ch. 38, §81–30.	Reports, rules and regulations, confidential information.
Ch. 38, §81–31.	Violations, penalties, unprofessional conduct.
Ch. 48, §138.16.	Rules and orders—Depositions—Subpoenas—Hospital Records, Court reporter, fees and charges.
Ch. 56–1/2, §1311.	Original and duplicate of prescription.
Ch. 56–1/2, §1312.	Dispensing controlled substances.
Ch. 82, §99.	Hospital Records—Examination—Furnishing Statement of Injuries.
Ch. 91–1/2, §§801–817.	Mental Health and Developmental Disabilities Confidentiality.
Ch. 110, §2–1101.	Subpoenas.
Ch. 110, §2–1113.	Medical malpractice, res ipsa loquitur.
Ch. 110, §8–802.	Physician and patient.
Ch. 110, §8–2001.	Examination of records.
Ch. 110, §8–2101.	Information obtained.
Ch. 110, §8–2102.	Admissibility as evidence.
Ch. 110, §8–2103.	Furnishing information.
Ch. 110, §8–2104.	Interviews.
Ch. 110, §8–2105.	Improper disclosure.
Ch. 111, §3402(2).	Necessity of license, acts not prohibited.
Ch. 111–1/2, §73–17.	New certificate of birth—prerequisites.
Ch. 111–1/2, §157–11.	Retention of x-ray or roentgen films as records, litigation.
Ch. 116, §59–64.	Uniform preservation of private business records.

Indiana:

Indiana Statutes Annotated

§16–4–2–3.	Information confidential, research use only, exceptions, identity withheld.

	§16–4–3–1.	Access to records and reports of patients by in-hospital medical staff, purposes.
	§16–4–3–2.	Use and publication of material from records, identity of patient.
	§34–1–14–5.	Who is incompetent.
	§34–3–15.5–1 et seq.	Hospital medical records.
	§34–4–12.6–1.	Definitions.
	§34–4–12.6–2.	Confidentiality and privilege.
Iowa:	*Iowa Code Annotated*	
	68A.7.	Confidential records.
	§135.40.	Collection and distribution of information.
	§135.41.	Publication.
	§135.42.	Unlawful use.
	§147.137.	General provisions regulating practice professions, malpractice, consent in writing.
	§622.10.	Communications in professional confidence, exceptions, application to court.
Kansas:	*Kansas Statutes Annotated*	
	§59–2928.	Restraints and seclusion.
	§59–2929.	Rights of patients.
	§60–245(d).	Subpoenas, service.
	§60–427.	Confidential communications statute.
	§65–177.	"Data" defined; study of diseases and deaths from maternity causes, confidentiality, use, admissibility as evidence, reports, contents.
	§65–2423.	Adoption cases.
	§65–504.	Licenses, terms and regulations, temporary licenses, refusal to grant licenses, revocation, notice, hearing, appeals, procedure.
Kentucky:	*Kentucky Revised Statutes Annotated*	
	§213.200.	Privileged communications.
	§311.377.	Waiver of claim for damages by applicant for or grantee of staff privileges, records confidential, exceptions.
	§311.595.	Causes for denial, probation, suspension or revocation of licenses and permits.
	§422.300.	Use of photostatic copies of medical records, originals held available.
	§422.305.	Subpoena of records, certification of copies, personal delivery.
	§422.310.	Personal attendance of custodian of hospital records, when.
	§422.315.	Patient may ask to prohibit or limit use of his medical records.
	§422.320.	Return of medical records to court clerk.
	§422.325.	Proper procedure for obtaining records required.
	§422.330.	Privileges not waived.

Louisiana: *Louisiana Revised Statutes Annotated*

§13:3714.   Charts or records of hospitals, admissibility of certified copy.

§13:3715.   Court order for chart or record of state-operated health care facilities, certified copy as sufficient compliance.

§13:3715.1.   Hospital records, procedure in an action in which the hospital is not a party.

§15:476.   Privileged communications between physician and patient, exceptions.

§28:94.   Transfer of patients between institutions.

§44:7.   Hospital records.

§44:39.   Microfilm records; use as evidence.

Maine: *Maine Revised Statutes Annotated*

Tit. 10, §3412.   Notice.

Tit. 10, §3413.   Duration.

Tit. 16, §101.   Subpoenas for witnesses.

Tit. 16, §357.   Hospital records and copies of records.

Tit. 22, §1711.   Patient access to hospital medical records.

Tit. 32, §3296.   Records of proceedings of hospital medical staff review committees confidential.

Tit. 34, §2253.   Medical restraints and seclusion.

Tit. 34, §2254.   Rights to communication and visitation.

Tit. 34, §2255.   Habeas corpus.

Tit. 34A, §3003.   Confidentiality of information.

Tit. 34B, §1207.   Confidentiality of information.

Maryland: *Maryland Code Annotated*

§4–301.   Disclosure of medical records.

§4–302.   Records of facilities.

§10–709.   Records.

§10–1002.   False application or certificate; unlawful detention.

§10–1004.   Records.

§14–601.   Medical review committees.

§14–602.   Confidential records of faculty and others.

§14–603.   Immunity from civil liability of certain persons providing information about physicians.

§16–604.   Inspection of hospital records.

§19–344.   Procedures for compliance.

Art. 15B, §1.   Definitions.

Art. 15B, §2.   Records may be destroyed after three years, exceptions.

Art. 15B, §3.   Preservation of reproductions.

Art. 15B, §4.   Authority of state officers to permit destruction unaffected.

Art. 15B, §5.   Uniformity of interpretation.

Art. 15B, §6.   Short title.

Massachusetts: *Massachusetts General Laws Annotated*

Ch. 111, §70.   Records of hospitals or clinics, custody, inspection, copies, fees.

Ch. 111, §70E.   Patients' rights.

Ch. 111, §111F.   Reciprocal duty of insurer and insured to furnish medical reports upon request.

Ch. 231, §85N.   Members of professional societies, medical staff committees, etc., immune from liability in certain cases, professional society defined.

Michigan: *Michigan Statutes Annotated*

§14.57[23].   Confidentiality of information.

§14.800[141].   Patients' records, contents.

§28.642.   Soliciting personal injury claims, exception. Unauthorized disclosure of identity or treatment of patient, misdemeanor.

Michigan Compiled Laws Annotated

§333.2623.   Results of health services research, demonstrations and evaluations, publication and dissemination.

§600.2157.   Physician-patient privilege; waiver.

§600.5833.   Malpractice by member of state licensed profession.

Minnesota: *Minnesota Statutes Annotated*

§144.34.   Investigation and control of occupational diseases.

§144.68.   Records and reports, hospitals and similar institutions, information without liability.

§144.69.   Information not available to the public.

§144.335.   Access to have records, patient access.

§144.651.   Patients and residents of health care facilities, bill of rights.

§145.30.   Superintendent of hospitals to transfer records.

§145.31.   Photostatic copies to be used as evidence.

§145.61.   Definitions.

§145.62.   Limitation on liability for persons providing information to review organization.

§145.63.   Limitation on liability for members of review organizations.

§145.64.   Confidentiality of records of review organization.

§145.65.   Guidelines not admissible in evidence.

§145.413.   Recording and reporting health data.

§145.423.   Abortion, live births.

§246.017.   Medical policy directional committee on mental health, system of records and statistics.

§253A.17.   Rights of patients.

§595.02.   Competency of witnesses.

Mississippi: *Mississippi Code Annotated*

§41–9–1.   Declaration of purpose.

§41–9–61.   Definitions.

§516.140.	What actions within two years.
§537.035.	Members of certain professional standards boards or committees exempt from action for damages, when.

Montana: *Montana Code Annotated*

§26–1–805.	Confidential communications statute.
§50–16–202.	Committees to have access to information.
§50–16–203.	Committee information and proceedings confidential and privileged.
§50–16–204.	Restrictions on use or publication of information.
§50–16–205.	Data confidential, inadmissible in judicial proceedings.
§50–16–302.	Definitions.
§50–16–311.	When consent is required to release or transfer confidential health care information.
§50–16–313.	Right of person affected regarding modifications and additions.
§50–16–314.	Privileged information—exemption for compulsory legal process.

Nebraska: *Nebraska Revised Statutes*

§25–12, 120.	Hospital records, examination and inspection, hospital medical staff committee, utilization review committee.
§25–12, 121.	Hospital records, hospital medical staff committee, utilization review committee, recommendations, not liable for damages.
§27–504. Rule 504.	Physician-patient privilege, definitions, general rule of privilege, who may claim privilege, exceptions to the privilege.
§71–3401.	Information, statement, data, furnish without liability.

Nevada: *Nevada Revised Statutes Annotated*

§41A.110.	Consent of patient, when conclusively established.
§49.215.	Definitions.
§49.225.	General rule of privilege.
§49.235.	Who may claim privilege.
§49.245.	Exceptions.
§49.025.	Required reports privileged by statute.
§51.125.	Hearsay exceptions: recorded recollection.
§51.135.	Hearsay exceptions: records of regularly conducted activity, affidavit of custodian or medical records.
§52.325.	Use of photographic copies, delivery to the clerk of court, authentication.
§108.640.	Hospital records, examination; copying.
§629.021.	"Health care records" defined.
§629.051.	Health care records: retention.
§629.061.	Health care records: inspection; use in public hearing; immunity from civil action.

New Hampshire:	*New Hampshire Revised Statutes Annotated*	
	§126–A:4–a.	Medical and scientific research information.
	§329:26.	Confidential communications.
	§337–A:1–A:6.	Preservation of private business records.
New Jersey:	*New Jersey Revised Statutes Annotated*	
	§2A:44–45.	Statement of hospital charges; examination of hospital records.
	§2A:82–41.	Person against whom claim is asserted, right of examination.
	§2A:84A–22.1.	Definitions.
	§2A:84A–22.2.	Patient and physician privilege.
	§2A:84A–22.8.	Utilization review committees of certified hospital or extended care facility, exceptions.
	§26:8–5.	Institutional records.
	§337–A:1.	Definitions.
	§337–A:2.	Destruction of records.
	§337–A:3.	Reproductions.
	§337–A:4.	Application.
	§337–A:5.	Construction.
	§337–A:6.	Citation.
New Mexico:	*New Mexico Statutes Annotated*	
	§14–6–1.	Health information, confidentiality, immunity from liability for furnishing.
	§14–6–2.	Hospital records, retention.
	§14–7–1.	Requiring notice of intent to gain access to records of financial institutions.
	§14–9–2.	Definitions.
	§14–9–3.	Limitation on liability for persons providing information to review organization.
	§14–9–4.	Limitation on liability for members of review organizations.
	§14–9–5.	Confidentiality of records of review organization.
	§14–9–6.	Penalty for violation.
	§14–9–7.	Protection of patient.
New York:	*New York Education Law*	
	§6527.	Special provisions.
	New York Mental Hygiene Law	
	§31.09.	Powers of the department regarding investigation and inspections.
	§31.11.	Certain duties of providers of services.
	§31.13.	Powers of subpoena and examination.
	§31.17.	Formal hearings, procedure.
	New York Lien Law	
	§189.	Liens of hospitals.

New York Public Health Law

§17.	Release of medical records.
§201.	Functions, powers and duties of the department.
§2801.	Definition.
§2803.1.a.	Commissioner and council, power and duties.
§2805–g.	Maintenance of records.
§4160.	Fetal deaths, registration.
§4161.	Fetal death certificates, form and content, physicians, midwives, and hospital administrators.
§4165.	Persons in institutions, registration.
§C2306:1.	Patients' records from hospital or governmental unit.
§C3121.7.	Hospital records authorization.

New York Civil Practice Law and Rules

Rule 4504.	Physician, dentist and nurse.
§2306.	Hospital records, medical records of department or bureau of a municipal corporation or of the state.
§2307.	Books, papers, and other things of a library, department, or bureau of a municipal corporation or of the state.

New York Penal Law

§265.25.	Certain wounds to be reported.

North Carolina: *North Carolina General Statutes*

§8–44.1.	Copies of medical records.
§8–53.	Communications between physician and patient.
§14–118.3.	Acquisition and use of information obtained from patients in hospitals for fraudulent purposes.
§48–25.	Recordation and information not to be made public, violation a misdemeanor.
§122–8.1.	Disclosure of information, records, etc.
§122–48.	Clerk to keep records of examinations and discharges.
§131–168.	Definitions.
§131–169.	Limited liability.
§131–175.	Findings of fact.
§131E–87.	Reports of disciplinary action, immunity from liability.
§131E–90.	Authority of administrator, refusal to leave after discharge.
§131E–95.	Medical review committee.

North Dakota: *North Dakota Century Code*

§23–01–12.	Hospital records to be kept at direction of state health officer.
§23–01–02.1.	Hospital utilization committees, internal quality assurance review committee, reports, immunity.
§25–03.1–43.	Confidential records.

§25–03.1–44.	Records of disclosure.
§25–03.1–45.	Expungement of records.
§23–16–09.	Information confidential.
§31–08–01.	Admissibility in evidence of business records, term "business records" defined, exception.

North Dakota Revised Evidence Code

Rules 501 and 503.	Confidential communications statute.

Ohio:

Ohio Revised Code Annotated

§2305.24.	Information disclosed to a hospital utilization review committee, immunity from liability.
[§2305.25.1]	Review committees' proceedings and records.
§2305.251.	
§2317.02.	Privileged communications and acts.
[§3701.26.1].	
§3701.261.	Information concerning malignant disease.
§3721.01.	Definitions and classification.
§3721.02.	Licensing by director of health; delegation of licensing authority; inspection; distribution of fees.
§3721.04.	Uniform rules for operation of homes, standards.
§3721.26.	Area training centers for employees of nursing homes.
[§3721.26.1]	Supervision of training centers.
§3721.261.	
§3727.01.	"Hospital" defined.
§3727.02.	Certification or accreditation requirements for hospitals.
§3727.03.	Rules for proving compliance and closing non-complying hospitals.
§3727.04.	Inspections.
§3727.05.	Injunctions.
§3727.06.	Admission and supervision of patients.
§3727.07.	Licensing of maternity and psychiatric units not affected.
§5122.31.	Disclosure of information.

Oklahoma:

Oklahoma Statutes Annotated

Tit. 12, §§2101–3103.	Evidence code.
Tit. 12, §2503.	Physician and psychotherapist-patient privilege.
Tit. 17, §19.	Access to medical records, copies, waiver of privilege.
Tit. 17, §20.	Refusing to furnish records, penalty.
Tit. 59, §509.	Unprofessional conduct, definition.
Tit. 63, §1–1709.	Information concerning condition and treatment of patients—restrictions—exemption from liability—review committees.
Tit. 67, §§251–256.	Uniform preservation of private business records act.
Tit. 76, §19.	Access to medical records, copies, waiver of privilege.

Oregon:	*Oregon Revised Statutes*	
	§41.675.	Inadmissibility of certain health care facility and training data.
	§192.525.	State policy concerning medical records.
	Oregon Rules of Evidence	
	Rule 504–1.	Confidential communications statute.
	Oregon Rules of Civil Procedure	
	Rule 55(H).	Hospital records.
Pennsylvania:	*Pennsylvania Statutes Annotated*	
	§835.	Depositions, hospital records, physician's certificate, medical and surgical data.
	§1522.	Rules of evidence, depositions, hospital records, physician's certificate, medical and surgical data.
	§4604.	Report of psychological examination.
	§4605.	Penalties.
	§5929.	Physicians not to disclose information.
	Tit. 63, §425.2.	Definitions.
	Tit. 63, §425.3.	Immunity from liability.
	Tit. 63, §425.4.	Confidentiality of review organization's records.
Rhode Island:	*Rhode Island General Laws*	
	[§5–37.3–1].	Short title–Confidentiality of Health Care Information Act.
	[§5–37.3–2].	Statement of purpose.
	[§5–37.3–3].	Definition of terms.
	§5–37.3–4.	Limitations on disclosure.
	§5–37.3–5.	Transfer and amendment of information.
	[§5–37.3–6].	Legal process.
	[§5–37.3–7].	Medical peer review.
	§5–37.3–8.	Guardian ad litem.
	§5–37.3–9.	Penalties, attorney's fees.
	§5–37.3–10.	Waiver.
	§5–37.3–11.	Severability.
	§9–3–8.	Hospital lien docket.
	§9–19–27.	Evidence of charges for medical and hospital services and for prescription and orthopedic appliances and evidence required from hospital medical records.
	§23–17–24.	Internal risk management program.
	§40.1–5–26.	Confidential information and records, disclosures.
	§40.1–5–27.	Information to person's family.
	§40.1–5–28.	Notice of disappearance of person.
	§40.1–5–29.	Records of disclosure.
	§40.1–5–30.	Statistical data.
South Carolina:	*South Carolina Code Annotated*	
	§40–71–20.	Confidentiality of certain proceedings, records, and information.
	§44–23–1010.	Treatment and medication of patients; shock treatment.

South Dakota:

Tennessee:

§68–11–401.	Definitions.
§68–11–402.	Furnishing copies of records in compliance with subpoenas.
§68–11–403.	Sealing, identification, and direction of copies.
§68–11–404.	Opening of sealed envelopes.
§68–11–405.	Affidavit of custodian as to copies, charges.
§68–11–406.	Admissibility of copies and affidavits.
§68–11–407.	Personal attendance of custodian, production of original record.
§68–11–408.	Substitution of copies for original records.

Texas:

Texas Revised Civil Statutes Annotated

Art. 4447D.	Providing state Department of Health with data on condition and treatment of persons.
Art. 4447D–1. §2.23.	Data on condition and treatment of persons.
Art. 4447D–1. §2.24.	Certificate of need requirement.
Art. 4495b, §5.08.	Physician-patient communication.
Art. 4590h, §1 et seq.	Natural Death Act.

Utah:

Utah Code Annotated

§26–15–58.	Licenses, minimum requirements.
§26–25–1.	Authority to provide data on treatment and condition of persons to designated agencies—Immunity from liability.
§26–25–3.	Data and findings as privileged communications.
§78–24–8.	Privileged communications.
§78–25–25.	Patient records, inspection and copying by attorneys.

Vermont:

Vermont Statutes Annotated

| Tit. 26, §1441. | Definitions and purpose. |
| Tit. 26, §1443. | Records immune from discovery. |

Virginia:

Virginia Code Annotated

§2.1–342.	Official records to be opened to inspection, procedure for requesting records and responding to requests, charges, exceptions to application of chapter.
§8.01–391.	Copies of originals as evidence.
§8.01–399.	Communications between physicians and patients.
§8.01–413.	Certain copies of hospital or physicians' records or papers of patient admissible, right of patient or his attorney to copies of such records or papers, subpoena, damages, costs, and attorney's fees.
§8.01–581.16.	Civil immunity for members of or consultants to certain boards or committees.
§8.01–581.17.	Privileged communications of certain committees.

§32.1–70.	Record of hospital and clinics may be applied to commissioner, statewide cancer registry.
§32.1–71.	Confidential nature of informations applied, publication.
§32.1–72.	Performance of laboratory tests.

Washington: *Washington Revised Code Annotated*

§4.24.250.	Health care provider filing charges or presenting evidence, immunity, records, members, employees, etc., of review committees or boards not subject to process.
§5.60.060.	Who is disqualified—privileged communications.
§18.108.180.	Inspection of massage premises by director, reports, and information.
§70.41.190.	Retention and preservation of records of patients.
§70.58.270.	Data on inmates of hospitals, etc.
§70.122.030(1).	Directive to withhold or withdraw life-sustaining procedures.

West Virginia: *West Virginia Code*

§27–5–9.	Right of patients.
§30–3C–3.	Confidentiality of review organization's records.

Wisconsin: *Wisconsin Statutes Annotated*

§51.45.	Prevention and control of alcoholism, confidentiality of records of patients.
§51.61.	Patients' rights.
§146.38.	Health care services review, confidentiality of information.
§804.10.	Physical and mental examination of parties, inspection of medical documents.
§895.045.	Contributory negligence.
§905.04.	Physician-patient, chiropractor-patient, or psychologist-patient privilege.

Wyoming: *Wyoming Statutes*

§1–12–101.	Privileged communications and acts.
§25–10–122.	Records to be kept confidential; exceptions.
§35–17–103.	Exemption from liability, exception.
§35–2–601.	Medical staff committees to have access to records, etc., purpose.
§35–2–602.	Reports, etc., to be confidential and privileged.
§35–2–603.	Immunity from liability.
§35–2–604.	Definitions.

State-by-State Analysis of Medical Records Statutes and Regulations

The following comprehensive compilation and analysis of state statutes and regulations affecting medical records sets forth significant language of the regulations. Although a high degree of similarity exists among the state regulations, each state has its peculiarities. Language applicable to records in uniform acts, such as the Uniform Narcotic Drug Act and the Interstate Compact on Mental Health, will not be reported, because the provisions of these acts are the same from state to state. This appendix should be used with caution. The authors have prepared an analysis of the materials they consider relevant; some materials have been omitted. Moreover, regulations change constantly. Some may not be found here; those discussed here may be revised. Therefore, this appendix should be used as a general guide to the regulatory treatment of medical records in the various states.

The regulations are analyzed in terms of the following categories (not all categories are represented in each state's analysis):

1. Creation and contents
2. Retention
3. Signature requirements
4. Disclosure authorized
5. Confidentiality
6. Other matters.

1. *Creation and Contents*: This category identifies regulations that make specific reference to the contents of the medical record and to the form it should take.
2. *Retention*: This category deals with requirements that specify the manner in which and the length of time the record must be kept. Provisions relating to completion of records are included also. These materials vary significantly from state to state.
3. *Signature Requirements*: The states vary in their requirements for physician signatures in the medical record, but the intent of a great majority of regulations and a number of statutes is that the physician sign or authenticate specified portions of the record as well as the record as a whole.
4. *Authorized Disclosures*: This category includes legal materials that specifically permit the disclosure of information from the record.
5. *Confidentiality*: This category analyzes regulations specifically declaring that records or certain portions of the information they contain are confidential.
6. *Other Matters*: This general category reports on regulations that deal with a variety of subjects, such as admissibility, ownership, and hospital lien laws.

ALABAMA

1. *Creation and Contents*: The *Rules, Regulations and Standards—Hospitals*, Department of Public Health (December, 1970), contains many references to the required contents and form of medical records. These regulations are contained in one extensive chapter of the *Alabama Administrative Code* (AAC). AAC ch. 420–5–7. AAC Rule 420–5–7.07(2)(b)(3)(a) *Admission Record*. This rule provides that an "adequate permanent record either typewritten or legibly written with pen and ink shall be kept for each patient." AAC Rule 420–5–7.07(2)(b)(3)(b) *Medical and Surgical Record*. Minimum requirements are set out in the rule. In addition to general information, the clinical section must include, when applicable, provisional diagnosis, laboratory and x-ray reports, consultations, medical and surgical treatment, operative report, tissue report, progress notes, final diagnosis, discharge summary (cases over 48 hours), and autopsy findings. AAC Rule 420–5–7.07(2)(b)(3)(c) *Obstetrical Record*. Prenatal, labor, and postpartum records must be maintained. AAC Rule 420–5–7.07(2)(b)(3)(d) *Newborn Record*. Birth record, physical examination, and nurses' record are required. AAC Rule 420–5–7.07(2)(b)(3)(e) *Physicians' Orders*. A specific record form for each patient is required for all physicians' orders. AAC Rule 420–5–7.07(2)(b)(3)(f) *Nurses' Record*. Personal services and observations shall be noted.

   With reference to physical medicine, AAC Rule 420–5–7.14(1)(d) requires written records for all orders, treatments, and procedures. Such records become a part of inpatients' medical records.

2. *Retention*: AAC Rule 420–5–7.07(1)(a) places primary responsibility for maintenance of records on the administrator. Rule 420–5–7.07(1)(b) requires that records be stored to ensure their safety from water or fire damage and unauthorized use. Rule 420–5–7.07(1)(c) provides that records be kept current. They must be stored for 22 years as either original records, abstracts, microfilm, or otherwise. Nurses' notes may be deleted from the permanent record.

3. *Signature Requirements*: Numerous rules require signatures. Rule 420–5–7.07(1)(g) requires that entries in the medical record be made in ink or by typewriter; they must be authenticated, and signed or initialed by the attending physician. Rule 420–5–7.07(2)(b)(3)(e) is to the same effect, requiring the signature or initials of the attending physician for all orders. Verbal or telephone orders must later be signed or initialed by the attending physician. Laboratory reports must be signed or initialed by the individuals performing the tests under Rule 420–5–7.09(1)(e). Mechanical restraints, according to Rule 420–5–7.12(1)(b), can be applied only when the attending physician deems them necessary. The restraint orders must be in writing and signed by the attending physician within 24 hours. Rule 420–5–7.12(1)(c) permits seclusion of patients only on the written orders of the attending physician.

4. *Disclosure Authorized*: No statute or regulation specifically authorizes the disclosure of information in medical records. Rule 420–5–7.05(2)(a)(2)(iv) requires that the medical staff bylaws provide for a monthly review and analysis of the medical staff's clinical experience using the patients' medical records as the basis for such review. However, Rule 420–5–7.07(1)(h) provides that the hospital governing board determine the persons who shall have access to medical records. The State Mental Health Board has the power to set standards for the transfer of patients and their records. Ala. Code §22–50–11 (1975).

5. *Confidentiality*: Rule 420–5–7.07(1)(h) of the health regulations specifically makes the contents of records confidential. Rule 420–5–7.07(1)(b) requires that the records be handled in such a manner as to ensure that they are safeguarded from unauthorized use.

6. *Other Matters*: Several statutes refer to the admissibility of records or copies in judicial proceedings. When the original would be admissible in any suit or proceeding, a certified copy of the hospital record will be admissible in its place. The record may include admission data, disease, injury, history, temperature and other charts, x-rays, written orders, directions, findings and reports, and interpretations of

physicians, doctors, surgeons, pathologists, radiologists, specialists, dentists, technicians and nurses as well as of employees of such hospitals, forming part of such hospital records as to the health, condition, state, injuries, sickness, disease, mental, physical and nervous disorders, duration and character of disabilities, diagnosis, prognosis, progress, wounds, cuts, contusions, lacerations, breaks, loss of blood, incisions, operations, injuries, medication, medicines, supplies, treatment and care and the cost, expenses, fees and charges. . . .

This information is admissible without further proof as business records of the hospital. Ala. Code §12–21–5 (1975).

Rule 420–5–7.07(1)(d) of the regulations provides that the records are the property of the hospital. Control of the records rests with the hospital administrator.

ALASKA

1. *Creation and Contents*: *General Acute Care Hospital Regulation*, Department of Health and Social Services (1984), contains many references to the contents and form of the medical record. These regulations are contained in one extensive section of the Alaska Administrative Code. Alas. Adm. Code tit. 7, §12.770.

   Sections 12.770(b) and (c) set out the requirements for medical records. All patients must have medical records. Minimum requirements for completeness include, where applicable, adequate identification data, admitting diagnosis, history and physical examination, consultation reports, progress notes, signed doctors' orders, operative notes, laboratory and x-ray reports, pathology reports, nurses' notes, discharge diagnosis, and autopsy report.

2. *Retention*: Section 12.770(b) provides that "originals or accurate reproductions of the contents of the originals of all records, including x-rays, must be maintained in a form which is legible." Section 12.770(d) requires that procedures be established to protect the information in medical records from loss, defacement, or tampering. Section 12.770(e) requires that patient records be completed within 15 days of discharge.

   Hospital records must be preserved for seven years following the discharge of the patient. Records of minors must be maintained for at least two years after the patient has reached the age of 19 or for seven years following the discharge of the patient, whichever is longer. X-ray film records must be retained for five years. If a hospital ceases operation, it must make arrangements for preserving its records. Alaska Stat. §18.20.085 (1983).

3. *Signature Requirements*: Section 12.770(e) requires that a record be "authenticated or signed by the attending physician or dentist." However, a signature stamp or computer key may be substituted for the physician's signature when "the physician has given a signed statement to the hospital administrator that he or she is the only person who (1) has possession of the stamp or key; and (2) may use the stamp or key." Section 12.110(c)(4) requires that a physician's order, including a telephone or other oral order, be reduced to writing and initialed or signed by the attending physician within 24 hours after the order is given.

   Alas. Stat. §47.30.140 (1983), dealing with the use of mechanical restraints in mental hospitals, provides that their use and reasons therefor shall be made part of the patient's clinical record over the signature of the head of the hospital, or his or her designee.

4. *Disclosure Authorized*: Section 12.770(b) requires that the records be readily available to the attending physician, medical staff, representative of the department, or, upon the patient's written request, to other practitioners.

   Section 12.770(d) requires that the information in medical records be protected from access by unauthorized persons.

6. *Other Matters*: The regulations also provide that a transfer summary, signed by the physician, must accompany the patient if he or she is transferred to another facility or to a different unit within the same facility. Section 12.770(g) sets out the information that must be contained in the transfer summary, including the patient's diagnosis, condition, medications, and treatment.

ARIZONA

1. *Creation and Contents*: Regulations providing complete references to the form and contents of medical records are contained in one detailed section of the *Official Compilation of Administrative Rules and Regulations*. Ariz. Admin. Comp. R9–10–221 (Supp. 1979).

    Section 221(B) provides that "a medical record shall be established and maintained for every person receiving treatment as an inpatient, outpatient, or on an emergency basis in any unit of the hospital."

    The contents of inpatient medical records are set out in section 221(N). Minimum requirements include, when applicable, identification information, history and physical examination, physicians' orders, laboratory and diagnostic reports, nursing notes, medication and treatment record, and admitting and discharge diagnosis. Section 221(O) provides that an outpatient's medical record must contain identification information, history and physical examination, physicians' orders, laboratory and diagnostic tests, diagnosis, treatment, and disposition. Section 221(P) requires that an emergency services record contain identification information, patient history, laboratory and x-ray reports, diagnosis, treatment, disposition, and the name of the physician who saw the patient in the emergency room.

    In addition, section 221(G) requires that the original or a signed copy of all clinical reports be filed in the medical record.

2. *Retention*: Section 221(M) provides that medical records of discharged patients shall be completed "within the time limit established by the medical staff."

    With regard to preservation, section 220(F) requires that medical records be readily retrievable for a period of not less than three years in order to comply with licensing standards. However, the section notes that Ariz. Rev. Stat. Ann. §36–343 (1974) requires that vital records and statistics be retained for ten years.

3. *Signature Requirements*: Section 221(L) provides that "the person responsible for each entry shall be identified by initials or signature." The section requires that, if initials are used, the person's signature appear on the page.

    Section 221(K) sets out regulations concerning patient histories and physicals. Histories and physicals shall be written in the medical record "by members of the medical or house staff." However, when authorized by medical staff bylaws, physician assistants and nurse practitioners may write medical histories and results of physical examinations, provided that such entries are countersigned by the attending physician. This section also requires that a physician's signature appear on each page of the record that bears his or her notation or a notation made by a physician assistant or nurse practitioner under the physician's direction.

4. *Authorized Disclosure*: Section 221(C) provides that only authorized personnel shall have access to the records. However, under section 221(B), the records are to be made available to any unit in the hospital engaged in the care and treatment of the patient.

5. *Confidentiality*: Section 221(D) is the only reference to confidentiality in the regulations. It permits medical record information to be released only "with the written consent of the patient, the legal guardian, or in accordance with law."

6. *Other Matters*: The hospital lien law found at Ariz. Rev. Stat. Ann. §§33–931 to 936 (1974) does not specifically require the institution to furnish copies of records.

    Pursuant to Ariz. Rev. Stat. Ann. §36–151 (Supp. 1975–1983), a home health agency is one that, among other things, "maintains clinical records on all patients."

ARKANSAS

1. *Creation and Contents*: The *Rules and Regulations for Hospitals and Related Institutions in Arkansas,* Department of Health, Part Six (1979), provides complete references to the form and contents of medical records.

   Record contents shall include complete identification data, family history, chief complaints, physical examinations, orders and progress notes (dated and signed), provisional and final diagnosis, and discharge summary. When applicable the record shall include laboratory and x-ray reports, consultation reports, complete surgical records, obstetrical records (prenatal, labor, postpartum), newborn records, physical therapy, autopsy findings, and nurses' notes. Medical records are also required for persons receiving outpatient or emergency treatment.

   The original or a copy of the original of all reports must be included in the medical record. The regulations provide that the record shall be permanent and either typewritten or legibly written in ink.

2. *Retention*: Patient records must be completed within 15 days of discharge. The regulations require that index cards and "a recognized system for the indexing of records by disease, operation, and physician shall be maintained and kept up-to-date." Patients' records must be kept in a fire-resistant place.

   With regard to preservation, the regulations state that "all records must be retained in either original form or microfilm for 10 years after the most recent admission." After the ten-year period, medical records may be destroyed provided that the following information is retained: basic identification information including dates of admission and discharge, name of physician or physicians, record of diagnosis and/or operations performed, operative reports, tissue reports, and discharge summaries. The complete medical records of minors must be retained for a period of seven years after the age of majority.

3. *Signature Requirements*: Included among the numerous provisions that require signatures are orders and progress notes (verbal orders must be signed within 24 hours), date and time of death, laboratory reports, x-ray reports, therapy reports, pathology reports, anesthetic reports, operative reports, and, of course, the various consent authorizations.

   The regulations provide that the attending physician must sign the medical record "with first initial and last name on either the admitting orders or initial progress note." All subsequent notations on the patient's record by the physician can be initialed.

   The regulations permit a physician to use a rubber stamp signature if this method is approved in writing by the hospital administrator and medical record committee. Furthermore, the regulations require "a signed statement by the physician, filed in the administrator's office, stating that he will use a rubber stamp on his hospital records and that the signature stamp will be in his possession at all times or locked in the Medical Record Department when not in use by the physician."

4. *Disclosure Authorized*: Only personnel authorized by the administrator may have access to medical records. However, the records are to be made available to health department personnel.

5. *Confidentiality*: The medical records are considered confidential material, but written consent of the patient or his or her legal guardian shall be presented as authority for the release of information.

6. *Other Matters*: Medical records shall not be removed from the hospital environment except on subpoena by a court having legal authority to issue such an order.

CALIFORNIA

1. *Creation and Contents*: The regulations of the state department of health (March 1980, as amended) require that records be kept on all patients admitted. All records are to be kept as

originals or as "accurate reproductions of the contents of such originals." Cal. Adm. Code tit. 22, §70751(a) (as amended 1980). This language has been interpreted to permit the application of electronic data processing techniques to the maintenance of required records.

Section 70749 specifies the contents of inpatient medical records, which must contain, among other things, identification information, dates of admission and discharge, initial and final diagnoses, history and physical examination, consultation reports, order sheets, progress notes, nurses' notes, laboratory and x-ray reports, operative reports, pathology reports, labor and delivery record, and a discharge summary.

2. *Retention*: The record must be safely preserved for seven years following the discharge of the patient, except that records of minors must be kept at least one year after the minor has reached the age of 18, and in any event not less than seven years. Cal. Adm. Code tit. 22, §§70751(b)–(c) (as amended 1980).

If a facility ceases to operate, section 70751(d) requires that the health department be notified of the arrangements made for safe preservation of the patients' records. Upon a change in ownership, both the previous licensee and the new licensee shall have custody of the patient's records and the records shall be available to both of them. The regulations also provide that arrangements must be made for the safe preservation of the records.

Section 70751(b) provides that the hospital shall safeguard the information in the record against loss, defacement, or tampering. Section 70751(g) requires that medical records be completed promptly.

3. *Signature Requirements*: Section 70751(g) requires that medical records be authenticated or signed by a physician, dentist, or podiatrist within two weeks following the patient's discharge. The section permits authentication by a signature stamp or computer key in lieu of a physician's signature "only when that physician has placed a signed statement in the hospital administrative offices to the effect that he is the only person who (1) has possession of the stamp or key and (2) will use the stamp or key." Pursuant to section 70263(g), no medication or treatment shall be given except on the signed order "of one lawfully authorized to prescribe." In emergencies a physician may give an order by telephone, but he or she must sign the order within 48 hours. Section 70577(j) requires a physician's signed order for the use of restraints. In cases of clear-cut emergency, a telephone order may be given, but the physician must sign the order on his or her next visit.

4. *Disclosure Authorized*: Pursuant to section 70751(a) records are required to be legible and readily available upon the request of the attending physician; the hospital; its medical staff or any authorized officer, agent, or employee; authorized representatives of the health department; as well as "any other person authorized by law to make such a request."

COLORADO

1. *Creation and Contents*: The contents of hospital records are specified in considerable detail by the Colorado licensing standards. *Standards for Hospitals and Health Facilities*, Department of Public Health, Ch. IV, §§4.1–4.9 (1982). The standards require that a complete medical record be maintained on every patient from the time of admission through discharge. Items to be included in the contents are identification data, medical-surgical data, and nurses' records. Medical-surgical data include personal and family history, physical examination reports, provisional diagnosis, clinical and pathology laboratory findings, x-ray reports, consultation reports, treatment and progress notes, complete surgical and dental reports (when applicable), final diagnosis, and autopsy protocol, if any.

The regulations for obstetric records provide an excellent example of the completeness required for medical records generally.

§4.7 CONTENT, OBSTETRIC. Records of all obstetric patients shall include, in addition to the requirements for medical records, the following:

Record of previous obstetric history and prenatal care including blood serology and RH factor determination. Admission obstetrical examination report describing conditions of mother and fetus.

Complete description of progress of labor and delivery, including reasons for induction and operative procedures.

Records of anesthesia, analgesia, and medications given in the course of labor and delivery.

Records of fetal heart rate and vital signs.

Signed report of consultants when such services have been obtained.

Names of assistants present during delivery.

Progress notes including descriptions of involution of uterus, type of lochia, condition of breast and nipples, and report of condition of infant following delivery.

2. *Retention*: Section 4.4 makes completion of the record the responsibility of the attending physician. Section 4.2 provides that "medical records shall be preserved as original records or on microfilm for no less than ten years after the most recent patient care usage, after which time records may be destroyed at the discretion of the facility." However, the medical records of minors must be preserved "for the period of minority plus ten years." Patients must be notified by the facilities before their records are destroyed. The regulation also provides that no records are to be destroyed prior to consultation with legal counsel.

Section 4.1 provides that medical records should be stored to provide protection from loss or damage.

3. *Signature Requirements*: Numerous references to signatures are found in the regulations. Section 4.4 relating to entries states that all orders for diagnostic procedures, treatments and medications, and all reports shall be entered into the medical record in ink or by typewriter. Such orders or reports are to be signed by the attending physician.

Authentication may be by written signature, identifiable initials, or computer key. However, the regulation provides that the use of rubber stamp signatures is acceptable if "the physician whose signature the rubber stamp represents is the only one who has possession of the stamp and is the only one who uses it" and if "the physician places in the administrative offices of the hospital a signed statement to the effect that he is the only one who has the stamp and is the only one who will use it."

Section 3.6 relating to the medical staff requires that each record be authenticated and signed by a licensed physician; those for dental treatment must also be signed by a licensed dentist. Section 19.23 provides that "medications and treatments shall be given only on the order of a physician." Orders must be written, although verbal orders are permitted if countersigned within 24 hours by the ordering physician. Section 3.6 provides that "only members of the medical or house staff shall write or dictate medical histories and physical examinations."

Sections 3.7 and 4.7 require the signatures of consulting physicians. Section 4.6 requires the attending surgeon to write a complete description of operative procedures and findings, including postoperative diagnosis, and to sign the record promptly following the operation. Section 4.8 requires that reports of physical examinations of newborns be signed by the attending physician. Section 19.26 provides that reports of medications administered shall be signed by the persons administering them. Section 24.4 provides that a written report of the findings and evaluations of each x-ray examination or treatment shall be signed by the physician responsible for the procedure.

4. *Disclosure Authorized*: Under section 3.6 the medical record committee of the medical staff is responsible for supervising and appraising the quality of medical records. Colo. Rev. Stat.

§25–4–505 (1982) requires pathology laboratories to report cases of tuberculosis to the department of public health. Section 25–4–508 (1982) permits health department employees to inspect and have access to all medical records of all institutions and clinics where tuberculosis patients are treated. Hospitals must establish policies and procedures for permitting patients access to their records. Colo. Rev. Stat. §25–2–801 (Supp. 1983). Section 27–10–120 (1982) lists those individuals authorized to have access to the records of the mentally ill.

CONNECTICUT

1. *Creation and Contents*: Section 19–13–D3(d) of the Public Health Code promulgated pursuant to Conn. Gen. Stat. §19–13 (1981) requires that a medical record be started for each patient at the time of admission. The regulation requires that all medical records include proper identification data, a complete history and physical examination, doctors' orders, nurses' notes, and charts.
2. *Retention*: The records must be filed in an accessible manner in the hospital and shall be kept for a minimum of 25 years after discharge of the patient, except that the original medical records may be destroyed sooner if they are microfilmed in an approved process. Medical records must be completed within 14 days after discharge of the patient. Persistent failure by a physician to maintain proper records of his or her patients, promptly prepared and completed, is grounds for suspension or withdrawal of medical staff privileges.
3. *Signature Requirements*: The regulation provides that all entries shall be signed by the person responsible for them.
4. *Disclosure Authorized*: Conn. Gen. Stat. Ann. §4–104 (West 1969) requires each public or private hospital, upon demand of a patient after discharge, to permit the patient, his or her physician, or his or her attorney to examine the patient's hospital record including history, bedside notes, charts, pictures, and plates. Copies may also be made.

   Conn. Gen. Stat. Ann. §4–105 (West 1969) indicates the procedure the patient may follow when his or her request to examine his or her records has been refused. The patient may obtain a court order that requires the officer authorized to act as manager of the hospital to bring the records, plates, notes, and charts to a judge of the superior court so that the patient or his physician or attorney may copy them.
6. *Other Matters*: Conn. Gen. Stat. Ann. §4–104 (West 1969) also provides for the admissibility into evidence of copies of hospital records if an affidavit accompanies the copy and certifies that the record was made in the regular course of business. This section further provides that the subpoena must be served not less than 24 hours before the time for production of the record.

DELAWARE

1. *Creation and Contents*: The *Rules and Regulations of the State Board of Health* (July, 1970 as amended October, 1981) contains no specific reference to medical records. In section 50.301, Delaware adopts as the official standards for the governing body, organization, and staff of hospitals the "Standards for Accreditation of Hospitals plus Provisional Interpretations," published by the JCAH, 1981 edition, and the "Requirements and Interpretive Guide for Accredited Hospitals," published by the American Osteopathic Hospital Association, and all codes or standards referred to under these adopted parts.
4. *Disclosure Authorized*: Several statutes relating to payment for care of the indigent specify that the hospital should keep records of patients on forms required by the county levy court. Investigators may inspect the records. Del. Code Ann. tit. 19, §2322 (1974) allows an employee making a claim for workmen's compensation to inspect, copy, and reproduce any medical records pertaining to the employee. Medical records are defined to include hospital records.

6. *Other Matters*: The Hospital Lien Law, Del. Code Ann. tit. 25, §§4301 to 4306 (1974), requires the hospital to make medical records pertaining to the injured person available to the party alleged to be liable for the injury.

DISTRICT OF COLUMBIA

1. *Creation and Contents*: The medical record requirements are found in *District of Columbia Regulations* tit. 8, ch. 7 (as amended 1967). References to medical records are found throughout section 8–7:124. It provides that medical records shall conform to the requirements of the 1960 standards of the JCAH. It is to be noted that new standards were approved in 1983.
2. *Retention*: Medical records must be filed in a safe place for not less than ten years after the patient's discharge, "either in the form of the original copy or in the form of a microfilm or photostatic copy."
3. *Signature Requirements*: Medication and treatment orders must be signed by a physician or dentist under section 8–7:108(f).

FLORIDA

1. *Creation and Contents*: The *Rules of the Department of Health and Rehabilitative Services,* Chapter 10D–28 (1977), provides at section 10D–28.59(2) that all clinical information pertaining to a patient shall be centralized in the patient's record. Under section 10D–28.59(3), the record is to contain identification data, complaint, present illness, past history, family history, physical examination, provisional diagnosis, clinical laboratory reports, x-ray reports, consultation reports, tissue reports, treatment (medical and surgical), progress notes, formal diagnosis, discharge summary, and autopsy findings. These requirements are repeated in Fla. Stat. Ann. §395.016 (West Supp. 1974–1983).
2. *Retention*: Section 10D–28.58(2)(e) makes the medical staff responsible for creating a committee to ensure that medical records are maintained in a sufficiently complete manner.
3. *Disclosure Authorized*: A listing of those persons authorized to have access to patient records is found at Fla. Stat. Ann. §395.017(3) (West Supp. 1974–1983). They include hospital personnel for use in connection with treatment and internal hospital administrative purposes, and the Hospital Cost Containment Board. This section also provides for the disclosure of medical records in any civil or criminal action, unless otherwise prohibited by law, upon the issuance of a subpoena from a court of competent jurisdiction. Finally, section 395.017(4) permits the department of health to examine patient records for the purpose of epidemiological investigations.
4. *Confidentiality*: Fla. Stat. Ann. §395.017(3) (West Supp. 1974–1983) provides that "patient records shall have a privileged and confidential status and shall not be disclosed without the consent of the person to whom they pertain."

GEORGIA

1. *Creation and Contents*: The *Rules and Regulations for Hospitals,* Department of Public Health (as amended 1977), contains comprehensive requirements for the contents of medical records at section 290–5–6–.11.
   Records must be kept on all patients. Sufficient information must be included so as to validate the diagnosis and provide a foundation on which the treatment is given. The normal contents should include, where applicable, admission and discharge data, admitting and final diagnosis, condition on discharge, attending physician's signature, history and physical examination,

treatment, physicians' orders, operation record, progress notes, nurses' notes, medication, special examinations and reports, consultation record, autopsy findings, and discharge summary. The admitting diagnosis must be recorded within 24 hours after admission.

2. *Retention*: Medical records are to be preserved in original form or microfilms, or "other useable forms." Hospitals must retain all medical records at least until the sixth anniversary of the patient's discharge. In the case of a minor the record must be maintained until his or her 27th birthday.

3. *Signature Requirements*: The regulation requires that all orders for patients be signed by the physician. Telephone orders must be signed within 48 hours by the doctor. The regulation further requires that "[p]ractitioner's progress notes signed by the attending practitioner shall be written for all patients as often as the need of the patient indicates. Such notes shall be entered at least weekly."

HAWAII

1. *Creation and Contents*: The *Public Health Regulations,* Board of Health, Chapter 12 (approved May 1973), pertains to hospitals. Section 10 provides that the hospital shall maintain adequate medical records for every person admitted. The medical records should contain identification data, diagnosis, treatment, physicians' orders, observations, and conclusions. Section 11 provides that all pathology reports should be made a part of the patient's medical record. Copies of legal process papers served on a patient in a psychiatric facility must be filed with his or her records pursuant to Haw. Rev. Stat. §334–62 (Supp. 1983).

2. *Retention*: Section 10 contains only one reference to retention. The medical records department shall be "directed, staffed, and equipped to facilitate the accurate processing, checking, indexing, and filing of all medical records."

4. *Disclosure Authorized*: Section 10 authorizes the department of health to inspect medical records as necessary to the execution of its responsibilities. However, the department is required to respect the confidentiality of all such records.

   The director of health may inspect records of patients in state hospital pursuant to section 334–35 (1976).

   The chief of police of Honolulu, any coroner, and the coroner's physician may examine the record of any hospital pertaining to any patient in connection with criminal investigations. The hospital may require written authority for such investigations. Haw. Stat. §841–17 (1976).

5. *Confidentiality*: Section 10 provides that all medical records shall be kept confidential.

IDAHO

1. *Creation and Contents*: The *Rules, Regulations, and Minimum Standards for Hospitals in Idaho,* Dept. of Health (1963, as amended 1968), specifies the required contents of medical records. The following items, in addition to general information, must be included in the record of each patient: special examination reports, x-ray and laboratory reports, consultation reports, nursing notes, treatment notes, progress notes, complete surgical and dental record (when applicable), graphic charts, final diagnosis, condition on discharge, and "signed permission for surgery, anesthesia, autopsy, and other procedures when necessary."

2. *Retention*: Records must be kept for a minimum of seven years. In the case of a minor the record must be kept for seven years after his or her 21st birthday. The regulation also requires that records be stored safely. "This shall be deemed to mean that medical records are handled in such manner as to assure reasonable safety from water or fire damage and are safeguarded from unauthorized use."

The regulation further provides that it is desirable that records be permanently preserved either as original records, abstracts, microfilms, "or other reproductions to afford a basis for a complete audit of professional services rendered. . . ." An elaborate procedure is spelled out for destruction of records at the closing of a hospital.

Completion of the medical record is the responsibility of the attending physician. The medical records committee is responsible for supervising the completion of medical records.

3. *Signature Requirements*: Physicians are required to sign treatment notes and progress notes. The anesthetist or anesthesiologist must sign the anesthesia record including postanesthetic condition.

The attending surgeon must record and sign the operative record including operative procedure, findings, and postoperative diagnostic impressions. Signature requirements are found in other regulations dealing with obstetrics and newborns.

Signatures for the use of restraints are required not only in the regulations but also by Idaho Code §66–345 (Supp. 1983).

4. *Disclosure Authorized*: With reference to the hospitalization of the mentally ill, Idaho Code §66–348 (1980) provides that records are confidential except that (1) the individual may consent to disclosure, (2) disclosure may be made to carry out the provisions of the act, and (3) the court may direct disclosure if necessary and if in the public interest. The section does not preclude disclosure "upon proper inquiry" to members of the patient's family, relatives or friends, abstracts, title insurance companies, lawyers, physicians, or authorized hospital personnel.

The regulations provide that the previous records are to be made available for the use of the physician attending a readmission.

ILLINOIS

1. *Creation and Contents*: The *Hospital Licensing Act and Requirements,* Department of Public Health (1981), sets forth the minimum requirements for medical records in Part XII:

12–1.2(b). For each patient there shall be an adequate, accurate, timely, and complete medical record. Minimum requirements for medical record content are as follows: patient identification and admission information; history of patient as to chief complaints, present illness and pertinent past history, family history, and social history; physical examination report; provisional diagnosis; diagnostic and therapeutic reports on laboratory test results, X-ray findings, any surgical procedure performed, any pathological examination, any consultation, and any other diagnostic or therapeutic procedure performed; orders and progress notes made by the attending physician and when applicable by other members of the medical staff and allied health personnel; observation notes and vital sign charting made by nursing personnel; and conclusions as to the primary and any associated diagnoses, brief clinical resume, disposition at discharge to include instructions and/or medications and any autopsy findings on a hospital death.

2. *Retention*: Original records or photographs of such records are required to be preserved in accordance with the recommendations of the American Hospital Association and legal opinions. Provision must be made for the safe storage of the record including safety from fire or water damage and unauthorized use. A committee of the organized medical staff is responsible for reviewing medical records to ensure "adequate documentation, completeness, promptness, and clinical pertinence."

3. *Signature Requirements*: Laboratory reports must be signed "or otherwise authenticated" and filed with the patient's record. Signed reports of tissue examinations are to be filed with the patient's record.

5. *Confidentiality*: The physician-patient privilege applies to any information the physician or surgeon may have acquired in attending the patient in a professional capacity that was necessary to enable him or her to treat the patient. It does not apply to homicide trials, mental illness inquiries, actions against a physician for malpractice, wills, criminal abortion trials, child abuse trials, and, of course, where the patient consents. Ill. Stat. Ann. ch. 110, §8–802 (Smith-Hurd 1966, as amended 1982).

INDIANA

1. *Creation and Contents*: The *Regulations for General and Special Hospitals*, Indiana State Board of Health, Section 9 (1977), sets forth the minimum requirements for medical records. Section 9.1 provides that accurate and complete records shall be maintained for all patients. Computerized records may be substituted for written reports. Inpatient hospital records must include identification data, chief complaint, history, physical examination, progress notes, consultation reports, x-ray and laboratory reports, operative reports, doctors' orders (signed and dated), notes and observations, treatment records, and final discharge summary.
2. *Retention*: Section 9.2 provides that medical records shall be filed in a safe and accessible manner in the hospital. Inactive records must be stored in a fire-resistant structure. The section also requires that all original records or microfilms thereof shall be stored in the hospital for a minimum of seven years. Microfilms may be substituted for original records after the original records have been on file for a period of at least three years. Upon closure of a hospital, the microfilmed records shall be transferred to a local public health department, a public hospital in the same geographic area, or to the state board of health. Section 7 requires the medical staff to review at regular intervals the completeness of medical records and the enforcement of requirements related thereto.

   Section 9.3 further provides that representatives of the medical staff shall work with the medical records librarian to ensure that the patient records are complete.
3. *Signature Requirements*: Section 9.1 requires that all medical records contain a summary sheet, giving final diagnosis, complications, and operative procedures, that must be signed by the attending physician. All physicians' orders for medication and "other specific services" must be in writing or acceptable computerized form and signed by hand or key by the attending physician within 24 hours. The section also provides that "entries in medical records may be made only by individuals given this right as specified by hospital and medical staff policies." Each entry in the record must be dated and authenticated by its author. Authentication may be by written signature, initials, or computer keys.
4. *Disclosure Authorized*: Section 9.2 provides that medical records shall be made available for inspection by a duly authorized representative of the board of health.

IOWA

1. *Creation and Contents*: The *Iowa Hospital Rules*, Department of Health (1977), appear in Chapter 51 of the Iowa Administrative Code. Section 470–51.5 (135B) contains a general requirement for the maintenance of accurate and complete medical records.
2. *Retention*: Records are to be filed and stored in an accessible manner in the hospital in accordance with the statute of limitations.
3. *Signature Requirements*: The regulations provide that accurate and complete medical records shall be written for all patients and signed by the attending physician.

KANSAS

1. *Creation and Contents*: The *Kansas Hospital Regulations,* Board of Health (1974), list the required contents of medical records:

   28–34–9 MEDICAL RECORD DEPARTMENT.

   * * *

   e. The medical record shall contain, when applicable, identification data, chief complaint, present illness, past history, family history, physical examination, provisional diagnosis, clinical laboratory reports, physician's orders, radiological reports, consultations, medical and surgical treatment, tissue reports, progress notes, care given, pertinent observations, final diagnosis, hospital dismissal summary, and autopsy findings.

   Regulation 28–34–9q specifically allows for automation of medical records: "Nothing in these regulations shall be construed to prohibit the use of properly automated medical records or use of other automated techniques, provided the regulations stated herein are met."

2. *Retention*: Regulation 28–34–9c provides that medical records are to be maintained "in retrievable form for the greater of ten years after the date of last discharge of the patient or one year beyond the date that patients who are minors reach the age of 18." The attending physician has the responsibility for completing the medical record.

3. *Signature Requirements*: Regulation 28–34–9f requires that each clinical entry be signed or initialed by the attending physician, who must be properly identified in the record. Nursing notes and observations must be signed by a registered nurse. Regulation 28–34–6g requires that all medical orders be signed or initialed by the attending physician. Written reports of findings and evaluation of radiological examinations must be signed by the physician responsible and must be made a part of the patient's permanent record per regulation 28–34–12m. Use of restraints must be authorized by the head of the hospital or a member of the medical staff and be accompanied by a statement of the necessity for the use of such restraints. The statement must be signed and made a part of the patient's record, pursuant to Kan. Stat. Ann. §59–2928 (1978).

4. *Disclosure Authorized*: Regulation 28–34–9b limits access to medical records to authorized personnel.

6. *Other Matters*: Regulation 28–34–9b provides that medical records are the property of the hospital.

KENTUCKY

1. *Creation and Contents*: The regulations for hospitals are found in Kan. Admin. Reg. tit. 902, §20.016 (1983). Section 3(11) provides that a medical record shall be maintained "in accordance with accepted professional principles" for every patient. Medical records shall contain identification data, medical history, report of special examinations or diagnostic procedures, provisional diagnosis, physicians' orders, medical, surgical, and dental treatment notes and reports, complete surgical record, physicians' progress notes and nurses' observations, final diagnosis, and discharge summary.

2. *Retention*: All medical records must be maintained for a minimum of 5 years from the date of discharge, or "in the case of a minor three years after the patient reaches the age of majority under state law, whichever is the longer." Records must be safely stored to protect against loss,

defacement, tampering, and particularly damage by fire or water. Section 4(1)(c) requires that the attending medical staff member complete the medical record within 15 days following the patient's discharge.

3. *Signature Requirements*: The regulation contains many references to signatures. Section 3(11) requires that all orders for diet, diagnostic tests, therapeutic procedures, and medications be written, signed, and dated by the medical staff members. If given verbally, the orders must be undersigned by the medical staff member upon his or her next visit to the hospital. Section 4(2)(c)(5) provides that telephone orders for medications shall be given only to registered nurses or pharmacists and shall be signed by the prescribing medical staff member within 24 hours. The complete surgical record must be signed by the attending surgeon and must include an anesthesia record signed by the anesthesiologist. Section 4(1)(c) provides that the attending physician must sign the records as soon as practical after discharge.

4. *Disclosure Authorized*: Only authorized personnel shall be permitted access to a patient's record under section 3(11). Patient information may be released only upon the authorization of the patient. The regulations specifically authorize the routing of records to physicians for consultation and the inspection of records by authorized representatives of the board of health.

In the case of involuntary hospitalization, hospitals in which patients were treated must send patient records to the receiving hospitals.

6. *Other Matters*: Section 3(11) provides that patients' medical records are the property of the hospital and shall not be taken from the facility except by court order.

LOUISIANA

1. *Creation and Contents*: *Rules, Regulations and Minimum Standards Governing Hospitals*, State Department of Hospitals, ch. VIII (1962), contains specific requirements for the contents of medical records.

Section 3 requires that an accurate and complete record be written for each patient. Sections 4 through 6 pertain to minimum contents. The medical record should include identifying and sociological data, medical history, physical examination, medical orders, progress notes, summary report of the patient's course, treatment records, reports of diagnostic procedures, nurses' record, and condition on discharge.

The medical record should also include, where applicable, consultation notes, consent forms, operative record, anesthesia report, pathology reports, and obstetrical records. Separate records for newborns are required.

2. *Retention*: No specific time limit for retention is given. The only requirement is that the record be "filed in an accessible manner in the hospital."

3. *Signature Requirements*: Chapter V, section 20, requires written orders signed by a member of the medical staff for all medications and treatments given to patients. Telephone orders for medication must be initialed by the prescribing physician within 24 hours of the time they were given.

Chapter VIII, section 5, requires that medical history, physical examination, medical orders, progress notes, summary report, and records of all medical care be written, dictated, or prepared by or under the supervision of the attending physician. The face sheet of the complete patient chart must be signed by the doctor.

4. *Disclosure Authorized*: Upon transfer of a patient to a mental institution, all of the patient's records or a full abstract must be sent. La. Stat. Ann. tit. 28, §94 (West Supp. 1984). Another statute requires the governing body of any public institution to make rules under which the charts, records, reports, documents, or other memoranda may be exhibited or copied by or for persons legitimately interested in the disease, mental or physical, or in the condition of patients. La. Rev. Stat. Ann. tit. 44, §7 (West 1982).

6. *Other Matters*: Certified copies of hospital records, signed by appropriate hospital officials, may be received in evidence as prima facie proof of their contents. However, opposing parties may still subpoena and examine the persons who made the original record. La. Rev. Stat. Ann. tit. 13, §§3714, 3715 (West Supp. 1984).

MAINE

1. *Creation and Contents*: The *Regulations for the Licensure of General and Specialty Hospitals in the State of Maine*, ch. XII, Department of Human Services (July, 1972), refers to medical records. The regulations require that all clinical information pertaining to a patient's stay be centralized in the patient's record. Medical records should contain the following information: identification, data, history, physical examination, provisional diagnosis, clinical laboratory reports, x-ray reports, consultation reports, medical and surgical treatment reports, tissue reports, progress notes, final diagnosis, discharge summary, and autopsy findings. They must also include the nursing care given. Another portion requires operative records to be kept. Limitations on the rights of mental patients are to be made part of their clinical records in accordance with Me. Rev. Stat. Ann. tit. 34, §2254 (1978 and Supp. 1983).
2. *Retention*: Records must be preserved, either in the original or by microfilm, for a period of time "not less than that determined by the statute of limitations in the respective State." Medical records must be completed promptly. Current records must be completed within 24–48 hours of admission. Records of patients discharged must be completed within 15 days of discharge. Chapter IX requires the medical records committee to supervise the maintenance of medical records at "the required standard of completeness" and to ensure that there is "proper filing, indexing, storage, and availability of all patient records."
3. *Signature Requirements*: Chapter XII provides that only members of the medical staff and the house staff are competent to write or dictate medical histories and physical examinations. All records must be authenticated and signed by a licensed physician. Every physician must sign each entry he or she makes, and the attending physician must countersign the history, physical examination, and summary written by the house staff. Chapter IX requires that a consultation report include a written opinion signed by the consulting physician and be filed in the medical record. Chapter XVII provides that operative reports must be written or dictated immediately following surgery and be signed by the surgeon.
4. *Disclosure Authorized*: Chapter XII provides that only authorized personnel have access to the record. Written consent of the patient is required for release of medical information.
5. *Confidentiality*: Chapter XII requires that all medical records are to be kept confidential.
6. *Other Matters*: The hospital lien law found at Me. Rev. Stat. Ann. tit. 10, §3412 (1980) requires hospitals to make their records available in order to determine the reasonableness of charges. The statute prohibits disclosure of records that indicate the nature of the injury to the patient, the nature of his or her condition, or the state of his or her recovery.

   Chapter XII of the regulations also provides that medical records are not to be removed from the hospital environment except upon subpoena.

MARYLAND

1. *Creation and Contents*: Hospital regulations governing medical records are found in Md. Admin. Code tit. 10, §07.02 (1978). Section 10.07.02.20 provides that records for all patients shall be maintained "in accordance with accepted professional standards." The records should contain identification data, provisional diagnosis, history, report of physical examination, diagnostic and therapeutic orders, consultation reports, observations, and progress notes, reports of treatments and clinical findings, and discharge summary.

2. *Retention*: Medical records must be retained for a period of not less than five years from the date of discharge or, in the case of a minor, "three years after the patient becomes of age or five years, whichever is longer." The regulations also provide that current medical records and those of discharged patients shall be completed promptly. Closed or inactive records shall be filed and stored in a safe, fire-resistant place that provides for confidentiality and retrieval when necessary.

3. *Signature Requirements*: The regulations contain numerous signature requirements. Section 10.07.02.20 provides that the record must contain authentication of hospital diagnoses, including "discharge summary, report from patient's attending physician, or transfer form." Section 10.07.02.15 provides that all medications administered to patients shall be ordered in writing by the patient's physician. Section 10.07.02.16 provides that all signed and dated reports of diagnostic services shall be filed with the patient's medical record.

   Section 10.07.02.10 and .11 contain provisions relating to verbal or telephone orders. A verbal order shall be given to "a duly authorized person functioning within his sphere of competence, with sufficient experience and responsibility to assure that it will be correctly received and interpreted." A verbal order shall be considered to be in writing if signed with the name of the physician per the name of the authorized person to whom it was dictated. However, the verbal order must be countersigned at the time of the physician's visit.

   Section 10.07.02.09 provides that a written physician's order is required for the use of protective devices.

6. *Other Matters*: The hospital lien law, Md. Com. Law Code Ann. §16–604 (1983), provides that persons against whom a claim for personal injuries is made shall be permitted to examine hospital records to ascertain changes with regard to the period of confinement and the itemization of departmental charges. Notice of such inspection must be mailed to the patient.

MASSACHUSETTS

1. *Creation and Contents*: Hospital regulations are contained in Mass. Admin. Code tit. 105, §130.000 (1984). Section 130.200 provides that each hospital shall meet all of the requirements of the Medicare Conditions of Participation, 42 C.F.R. 405.1011 through 405.1040, and as they may be amended from time to time, except the requirement for utilization review (42 C.F.R. 425.1035) and the requirement of compliance with the Life Safety Code (42 C.F.R. 425.1022(b)).

2. *Retention*: Mass Gen. Laws Ann. Ch. 111, §70 (West 1983), requires licensed hospitals or clinics and those supported in whole or part by the Commonwealth to keep records and medical histories of the treatment of cases under their care. The section permits records to be photographed or microphotographed and provides for the destruction of the original from which they were made. The section further provides that the records may be destroyed 30 years after the discharge or final treatment of the patient.

MICHIGAN

1. *Creation and Contents*: The requirements for medical records appear in *Rules and Minimum Standards for Hospitals*, Mich. Dept. of Public Health, Rule 325.1028 (1960, as amended 1977). Section 8.1 requires "accurate and complete" medical records for each patient admitted. The regulations specify the contents:

   8.2   Patients   records shall include the following:
   8.21 Admission date.
   8.22 Admitting diagnosis.

8.23 History and physical examination.
8.24 Physician's progress notes.
8.25 Operation and treatment notes and consultations.
8.26 The physician's orders.
8.27 Nurse's notes including temperature, pulse, respiration, conditions observed and medication given.
8.28 Record of discharge or death.
8.29 Final diagnosis.
8.3   Additional records of patients having surgery shall include the following:
8.31 Details of the pre-operative study and diagnosis.
8.32 The pre-operative medication.
8.33 The name of the surgeon and his assistants.
8.34 Repealed.
8.341 The method of anesthesia.
8.342 The amount of anesthetic when measurable.
8.343 The name of the anesthetist.
8.35 The post-operative diagnosis, including pathological findings.
8.4   The report of special examinations such as laboratory, x-ray, and pathology shall be kept in the patient's record.

2. *Retention*: No specific time limit is indicated in the regulations; however, they do provide that medical records shall be preserved as original records, abstracts, microfilms or otherwise.
3. *Signature Requirements*: Section 7.13 provides that medication or treatment can only be given on the written order of a physician. Sections 7.14 and 7.15 provide that verbal orders for medication be entered in the record as such by the person receiving the order, "initialed by the physician's initials per the receiver's initials and countersigned by the physician at the time of the next visit."

MINNESOTA

1. *Creation and Contents*: Minnesota has adopted all of the requirements of the Medicare Conditions of Participation, 42 C.F.R. 405.1011 through 405.1040.
2. *Retention*: The chief administrative officer of any public or private hospital, with the approval of the governing board, may destroy records that are more than three years old, provided the records shall first have been transferred and recorded on photographic film. Those portions of an individual's hospital medical record that comprise an individual's permanent medical record as defined by the commissioner of health must be retained. Other portions of an individual's medical record may be destroyed after seven years without transfer to photographic film. All portions of a minor's medical record must be maintained for seven years following the age of majority. Minn. Stat. Ann. §145.32 (West Supp. 1984).
3. *Signature Requirements*: In mental hospitals, each use of restraints and the reason therefor must be made part of the patient's record, along with the signature of the head of the hospital or a member of the medical staff. Minn. Stat. Ann. §253A.17 (West 1982).
6. *Other Matters*: Photographic or photostatic copies, when certified by the custodian of the records, are admissible in evidence. Minn. Stat. Ann. §145.31 (Supp. 1984).

MISSISSIPPI

1. *Creation and Contents*: Minimum Standards of Operation for Mississippi Hospitals, Mississippi Health Care Commission, chapter 17 (1979), contains the specific requirements for medical

records. A medical record shall be maintained "in accordance with accepted professional principles" for each patient admitted.

The minimum requirements for medical records include identification data, history, physical examination, clinical laboratory reports, x-ray reports, consultations, medical and surgical treatment, tissue reports, physicians' orders, progress notes, provisional and final diagnosis, discharge summary, and autopsy findings. Special provisions for emergency medical records are set forth in Chapter 7, Section 705.

2. *Retention*: Miss. Code Ann. §41–9–61 to –83 (1981) provides minimum standards for preparing, maintaining, and retiring hospital records. It is a comprehensive statute. Section 41–9–69, relating to retention, provides:

> Section 41–9–69 PERIOD OF RETENTION OF HOSPITAL RECORDS.—Hospital records shall be retained, preserved and properly stored by hospitals for such periods of reasonable duration as may be prescribed in rules and regulations adopted by the licensing agency. Such rules and regulations may provide for different periods of such retention for the various constituent parts of any hospital records, and such rules and regulations may require that an abstract be made of pertinent data from any hospital records that may be retired as provided herein. Such rules and regulations may also provide for different periods of such retention for the various injuries, diseases, infirmities or conditions primarily causing or associated with the hospitalization. However, complete hospital records shall be retained for a period after discharge of the patient of at least (a) seven (7) years in cases of patients discharged at death, except as may be otherwise hereinafter provided; (b) ten (10) years in cases of adult patients of sound mind at the time of discharge, except as may be otherwise hereinafter provided; (c) for the period of minority or other known disability of the patient plus seven (7) additional years, but not to exceed twenty-eight (28) years, in cases of patients under disability of minority or otherwise; or (d) for the period of minority or other known disability of any survivors hereinafter mentioned plus seven (7) additional years, but not to exceed twenty-eight (28) years, in all cases where the patient was discharged at death, or is known by the hospital to have died within thirty (30) days after discharge, and the hospital knows or has reason to believe that such patient or former patient left one or more survivors under disability of minority or otherwise who are or are claimed to be entitled to damages for wrongful death of the patient under Section 11–7–13, Mississippi Code of 1972, or laws amendatory hereof. Upon the expiration of the applicable period of retention, any hospital may retire the hospital record.

Section 41–9–77 permits a hospital to reproduce any hospital record on film or other reproducing material by microfilming, photographing, photostating, or other appropriate process and to retire the original documents so reproduced after three years from discharge of the patient.

Upon closure of a hospital, section 41–9–79 provides that its hospital records should be delivered to another hospital in the vicinity or to the licensing agency.

The regulations in section 1702 also make reference to the time periods quoted above and require that medical records be retained for those periods, either in the original or by microfilm.

Section 1710 of the regulations requires that current records be completed within 24–48 hours of admission. Records of patients discharged must be completed within 30 days of discharge. Section 503.3 provides that it is the responsibility of the medical staff to ensure that medical records meet "the required standards of completeness, clinical pertinence, and promptness of completion following discharge." Section 1710 further provides that staff regulations at the hospital must provide for suspension or termination of staff privileges where a physician is persistently delinquent in completing records.

3. *Signature Requirements*: Section 1708 provides that only members of the medical staff and the house staff are permitted to write or dictate medical histories and physical examinations. Section 1709 requires that medical records be authenticated and signed by a licensed physician. Every physician must sign each entry he or she makes, and the attending physician must countersign the history, physical examination, and summary written by the house staff.

4. *Disclosure Authorized*: Section 1701 provides that only authorized personnel shall have access to the records. The written consent of the patient is required for release of medical information. The statute setting forth minimum standards provides that the records are the property of the hospital, subject to reasonable access to the information they contain where good cause is shown by the patient, his or her personal representatives, heirs, attending medical personnel, or duly authorized nominees. Miss. Code Ann. §41–9–65 (1981).

5. *Confidentiality*: Section 1701 requires that all medical records be kept confidential.

MISSOURI

1. *Creation and Contents*: Mo. Admin. Code tit. 13, §50–20–.021 (1982), contains specific requirements for the contents of records.

   The regulations will be deemed to have been satisfied if the patient's records include identification data, present illness, past history, family history, history of present complaint, physical examination, provisional diagnosis, physicians' or dentists' orders, progress notes, nurses' notes, final diagnosis, and discharge summary. When applicable, medical records should also contain reports such as clinical laboratory, x-ray, consultation, electrocardiogram, surgical procedures, therapy, anesthesia, pathology, autopsy, and any other reports pertinent to the patient's care.

2. *Retention*: The regulations provide that medical records are to be retained for at least the minimum period established by statutes of limitations. Medical records may be preserved either in the original or on microfilm. The records should be stored in such a way as to safeguard against loss, defacement, and tampering, and to prevent damage from fire and water.

   The administrator is responsible for the completeness of the records.

3. *Signature Requirements*: The regulations provide that "patient care by members of the medical staff, nursing staff, and allied health professionals shall be entered in the patient's medical record in a timely manner." Documentation must be legible, dated, authenticated, and be recorded in ink, typewritten, or recorded electronically.

   Verbal and written orders must be dated and authenticated by the attending physician as soon as possible after the order is given. Authentication may be by written signature, initials, computer-generated signature codes, or rubber-stamp signatures. The regulations state that the use of rubber stamps is discouraged. However, where their use is authorized, a signed statement must be maintained in the administrative offices, with a copy in the medical records department, stating that "the medical staff member whose stamp is involved is the only one who has possession of the stamp and is the only one authorized to use it." The regulations prohibit the duplication of signature stamps and the delegation of their use.

4. *Disclosure Authorized*: Only authorized personnel have access to medical records. The written consent of the patient is required for release of information from the medical records to persons not so authorized.

6. *Other Matters*: Medical records are the property of the hospital and are not to be removed from the hospital premises except by court order or subpoena.

MONTANA

1. *Creation and Contents*: Mont. Admin. Rule 16.32.320 (1980), requires that each hospital comply with the Medicare Conditions of Participation as set forth in 42 C.F.R. 405, Subpart J. However, the Administrative Rules of Montana do contain several specific references to medical records. Rule 16.32.328 sets out requirements for obstetrical records and records for newborns.
2. *Retention*: Rule 16.32.328 provides that a hospital patient's medical records must be maintained "no less than 25 years following the date of a patient's discharge or no less than 5 years following the date of a patient's death." Records may be microfilmed provided that the reproduction is done on the premises. Medical records must be stored in a safe manner and in a safe location.
3. *Signature Requirements*: Rule 16.32.308 provides that a signature of a physician may not be stamped on a medical record "unless there is a statement in the facility administrator's or manager's file signed by the physician stating that the physician is responsible for the content of any document signed with his rubber stamp."

NEBRASKA

1. *Creation and Contents*: *Regulations and Standards for Hospitals,* Department of Health, Rule 30 (1979), provides a general description of medical record contents. Medical records should contain identification data, history and physical examination, provisional diagnosis, clinical pathology and laboratory reports, radiology reports, consultation, medical and surgical treatment reports, tissue reports, progress reports, discharge summary, and autopsy findings. A medical record must be maintained for each newborn infant.
2. *Retention*: Medical records must be maintained in original, microfilm, or other approved copy for a period of at least ten years following discharge. In the case of minors, records must be maintained until three years after the age of majority has been attained.
3. *Signature Requirements*: The regulations provide that all physicians' orders shall be written and dated in ink or indelible pencil, or be entered into a computer using a physician code system. Such orders shall be signed by the physician and preserved on the patient's record.

    The regulations permit facsimiles of physicians' signatures and initials "where appropriate safeguards have been taken to limit access and use of the facsimiles or code to the individual physician." Special provisions exist for prescriptions made by means of a computer.

    When a physician's assistant has authority to write orders and progress reports, such orders must be signed in the supervising physician's name, followed by the physician's assistant's name. Telephone or verbal orders must be signed or initialed, and dated by the attending physician within 48 hours.
4. *Disclosure Authorized*: Under the regulations medical records are available only for use by authorized persons and for examination by authorized representatives of the department of health. Medical records may not be removed from the hospital premises except by court order.
5. *Confidentiality*: The regulations provide that medical records are confidential and privileged.

NEVADA

1. *Creation and Contents*: *Operational Rules and Regulations for Health Facilities,* State Board of Health, Section VI (1969, as amended 1974), contains the medical records provisions. The relevant provisions appear at Nev. Admin. Code §449.379 (1982). Medical records must contain "sufficient information to justify the diagnosis, warrant treatment and vindicate the end results."

    The record must be either printed, typewritten, or legibly written. Records must include, where applicable, identification data, admissions diagnosis, progress notes by the physician, chief complaint, consultations, nurses' notes, medication and treatment orders, diet orders, history and physical examination, laboratory and x-ray reports, complete surgical record, complete obstetrical record, and condition and diagnosis of patient when discharged.

2. *Retention*: Medical histories must be retained for 25 years; they may be microfilmed after 3 years if stored on rolls. If unitized jackets or cards are used, they may be microfilmed at the time of discharge. Current records must be completed within 24 hours, and records of discharged patients must be completed within 15 days of discharge.

3. *Signature Requirements*: Records must be authenticated and signed by a licensed physician. Only members of the medical and house staff may write or dictate medical histories and physical examinations. Medication orders must be in writing and signed by the attending physician. Nev. Admin. Code §449.379(4) (1982). In an emergency a verbal order may be given to a licensed nurse who must write it down and sign it. The physician must countersign the order within 72 hours. Nev. Admin. Code §449.343 (1982). The regulation relating to medication also contains the following language: "Each medication shall be properly recorded in the patient's medical record and signed by the individual responsible."

   Laboratory reports must be signed and filed with the patient's record. Tissue reports must be signed by the pathologist. X-ray reports must be signed by the radiologist and filed with the patient's record.

6. *Other Matters*: The lien law permits anyone against whom a claim is asserted for damages for injuries to examine and copy all records related to the injured person. Nev. Rev. Stat. §108.640 (1983).

NEW HAMPSHIRE

1. *Creation and Contents*: *Licensure Rules and Regulations—Hospitals*, Dept. of Health and Welfare (1982), contains the general requirements for the content of medical records. The regulations provide:

   He–P 802.11 Medical Records
   (a) There shall be accurate and complete records written for all patients and filed in an accessible manner in the hospital, a complete medical record being one which includes identification data; complaint; personal and family history; history of present illness; physical examination; special examinations, such as consultations, clinical laboratory, X-ray and other examinations; provisional or working diagnosis; medical or surgical treatment; gross and microscopical pathological findings; progress notes; final diagnosis; condition on discharge; followup; and autopsy findings.

   The department further directs in He–P 802.12 that the record system conform with the recommendations of the JCAH.

2. *Retention*: Original records, or photographs of such records, must be retained for a minimum of seven years. Records of minors must be retained for a minimum of seven years after the age of majority has been attained. The regulations require that each hospital formulate a written policy with regard to the disposition of records. All records must be safely stored.

NEW JERSEY

1. *Creation and Contents*: The current hospital regulations are contained in the *Manual of Standards for Hospital Facilities*, New Jersey State Department of Health (1969, as amended 1981). Section 7 lists the minimum requirements for medical records. Records must be "accurate and

complete.'' Patients' records must include date of admission, provisional diagnosis, history, physical findings, physicians' progress notes, record of operation, laboratory and x-ray reports, nurses' notes, consultations, medication and treatment records, physicians' orders, final diagnosis, and discharge summary.

2. *Retention*: Section 701 provides that medical records must be preserved, either in the original or by microfilm, for a period of not less than ten years following the most recent discharge of the patient or until the patient reaches the age of 23, whichever is the longer period. X-ray films must be retained for five years.

   The attending physician is responsible for completing the record. Histories and physical examinations must be completed within 24–48 hours of admission. Records of patients discharged must be completed within 15 days of discharge.

3. *Signature Requirements*: Section 702 requires that all medical records be authenticated by a licensed physician. All orders for medication and treatments must be in writing, signed and dated. This requirement is repeated in section 602. Section 702 also provides that all telephone and verbal orders must be countersigned by the physician within 24 hours. Progress notes may be written by physicians engaged in an approved intern or residency training program and do not require the countersignature of a licensed physician. However, physicians' orders for patient care written by such individuals must be countersigned by a licensed physician.

4. *Disclosure Authorized*: Section 701 provides that medical records shall be accessible to authorized personnel. Authorized representatives of the department of health may inspect patient records at any time. The written consent of the patient is required for the release of medical information to any other individuals.

   Section 701 also provides that medical records should not be removed from the hospital premises except upon subpoena. Section 704 requires that each facility formulate policies regarding a patient's access to his or her own medical record.

5. *Confidentiality*: Section 701 provides that all medical records shall be kept confidential.

6. *Other Matters*: The hospital lien law provides that the hospital must allow the party against whom the claim has been made to inspect the records. N.J. Stat. Ann. tit. 2A, §§44–45 (West 1983).

NEW MEXICO

1. *Creation and Contents*: *Rules, Regulations and Standards for Hospitals and Related Facilities*, Department of Public Health (1964, as amended 1965), contains the record requirements. Medical records must be written and kept for all patients and newborn infants. To be sufficient, a medical record must include identification data, complaint, relevant histories, physical examination, nursing notes, special examinations and reports, working diagnosis, medical, surgical, and dental treatment, tissue reports, progress notes, final diagnosis, condition on discharge, and followup. All orders must be written by the attending physician and be included in the patient's medical record.

2. *Retention*: The retention provision makes reference to various statutes of limitations. No time is fixed by law for the preservation of hospital records. However, records of adults may be needed to collect hospital bills within the six-year period for written contracts and four-year period for unwritten contracts, or for a three-year period to defend the hospital against personal injury claims, and it is desirable to retain records of children for one year after the child has attained the age of 21. The licensing agency has no objection to microfilming of hospital records, provided that pertinent state statutes are not violated.

   Records must be preserved for a period of ten years following the last discharge of the patient. Records may be preserved in microfilm or other photographically reproduced form. N.M. Stat. Ann. §14–6–2 (1983). The regulations also require that the records be safely stored.

3. *Signature Requirements*: The order for discharge must be written in ink and signed by the attending physician or dentist or countersigned by that person within 24 hours. Drugs and medications may not be given without a written order signed by the prescribing physician or dentist.

NEW YORK

1. *Creation and Contents*: New York has adopted the standards with regard to medical records contained in the Medicare Conditions of Participation, 42 C.F.R. 405.1026.
6. *Other Matters*: N.Y. Civ. Prac. Law §2306 (Consol. 1978) authorizes the head of the hospital to send a certified transcript or reproduction of the record in response to a subpoena. Another section permits court-ordered medical examinations and allows the parties to obtain copies of hospital records of such examinations.

   The hospital lien law permits persons against whom a claim is asserted to examine the hospital records with reference to the treatment, care, and maintenance of the injured person. The section excepts confidential communications or privileged records, unless the privilege is waived. N.Y. Lien Law §189 (Consol. 1979).

   Other provisions relating to information in the record are found in the Mental Hygiene Law, Public Health Law, Social Service Law, and Workman's Compensation Law.

NORTH CAROLINA

1. *Creation and Contents*: The requirements for medical records are specified in *Laws, Regulations and Procedures Applying to the Licensing of Hospitals in North Carolina*, Department of Human Resources, Section 3C.1400 (1980). These regulations are contained in one detailed section of the North Carolina Administrative Code. N.C. Admin. Code tit. 10, §3C.1400 (1980). All patients must have adequate and complete written records. The information contained in the records should "justify the diagnosis, verify the treatment and warrant the end results."

   Those items specified to be contained in the record are identification data, dates for admission and discharge, personal and family history, chief complaint, history of present illness, physical examination, special examinations, provisional diagnosis, medical treatment, a complete surgical record, progress and nurses' notes, charts, final diagnosis, summary, and condition on discharge. N.C. Gen. Stat. §130A–117 (Supp. 1983) also requires that hospitals maintain a record of personal data concerning each patient admitted.
2. *Retention*: Section 3C.1405 of the regulations states that,

   > All original medical records or photographs of such records shall be preserved or retained for at least the period outlined in the North Carolina Statute of Limitations and in accordance with hospital policy based on American Hospital Assocation recommendations and guidance of the hospital's legal advisers. N.C. Admin. Code tit. 10, §3C.1405 (1980).

   N.C. Gen. Stat. §130A–117 (Supp. 1983) provides that records must be maintained for a period of not less than three years.

   The medical record must be completed within a reasonable time after the discharge of the patient. The responsibility for completion is on the attending physician. Section 3C.1403(c) requires that the medical staff appoint a committee whose responsibility it will be to ensure that the medical records are adequate and up to date.

Section 3C.1401 requires that medical records be safely stored in a fire-resistant structure. The hospital must safeguard the information in the records against loss, tampering, or use by unauthorized persons.

3. *Signature Requirements*: Section 3C.1404 requires that records of medical treatment be signed or initialed by the person giving the medication or treatment. Section 3C.0405 provides that orders for medication or treatment shall be dated and recorded directly in the patient chart or "in a computer or data processing system which provides a hard copy printout of the order for the patient chart." Each hospital must establish a method to identify all persons who record such orders and to safeguard against fraudulent recordings.

All orders for medication or treatment must be authenticated at the time they are recorded by the ordering physician. Verbal orders must be authenticated within 24 hours by "the ordering physician or by a physician involved with the care of the patient." Authentication may be accomplished by "signature, initials, computer entry or code, or other method(s) not inconsistent with the laws, rules and regulations of any other applicable jurisdictions." Section 3C.0505 also refers to these procedures for recording and authenticating physicians' orders for medication and treatment.

Section 3C.1403(f) provides that only physicians, members of the house staff, physician assistants, and nurse practitioners are allowed to write or dictate medical histories and physical examinations. Histories and physicals performed by a physician assistant or nurse practitioner must be countersigned by the responsible physician. Radiology reports must also be signed by the physician responsible for the procedure.

When a surgical operation is to be performed on an inmate of a state institution, the chief medical officer and the medical staff of the institution must keep a careful and complete record of the measures taken to obtain consent, and the complete medical record must be signed by the medical superintendent, the surgeon performing the operation, and all surgical consultants. N.C. Gen. Stats. §148–22.2 (1982).

4. *Disclosure Authorized*: Records shall be made available for inspection by the state registrar upon request. N.C. Gen. Stat. §130A–117 (Supp. 1983).

6. *Other Matters*: Section 3C.1403(d) provides that records of patients are the property of the hospital and shall not be taken from the hospital except under subpoena.

NORTH DAKOTA

1. *Creation and Contents*: The medical record requirements are contained in *Rules and Regulations for Hospitals in North Dakota*, Dept. of Health, Sec. 33–07–01–16 (1979, as amended 1980). A medical record must be maintained for every patient admitted for care in the hospital. The medical records must contain "sufficient information to justify the diagnosis and warrant the treatment and end results."

The regulations provide that, at a minimum, the medical record must contain identification data, chief complaint, present illness, past history, family history, physical examination, provisional diagnosis, clinical laboratory reports, x-ray reports, consultations, medical and surgical treatment, tissue reports, progress notes, final diagnosis, discharge summary, nurses' notes, and, when applicable, autopsy findings.

2. *Retention*: Current records must be completed within 48 hours of admission. Records of discharged patients must be completed within 15 days of discharge.

Medical records must be preserved "either in original or any other method of preservation, such as microfilm" for a period of 25 years from date of discharge. The medical records of deceased patients may be destroyed after 7 years have passed from the date of death. The regulations further provide:

It shall be the governing body's responsibility to determine which record has a research, legal, or medical value and to preserve such records beyond the twenty-five year or seven-year requirement until such time in the board's determination the record no longer has a research, legal, or medical value.

3. *Signature Requirements*: The regulations require that all records be authenticated and signed by a licensed physician. Every physician must sign the entries he or she personally makes. A single signature on the face sheet of the record will not suffice to authenticate the entire record. In hospitals with house staff, the attending physician must countersign the history, physical examination, and summary when written by the house staff. Consultation reports must be in writing and be signed by the consultant.
4. *Disclosure Authorized*: The regulations provide that only authorized personnel shall have access to the record. The written consent of the patient is required for release of medical information.
5. *Confidentiality*: The regulations require that all medical records be kept confidential.
6. *Other Matters*: The regulations provide that medical records generally shall not be removed from the hospital environment except upon subpoena.

OHIO

1. *Creation and Contents*: Ohio has no official instrumentality that licenses hospitals within the state and, as such, has no formal requirements for medical records. The Ohio Revised Code does, however, provide that no hospital may operate unless it is certified under Title XVIII of the "Social Security Act," 49 Stat. 620 (1935), 42 U.S.C. 301, as amended (Medicare Conditions of Participation), or is accredited by the JCAH or the American Osteopathic Association. Ohio Rev. Code Ann. §3727.02 (Supp. 1983).

   Maternity and pyschiatric hospitals are considered separately and are subject to the licensure requirements found in chapters 3711 and 5119, respectively, of the revised code. Consequently, the department of health has promulgated a set of regulations pertaining to maternity hospitals in chapter 3701–7 of the *Rules of the Ohio Department of Health Public Council* (1976). Sec. 3701–7–24 requires that separate records be maintained for each maternity patient and each newborn infant. Sec. 3701–7–35 prescribes requirements for the maintenance of medical records in maternity homes.

   The department of mental health and mental retardation has also adopted a set of regulations for psychiatric hospitals. *Rules for Licensure of Private Psychiatric Hospitals* (1978). Sec. 5119:1–5–15 pertains to the contents of medical records. A complete medical record must be maintained for each patient. At a minimum, the records must contain identification information, patient history, chief complaint, reports of psychiatric and physical examinations, individualized treatment plan, medical orders, observations, reports of actions, findings, conclusions, and a discharge summary.
2. *Retention*: Sec. 3701–7–24 of the maternity hospital regulations requires that maternity hospitals retain all records and reports as directed by the state director of health for at least two years. The section further provides that such records and reports must be made available for inspection by the director or his authorized representative.

   Sec. 5119:1–5–15 of the psychiatric hospital regulations provides that each hospital shall maintain records in accordance with all applicable federal and state regulations.
5. *Confidentiality*: Sec. 5119:1–5–17 of the psychiatric hospital regulations provides with regard to confidentiality that each hospital must maintain records in accordance with all applicable state and federal regulations regarding its security.

OKLAHOMA

1. *Creation and Contents*: The requirements for medical records are contained in *Standards and Regulations for Licensure of Hospitals and Related Institutions*, Department of Health (1976). Each medical record must be "accurate and complete." The records shall include identification data, medical history of current illness, physical examination, doctors' orders, progress notes, consultations, nurses' notes, diets, requests and results of clinical tests, and a note of patient's condition when discharged. Complete records of surgery, obstetrical procedures, and anesthesia are also required when applicable.
2. *Retention*: The regulations provide that microfilming of records, including x-ray reports, may be used to conserve storage space.
3. *Signature Requirements*: Orders for medication, treatment, and tests must be written in ink and be signed by the physician in charge. Signature stamps must not be used as a substitute for the signature of the authorizing doctor. All orders taken from the doctor, for entry by authorized others, must be countersigned within 24 hours. Orders for emergency use of restraints must be signed by the physician as soon as possible.
4. *Disclosure Authorized*: Information may be disclosed for purposes of research and study by, among other groups, in-hospital staff committees. No liability will follow such disclosure.

OREGON

1 *Creation and Contents*: The *Rules, Regulations and Standards for Health Care Facilities in Oregon*, Board of Health (1981), contains general requirements for the contents of medical records. These regulations appear in one detailed section of the *Oregon Administrative Rules*. Or. Admin. R. 333–23–190 (1981). A "legible medical record in ink or typescript" must include identification data, relevant histories, physical examination report, provisional diagnosis, clinical laboratory reports, x-ray reports, consultation reports, physicians' orders, final diagnosis, and discharge summary. Records of surgical patients shall also include preoperative history, anesthesia record, record of operation and pathology reports.
2. *Retention*: The attending physician is responsible for completing the medical record. Medical records must be completed within four weeks following the patient's discharge.

   Medical records must be protected against unauthorized access, fire, water, and theft.

   All medical records must be kept for at least ten years after the date of last discharge. Original medical records may be replaced with microfilmed copies. Original clinical records or photographic or electronic facsimiles thereof, not otherwise incorporated in the medical record, "such as x-rays, electrocardiograms, electroencephalograms, and radiological isotope scars" need only be retained for seven years after the patient's last discharge if professional interpretations of such graphics are included in the medical records. If a hospital is closed, its medical records should be turned over to another hospital in the vicinity.
3. *Signature Requirements*: The regulations provide that "the appropriate individual shall separately sign or authenticate the history and physical examination, operative report, progress notes, orders and summary." The attending physician must countersign all entries written by unlicensed house officers. Physicians must also sign any clinical entries they make themselves. The regulations provide that "a single signature or authentication of the physician on the face sheet of the medical record does not suffice to cover the entire content of the record."

   Clinical laboratory reports must be signed, initialed, or authenticated, and filed in the patient's medical record. X-ray reports shall be filed in the medical records and authenticated by the originator of the interpretation. Consultation reports must also be signed. Physicians' orders must be signed by the physician or authenticated "by a signature stamp or computer key." A signed stamp or computer key may be used in lieu of a signature only when "that person has placed a signed statement in the hospital administrative offices to the effect that he is the only person who: (i) has possession of the stamp or key; and (ii) will use the stamp or key.'' Verbal orders accepted by authorized individuals must be countersigned or authenticated by the prescriber within 24 hours.

Dated progress notes must be signed or authenticated by the person making the entry. Anesthesia records must also be signed or authenticated by the person making the entry. Rule 333–23–178 provides that drugs will not be dispensed without a written order signed or authenticated by the prescribing physician.

4. *Disclosure Authorized*: The regulations provide that only authorized personnel be permitted to review medical records. Rule 333–23–190.
6. *Other Matters*: Medical records are the property of the hospital and may not be removed from the institution except where necessary for a judicial or administrative proceeding.

PENNSYLVANIA

1. *Creation and Contents*: The specific requirements for medical records are contained in *Rules and Regulations for Hospitals*, Department of Health, ch.115 (1982). Section 115.31 provides that an adequate medical record shall be maintained for every patient. The record shall contain data "from all episodes of care and treatment of the patient, whether services were performed on an inpatient basis, on an outpatient basis, or in the emergency unit."

Section 115.31 requires that each record include an admission history and physical examination, physicians' notes, consultation reports, nurses' notes, pathology or clinical laboratory reports, radiology reports, medical and surgical treatment, other diagnostic or therapeutic procedures, provisional and final diagnoses, and a clinical resume.
2. *Retention*: Section 115.22 requires that medical records be stored in such a manner as to provide protection from loss, damage, and unauthorized access. Section 115.23 provides that medical records, "whether original, reproductions, or microfilm," must be kept on file for a minimum of seven years following the discharge of a patient. Records of minors shall be kept on file until they reach majority and then "for seven years or as long as the records of adult patients are maintained." The section also includes provisions for the storage of medical records in the event a hospital discontinues operation.

Section 115.24 permits medical records to be microfilmed immediately after completion. Section 115.26 encourages the use of automation in the medical records service and innovations in medical record formats, compilation, and data retrieval.

Section 115.33 requires that records of patients discharged be completed within 30 days of discharge.

Section 107.26 creates a medical records committee to supervise the maintenance of medical records "at the required standard of completeness." The medical records committee shall establish a disciplinary system for those who do not complete records in a timely manner. These provisions are repeated in section 115.34.
3. *Signature Requirements*: Section 115.33 provides that all entries in the record shall be dated and authenticated by the person making the entry. Sections 107.61 through .65 set forth the requirements pertaining to medical orders. Medication or treatment shall be administered only upon written, dated, and signed orders of a practitioner "acting within the scope of his license and qualified according to the medical staff bylaws." Oral orders may be taken only by personnel qualified according to medical staff bylaws. The order shall include the date, time, and full signature of the person taking the order and shall be countersigned by a practitioner within 48 hours. Section 115.33 provides that each entry must be individually authenticated. A single signature on the face sheet of the record shall not suffice to authenticate the entire record.

Section 109.65 provides that each dose of drug shall be recorded in the patient's medical record, which shall be properly signed after the drugs have been administered. Section 127.35 requires that authenticated reports of radiology interpretations, consultations, and therapy be made a part of the patient's medical record.

4. *Disclosure Authorized*: Section 115.27 provides that only authorized personnel shall have access to the records. The written authorization of the patient is required for release of medical record information outside the hospital. Section 115.31 requires that each patient's medical record be readily accessible and available to the professional staff concerned with the care and treatment of the patient. Section 115.28 provides that copies of the records may be made available for authorized appropriate purposes such as insurance claims and physician review.

5. *Confidentiality*: All medical records shall be treated as confidential under section 115.28.

6. *Other Matters*: Section 115.28 provides that medical records are the property of the hospital and shall not be removed from the hospital premises except upon subpoena.

RHODE ISLAND

1. *Creation and Contents*: The *Rules and Regulations for Licensing of Hospitals*, Department of Health, Section R23–17–HOSP (1973, as amended 1982), contains the regulations pertaining to medical records. Section 25.3 requires that a medical record be established for every person treated on "an inpatient, outpatient, or emergency basis in any unit of the hospital." Section 25.6 provides that "the medical record shall contain sufficient information to identify the patient and the problem, and to describe the treatment and document the results." Section 25.7 provides that the contents of all medical records shall conform with the applicable standards of the JCAH. Section 22.17 contains special requirements for the medical records of patients seeking emergency care.

2. *Retention*: Section 25.8 requires that provisions be made for the safe storage of medical records in accordance with the standards of the National Fire Protection Association. Section 25.9 provides that all medical records, "either original or accurate reproductions," must be preserved for a minimum of five years following discharge. Records of minors must be kept for at least five years after such minor has reached the age of 18.

3. *Signature Requirements*: Section 25.5 provides that entries in the medical record shall be made by the responsible person in accordance with hospital policies and procedures. Under Section 17.3, no medication or treatment may be given except on the signed order of a lawfully authorized person. Emergency telephone orders must be signed within 24 hours.

Section 24.10 requires that authenticated and dated reports of all pathology and clinical laboratory examinations be made a part of the patient's medical record. Section 30.6 requires that authenticated reports of radiological interpretations, consultations, and therapy be made a part of the record. Section 34.9 provides that an accurate and complete description of operative procedure must be recorded within 48 hours after the surgery is completed.

6. *Other Matters*: The hospital lien law allows persons against whom a claim has been asserted to examine the records of the hospital with reference to the claimed treatment, care, and maintenance of the injured person. R.I. Gen. Laws §9–3–7 (Reenact. 1969).

A provision of a statute dealing with evidence permits defendants to subpoena records to refute claimed charges for medical and hospital services. R.I. Gen. Laws §9–19–27 (Supp. 1983).

SOUTH CAROLINA

1. *Creation and Contents*: The requirements for medical records appear in section 601 of *Minimum Standards for Licensure of Hospitals and Institutional General Infirmaries in South Carolina*, Department of Health and Environmental Control (1979, as revised 1982). Section 601.5.A.

provides that an adequate and complete medical record shall be written for all patients admitted to the hospital. All notes shall be legibly written or typed. At minimum, a medical record must include: identification data, date of admission and discharge, history and physical examination, special examinations, provisional diagnosis, preoperative diagnosis, medical treatment, complete surgical record, report of anesthesia, nurses' notes, progress notes, pathological findings, charts, final diagnosis, condition on discharge, and autopsy findings in case of death.

Adequate medical records must also include a medication administration record for recording medications, treatments, and other pertinent data. Nurses shall sign this record after each medication administered or treatment rendered.

2. *Retention*: Section 601.1 provides that each attending physician shall be responsible for completing the medical record within "a stipulated time after the discharge of the patient consistent with good medical practice." Section 601.7 contains regulations concerning storage and microfilming. Medical records must be stored in an environment that will prevent unauthorized access and deterioration. The records must be retained for ten years. Records may be destroyed after ten years provided that "the hospital retains an index, register, or summary cards providing such basic information as dates of admission and discharge, name of responsible physician, and record of diagnoses and operations for all records so destroyed." However, records of minors must be retained until after "the expiration of the period of election following achievement of majority as prescribed by statute." Records may be placed on microfilm before ten years have expired provided that the entire record is filmed. Upon closure of a hospital, the facility must arrange for preservation of records.

3. *Signature Requirements*: Section 601.1 provides that each attending physician must sign the medical record. The use of a rubber stamp signature is acceptable only if (a) the physician whose signature the rubber stamp represents is the only one who has possession of the stamp and is the only one who uses it, and (b) the physician places in the administrative offices of the hospital a signed statement to that effect. However, the use of rubber stamp signatures is prohibited on orders for drugs listed as controlled substances under "Rules and Regulations Pertaining to Controlled Substances," R61–4 of the South Carolina Code of 1976.

Section 601.5A requires that all notes be signed. The use of initials in lieu of licensed nurses' signatures is discouraged but will be acceptable provided "such initials can be readily identified within the medical record."

Section 601.6 provides that all medical records shall contain orders for medication and treatment written in ink and signed and dated by the prescriber or his or her designee. All orders, including verbal orders, must be properly recorded in the medical record and dated and signed by the prescriber or his or her designee within 48 hours. These provisions are repeated in section 404.3, which also provides that verbal and telephone orders shall be given only to a licensed nurse and immediately recorded, dated, and signed. Verbal orders must be countersigned by the prescriber or his or her designee within 48 hours.

Section 602.2 provides that a written and signed report of each laboratory test and examination shall be made a part of the patient's record. This section also provides that initials in lieu of signatures will be accepted "provided such initials can be identified readily from a roster of individual initials with signature on permanent file."

5. *Confidentiality*: Section 601.7 provides that medical records shall be kept confidential.

6. *Other Matters*: Section 601.4 provides that patient records remain the property of the facility and that they not be taken from the hospital except by court order.

SOUTH DAKOTA

1. *Creation and Contents*: Hospital licensure requirements are contained in the *Administrative Rules of South Dakota*, Dept. of Health, tit. 44 (1980). Section 44:04:09:05 requires that each medical

record include identification data, consent forms, history, report of physical examination, diagnostic and therapeutic orders, observations, reports of actions and findings, and conclusions.

2. *Retention*: Section 44:04:09:04 requires that each hospital formulate written policies and procedures pertaining to requirements for completion of medical records.

3. *Signature Requirements*: Section 44:04:05:02 provides that all medical orders shall be in writing and be signed by the physician or the physician extender. Telephone orders may be taken only in an emergency and the physician or physician extender must sign or initial the orders on his or her next visit. The attending physician shall be responsible for documenting written orders and progress notes on each patient's medical record. Section 44:04:08:03 sets forth the same requirements with regard to medications or drugs. Section 44:04:10:08 requires that complete, signed reports of physician interpretations of all radiological examinations be made a part of the patient's medical record.

5. *Confidentiality*: Section 44:04:09:04 requires that each hospital formulate written policies and procedures pertaining to the confidentiality and safeguarding of medical records.

6. *Other Matters*: The lien law permits anyone against whom a claim is asserted for damages for personal injuries to examine and copy all hospital records related to the injured person. S.D. Codified Laws Ann. §44–12–9 (1983).

TENNESSEE

1. *Creation and Contents*: The requirements for medical records appear in chapter 1200–8–3 of the *Rules of the Tennessee Department of Public Health* (1974). Section 1200–8–3–.05 requires "individual, separate, and complete" medical records for all patients admitted to the hospital. Minimum contents of medical records include identification data, date of admission and discharge, medical history and physical examination, special examinations, provisional diagnosis, medical orders, complete surgical record, anesthesia report, physicians' progress and nurses' notes, pathology findings, charts, final diagnosis, condition on discharge, and discharge summary.

2. *Retention*: The attending physician is responsible for completing and signing the medical record of each patient as soon as practicable after discharge.

   All medical records, "either original records or microfilm of the same," must be stored in the hospital for a minimum of 22 years. After 22 years, records may be destroyed, but the date and time and circumstances of such destruction must be recorded "with the appropriate entry made on the patient index card." Upon the closing of any hospital, medical records may be stored with the Tennessee Department of Public Health.

   Section 1200–8–3–.02 requires that the discharge summary be recorded no later than 15 days after discharge. This section also requires physicians to record a detailed history and physical examination within 24 hours after admission. A medical staff committee is responsible for reviewing the medical records "to ensure that the recorded clinical information is sufficient for the purposes of medical care evaluation."

3. *Signature Requirements*: Section 1200–8–3–.05 provides that all entries shall be legibly recorded, dated, and signed by "the appropriate person responsible for recording." Section 1200–8–3–.02 requires that all orders for "diagnostic procedures, treatments, medications and transfer or disposition" be recorded legibly in ink or be typewritten, and that they be dated and signed by the physician. Telephone orders may be taken only by licensed nurses and must be countersigned by the physician no later than his or her next visit to the institution. Verbal orders recorded by someone other than the physician must also be countersigned by the physician at the time they are recorded. The person recording the orders should sign his or her name and title.

   Section 1200–8–3–.05 similarly provides that all medical records must contain medication and treatment orders written in ink and signed by the prescribing physician. This section also requires that a written and signed report of each laboratory test and examination and of each x-ray and therapy treatment be made a part of the patient's record.

The use of restraints requires the signed order of a physician under section 1200–8–3–.03, unless the patient's safety is in jeopardy and an immediate attempt has been made to notify the physician.

4. *Disclosure Authorized*: Section 1200–8–3–.05 provides that medical records shall be made available for inspection by an authorized representative of the Hospital Licensing Board or the Tennessee Department of Public Health. Records may be routed to physicians for consultation. Section 1200–8–3–.03 requires that the medical staff periodically review and analyze the clinical experience of the hospital based upon the medical records of patients. Written records of such meetings shall be kept confidential.

5. *Confidentiality*: Section 1200–8–3–.05 provides that "records of patients are the property of the institution and must not be taken from the property and must be held in confidence by the hospital and members of the medical staff except by court order."

TEXAS

1. *Creation and Contents*: *Hospital Licensing Standards*, State Department of Health (Hospital Licensure Division, 1969), contains few clear references to medical records. There is no section specifically dealing with contents.
2. *Retention*: *Hospital Licensing Standards* contains no reference to retention.
3. *Signature Requirements*: *Hospital Licensing Standards* prohibits giving any medication or treatment except on the signed order of "one lawfully authorized to give such order." In emergencies the physician can give the order by telephone, provided that he or she signs it on his or her next visit. Radiological reports must "indicate" the individual who performed the tests.

UTAH

1. *Creation and Contents*: *Hospital and Psychiatric Hospital Rules and Regulations*, Department of Health (1984), contains an extensive and detailed section on medical records in chapter 7. A medical record must be maintained for every patient admitted to the hospital or accepted for treatment.

   Section 7.407 requires that all medical records contain identification data, medical history, physical examination, provisional and final diagnoses, laboratory and x-ray reports and consent forms, diagnostic and therapeutic orders by physicians and other authorized practitioners, medical staff orders for medications and treatments, anesthesia record, pathology report, clinical observation including progress notes, consultation reports, and nursing notes, discharge summary, autopsy findings, reports of procedures, tests, and results, and physician identification.

   In addition to the above requirements, which apply to all medical records, special requirements are provided for obstetrical records (sec. 7.408), newborn infant records (sec. 7.409), emergency room records (sec. 7.410), and outpatient records (sec. 7.411).
2. *Retention*: Sec. 7.402 requires each hospital to provide for the filing, safe storage, and easy accessibility of medical records. The records must be safeguarded from loss, defacement, tampering, fires, floods, and unauthorized access.

   Sec. 7.406 provides that complete medical records for all patients must be retained for ten years after the last date of patient care. Before a patient's record may be destroyed, the hospital must make and retain a summary that includes the following data: name; medical record number; date of birth, admission, and discharge; nearest relative, if any; attending physician; final diagnosis; surgical procedure(s); and pathology findings. Medical records should be completely destroyed in order to maintain confidentiality. If a hospital ceases operation, it must make arrangements for the safe storage and prompt retrieval of all of its medical records.

Sec. 7.405 requires that records of discharged patients be completed within a reasonable time, not exceeding 30 days after discharge. Under the regulations, a medical record will be considered complete "when the required contents are assembled and authenticated." The attending physician is responsible for completing the medical record.

3. *Signature Requirements*: Sec. 7.405 requires that all entries in medical records be dated and "authenticated including the identity of the authors." Identification may include signatures, initials, or computer key. The regulations further provide that delegating the use of rubber stamps to other individuals is prohibited.

Sec. 7.407 contains numerous signature requirements pertaining to the general contents of the medical records. Medical staff orders for medications and treatments must be written in ink and signed by the prescribing physician within 24 hours. Verbal orders may be accepted and transcribed by qualified personnel.

Sec. 4.303 also provides that all medical orders must be in writing and be signed by a member of the medical staff. Sec. 6.303 requires that reports of all examinations performed by the pathology or laboratory be authenticated, dated, and made a part of the patient's medical records. Similarly, Sec. 6.604 requires that authenticated reports of all radiologic examinations be filed in the patient's medical record.

4. *Disclosure Authorized*: Sec. 7.404 provides that all medical records shall be readily available upon the request of the attending physician; the hospital or its medical staff or any authorized officer, agent or employee of either; authorized representatives of the department of health for determining compliance with licensure regulations; and any other person authorized by consent form.

Only authorized personnel have access to the records. The patient or his or her legal representative must consent in writing to the release of medical information to any unauthorized person.

When a patient is transferred to another facility, a copy of the patient's discharge summary and other appropriate information must be sent to that facility no later than four working days after discharge.

5. *Confidentiality*: Sec. 7.404 provides that all records shall be kept confidential.
6. *Other Matters*: The regulations also state in sec. 7.404 that medical records are the property of the hospital and may not be removed from the hospital's control except by court order or subpoena.

VERMONT

1. *Creation and Contents*: The *Hospital Licensing Procedure*, promulgated by the state department of health, provides regulations for medical records in section 3–946.

The present standards require complete and accurate records for each patient admitted to the hospital. The records must include identification data, complaint, the various histories, physical examination, special examinations, working diagnosis, medical or surgical treatment, pathology findings, progress notes, final diagnosis, condition on discharge, followup, and autopsy findings. Medical records must be permanent and be either typewritten or legibly written with pen and ink.

2. *Retention*: Records must be filed in a manner approved by the Department of Health and retained for at least ten years following the patient's discharge.
3. *Signature Requirements*: No medication or treatment can be given except on the written order of a practicing physician. All medical records must be signed by the attending physician.

VIRGINIA

1. *Creation and Contents*: The *Rules and Regulations for the Licensure of Hospitals in Virginia*, Department of Health (1982), contains the regulations for medical records. Section 208.2 requires that a medical record be established for every person treated on an inpatient, outpatient, or emergency basis. Separate medical records must be maintained for each newborn infant. Section 208.5 provides that the content of all medical records shall conform with the applicable standards of the JCAH.

2. *Retention*: Section 208.7 requires that each hospital make provisions for the safe storage of medical records or accurate and legible reproductions thereof in accordance with the National Fire Protection Association. Section 208.8 provides that all medical records, "either original or accurate reproductions," be preserved for a minimum of five years following discharge of the patient. Records of minors must be retained for a minimum of five years after such minor has reached the age of 18. Birth and death information must be retained for ten years.

    Section 208.3 requires that each hospital establish written policies and procedures regarding content and completion of medical records.

3. *Signature Requirements*: Section 208.4 provides that entries in the medical record be made by the responsible person in accordance with hospital policies and procedures. Section 201.3 requires that no medication or treatment be given except on the signed order of "a person lawfully authorized by state statutes." Telephone and verbal orders must be signed within 24 hours.

4. *Disclosure Authorized*: Section 208.6 deals with authorized disclosure. Only authorized personnel may have access to the records. Copies of a patient's medical record shall be released only with the written consent of the patient, his or her legal representative, or duly authorized state or federal health authorities. The hospital's permanent records may be removed from the premises only in accordance with a court order, subpoena, or statute.

WASHINGTON

1. *Creation and Contents*: *Hospital Rules and Regulations*, Department of Health (1983, as amended January, 1984), contains specific medical record requirements as they appear in the Washington Administrative Code (WAC).

    WAC 248–18–440 provides that the following minimum data shall be kept on all patients: admission data, dates of admission and discharge, medical history, physical examination and findings, medical orders, progress notes, operative reports, record of all medical care or treatments, reports of diagnostic procedures such as laboratory tests, x-ray, etc., nurses' records of care given to patients, and summary report of patient's course in the hospital and condition on discharge. The regulations provide that an accurate and complete medical record shall be written for each patient. All entries in a patient's medical record must be legibly written in ink or by typewriter or be recorded on a computer terminal designed to receive such information.

2. *Retention*: Patients' individual medical records must be handled and stored so that "they are not accessible to unauthorized persons, are protected from undue deterioration or destruction, and are easily retrievable for medical or administrative purposes."

    Medical records must be preserved for a minimum of ten years following the most recent discharge of the patient. However, the records of minors must be retained for at least three years after the patient reaches the age of 18 or for ten years following the patient's most recent discharge, whichever is longer. Records may be preserved in original form or photographic form. If a hospital ceases operation, it must make arrangements for the preservation of its medical records.

WAC 248–18–190 requires that a physical examination and medical history be documented within 48 hours of admission.

3. *Signature Requirements*: WAC 248–18–440 provides that each entry in a patient's medical record shall be dated and authenticated by the person who gave the order or provided the care to which the entry pertains. WAC 248–18–190 requires written orders or prescriptions by members of the medical staff for all medications administered to patients. Verbal and telephone orders must be authenticated by the medical staff within 48 hours.

WAC 248–18–440 requires that a patient's medical record include authenticated orders for any drug, therapy, restraint, or diet administered to a patient. Standing medical orders must be authenticated and entered into the record.

4. *Disclosure Authorized*: WAC 248–18–440 requires that each hospital establish written policies and procedures "which govern access to and release of data in patients' individual medical records and other medical data taking into consideration the confidential nature of these records."

WEST VIRGINIA

1. *Creation and Contents*: *West Virginia Regulations and Law for Licensing Hospitals*, State Department of Health (1969), contains the regulations for medical records as PART VI, Section C. Regulation 603.1(b) requires accurate and complete written medical records on all patients.

> 603.1(b)
> A complete medical record is one which includes patient identification data, complaints, history of present illness, personal and family history, physical examination, doctor's orders including dietary orders, special examinations and consultations, clinical laboratory, x-ray and other examinations, provisional or working diagnosis, treatment and medications given, surgical reports including operative and anesthesia records, gross and microscopic pathological findings, progress notes, final diagnosis, condition on discharge, discharge summary and autopsy findings, if performed.

The same regulation provides for a "short form medical record," that may be used for patients staying in the hospital less than 48 hours. Maternity and newborn patients are excluded from this type of record. The short form need contain only sufficient information for proper diagnosis and treatment.

2. *Retention*: Regulation 603.1(e) provides that records "shall be preserved either in the original form or by microfilm or electronic data process." Since this is the only reference to retention, the implication is that records are to be permanently preserved.

Medical records must be completed promptly, within 15 days, but not more than 45 days, following discharge of the patient.

3. *Signature Requirements*: All orders for medication or treatment are to be in writing and signed by the physician in ink. Telephone or verbal orders given to a registered nurse must be signed by the physician as soon as possible thereafter. All orders, reports, and entries are to be typewritten or written in ink and signed by the person making the entry. The records must be authenticated and signed by the physician or dentist.

WISCONSIN

1. *Creation and Contents*: The *Rules of the Division of Health, General and Special Hospitals*, Department of Health and Social Services, ch. H 24 (June 1968), provides general and specific requirements for the contents of records, including the requirement that all clinical information

pertaining to the patient's stay shall be centralized in the patient's record. H 24.07 provides that the medical records should contain identification data, chief complaint, present illness, past and family history, physical examination, provisional diagnosis, clinical laboratory and x-ray reports, consultations, medical and surgical treatment, tissue reports, progress notes, final diagnosis, discharge summary, and autopsy findings.

A specific reference to automation provides the following:

ADMINISTRATIVE RESPONSIBILITIES

* * *

(f) records shall be indexed according to disease, operation, and physician and shall be kept up-to-date. For indexing, any recognized system may be used.

* * *

3. In hospitals using automatic data processing, indexes may be kept on punch cards or reproduced on sheets kept in books. Wis. Adm. Code, ch. H 24, §24.07 (1968).

2. *Retention*: The regulations provide that the hospital should have a written policy for the preservation of medical records, either in the original or by microfilm, for a period of time determined by each hospital based on historical research, legal, teaching, and patient care needs. Current records must be completed within 24–48 hours of admission. Records of discharged patients must be completed within 15 days of discharge. H 24.04 provides that the medical records committee shall supervise the maintenance of medical records at "the required standard of completeness."

3. *Signature Requirements*: The regulations, in that portion relating to medical staff responsibilities, require signatures for reports of consultations. They also require that licensed practitioners authenticate and sign records. Every physician must sign the entries he or she makes; a single signature on the face sheet is insufficient. The regulations also provide that only members of the medical house staff are competent to write or dictate medical histories and physical examinations. The attending physician must countersign at least the history and physical examination and the summary written by members of the house staff. Telephone orders must be signed or initialed by the physician within 24 hours. Nurses' notes shall be signed, not initialed.

4. *Disclosure Authorized*: Only authorized personnel shall have access to the records. The regulations provide that the written consent of the patient shall be presented as authority for release of medical record information.

5. *Confidentiality*: The regulations provide that the medical records shall be kept confidential.

6. *Other Matters*: Medical records generally shall not be removed from the hospital environment except upon subpoena.

WYOMING

1. *Creation and Contents*: *Standards, Rules and Regulations for Hospitals and Related Facilities*, Department of Health and Social Sciences (1979), contains extensive medical records requirements in chapter III, section 7. Medical records must be maintained on all patients and must contain sufficient information to justify the diagnosis and to warrant the treatment and end results. The records shall include identification data, chief complaint, present illness, past and family history, physical examination, provisional diagnosis, clinical laboratory and x-ray reports, consultations, medical and surgical treatment, progress notes, final diagnosis, discharge summary, and autopsy findings.

2. *Retention*: Medical records of public hospitals shall be preserved, either in the original form or on microfilm, for "a period of time determined by the hospital administrator and the Archives, Records Management, and Centralized Microfilm Division of the State of Wyoming Archives and Historical Department." Final legal authority for the destruction of any records must be obtained from the department's records committee. Private hospitals may preserve and destroy records at their discretion.

Chapter I, section 5, provides that the medical records committee shall supervise the maintenance of medical records at "the required standard of completeness."

Current records shall be completed within 24 to 48 hours of admission, while records of discharged patients must be completed within 15 days.

3. *Signature Requirements*: The regulations provide that "every physician shall sign or initial all entries which he himself makes." The regulation makes it clear that a single signature on the face sheet of the medical record shall not suffice to authenticate the entire record. The attending physician must countersign at least the history, physical examination, and summary written by the house staff. Chapter I, section 5, also requires that all orders be recorded and signed. Consultation reports must be signed by the consultant. Radiology and laboratory reports must also be signed.

4. *Disclosure Authorized*: The records are to be kept confidential and only authorized personnel shall have access to them. Written consent of the patient must be presented for the release of medical information.

6. *Other Matters*: Original medical records must not be removed from the hospital except upon subpoena.

State-by-State Analysis: Discoverability and Admissibility of Medical Staff Committee Records

This state-by-state analysis consists of a listing of the applicable statutes and more important cases dealing with the discoverability and admissibility of medical staff committee records. The list of cases for each state is not exhaustive, and additional citations may be encountered in legal research. The state-by-state analysis does not constitute an exhaustive treatment of statutory protection in each state.

ALABAMA

Statutory Provisions

Ala. Code tit. 34 §24–58.

The decisions, opinions, actions, and proceedings of utilization review committees or committees of similar nature or purpose are privileged if they are rendered, entered, or acted upon in good faith and without malice and on the basis of facts reasonably known or reasonably believed to exist.

ALASKA

Statutory Provisions

Alaska St. §§18.23.030 and 18.23.070.

All data and information on quality assurance, mortality and morbidity, cost control, and similar committees shall be held in confidence and shall not be disclosed to anyone except to the extent necessary to carry out the purposes of the review committee. Such data and information are not subject to subpoena or discovery. Records and proceedings of review organizations are not subject to discovery or introduction into evidence in civil actions against health care providers arising out of matters that are the subject of evaluation and review. However, information that is otherwise available from original sources is not immune from discovery and introduction into evidence simply because it was presented to a review committee. In addition, a person whose conduct or competence has been reviewed by a committee may obtain information for purposes of appellate review of the committee's action. Similarly, discovery proceedings may be brought by a plaintiff who claims that

(1) information provided to a review organization was false, and (2) the person providing the information knew or had reason to know it was false.

ARIZONA

Statutory Provisions

Ariz. Rev. Stat. Ann. §36–445.01, *as amended by* S.B. 1264 (Laws 1982).

All proceedings, records, and materials prepared in connection with committees that review the nature, quality, and necessity of care provided in a hospital and the preventability of complications and deaths occurring in a hospital, including all peer reviews of individual health care providers practicing in and applying to practice in hospitals, and the records of such reviews, are confidential and not subject to discovery. Discovery is allowable in proceedings before the board of medical or osteopathic examiners, or in an action by an individual health care provider against a hospital or its staff arising from discipline of that health care provider or refusal, termination, suspension, or limitation of his or her privileges.

Selected Cases

Tucson Medical Center, Inc. v. Misevch, 113 Ariz. 34, 545 P. 2d 958 (1976). Statements and information considered by a medical review committee are subject to subpoena, but reports and minutes of the committee are not.

ARKANSAS

Statutory Provisions

Ark. Stat. Ann. §82–357.

All information, interviews, reports, statements, memoranda, and other data used by hospital staff committees and other committees in the course of medical studies, the purpose of which is to reduce morbidity and mortality, and any findings or conclusions resulting from such studies, are privileged and may not be received in evidence in any legal proceeding. This statute does not apply to original medical records pertaining to patients.

Selected Cases

Baxter County Newspapers v. Medical Staff of Baxter General Hospital, 273 Ark. 511, 622 S.W. 2d 495 (Ark. 1981). The state Freedom of Information Act (FOIA) was held to permit public access to medical review committee proceedings because such proceedings were not expressly exempted from the FOIA.

CALIFORNIA

Statutory Provisions

Cal. Evid. Code §1157.

The proceedings and records of organized medical staff and podiatric and registered dietician committees, the function of which is to evaluate and improve the quality of care rendered in a hospital, are not subject to discovery. In addition, the prohibition shall not apply to the statements made by any person in attendance at a committee meeting and who is a party to an action or proceeding, the subject of which was reviewed at the meeting, or to any person requesting staff privileges. Other exceptions are noted.

Prohibitions contained in this section shall not exclude the discovery or use of relevant evidence in a criminal action.

Selected Cases

Kenney v. Superior Court, 255 Cal. App. 2d 106, 63 Cal. Rptr. 84 (1967). Records and documents in hospital files concerning disciplinary proceedings against a physician are discoverable in a malpractice suit upon the showing of good cause. (This was decided prior to the enactment §1157 of the California Evidence Code.)

Matchett v. Superior Court of Yuba, 40 Cal. App. 3d 623, 115 Cal. Rptr. 317 (1974). Reports of various medical staff committees are immune from discovery in a malpractice suit, but records of hospital management administration are discoverable.

Schulz v. Superior Court for County of Yolo, 66 Cal. App. 3d 440, 136 Cal. Rptr. 67 (1977). Discovery of reports of the hospital's medical advisory board was denied in a malpractice action.

Roseville Community Hospital v. Superior Court, 70 Cal. App. 3d 809, 139 Cal. Rptr. 170 (1977). Statements made by individuals at a committee meeting of the hospital's medical staff are discoverable by persons whose requests for hospital staff privileges were denied.

Henry Mayo Newhall Memorial Hospital v. Superior Court, 81 Cal. App. 3d 626, 146 Cal. Rptr. 542 (1978). A hospital's filing of the transcript of a staff committee hearing in an unrelated administrative mandamus action does not constitute a waiver of immunity from discovery under §1157 of the California Evidence Code.

County of Kern v. Superior Court of Kern County, 82 Cal. App. 3d 396, 147 Cal. Rptr. 248 (1978). The court found the trial court's order granting a discovery motion in a malpractice action to be overbroad and in violation of §1157 of the California Evidence Code.

COLORADO

Statutory Provisions

Colo. Rev. Stat. §12-43.5-102.

The records of peer review committees or other committees that perform similar review services are not subject to subpoena in any civil suit against a physician. However, the Colorado State Board of Medical Examiners may obtain a summary of the findings, recommendations, and disposition of actions taken by a review committee.

Selected Cases

Posey v. District Court, 196 Colo. 396, 586 P. 2d 36 (1978). Section 12–43.5–102 of the Colorado Revised Statutes is applicable to civil suits against hospitals as well as physicians.

Davidson v. Light, 79 F.R.D. 137 (D. Colo. 1978). Section 12–43.5–102 is designed to confer immunity on professional review committees, not on hospital infection control committees.

Franco v. District Court, 641 P. 2d 922 (Colo. 1982). Records of peer review committees are not discoverable by a physician who seeks to compel a hospital to restore his or her surgical privileges.

Sherman v. District Court, City and County of Denver, 637 P. 2d 378 (1981). Surveys conducted by hospital inspection committees are privileged and free from discovery only if they were furnished to a committee formed for the purpose of evaluating quantity, quality, and timeliness of medical services and if open communication between hospitals and hospital inspection committees is not substantially impaired by public disclosure.

CONNECTICUT

Statutory Provisions

Conn. Gen. Stat. Ann. §38–19a.

Opinions of peer review, utilization review, medical audit, and similar committees are not subject to discovery and are not admissible into evidence in any civil action arising out of matters that are the subject of committee evaluation and review.

Selected Cases

Morse v. Gerity, 520 F. Supp. 470 (D. Conn. 1981). Peer review documents are nondiscoverable regardless of whether they pertain to the subject matter of a lawsuit.

DELAWARE

Statutory Provisions

Del. Code Ann. tit. 24, §1768.

Records and proceedings of hospital and nursing home quality review committees are confidential and are not available for court subpoena or subject to discovery.

Selected Cases

Register v. Wilmington Medical Center, Inc., 377 A. 2d 8 (Del. 1977). Staff reports concerning performance of a resident physician are discoverable in a malpractice action.

FLORIDA

Statutory Provisions

Fla. Stat. Ann. §768.40.

The proceedings and records of quality assurance and utilization review committees are not subject to discovery or admissible into evidence in any civil action against a health care provider arising out of matters that are the subject of committee evaluation and review. However, material otherwise available from original sources is not immune from discovery or use in civil actions.

Selected Cases

Carter v. Metropolitan Dade County, 253 So. 2d 920 (Fla. App. 1971), *cert. denied,* 263 So. 2d 584 (Fla. 1972). Minutes of a hospital teaching session are admissible.

Good Samaritan Hospital Ass'n v. Simon, 370 So. 2d 1174 (Fla. App. 1979). Discovery is allowed where plaintiff physician alleges that the medical review committee acted fraudulently and maliciously in denying him or her staff privileges.

Dade County Medical Association v. Hlis, 372 So. 2d 117 (Fla. App. 1979). Discovery of ethics committee records in a context different from the civil action against a health care provider is prohibited on public policy grounds.

Segal v. Roberts, 380 So. 2d 1049 (Fla. App. 1979), *cert. denied,* 388 So. 2d 1117 (Fla. 1980). Section 768.40 of the Florida statute is not applicable where the subject considered by the medical review committee, but discovery of the committee's records is prohibited nevertheless on public policy grounds.

Gadd v. News-Press Publishing Co., 412 So. 2d 894 (Fla. App. 1982). Minutes and documents of a public hospital's utilization review committee are subject to public inspection under the Florida Public Records Act because no specific exemption or confidentiality requirement for such files is provided by statute.

Somer v. Johnson, 704 F. 2d 1473 (11th Cir. 1983). The proceedings and records of medical committees are not subject to discovery or introduction into evidence against a provider of professional health services in an action between citizens of different states when such action alleges medical malpractice.

Holly v. Auld, 450 So. 2d 217 (Fla. 1984). Physician is not permitted to discover credentials committee records in defamation action against persons who submitted information to the committee.

City of Williston v. Roadlander, 425 So. 2d 1175 (Fla. App. 1983). Florida's medical staff committee records confidentiality statute may not be circumvented by claiming that, in a public hospital, medical review committee records are public records.

GEORGIA

Statutory Provisions

Ga. Code Ann. §88–3204.

Records and proceedings of committees, the function of which is to evaluate and improve the quality of health care rendered by health care providers or to determine that services rendered were professionally indicated or that the cost of services rendered was reasonable, are not subject to discovery or introduction into evidence against a provider of professional health care services arising out of matters that are the subject of evaluation and review. However, information, documents, and records otherwise available from original sources are not immune from discovery or use in civil actions simply because they were presented to a committee.

Selected Cases

Hollowell v. Jove, 247 Ga. 678, 279 S.E. 2d 430 (1981). Medical review committee records concerning a physician's care of a particular patient, that physician's care of other patients—and even a listing of the persons who were present at those review meetings—are totally exempt from discovery in Georgia.

HAWAII

Statutory Provisions

Hawaii Rev. Stat. §624–25.5, as amended by Act 227 (1982).

Proceedings and records of peer review committees are not subject to discovery. However, this prohibition does not apply to the statements made by any person in attendance at a committee meeting who is a party to an action or proceeding, the subject of which was reviewed at such meeting, or to any person who has requested hospital staff privileges. Other exceptions are noted.

The prohibitions contained in this section shall apply to investigations and discovery conducted by the board of medical examiners.

IDAHO

Statutory Provisions

Idaho Code §39–1392a, b, and e.

Written records of interviews, reports, statements, minutes, memoranda, charts, and materials of any hospital medical staff committee, the function of which is to conduct research concerning (1) hospital patient cases or (2) medical questions or problems arising from hospital patient cases, are neither discoverable nor admissible. This section does not affect the use nor prohibit the dissemination of documents that are to be used for medical purposes. Other exceptions are noted.

Selected Cases

Murphy v. Wood, 105 Idaho 180, 667 P. 2d 859 (1983), statute requiring disclosure of names of persons having direct knowledge concerning a claimant's case, was not a basis for permitting physicians in medical malpractice action to obtain disclosure of peer review records.

ILLINOIS

Statutory Provisions

Ill. Ann. Stat. ch. 110, §§2101 and 8–2102.

Information, interviews, reports, statements, or other data of patient care audit, medical care evaluation, utilization review, and similar committees are strictly confidential and are not admissible. However, the claim of confidentiality cannot be invoked in any hospital proceeding concerning a physician's staff privileges or in a judicial review of such a proceeding.

Selected Cases

Matviuw v. Johnson, 70 Ill. App. 3d 481, 388 N.E. 2d 795 (1979). Plaintiff physician is permitted to discover and use medical staff committee data in a defamation action

Walker v. Alton Memorial Hospital Association, 91 Ill. App. 3d 310, 414 N.E. 2d 850 (1980). The hospital was ordered to submit peer review records to a judge for private examination to determine whether the material was inadmissible at trial.

Mennes v. South Chicago Community Hospital, 100 Ill. App. 3d 1029, 427 N.E. 2d 952 (1981). Private judicial examination of peer review committee material relating to the granting of physicians' privileges or physician reappointment is not necessary because such information is nondiscoverable, regardless of the content of such material.

INDIANA

Statutory Provisions

Ind. Code Ann. §§34–4–12.6–1 and 34–4–12.6–2.
Records of the determinations of or communications to a peer review committee are not subject to discovery or admissible into evidence. Information otherwise discoverable or admissible from original sources is not immune from discovery or use simply because it was presented during committee meetings. In addition, any professional health care provider who is under investigation has the right to see any records pertaining to his or her personal practice.

IOWA

Statutory Provisions

Iowa Code Ann. §§135.40 and 135.42.
Information, interviews, reports, statements, memoranda, and other data used by hospital staff committees in the course of any study the aim of which is to reduce morbidity are not to be used, offered, or received in evidence. This section does not affect the admissibility of a patient's primary medical or hospital records.

Selected Cases

Boger v. Lee, No. 49568 (D. Iowa, June 16, 1982). Information produced by the activities of a professional standards review organization (PSRO) or a hospital performing the function of a PSRO is not subject to subpoena or discovery in a civil action except to the extent that the hospital contemplates using the information at trial.

KANSAS

Statutory Provisions

Kan. Stat. Ann. §65–177.
Opinions based on data collected in medical research studies conducted by the state health officer on the subject of reducing mortality and morbidity from maternal, perinatal, and anesthetic causes are not admissible in any action in any court. However, statistics or tables resulting from such studies are admissible.

KENTUCKY

Statutory Provisions

Ky. Rev. Stat. §311.377.

The proceedings, records, opinions, conclusions, and recommendations of any committee, board, commission, PSRO, or other entity, the purpose of which is to review and evaluate the health care acts of other health care personnel, are confidential and privileged; they are not subject to discovery, subpoena, or introduction into evidence in any civil action, court, or administrative proceeding. This statute does not protect materials that are independently discoverable or admissible, nor does it restrict or prevent the presentation of records and other materials in any statutory or administrative proceeding relating to the function of any committee or other review body. Other exceptions are noted.

Selected Cases

Nazareth Literary and Benevolent Institution v. Stephenson, 503 S.W. 2d 177 (Ky. 1973). Medical staff reports concerning the professional activities of a physician are discoverable in the absence of clear statutory intent to the contrary. (This case was decided prior to the enactment of §311.377.)

Ott v. St. Luke Hospital of Campbell County, Inc., 522 F. Supp. 706 (E.D. Ky. 1981). Deliberations of the peer review committee of the defendant hospital are subject to discovery by plaintiff doctor challenging denial of his or her application for staff privileges.

LOUISIANA

Statutory Provisions

La. Rev. Stat. Ann. §44.7.

The records and proceedings of any hospital committee, medical organization committee, or extended care facility are not available for court subpoena.

MAINE

Statutory Provisions

Me. Rev. Stat. Ann. tit. 32, §3296.

All proceedings and records of proceedings of mandatory medical staff review committees and hospital review committees are exempt from discovery without a showing of good cause

MARYLAND

Statutory Provisions

Md Health Occ. Code §14–601.

The proceedings, records, and files of a medical review committee are neither discoverable nor admissible into evidence in any civil action arising out of matters that are the subject of committee evaluation and review.

Selected Cases

Unnamed Physician v. Commission on Medical Discipline, 285 Md. 1, 400 A. 2d 396, *cert. denied*, 444 U.S. 868 (1979). The proceedings, records, and other documents of medical staff committees are discoverable in physician disciplinary proceedings but not in civil suits.

Kappas v. Chestnut Lodge, Inc., *709 F. 2d 878 (4th Cir.), *cert. denied*, 104 S.Ct. 164 (1983). Immunity provided by statute is not limited solely to records concerning disciplinary matters, but applies also to matters involving quality of health care, and evaluating need for and level of performance of health care rendered.

MASSACHUSETTS

Statutory Provisions

Mass. Gen. Laws Ann. ch. 231, §85 N.

Members of professional committees are not liable in civil actions except for bad faith or reckless decisions.

MICHIGAN

Statutory Provisions

Mich. Stat. Ann. §14.57 (23).

All proceedings, reports, findings, and conclusions of review entities are confidential and shall not be discoverable or used as evidence in an action for personal injuries based upon malpractice, lack of informed consent, or negligence.

Selected Cases

Marchand v. Henry Ford Hospital, 398 Mich. 163, 247 N.W. 2d 280 (1976). Information collected by individuals other than those sitting as a professional practices review committee is discoverable.

MINNESOTA

Statutory Provisions

Minn. Stat. Ann. §§145.61 through 145.65.

Data and information of quality assurance, mortality and morbidity, cost control, and similar committees are not subject to subpoena or discovery. The proceedings and records of these committees are not subject to discovery or introduction into evidence in any civil action against a health care professional arising out of matters that are the subject of evaluation and review. However, documents or records otherwise available from original sources are not immune simply because they were presented during the proceedings of review organization. This statute does not apply to committees that function to grant or deny staff privileges.

Selected Cases

Kalish v. Mt. Sinai Hospital, 270 N.W. 2d 783 (Minn. 1978). Guidelines of a hospital medical staff committee are discoverable but not admissible.

MISSISSIPPI

Statutory Provisions

Miss. Code Ann. §41–63–9.

The proceedings and records of committees the function of which is to evaluate and improve the quality and efficiency of medical care are not subject to discovery or introduction into evidence in any civil action against a health care provider arising out of matters that are the subject of evaluation and review. However, information, documents, and records that are otherwise discoverable from original sources are not immune from discovery merely because they were presented to a committee. This statute does not apply to legal actions brought by a committee to restrict or revoke a physician's license or privileges, or in any action brought against a committee or its members for actions alleged to be malicious.

MISSOURI

Statutory Provisions

Mo. Ann. Stat. §537.035.

Members of medical review, peer review, utilization review, pharmacy review, and similar committees are not liable in damages to any person subject to the actions of such committees unless the actions were malicious or unsupportable.

MONTANA

Statutory Provisions

Mont. Code Ann. §§50–16–201, 50–16–203, and 50–16–205.

Data (written reports, notes, and records) of tissue committees and committees that function to assist in the training, supervision, and discipline of health care professionals are confidential and are not admissible in evidence in any judicial proceeding. This statute does not affect the admissibility of records dealing with a patient's hospital care and treatment.

NEBRASKA

Statutory Provisions

Neb. Rev. Stat. §§71–2046 and 71–2048.

The proceedings, records, minutes, reports, and communications of medical staff committees and utilization review committees are not subject to discovery except upon court order after a showing of good cause arising from extraordinary circumstances. This statute does not preclude or affect discovery of or production of evidence relating to the hospitalization or treatment of any patient in the ordinary course of hospitalization of such patient.

Selected Cases

Oviatt v. Archbishop Bergan Mercy Hospital, 191 Neb. 224, 214 N.W. 2d 490 (1974). The proceedings of a hospital medical staff committee are privileged in the absence of a showing of good cause arising from extraordinary circumstances.

NEVADA

Statutory Provisions

Nev. Rev. Stat. §49.265.

The proceedings and records of medical review committees and organized medical staff committees responsible for evaluating and improving the quality of care rendered in hospitals are not subject to discovery. In addition, persons in attendance at such committee meetings may not be required to testify about the proceedings at the meetings. However, this statute does not apply to any statement made by an applicant for hospital staff privileges; nor does it apply to any statement made by a person in attendance at a committee meeting who is a party to an action or proceeding the subject of which is reviewed at such meeting. The privilege does not extend to certain actions against insurance carriers and to information included in health care records made available to either the patient, the board of medical examiners, or the attorney general under other provisions of Nevada law.

NEW HAMPSHIRE

Statutory Provisions

N.H. Rev. Stat. Ann. §329–29.

All proceedings, records, findings, and deliberations of duly established state and county medical society medical review committees are confidential and privileged and are not to be used, available for use, or subject to process in any other proceeding. This privilege also includes, specifically, the manner of deliberation and voting of the committee and members thereof.

NEW JERSEY

Statutory Provisions

N.H. Stat. Ann. §2A:84A–22.8.

Information and data secured by utilization review committees may not be revealed or disclosed in any manner or in any circumstances except to (1) a patient's attending physician, (2) the chief administrative officer of a hospital that such committees serve, (3) the medical executive committee of a hospital, (4) representatives of governmental agencies in the performance of their duties, or (5) insurance companies, hospital service corporations, and medical service organizations, under certain circumstances.

Selected Cases

Myers v. St. Francis Hospital, 91 N.J. Super. 377, 220 A. 2d 693 (1966). Discovery rules are to be construed liberally in the absence of any indication therein to the contrary. (This case was decided prior to the enactment of section 2A:84A–22.8.)

Gureghian v. Hackensack Hospital, 109 N.J. Super. 143, 262 A. 2d 440 (1970). Records of a perinatal mortality committee are discoverable. (This case was decided prior to the enactment of section 2A:84A–22.8.)

Young v. King, 136 N.J. Super. 127, 344 A. 2d 792 (1975). Section 2A:84A–22.8 applies to information and data of utilization committees, but not to information and data of medical records committees, tissue committees, or infection control committees.

Garrow v. Elizabeth General Hospital and Dispensary, 79 N.J. 549, 401 A. 2d 533 (1979). A physician is entitled to discover data used by a hospital medical staff in its decisions to reject his or her application for staff privileges.

NEW MEXICO

Statutory Provisions

N.M. Stat. Ann. §§41–9–2 and 41–9–5.

Data and information on cost control, quality assurance, mortality and morbidity, and similar committees are confidential and not subject to discovery. However, information, documents, and records otherwise available from original sources are not immune from discovery or use in any civil action merely because they were present during the proceedings of a review organization. Material is not protected if it is sought to be used in a judicial appeal from an action of a review organization.

Selected Cases

University Heights Hospital, Inc. v. Ashby, No. 14284 (N.M. Sup. Ct., June 16, 1982). Constitutionality of state peer review act reinstated after a trial court erroneously invalidated the confidentiality provisions of the act.

NEW YORK

Statutory Provisions

N.Y. Educ. Law §6527.

Proceedings and records of utilization review, quality control, and similar committees are not subject to disclosure. This exception from disclosure does not apply to statements made by any person in attendance at a committee meeting who is a party to an action or proceeding the subject of which was reviewed at the meeting. Other exceptions are noted.

Selected Cases

Judd v. Park Avenue Hospital, 37 Misc. 2d 614, 235 N.Y.S. 2d 843 (Sup. Ct. 1962). Hospital medical staff committee discussions are considered hearsay and, therefore, not subject to discovery. (This case was decided prior to the enactment of section 6527.)

Salmonsen v. Brown, 62 Misc. 2d 623, 309 N.Y.S. 2d 535 (Sup. Ct. 1970). The hospital's failure to apply for a protective order constitutes a waiver of immunity from discovery. (This case was decided prior to the enactment of section 6527.)

Gourdine v. Phelps Memorial Hospital, 40 A.D. 2d 694, 336 N.Y.S. 2d 316 (1972). The court will not compel disclosure of documents of medical staff meetings where it is apparent that no such documents exist.

Pindar v. Parke Davis & Co., 71 Misc. 2d 844, 337 N.Y.S. 2d 452 (1972). Section 6527 does not protect statements of a person in attendance at a medical staff committee meeting who is a party to an action or proceeding the subject of which was reviewed at such meeting.

Lang v. Abbott Laboratories, 59 A.D. 2d 734, 398 N.Y.S. 2d 577 (1977). Discovery of hospital records concerning quality of intravenous fluid is not barred by section 6527.

Lenard v. New York University Medical Center, 83 App. Div. 2d 860, 442 N.Y.S. 2d 30 (1981). Statements by members of a hospital's medical review committee are not discoverable if the hospital, by itself, is a party to a medical malpractice suit, but would be discoverable if a member of the committee were a party to the lawsuit.

Daly v. Genovese, 96 App. Div. 2d 1027, 466 N.Y.S. 2d 428 (1983). N.Y. Education Law §6527 excepts from the peer review committee confidentiality privilege statements made during a peer review meeting about medical malpractice actions specifically reviewed by the committee. However, this exception does not allow in, over the privilege, allegedly slanderous statements made during peer review meetings but unrelated to medical malpractice actions.

Farley v. County of Nassau, 92 App. Div. 2d 583, 459 N.Y.S. 2d 470 (1983). Persons seeking the medical records of utilization and review committees cannot circumvent the privilege accorded such records by claiming to seek only the underlying facts involved, as opposed to the actual proceedings. The underlying facts incorporated in medical records of utilization and review committees, as well as the actual proceedings of such committees, are privileged.

Palmer v. City of Rome, 120 Misc. 2d 558, 466 N.Y.S. 2d 238 (1983). Evaluations received by hospitals from independent external medical centers are privileged when related to the performance and employment of physicians. Failure to establish a formal review committee is not fatal to the privilege.

Wiener v. Memorial Hospital, 114 Misc. 2d 1013, 453 N.Y.S. 2d 142 (1982). For medical malpractice actions, postincident and investigative reports do not fall within the definition of medical review functions and therefore are not privileged and are discoverable. However, peer review committee investigations are not discoverable.

NORTH CAROLINA

Statutory Provisions

N.C. Gen. Stat. §131E–95 (1983).

Members of duly appointed medical review committees are not subject to liability in civil actions when acting within the scope of the committee's function, except in cases of malice or fraud. In a civil action against a provider of professional health services, records and materials either considered or produced by a committee are not subject to discovery or introduction into evidence where the action arises out of matters that are the subject of evaluation and review by the committee.

NORTH DAKOTA

Statutory Provisions

N.D. Cent. Code §23–01–02.1, *as amended by* H.B. 1130 (New Laws 1983).

H.B. 1130 has amended §23–01–02.1 to ensure the confidentiality of all information, documents, and records of internal quality assurance review committees. The law previously referred only to utilization review committees. The amendment further provides that information, documents, or records that are otherwise discoverable will not be confidential merely because they were presented at a review committee hearing, nor can witnesses be prevented from testifying in a suit merely because they testified before the committee. However, the witnesses may not be questioned about testimony given before the committee.

OHIO

Statutory Provisions

Ohio Rev. Code Ann. §§2305.25 and 2305.25.1.

Proceedings and records of tissue, utilization review, and similar committees are confidential and are not subject to discovery or introduction into evidence in any civil action arising out of matters that are the subject of evaluation and review. However, information, documents, or records otherwise available from original sources are not immune from discovery or use merely because they were presented during committee meetings.

Selected Cases

Samuelson v. Susen, 576 F. 2d 546 (3d Cir. 1978). The Ohio statute protecting committee records does not deprive a litigant of Fifth and Fourteenth Amendment due process rights.

Young v. Gersten, 56 Ohio Misc. 1, 381 N.E. 2d 353 (1978). The Ohio statute protecting committee records does not violate the Ohio constitution.

Rees v. Doctor's Hospital, No. CA–5226 (Ohio App., Stark County, Feb. 6, 1980). Hospital incident reports are discoverable in a civil action against a hospital.

Gates v. Brewer, 2 Ohio App. 3d 347, 442 N.E. 2d 72 (1981). When an individual attempts to prevent the discovery of information by asserting the privilege provided by the Ohio statute that prohibits the discovery of review committee records, it is incumbent on the trial court to hold an *in camera* inspection of the information, documents, and records in question to ensure that all the material sought to be discovered is in fact protected under the statute.

Specifically protected under the Ohio statute are

(1) records or transcripts of the proceedings of the review committee that considered the conduct of the defendant

(2) any evidence produced or presented at such proceedings, unless such evidence is available to the subpoenaed witness in any capacity other than as a committee member

(3) any finding, recommendation, evaluation, opinion, or other action of said committee.

Atkins v. Walker, 3 Ohio App. 3d 427, 445 N.E. 2d 1132 (1981). The provisions of the Ohio peer review committee privilege statute reach and are applicable to slander actions, where a doctor sued members of a hospital's credentials committee for libelous statements. Therefore, delivery of the privileged document, in a slander action, from such a committee does not operate as a waiver of the privilege as to the writer-defendant who is the "original" source.

OKLAHOMA

Statutory Provisions

Okla. Stat. Ann. tit. 63, §1–1709.
All information, interviews, reports, statements, memoranda, findings, and conclusions of committees formed for the purpose of advancing medical research or medical education in the interest of reducing morbidity and mortality are not to be used, offered, or received in evidence in any legal proceeding.

Selected Cases

City of Edmond v. Parr, 587 P. 2d 56 (Okla. 1978). Records kept by a hospital infectious disease control committee and records pertaining to an investigation concerning infection in the hospital or among patients and employees are inadmissible in a malpractice action.

OREGON

Statutory Provisions

Or. Rev. Stat. §41.675.
All data of tissue, utilization review, and similar committees are confidential and are not admissible in evidence in any judicial proceeding. In addition, communications to such committees are privileged and members of the committee and individuals communicating to the committees cannot be examined on such communication. This statute, however, does not affect the admissibility in evidence of records dealing with a patient's hospital care and treatment.

Selected Cases

Straube v. Larson, 287 Or. 357, 600 P. 2d 371 (1979). Section 41.675 is applicable to medical staff disciplinary committees as well as to hospital tissue committees.

PENNSYLVANIA

Statutory Provisions

Pa. Stat. Ann. tit. 63, §§425.2 and 425.4.
The proceedings and records of peer review, utilization review, medical audit, claims review, and similar committees are not subject to discovery or introduction into evidence in

any civil action against a professional health care provider arising out of matters that are the subject of evaluation and review. However, information, documents, or records otherwise available from original sources are not immune simply because they were presented during committee proceedings.

Selected Cases

Baldwin v. McGrath, 8 Pa. D. & C. 3d 341 (1978). There must be some definitive establishment of a peer review committee, or at least the granting of the power to sanction, based upon evaluation, for the Pennsylvania statute's privilege to attach.

Robinson v. Magovern, 83 F.R.D. 79 (W.D. Pa. 1979). Pursuant to Rule 501 of the Federal Rules of Evidence, records of hospital medical staff credentials and executive committees are discoverable in federal antitrust action and in a pendent state claim, despite section 425.4.

RHODE ISLAND

Statutory Provisions

R.I. Gen. Laws §5–37.3–7.

Proceedings and records of medical peer review committees are not subject to discovery or introduction into evidence. However, information otherwise discoverable or admissible from original sources is not immune simply because it was presented during committee proceedings. The statute does not prohibit discovery in legal actions brought by a medical review committee to restrict or revoke a physician's license or staff privileges or in legal actions brought by aggrieved physicians. Other exceptions are noted.

Selected Cases

In re Board of Medical Review, 463 A. 2d 1373 (R.I. 1983). When the board of medical review, for the state, conducts an ongoing investigation, it can seek peer review committee material that would ordinarily be privileged.

SOUTH CAROLINA

Statutory Provisions

S.C. Code §40–71–20.

All proceedings and all data and information acquired by committees formed to maintain professional standards are not subject to discovery, subpoena, or introduction into evidence except upon appeal from a committee's action. Also, information, documents, and records that are otherwise available from original sources are not immune from discovery or use simply because they were presented before a committee.

SOUTH DAKOTA

Statutory Provisions

S.D. Codified Laws Ann. §36–4–26 and §36–4–26.1.

The proceedings, records, reports, statements, minutes, or other data of committees, the function of which is to review the quality, type, or necessity of care rendered by a health care provider, or to evaluate the competence, character, experience, and performance of a physician, are not subject to disclosure or introduction into evidence. However, the prohibition relating to discovery of evidence does not apply in situations in which a physician seeks access to information upon which a decision regarding his or her staff privileges was based.

TENNESSEE

Statutory Provisions

Tenn. Code Ann. §63–6–219.

All information furnished to health care quality assurance, cost containment, and utilization review committees is not available for subpoena or discovery. However, material that is otherwise available from original sources is not protected merely because it was presented before a committee. Other exceptions to the general rule of nondiscoverability are noted.

TEXAS

Statutory Provisions

Tex. Rev. Civ. Stat. Ann. art. 4447d.

The records and proceedings of committees formed to reduce morbidity or mortality or to identify persons who may be in need of immunization are confidential and are not available for court subpoena. However, this statute does not apply to records kept by a hospital in the regular course of its business.

Selected Cases

Karp v. Cooley, 493 F. 2d 408 (5th Cir. 1974), *cert. denied*, 419 U.S. 845 (1974), *rehearing denied*, 496 F. 2d 878 (5th Cir. 1974). Records of medical school investigating committees are protected by article 4447d.

Texarkana Memorial Hospital, Inc. v. Jones, 551 S.W. 2d 33 (Tex. 1977). Minutes of medical staff meetings are protected by article 4447d from discovery in a medical malpractice action (overruling *French v. Brodsky*, 521 S.W. 2d 670 (Tex. App. 1975)) Records of hospital advisory boards are not protected by article 4447d.)

Hood v. Phillips, 554 S.W. 2d 160 (Tex. 1977). A physician's private records are not protected by article 4447d.

Guidry v. Harris County Medical Society, 618 S.W. 2d 844 (Tex. App. 1981). Hospital and county medical society grievance records are privileged and confidential and cannot be discovered. However, the individuals responsible for the records could testify as to matters of which they had knowledge.

UTAH

Statutory Provisions

Utah Code Ann. §§26–25–1 and 26–25–3.

All information, interviews, reports, statements, memoranda, and other data of committees, the function of which is to reduce morbidity or mortality or to evaluate and improve the quality of hospital and medical care, are privileged and are not to be used or received into evidence in any legal proceeding.

VERMONT

Statutory Provisions

Vt. Stat. Ann. tit. 26, §§1441 and 1443.

The proceedings, reports, and records of committees formed to evaluate and improve the quality of health care rendered by providers of health care services or to determine whether services were professionally indicated and performed or whether their cost was reasonable are neither discoverable nor admissible in any civil action against a health care provider arising out of matters that are the subject of evaluation and review. However, information, reports, or documents otherwise available from original sources are not immune from discovery or use in civil actions simply because they were presented before a committee.

VIRGINIA

Statutory Provisions

Va. Code Ann. §§8.01–581.16 and 8.01–581.17.

The proceedings, records, minutes, reports, and oral and written communications of cost control, utilization review, quality control, peer review, and similar committees are privileged and are not discoverable except upon court order after a showing of good cause arising from extraordinary circumstances. This statute does not immunize hospital records kept with respect to any patient in the ordinary course of the business of operating a hospital.

WASHINGTON

Statutory Provisions

Wash. Rev. Code Ann. §4.24.250.

Written records of committees formed to evaluate the competence and qualifications of members of the health care profession are not subject to subpoena or discovery in any civil action, except actions arising out of a committee's recommendations involving the restriction or revocation of the clinical or staff privileges.

WEST VIRGINIA

Statutory Provisions

W. Va. Code §30–3C–3.

The proceedings and records of peer review, utilization review, medical audit, claims review, and similar committees are privileged and are not subject to subpoena, discovery, or introduction into evidence in any civil action arising out of matters that are the subject of evaluation and review. However, documents, information, and records that are otherwise available from original sources are not protected simply because they were presented during committee proceedings. Furthermore, material is available in civil actions to individuals whose activities are under committee scrutiny. Other exceptions are noted.

WISCONSIN

Statutory Provisions

Wis. Sta⁺ Ann §146.38

Records of organizatioᴎs formed to review and evaluate the services of healtn caᴎe providers may not be used in civil actions against health care providers or facilities. However, information, documents, and records are not to be construed as ᴉmmune from discovery or use in civil actions merely because they were presented to a committee Information can be released for medical and other specified purposes as long as the names ot patients are withheld.

Selected Cases

Davison v. St. Paul Fire & Marine Ins. Co., 75 Wis. 2d 190, 248 N.W. 2d 433 (1977). There is no statutory or common law immunity from discovery for medical staff committee records. (This case was decided prior to the enactment of section 146.38.)

Shibilski v. St. Joseph's Hospital of Marshfield, Inc , 83 Wis. 2d 459, 266 N.W. 2d 264 (1978). Inadmissibility of medical staff committee records is not a bar to their discovery. (This case was decided prior to the enactment of section 146.38.)

WYOMING

Statutory Provisions

Wyo. Stat. §35–17–103.

Members of PSROs are liable only for malicious or grossly negligent action.

FEDERAL LAW

Rules

Rule 501, Federal Rules of Evidence, 28 U.S.C. Federal common law is controlling with respect to discovery questions, except where state law supplies the rule of decision, in which case state laws governing privilege are controlling.

Selected Cases

Bredice v. Doctor's Hospital, Inc., 50 F.R.D. 249 (D.D.C. 1970), *aff'd*, 51 F.R.D. 187 (D.D.C. 1970), 479 F. 2d 920 (D.C. Cir. 1973). Minutes of a hospital medical staff committee are not subject to discovery without a showing of exceptional necessity.

Gillman v. United States, 53 F.R.D. 316 (S.D.N.Y. 1971). Minutes and reports of a committee inquiring into hospital procedures and behavior of hospital personnel are not discoverable in an action under the Federal Tort Claims Act.

Robinson v. Magovern, 83 F.R.D. 79 (W.D. Pa. 1979). Under Rule 501 of the Federal Rules of Evidence, hospital medical staff committee records are discoverable even though privileged under a state statute.

Memorial Hospital v. Shadur, 664 F. 2d 1058, 33 F.R.Serv. 2d 115 (7th Cir. 1981). Federal courts are not bound by state privilege law. They should, however, look at and weigh any state privileges. They should also take into account the overall preference for admissibility of evidence and construe the state confidentiality privileges narrowly.

Glossary of Selected Legal Terms

Action: A proceeding of a civil or criminal nature in a court of law. A civil action is a proceeding by which one party makes demand upon another party for the redress or prevention of an alleged wrong. A criminal action is a proceeding instituted by the state making demand for punishment of one who is alleged to have committed a crime.

Adjudication: A determination by a court of law or an administrative body with quasi-judicial functions. Also, the written document embodying such determination.

Affirmed: Action of an appellate court by which it declares that a judgment, decree, or order of an inferior tribunal is valid and correct and must stand as rendered by the tribunal.

Amicus Curiae: A friend of the court. A person who has no right to appear in a suit, but is allowed, as an exercise of discretion by the court, to introduce argument, authority, or evidence.

Appellant: The party who seeks review of a decision of an inferior tribunal by an appellate court. An appellate court is one invested with jurisdiction to review and correct and otherwise dispose of decisions of inferior tribunals, whether such tribunals are lower courts or administrative agencies. Appellant is usually the loser in the court below and is sometimes referred to as plaintiff in error.

Appellee: The party against whom an appeal to a higher court is taken. Appellee is usually the winner in the court below and is sometimes referred to as defendant in error.

Cause of Action: A cause of action is an event or set of circumstances upon which a court may grant relief in a civil proceeding.

Certiorari: The name of a writ directing an inferior tribunal to transmit the record of a proceeding to an appellate court for review. When a petition for a writ of certiorari is granted, it means the appellate court will review the prior determination.

Charge: The final address by a judge to the jury, in which the judge sums up the case and instructs the jury as to the rules of law that it must apply to the various issues in the case. See also: Instructions to Jury.

Complaint: The written statement of plaintiff in a civil action that sets forth his or her claims and commences the action. In a criminal action it is the charge made before a magistrate with the intention that a prosecution be instituted against the person named in such complaint as allegedly committing an offense.

Damages: Monetary compensation for one who has sustained loss, detriment, or injury to his or her person or property through the unlawful act, omission, or negligence of another.

Defendant: In a criminal case, the defendant is the person accused of committing a crime. In a civil suit, the defendant is the party against whom relief is sought.

Directed Verdict: The instructions by a judge to the jury directing that the jury return a verdict in favor of one of the parties to the proceeding.

Equitable Remedy: An injunction, decree of specific performance, or other type of remedy not available in a strictly common law proceeding.

Habeas Corpus: A writ that lays the basis for an action to determine the legality of the custody or confinement of a person.

Hearsay Rule: A rule that bars in a legal proceeding the admissibility of evidence that is not the personal knowledge of the witness.

Injunction: Equitable remedy that would ordinarily restrain a person from performing a certain act or acts. Injunctions are of various types. A mandatory injunction requires a person to perform a certain act or acts. An injunction may either be preliminary (temporary) or permanent. A preliminary injunction is awarded prior to trial on the merits of the contentions of the parties. A permanent injunction is awarded after the trial and is in the nature of a final order or decree.

Instructions to Jury: The judge's statement to the jury authoritatively setting forth the law applicable to the facts of the case. See also: Charge.

Judgment N.O.V.: Judgment *non obstante verdicto* (notwithstanding the verdict). A judgment entered by order of the court in favor of one party, notwithstanding the verdict by the jury in favor of the other party.

Jurisdiction: The power of a tribunal to hear and determine controversies. There are two types of jurisdiction. Jurisdiction over the subject matter is the power of a tribunal to hear and determine a certain class of controversy. Personal jurisdiction refers to a tribunal's power legally to bind a party to the outcome of the proceeding.

Laches: A defense to an equitable proceeding, as distinguished from a legal proceeding, predicated upon the unreasonable delay of the plaintiff in bringing the action. Laches is an appropriate equitable defense in circumstances where the delay in bringing proceedings would make it unjust to grant the plaintiff relief.

Legal Remedy: An award of compensatory and/or punitive damages. Other examples of legal remedies are the granting of writs of habeas corpus.

Mandamus: An order of court commanding the performance of an act, the performance of which constitutes a legal duty. Mandamus is usually the remedy available to compel public officers to perform nondiscretionary duties imposed upon them by law.

Per Curiam: A Latin phrase indicating that the opinion of the court is made by the entire court.

Plaintiff: Person who initiates a lawsuit.

Pleading: A document filed in court by a party to a proceeding either to commence the proceeding or in response to such initial pleading. Pleadings that commence action are called complaints, petitions, or bills. A responsive pleading is generally called an answer or an affidavit of defense. Pleadings set forth the nature of a plaintiff's claim and the remedy plaintiff is seeking or the defendant's denial or other type of answer to plaintiff's claim.

Remedy: The means the law affords a party to enforce a right or redress a wrong. Remedies are either criminal or civil. A civil remedy is one the law affords private parties. Civil remedies are either legal or equitable in nature. A criminal remedy is the penalty the law imposes for the commission of an offense against the public order (crime).

Remittitur: A court-ordered reduction in an award of damages.

Res Judicata: A rule that a final judgment or decree on merits by a court of competent jurisdiction is conclusive of the rights of the parties in all later suits on points and matters determined by that judgment.

Respondeat Superior: "Let the master answer." The legal principle that the employer is responsible for those acts of his or her employee that are performed within the scope of employment.

Respondent: A respondent is the defendant in an equitable proceeding. Sometimes the term is synonymous with appellee.

Restraining Order: An order issued by the court upon the filing of an application for an injunction forbidding the defendant to do the threatened act until a hearing on the application can be had. The term is sometimes used as a synonym for injunction. However, a restraining order is properly distinguishable from an injunction in that the former is intended only as a restraint upon the defendant until the propriety of granting an injunction can be determined, and it does no more than restrain activity until such determination.

Reversed and Remanded: The action of an appellate court in correcting a decision of a lower tribunal and returning the case to that tribunal for the purpose of taking action in conformity with the law as expressed in the opinion of the appellate court.

Stare Decisis: (To stand by the decided cases). A doctrine that means that a court, once it has laid down a principle of law applicable to a certain state of facts, will apply that principle in all future cases where the facts are substantially the same.

Statute of Limitation: A statute that provides that a legal proceeding may only be brought within a specified time after the cause of action arises. Proceedings after such time are subject to being dismissed.

Subpoena: A court order requiring one to come before tne court to give testimony.

Subpoena Duces Tecum: A subpoena that commands a person to come before the court and to bring with him or her documents or other tangible matter named in the order.

Summons: An official notification to the defendant that an action has been filed against him or her and that he or she is required to appear, on a day named, and answer the complaint.

Tort: An injury to a legally protected interest, arising from the conduct of an actor, which the law characterizes as·
   (1) negligence—i.e., failure to use due care under the circumstances;
   (2) intentional infliction of harm or intentional interterence with legally protected interests; or
   (3) ultrahazardous activity.
A tort may involve damage to one's interest in his or ner own personal well-being or that of his or her family, damage to reputation, interference with a contractual relationship, or an interest in property.

Verdict: The definitive answer given by the jury to the court concerning the matters of fact committed to the jury for its deliberation and decision.

Warrant: An order or direction from a competent legal authority pursuant to law, addressed to an officer or other competent person directing him or her to perform an act, and affording him or her protection from damage, if injury results from acting pursuant to the warrant. There are two types of warrants: an arrest warrant and a search warrant. An arrest warrant authorizes the taking into custody of a person accused of a crime for the purpose of formally charging such person with the offense. A search warrant authorizes the search of named premises for stolen goods or implements or fruits of crime. It also may authorize an inspection to determine whether certain legal standards, primarily applicable to health or safety, have been met.

Table of Cases

Note: Numbers following the name of each case refer to the page number on which reference to the case may be found. Numbers in italics refer to the page on which reference to the case may be found in a footnote.

Index

A

Abortion
  access to records and, 88, 107-108, 112
  minors and consent and, 167
  warrantless searches of clinics and, 102-103
Abuse of children. *See* Child abuse
Access to records
  abortion and, 88, 107-108, 112
  abortion clinics and, 102-103
  adoption and, 49-54
  alcohol abuse patients and, 62, 72-76, 94
  blood transfusion fatalities and, 96
  cancer and, 88-89
  child abuse and, 86-87, 106
  communicable diseases and, 89
  computerization and, 108-110
  day-care centers and, 102-103
  driver's records and, 106, 107
  drug abuse patients and, 62, 72-76, 87, 88, 94
  FOIA and, 59, 78-82, 83, 84, 85, 86
  government agencies and, 98-100
  hospital staff and, 90-91, 109, 110, 115, 116
  judicial approach to, 104-105
  law enforcement agencies and, 105-108
  legal process response to
    compliance and, 114-16
    court orders and, 113
    subpoenas and, 110-13
  medical research and, 91-95
  nursing homes and, 100-101, 104
  overview of, 59-60
  patient
    confidentiality and, 62-63, 66
    duplication of, 116
      fees for, 70
    general rules for, 62
    minors and, 67-70
    psychiatric records and, 62, 63, 66-67, 94, 112-13
    security of records and, 71, 110
    state statutes and, 63-67
  pharmacies and, 102, 104
  privacy act and, 77-78, 80
  PROs and, 59, 82-83, 95-96

Subpoenas
  compliance and, 114-16
  law enforcement agencies and, 105
  legal analysis of, 110-13
  medical staff and, 116
Sullivan v. Montgomery, 161
Sullivan v. State, 67
Supreme Court, 196-97, 200
Surgery
  consent and, 161, 171
  licensing regulations and, 3
  tissue committee and, 127
Surprise inspections, 100, 101,
  102-103, 104-105

T

Tatham v. Hoke, 174
Teaching hospitals, invasion of privacy
  and, 150
Telephone orders, 23
Telephone surveillance (bugging), 148
Teletype machines, 24
Tennessee, 234-35, 266-67, 289
Terminally ill patients. *See also* Patients
  do-not resuscitate orders (DNR) and,
    40-43
  natural death acts and, 43-46
Terminology (glossary), 293-96
Testimony. *See* Courtroom disclosure
Texas, 235, 267, 289-90
Tissue committee (surgery), 127
Touching, 160
Treatment, 14, 21-22, 23
  consent and alternative, 159, 172
Trial courts, 198-99, 200. *See also*
  Court system
Trials. *See* Courtroom disclosure
Truman v. Thomas, 160

U

Uniform Preservation of Private
  Business Records Act, 6-7

United States v. Banks, 75-76
United States v. Biswell, 99-100
University Group Diabetes Program
  (UGDP), 81
Utah, 235, 267-68, 290
Utilization review, 91, 95-98
Utilization review committee, 127
Uzzilia v. Commissioner of Health, 102

V

Venereal disease
  minors and, 167
  reporting of suspicions of, 144
Verbal orders, 23, 25-26
Vermont, 235, 268, 290
Veterans Administration
  fraudulent concealment case and, 217
  terminally ill and emergency
    resuscitation, 43
Virginia, 235, 269, 290

W

Waits v. United States, 217
*Wallace v. University Hospitals of
  Cleveland*, 64
Warrantless search, 100, 101, 102-103,
  104-105, 108
Washington, 235-36, 269-70, 290
*Washington Massage Foundation v.
  Nelson*, 105
West Virginia, 236, 270, 291
Whalen v. Roe, 88
*Weiner v. Memorial Hospital for Cancer
  and Allied Diseases*, 138
Wills (living), 43-46
Wisconsin, 236, 270-71, 291
Wounds, access to records and, 106
Writ of certiorari, 200
Wyoming, 236, 271-72, 291

Y

Young v. Gersten, 129
Young v. Madison General Hospital, 70
Young v. Yarn, 164

About the Authors

William H. Roach, Jr., J.D., is a partner of the law firm of Gardner, Carton & Douglas, a large multi-specialty firm with offices in Chicago, Washington, D.C., Denver, and Libertyville, Illinois. Mr. Roach's health-law practice specialties include corporate restructuring, tax-exempt organizations, health finance, certificate of need, medical staff bylaws and contracts, medical records, patient rights and responsibilities, health industry joint ventures, and legal audits. Before entering private practice, Mr. Roach was vice president for legal affairs at Rush-Presbyterian-St. Luke's Medical Center (1976–1980) and senior staff counsel at Michael Reese Hospital and Medical Center (1974–1976), both large Chicago teaching hospitals. He received an A.B. from Columbia College of Columbia University in 1966, a J.D. from Vanderbilt University in 1972, and an M.S. from the Health Law Training Program of the University of Pittsburgh in 1973. He is a member of the editorial board of *Topics in Health Record Management* and a contributing editor of the *Hospital Law Manual*. Mr. Roach is a former president and founding director of the Illinois Association of Hospital Attorneys and is a member of the American, Illinois, and Chicago Bar Associations, the American Academy of Hospital Attorneys, the National Health Lawyers Association, and the American Society of Law and Medicine.

Susan N. Chernoff, M.B.A., J.D., is an associate of the law firm of Gardner, Carton & Douglas, specializing in health and hospital law. Ms. Chernoff received her A.B. degree, with honors, in 1978 from Duke University. She received a J.D. and an M.B.A. in 1983, both from Washington University in St. Louis. Ms. Chernoff is a member of the American, Illinois, and Chicago Bar Associations, and the American Academy of Hospital Attorneys. She also has been a contributing author to *Topics in Health Record Management*.

Carole Lange Esley, R.R.A., is vice president for corporate management information systems of the NorthEast Health Corporation in Camden, Maine. She is the past editor of *Topics in Health Record Management* and currently serves on the editorial board of *Health Care Management Review*. Mrs. Esley has previously served as director of medical information service at the University Hospital in Tucson, Arizona, Boston University Medical Center, and the U.S. Public Health Service Indian Health Service Hospital in Shiprock, New Mexico. She received an A.B. degree in 1959 from Stetson University in Deland, Florida, and is a graduate of the University of Pennsylvania Graduate Hospital Medical Record Administration program. Mrs. Esley is a member of the American Medical Record Association and has served that organization in numerous capacities, including three years on its executive board of directors.

Providing special assistance in the preparation of this book were:

Chris J. Mollet, J.D., is an associate of the law firm of Gardner, Carton & Douglas, specializing in health and hospital law. Prior to entering private practice, he was staff counsel at Michael Reese Hospital and Medical Center (1980 to 1982). Mr. Mollet received his B.A., with distinction, in 1976 and his J.D. in 1979, both from the University of Wisconsin. He is a member of the American, Illinois, and Wisconsin Bar Associations, a member of the board of directors of the Young Lawyers Section of the Chicago Bar Association, the immediate past chairman of the Health and Hospital Law Committee of the Chicago Bar Association (Young Lawyers section) (1983–1984), and is a member of the American Academy of Hospital Attorneys, the National Health Lawyers Association, the American Bar Association Forum Committee on Health Law, and the Illinois Association of Hospital Attorneys.

David A. Rubenstein, J.D., is an associate of the law firm of Gardner, Carton & Douglas, specializing in the areas of federal taxation and ERISA. Mr. Rubenstein received his B.A. in economics from the University of Illinois in 1980, where he was a member of Phi Beta Kappa, and received his J.D., magna cum laude, from the University of Michigan in 1983. He is a member of the American, Illinois, and Chicago Bar Associations.